AUTOCAD 2000

NO EXPERIENCE REQUIRED

AUTOCAD® 2000

NO EXPERIENCE REQUIRED™

David Frey

SYBEX®

San Francisco • Paris • Düsseldorf • Soest • London

Associate Publisher: Amy Romanoff
Contracts and Licensing Manager: Kristine O'Callaghan
Developmental Editor: Melanie Spiller
Editor: Raquel Baker
Technical Editor: Scott Onstott
Book Designers: Patrick Dintino, Catalin Dulfu, Maureen Forys
Graphic Illustrator: Tony Jonick
Electronic Publishing Specialist: Cynthia Johnsen
Production Coordinator: Susan Berge
Indexer: Lynnzee Elze
Cover Designer: Design Site
Cover Photographer: Jack D. Myers

Library of Congress Card Number: 99-61305
ISBN: 0-7821-2498-4

Manufactured in the United States of America

20 19 18 17 16 15 14 13

*To my dad, Hugh, who believed he could fly...
and did. His patience, determination, and
delightfully positive spirit have been an
inspiration to me.*

Acknowledgments

There are many people who deserve acknowledgment and gratitude for their contribution to the development and publication of this book.

Many thanks to the folks at Sybex who were involved in this project. Adrienne Crew, a member of the Contracts and Licensing Team, patiently negotiated with me to finalize the contract. Thanks also to Amy Romanoff, Associate Publisher, for her leadership and support in the formation of the group of Sybex AutoCAD authors currently writing books. Melanie Spiller, Acquisitions and Developmental Editor, has given encouragement and inspiration throughout the process. Raquel Baker has been fun to work with, has been thorough and supportive as an editor, and has been an excellent guide as well. Also, thanks to Scott Onstott, who served as the technical editor. His edits and intelligent suggestions have significantly added to the quality of the book.

I also want to mention the production team at Sybex: Susan Berge, Production Coordinator; Cyndy Johnsen, Electronic Publishing Specialist; and Dan Schiff, Production Assistant. They've been successful in maintaining the standards of high quality that Sybex is known for, and I appreciate their ability and effort in putting together such a good-looking book.

Thanks to George Omura, Bob Calori, and Bill Hill—the AutoCAD authors writing for Sybex. It's been a pleasure to meet them and feel the support we give to each other in our work.

Contents at a Glance

Introduction   *xv*

skills

1   Getting to Know AutoCAD   1
2   Basic Commands to Get Started   21
3   Setting Up a Drawing   49
4   Gaining Drawing Strategies: Part 1   67
5   Gaining Drawing Strategies: Part 2   121
6   Using Layers to Organize Your Drawing   161
7   Using Blocks and Wblocking   205
8   Generating Elevations   253
9   Working with Hatches and Fills   289
10 Controlling Text in a Drawing   319
11 Dimensioning a Drawing   369
12 Managing External References   415
13 Using Layouts to Set Up a Print   443
14 Printing an AutoCAD Drawing   493
Appendix A: A Look at Drawing in 3D   521
Appendix B: An Introduction to Attributes   565
Glossary   591

Index   *603*

Table of Contents

Introduction xv

Skill 1 Getting to Know AutoCAD **1**

Starting Up AutoCAD 2

Introduction to the AutoCAD Graphics Window 4

The Command Window 9

Drop-Down Menus 10

Toolbars 11

Toolbar Flyouts 11

Calling Up and Arranging Toolbars 13

Custom Toolbars 18

The Keyboard 19

The Mouse 19

Are You Experienced? 20

Skill 2 Basic Commands to Get Started **21**

The Line Command 22

Coordinates 27

Relative Coordinates 29

Drawing the Box 32

Using Relative Cartesian Coordinates 32

Using Relative Polar Coordinates 33

The Offset Command 34

The Fillet Command 37

Completing the Box 40

Offsetting Lines to Mark an Opening 40

Extending Lines 42

Trimming Lines 43

If You Would Like More Practice... 48

Are You Experienced? 48

Skill 3 Setting Up a Drawing **49**

Drawing Units 50

Drawing Size 54

The Grid 54

Drawing Limits 56

Drawing with Grid and Snap 59

Saving Your Work 63

Are You Experienced? 65

Skill 4   Gaining Drawing Strategies: Part 1   67

Laying Out the Walls 69

The Exterior Wall Lines 70

The Interior Walls 74

Cutting Wall Openings 83

Creating Doors 91

Drawing Swinging Doors 91

Copying Objects 101

Mirroring Objects 104

Finishing the Swinging Doors 106

Drawing a Sliding Glass Door 109

Are You Experienced? 120

Skill 5   Gaining Drawing Strategies: Part 2   121

Drawing the Steps and Thresholds 123

The Front Step 124

The Back Step 128

The Thresholds 130

The Balcony: Drawing Circles 133

Laying Out the Kitchen 137

The Counter 138

The Stove and Refrigerator 141

The Kitchen Sink 147

Constructing the Bathroom 149

Setting Running Object Snaps 149

Drawing a Shower Unit 151

The Bathroom Sink 153

Positioning a Toilet 154

Are You Experienced? 159

Skill 6   Using Layers to Organize Your Drawing   161

Layers as an Organization Tool 162

Setting Up Layers 164

The Layer Properties Manager Dialog Box 165

Assigning Objects to Layers 173

Freezing and Turning Off Layers 183

Drawing the Headers 186

Drawing the Roof 189

Color, Linetypes, and Layers   200
Assigning a Color or Linetype to an Object   201
Making a Color or Linetype Current   201
Assigning an Individual Linetype Scale Factor   202
Are You Experienced?   203

Skill 7   Using Blocks and Wblocking   **205**
Making a Block for a Door   207
Inserting the Door Block   211
Finding Blocks in a Drawing   219
Using Grips to Detect a Block   220
Using the List Command to Detect a Block   220
Using the Properties Dialog Box to Detect a Block   223
Creating a Window Block   224
Inserting the Window Block   228
Rotating a Block during Insertion   229
Using Guidelines When Inserting a Block   232
Using Point Filters to Insert a Block   235
Using Blips to Help in Inserting Blocks   238
Finishing the Windows   240
Revising a Block   244
Wblocking   247
Inserting a .Dwg File into Another .Dwg File   249
Are You Experienced?   252

Skill 8   Generating Elevations   **253**
Drawing the Front Elevation   254
Setting Up Lines for the Heights   256
Trimming Lines in the Elevation   261
Drawing the Roof in Elevation   263
Putting in the Door, Step, and Windows   267
Finishing Touches   273
Generating the Other Elevations   274
Making the Rear Elevation   274
Making the Left and Right Elevations   279
Drawing Scale Considerations   285
Interior Elevations   286
Are You Experienced?   287

Skill 9   Working with Hatches and Fills   **289**
Hatching the Front Elevation   290
Looking at Hatch Patterns   294

Hatching the Rest of the Front Elevation 296
Special Effects 300
Modifying a Hatch Pattern 306
Using Hatches in the Floor Plan 308
Hatching the Floors 308
Finishing the Hatches for the Floors 312
Hatching the Walls in the Floor Plan 313
Modifying the Shape of Hatch Patterns 315
Are You Experienced? 317

Skill 10 Controlling Text in a Drawing   **319**
Setting Up Text Styles 320
Text and Drawing Scale 321
Defining a Text Style for Room Labels 322
Using Single Line Text 324
Placing Titles of Views in the Drawing 325
Placing Room Labels in the Floor Plan 328
Using Text in a Grid 334
Creating a Title Block and Border 344
Using Multiline Text 360
Are You Experienced? 368

Skill 11 Dimensioning a Drawing   **369**
Dimension Styles 370
Making a New Dimension Style 371
Placing Dimensions on the Drawing 380
Horizontal Dimensions 381
Vertical Dimensions 388
Other Types of Dimensions 392
Radial Dimensions 392
Leader Lines 396
Angular and Aligned Dimensions 398
Modifying Dimensions 400
Modifying Dimension Text 401
Dimension Overrides 406
Dimensioning Short Distances 408
Are You Experienced? 414

Skill 12 Managing External References   **415**
Drawing a Site Plan 416
Using Surveyor Units 417
Drawing the Driveway 420

Setting Up an External Reference   424
   The External Reference Dialog Box   424
   Controlling the Appearance of an Xref   426
Modifying an Xref Drawing   429
   Modifying an Xref by Making It the Current Drawing   430
   Modifying an Xref from within the Host Drawing   434
Applications for Xrefs   437
Additional Features of External References   438
   The Xref Path   438
Binding Xrefs   440
   Other Features of Xrefs   441
Are You Experienced?   442

Skill 13 Using Layouts to Set Up a Print   **443**
Setting Up Layouts   444
   Drawing a Border on a Layout   450
   Designing a Title Block for a Layout   452
   Adjusting a Viewport   456
   Switching between Model Space and a Layout   458
Working with Multiple Viewports in a Layout   460
   Setting Up Multiple Viewports   461
   Aligning Viewports   466
   Finishing the 11×17-Inch Drawing   467
   Setting Up Viewports in Different Scales   471
   Adding Multiple Viewports to a Layout   477
   Adding Text to Paper Space   486
   Turning Off Viewports   490
Are You Experienced?   491

Skill 14 Printing an AutoCAD Drawing   **493**
The Plot Dialog Box   495
   Paper Size and Paper Units   497
   Drawing Orientation and Plot Scale   498
   Plot Offset and Plot Options   499
   Plot Area   501
Printing a Drawing   506
   Determining Lineweights for a Drawing   506
   Setting Up the Other Parameters for the Print   509
   Previewing a Print   510

Printing a Drawing Using Layouts 513
Printing a Drawing with Multiple Viewports 514
Printing the Site Plan 516
Are You Experienced? 519

Appendix A: A Look at Drawing in 3D **521**
Surface Modeling 523
Viewing a Drawing in 3D 523
Creating a Wireframe 3D Model 525
Extruding Lines 527
Making the Doorway Openings 532
Putting 2D Drawings on 3D Surfaces 547
Getting the Roof into 3D 551
Making a 3D Balcony 555
Finishing Up the 3D Surface Model 557
Using 3D Orbit 558
Solid Modeling 561
Summary 564

Appendix B: An Introduction to Attributes **565**
Using Attributes for a Grid 566
Defining Blocks with Attributes 571
Inserting Blocks with Attributes 572
Editing Attribute Text 574
Setting Up Multiple Attributes in a Block 575
Defining a Block with Multiple Attributes 578
Inserting the Room_Info Block 581
Controlling the Visibility of Attributes 583
Editing Attributes 584
Extracting Data from an AutoCAD Drawing 586
Creating a Template File for Data Extraction 586
Extracting Attribute Data 587
Summary 590

Glossary **591**

Index *603*

Introduction

This book was born out of the need for a simple yet engaging tutorial that would help beginners step into the world of AutoCAD without feeling intimidated. That tutorial has evolved over the years into a full introduction to the way in which architects and civil and structural engineers use AutoCAD to increase their efficiency and capacity to produce state-of-the-art computerized production drawings and designs.

This book is directed towards AutoCAD novices—users who know how to use a computer and do basic file-managing tasks, like creating new folders and saving and moving files, but who know nothing or very little about AutoCAD. If you are new to the construction and design professions, this book will be an excellent companion as you're learning AutoCAD. If you're already practicing in those fields, you'll be immediately able to apply the skills you'll pick up from this book to real-world projects. The exercises included herein have been successfully used to train architects, engineers, and contractors, as well as college and high school students, in the basics of AutoCAD.

What Will You Learn from This Book?

Learning AutoCAD, as in learning any complex computer program, requires a significant commitment of time and attention, and, to some extent, repetition. Although there are new concepts you must understand to operate the program and to appreciate its potential as a drafting and design tool, becoming proficient at AutoCAD also requires that you use the commands enough times to gain an intuitive sense of how they work and how parts of a drawing are constructed.

In this tutorial, each chapter is designated as a *skill*. At the end of each skill, you will find a checklist of the tools you have learned (or should have learned!). The steps in the tutorial have a degree of repetition built into them that allows you to work through new commands several times and build up confidence before you move on to the next skill.

Progressing through the book, the skills break into four general areas of study:

- Skills 1 through 3 will familiarize you with the organization of the screen, go over a few of the most basic commands, and equip you with the tools necessary to set up a new drawing.

- Skills 4 and 5 develop drawing strategies that will help you use commands efficiently.

- Skills 6 through 11 work with the major features of AutoCAD.

- Skills 12 through 14 and Appendices A and B look into more intermediate and advanced features of AutoCAD.

In the process of exploring these elements, you will follow through the steps involved in laying out the floor plan of a small, three-room cabin. Then you will learn how to generate elevations from the floor plan and, eventually, how to set up a title block and print out your drawing. Along the way, you will also learn how to:

- Use the basic drawing and modifying commands in a strategic manner.

- Set up layers.

- Put color into your drawing.

- Define and insert blocks.

- Generate elevation views.

- Place hatch patterns and fills on building components.

- Use text in your drawing.

- Dimension the floor plan.

In the latter part of the book, the skills touch on some of the more intermediate and advanced features of AutoCAD, including:

- Drawing a site plan

- Using external references

- Setting up a drawing for printing with Layouts

- Making a print of your drawing

- Working in three dimensions

- Defining attributes and extracting data from the drawing

All of these features are taught with the cabin as a continuing project. As a result, you will build up a set of drawings that document your progress through the project and that can be used as reference material later if you find that you need to refresh yourself with material in a specific skill. If you are already somewhat familiar with AutoCAD and reading only some of the skills included, you can pull accompanying files for this book off of Sybex's Web page, at `http://www.sybex.com`.

At the end of the book, there is a glossary of terms that are used in the book and are related to AutoCAD and building design. Finally, there is an index.

Hints for Success

Because this book is essentially a step-by-step tutorial, it has a side effect in common with any tutorial of this type: After you finish a skill and see that you have progressed further through the cabin project, you may have no idea how you got there and are sure you couldn't do it again without the help of the step-by-step instructions. This feeling is a natural result of this kind of learning tool, and there are a couple of things you can do to get past it. You can do the chapter over again. This may seem tedious, but it has a great advantage: You gain speed in drawing. You'll accomplish the same task in half the time it took you the first time. If you repeat a skill for the third time, you'll halve your time again. Each time you repeat a skill, you can skip more and more of the explicit instructions and eventually you'll be able to execute the commands and finish the skill by just looking at the figures and reading a minimum of the text. In many ways, this is just like learning a musical instrument: You must go slow at first, but over time and through practice, your pace picks up.

Another suggestion for honing your skills is to follow the course of the book, but apply the steps to a different project. Possibly draw your own living space, or design a new one. If you have a real design project that is not too complex, that's even better. The probability of learning AutoCAD, or any computer program, is greatly increased when you are highly motivated, and a real project of an appropriate size can be the perfect motivator.

Ready, Set...

When I started learning AutoCAD 14 years ago, I was at first surprised how long I could sit at a workstation and be unaware of time passing. Then, shortly afterwards, I experienced a level of frustration that I never thought I was capable of feeling. When I finally "got over the hump" and began feeling that I could successfully draw with this program after all, I told myself that I would someday figure out a way to help others get over the hump. That was the primary motivating force for writing this book. I hope it works for you and that you too get some enjoyment while learning AutoCAD. As the title says, "No experience is required," only an interest in the subject and a willingness to learn!

Getting to Know AutoCAD

- → **Opening a new drawing**
- → **Getting familiar with the AutoCAD Graphics window**
- → **Modifying the display**
- → **Calling up and arranging toolbars**

Your introduction to AutoCAD begins with a tour of the features of the AutoCAD screen. In this skill, you will also learn some tools to help you control its appearance, and how to find and start commands. Starting up AutoCAD is the first task at hand.

Starting Up AutoCAD

If you have installed AutoCAD using the default settings for the location of the program files, start AutoCAD by selecting Programs ➤ AutoCAD 2000➤ AutoCAD 2000 from the Start menu. If you have customized your installation, find and select the AutoCAD 2000 icon to start the program.

When AutoCAD first opens, the Startup dialog box appears (Figure 1.1). Dialog boxes are used extensively in AutoCAD for many different functions. They have various combinations of buttons and text boxes that you will learn about as you progress through the book.

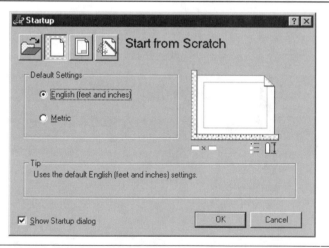

FIGURE 1.1: The Startup dialog box

The four buttons at the upper-left corner of the Startup dialog box give you options for setting up a new drawing or choosing an existing drawing to revise or update. The two buttons on the right—for Templates and Wizards—initiate advanced setup routines. The middle portion of the dialog box changes depending on which of the four buttons you choose. Let's start out by beginning a new drawing.

1. Click the Start from Scratch button, the second button from the left.

2. Select the English (Feet and Inches) radio button in the rectangular area titled Default Settings.

NOTE NOTE NOTE NOTE NOTE NOTE NOTE NOTE NOTE NOTE NOTE NOTE NOTE NOTE

Radio buttons are round, come in a list, and only one item can be activated at a time.

3. Click OK. The dialog box disappears, and your monitor displays the Auto-CAD Graphics window, sometimes called the Graphical User Interface or GUI (see Figure 1.2).

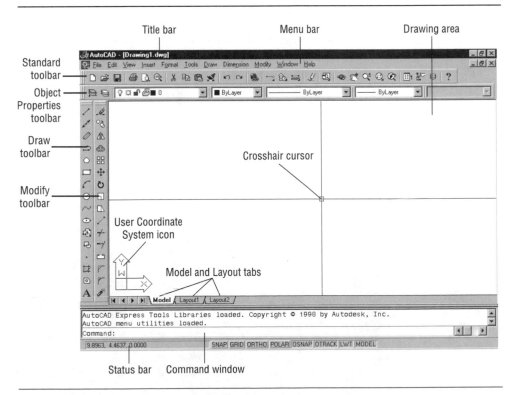

FIGURE 1.2: The AutoCAD Graphics window

Introduction to the AutoCAD Graphics Window

At the top of the Graphics window sits the *title bar*, the *menu bar*, and two *toolbars*.

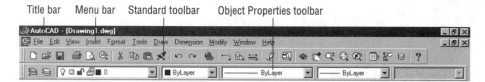

The title bar is analogous to the title bar on any Windows program. It contains the program name (AutoCAD) and the title of the current drawing. Below the title bar is the menu bar, where you will see the drop-down menus. Among the drop-down menus, the first two on the left and the last one on the right are Microsoft menus (meaning that they appear on most Windows applications). These Microsoft menus also contain a few commands specific to AutoCAD. The rest of the menus are AutoCAD menus. Below these menus is the *Standard toolbar*, which contains 27 command buttons. Several of these buttons will be familiar to Windows users; the rest are AutoCAD commands. Just below this toolbar is the *Object Properties toolbar*, which contains two command buttons and five drop-down lists.

The blank middle section of the screen is called the *drawing area*. Notice the movable *crosshair cursor*.

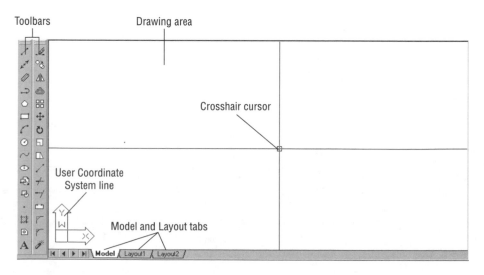

Notice the little box at the intersection of the two crosshair lines. This is one of several forms of the AutoCAD cursor that is moved and controlled by the mouse. When you move the cursor off the drawing area, it changes to the standard Windows pointing arrow. As you begin using commands, it will take on other forms, depending on which step of a command you are in. There is also an icon with a double-arrow in the lower-left corner of the drawing area. This is called the *User Coordinate System icon* and is used to indicate the positive direction for *x* and *y* coordinates. You won't need it for most of the skills in this book, so you'll learn how to make it invisible in Skill 3, *Setting Up a Drawing*. At the bottom of the drawing area, there are three tabs: a Model tab and two Layout tabs. These are used for switching between viewing modes and will be discussed in Skill 13, *Using Layouts to Set Up a Print*. Our example shows no toolbars floating in the drawing area, but there are two docked toolbars on the left of the drawing area. Your screen may or may not have them, or they may be in a different position. If the toolbars are on top of the drawing area, they will have a colored title bar. For more specifics, see the section titled "Toolbars" later in this skill.

Below the drawing area is the *Command window*.

The Command window is where you tell the program what to do, and where the program tells you what's going on. It's an important area and you will need to learn about how it works in detail. There should be three lines of text visible. If your screen has fewer than three lines showing, you will need to make another line or two visible. You'll learn how to do this later in this skill in the section titled "The Command Window."

Below the Command window is the *Status bar*.

On the left end of the Status bar, you'll see a coordinate readout window. In the middle there are eight readout buttons that indicate various drawing modes. It is important to learn about the coordinate system and most of these drawing aids (Snap, Grid, Ortho, and Osnap) early on as you learn to draw in AutoCAD. They will help you create neat and accurate drawings. Polar and Otrack are advanced drawing tools and will be introduced in Skill 5. Lwt stands for Lineweight and will be mentioned in Skill 14 in the discussion on plotting. The Model button is an advanced aid that will be covered later in Skill 13.

This has been a quick introduction to the various parts of the Graphics window. There are a couple of items I didn't mention which may be visible on your screen. You may have scroll bars below and to the right of the drawing area. And you may have a menu on the right side of the drawing area. Both of these features can be useful, but they may also be a hindrance and can take up precious space in the drawing area. They won't be of any use while working your way through this book, so I suggest that you remove them for now.

To temporarily remove these features, follow these steps:

1. From the menu bar, click Tools ➤ Options. The Options dialog box appears (shown in Figure 1.3). It has nine tabs across the top that act like tabs on file folders.

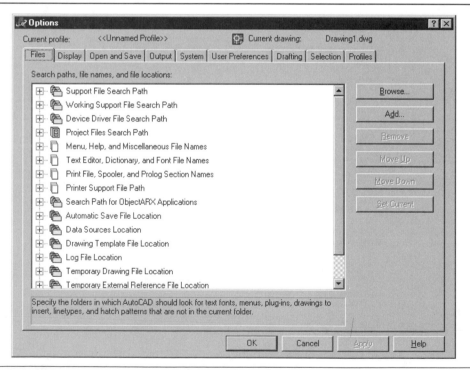

FIGURE 1.3: The Options dialog box

2. Click the Display tab. The display settings come up (Figure 1.4). Focus in on the rectangular area titled Window Elements. If you have scroll bars visible on the lower and right edges of the drawing area, the first checkbox, Display Scroll Bars in Drawing Window, should be selected.

3. Click the checkbox to remove the checkmark, as you will not be using the scroll bars. This turns off the scroll bars. Do the same for the second checkbox, named Display Screen Menu, to turn off the screen menu. Don't click the OK button yet.

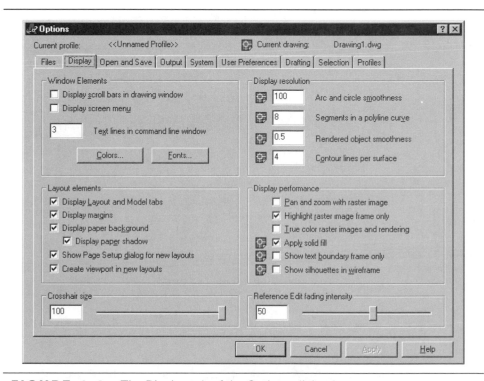

FIGURE 1.4: The Display tab of the Options dialog box

Another display setting that you may want to change at this point controls the color of the cursor and the drawing area background. The illustrations in this book show a white background and black crosshair cursor, but you may prefer to have the colors reversed. To do this, follow the steps on the next page.

1. Click the Colors button in the bottom of the Window Elements area of the Options dialog box. The AutoCAD Color Options dialog box comes up (Figure 1.5). In the middle of the dialog box, there is a drop-down list titled Window Element, Model tab background should be visible. If it's not, open the drop-down list and select it.

2. Move to the Color drop-down list, which is below the Window Element drop-down list. If your drawing area background is currently white, a square followed by White will be displayed. Open the Color drop-down list. Scroll to the color Black (or the background color you want) and select it. The drawing area will now have that color, and the cursor color will change to white, as shown in the Model Tab preview window in the upper-left corner of the dialog box.

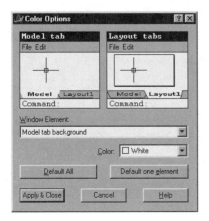

FIGURE 1.5: The AutoCAD Color Options dialog box

3. Click the Apply & Close button to close the AutoCAD Color Options dialog box.

4. Click OK to close the Options dialog box.

Your screen and crosshair cursor will take on their newly assigned colors.

TIP TIP TIP TIP TIP TIP TIP TIP TIP TIP TIP TIP TIP TIP TIP TIP TIP TIP TIP TIP TIP TIP TIP

If you choose a color other than black as the Model tab background color, the color of the crosshair cursor remains the same as it was (black). To change the crosshair color, stay in the AutoCAD Color Options dialog box, open the Window Element drop-down list, and select "Model tab pointer." Then select a color from the Color drop-down list.

The Command Window

Just below the drawing area is the Command window. This window is actually separate from the drawing area and behaves like a Microsoft Windows window; that is, you can drag it to a different place on the screen and resize it, although I don't recommend you do this at first. If you currently have fewer than three lines of text in the window, you will need to increase its vertical size. To do this, move the cursor to the horizontal boundary between the drawing area and the Command window until it changes to an up-and-down arrow broken by two parallel horizontal lines.

Hold down the left mouse button and drag the cursor up by approximately the amount that one or two lines of text would take up, then release the mouse. You should get more lines of text showing, but you may have to try it a couple of times to get exactly three lines visible. When you close the program, the new settings will be saved, and it will be right next time you start up AutoCAD.

TIP TIP TIP TIP TIP TIP TIP TIP TIP TIP TIP TIP TIP TIP TIP TIP TIP TIP TIP TIP TIP TIP TIP

The number of lines of text in the Command window can also be set in the Options dialog box. Click Tools ➤ Options ➤ Display. In the Window Elements area, set the Text Lines in Command Line Window setting to 3. Then click the Apply button and the OK button.

The Command window is very important. It is here where you will give information to AutoCAD, and where AutoCAD will prompt you as to the next step in executing a command. It is a good practice to get into the habit of keeping one eye on it as you work on your drawing. Most errors are made from not watching it often enough.

Before you begin to draw, you should take a close look at the menus, toolbars, and keyboard controls.

NOTE NOTE NOTE NOTE NOTE NOTE NOTE NOTE NOTE NOTE NOTE NOTE NOTE NOTE NOTE

In many cases, AutoCAD offers you a number of ways to start up commands. There are ways to get to most of the commands either from drop-down menus, from the toolbars, or from the keyboard. When you get used to drawing with AutoCAD, you will learn some of the shortcuts available to start commands quickly, and you will find the way that is most comfortable for you.

Drop-Down Menus

The menu bar, just below the title bar (see Figure 1.2), consists of eleven words and an icon. Click any of these and you will find a drop-down menu. The icon on the left end, as well as the File, Edit, and Help options, are Microsoft menus that come with all Windows-compatible applications, although they are somewhat customized to work with AutoCAD. The menu associated with the icon contains commands that allow you to control the appearance and position of the drawing area. Commands in the File menu are for opening and saving new and existing drawing files, printing, exporting files to another application, choosing basic utility options, and exiting the application. The Edit menu contains the Undo and Redo commands, the Cut and Paste tools, and options for creating links between AutoCAD files and other files. The Help menu (the last menu on the right) works like all Windows help menus.

The other eight menus contain the most often-used AutoCAD commands. You will find that if you can master the logic of how the commands are organized by menu, it will be immensely helpful in finding the command you want. Here is a short description of each of the AutoCAD drop-down menus:

View   Contains tools for controlling the display of your drawing file.

Insert   Has commands for placing drawings and images, or parts of them, inside other drawings.

Format   Is where you'll find commands for setting up the general parameters for a new drawing.

Tools   Contains special tools for use while you are working on the current drawing, such as those for finding how long a line is or for running a special macro.

Draw   Holds the commands for putting new objects (like lines or circles) on the screen.

Dimension   Is where you'll find commands for dimensioning a drawing.

Modify   Has the commands for making changes to objects already existing in the drawing.

Window   Has options for displaying currently open windows and lists currently open drawing files.

Toolbars

Just below the drop-down menus is the most extensive of the toolbars—the Standard toolbar.

The 27 icons don't appear as buttons until you put the pointer arrow on them, and then they are highlighted. They are arranged into 11 logical groups. The icons on the left half of the Standard toolbar are for commands used in all Windows-compatible applications, so you may be familiar with them. The icons on the right half of the Standard toolbar are AutoCAD commands that you will use during your regular drawing activities for a variety of tasks. These commands can do a number of things, including:

- Change the view or orientation of the drawing on the screen

- Change the properties of an object, such as color or linetype

- Force a line you are drawing to meet another line or geometric feature at specified points

Toolbar Flyouts

Notice that some icons on the Standard toolbar have a little triangular arrow in the lower-right corner. These arrows indicate that more than one command can be found through these icons. Follow the next six steps to see how these special icons work.

1.   Move the cursor up to the Standard toolbar and place the arrow on the icon that has a yellow ruler with a dimension line above it.

2. Rest the arrow on the button for a moment without clicking. A small window opens just below it, revealing what command the button represents. In this case, the window should say "Distance." This is a tool tip—all buttons have them. Notice the small arrow in the lower-right corner of the icon. This is the multiple command arrow mentioned above.

3. Place the arrow cursor on the button and hold down the left mouse button. As you hold the mouse button down, a column of five buttons drops down vertically below the original button. The top button in the column is a duplicate of the button you clicked. This column of buttons is called a *toolbar flyout*.

4. While still holding the mouse button down, drag the arrow down over each button until you get to the one that has a white paper scroll on it. Hold the arrow there until you see the tool tip. It should say "List." Now release the mouse button. The flyout disappears and the List command has started. Look in the Command window at the bottom of the screen.

 NOTE NOTE NOTE NOTE NOTE NOTE NOTE NOTE NOTE NOTE NOTE NOTE NOTE NOTE NOTE

The List command queries AutoCAD about the objects you select after the command has started. AutoCAD then displays information about the selected objects.

The middle line of text says "Command: _list." This tells you that you have started the List command. The bottom line says "Select objects:." This prompt tells you what you need to do next: select the objects about which you want information. This flyout is called the Inquiry flyout because it contains tools for asking questions about parts of the drawing.

5. Look at the Standard toolbar where the Distance button was previously located. Notice that it's been replaced by the List button.

On a toolbar flyout, the button you select replaces the button that was on the toolbar. This is handy if you are going to be using the same command several times, because now the button for the command is readily available and you don't have to open the flyout to select it again. The order of the flyout buttons remains the same, so when you open the Inquiry flyout again, the Distance button will be at the top of the list. You will need to become familiar with any flyout buttons you use, because the last one used becomes the representative button on the home toolbar.

6. Press Esc to cancel the List command.

By taking a look at the Inquiry flyout on the Standard toolbar, you have been introduced to the mechanisms that govern the behavior of flyouts in general.

NOTE NOTE NOTE NOTE NOTE NOTE NOTE NOTE NOTE NOTE NOTE NOTE NOTE NOTE NOTE
Whenever you start up AutoCAD for a new drawing session, the toolbars will be reset and contain the flyout buttons that were originally there.

The toolbar flyouts are actually regular toolbars that have been attached to another toolbar. There are 24 toolbars in all, and only six are flyouts. Five of these are attached to the Standard toolbar, and one is attached to the Draw toolbar. Any of these flyouts can be called up as a regular toolbar, independent from the Standard or Draw toolbars.

Calling Up and Arranging Toolbars

We'll use the Inquiry toolbar as an example of some ways in which toolbars can be controlled and manipulated.

1. From the View menu, select Toolbars. The Toolbars dialog box comes up (Figure 1.6). On the left side is a scrolling list box with all 24 toolbars listed.

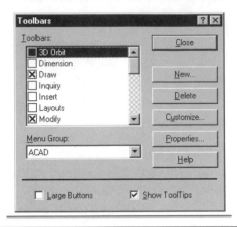

FIGURE 1.6: The Toolbars dialog box

2. In the Toolbars list box, find the Inquiry checkbox and select it. The Inquiry toolbar will appear in the form of a floating box in the drawing area (Figure 1.7).

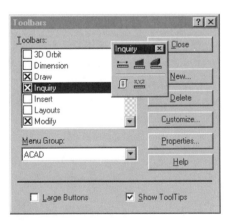

FIGURE 1.7: The Inquiry toolbar

3. Click the Close button in the Toolbars dialog box. Notice that the Inquiry toolbar now has a title bar. Toolbars which are positioned on the drawing area have title bars. By putting the cursor on the title bar and holding down the left mouse button, you can drag the toolbar around on the screen. Try this with the Inquiry toolbar.

4. Click and drag the Inquiry toolbar to the right side of the screen. You will notice that as you drag it, the toolbar stays put and you are dragging a rectangle of the same size as the toolbar (see Figure 1.8). As you drag the rectangle to the top of the drawing area and begin to move it off the drawing area onto the right side of the screen, the rectangle changes size to become taller and thinner.

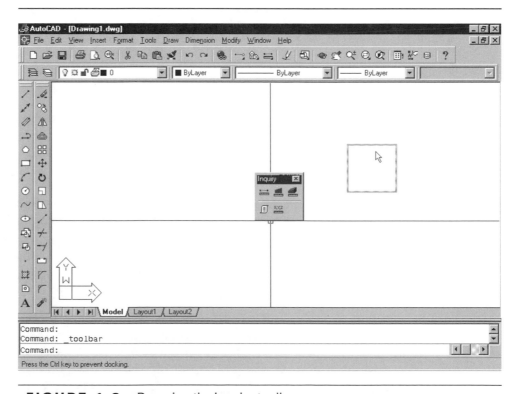

FIGURE 1.8: Dragging the Inquiry toolbar

5. Release the left mouse button once the toolbar is out of the drawing area. The rectangle changes to the Inquiry toolbar, which is now positioned off the drawing area without its title bar.

This procedure is called *docking* a toolbar. Notice how the Standard and Object Properties toolbars have no title bars—they are docked.

6. Move the cursor arrow to the left end of the Standard toolbar so the point of the arrow is on the two vertical grab bars.

7. Hold down the left mouse button while on the grab bars and drag the Standard toolbar onto the drawing area. Release the mouse button. The Standard toolbar now has a title bar, and the space it was occupying at the top of the screen has been filled in, making the drawing area a little larger, as you will see in Figure 1.9. The Standard toolbar is now a *floating* toolbar and can be moved around the drawing area.

Floating toolbars don't affect the size of the drawing area, but they cover your drawing. Each docked toolbar takes up a little space that would otherwise be drawing area. You have to decide how many docked and floating toolbars you need on the screen at a time. A good way to start out is to leave the Standard and Object Properties toolbars docked at the top of the screen, and the Draw and Modify toolbars docked on the left side of the screen, as in Figure 1.2.

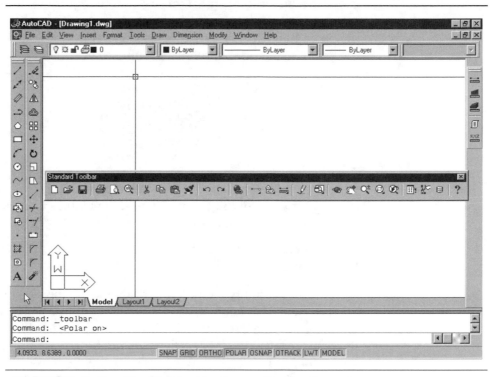

FIGURE 1.9: The Standard toolbar on the drawing area

Now, to put the Standard toolbar back where it was, and delete the Inquiry toolbar, follow these steps:

1. Drag the Standard toolbar up to its former position above the Object Properties toolbar.

2. Drag the Inquiry toolbar back onto the drawing area, using the grab bars. You can easily change the shape of any floating toolbar by dragging its edge. Let's change the shape of this toolbar.

3. Move the cursor to the far-right edge of the Inquiry toolbar until the crosshair cursor changes into a two-way arrow. Then hold down the left mouse button with the cursor on the right edge of the toolbar and drag the arrow to the right until the rectangle changes shape. Then release the mouse button.

Each floating toolbar can be reshaped and repositioned to fit on the drawing area just how you like it. You won't need the Inquiry toolbar just now, so remove it.

4. Move the cursor up to the title bar and click the box with an × in it. The Inquiry toolbar disappears.

If your Draw and Modify toolbars are positioned on the left side of the drawing area as in Figure 1.2, go on to the next section. If these toolbars are in another location on the drawing area, try out the steps you have used in this section to dock them on the left side. If the toolbars are not visible, select View ➤ Toolbars and use the Toolbars dialog box to bring them onto the screen. Then drag the Draw toolbar to the left side of the drawing area and dock it. Do the same with the Modify toolbar, positioning it next to the Draw toolbar.

This arrangement of the toolbars will be convenient because commands on these four toolbars are used often. When you need other toolbars temporarily, you can use the Toolbars dialog box to bring them onto the drawing area.

Custom Toolbars

Each toolbar can be customized and you can build your own custom toolbars with only the command buttons you need for your drawing. You can even design your own buttons for commands that aren't already represented by buttons on the toolbars. These activities are for more advanced users, however, and are not covered in this book. To find out more about how to work with toolbars, see *Mastering AutoCAD 2000* by George Omura (Sybex, 1999).

The Keyboard

Getting used to using the keyboard with AutoCAD is a good skill to master. The keyboard is an important tool for entering data and commands. If you are a good typist, you will gain a lot of speed in working with AutoCAD by learning how to use keyboard commands. AutoCAD provides what are called *alias keys*—single keys or key combinations that will start any of several often-used commands, and you can add more or change the existing aliases as you get more familiar with the program.

In addition to the alias keys, several of the F keys (function keys) on the top of the keyboard can be used as two-way or three-way toggles (switches) to turn AutoCAD functions on and off. Although there are buttons on the screen that duplicate these functions (Snap, Grid, etc.), it is often faster to use the F keys.

Finally, you can activate commands on the pull-down menus from the keyboard, rather than using the mouse. Notice that each menu has an underlined letter, called a *hotkey*. By holding down the Alt key while pressing the underlined letter, the menu is activated. Each command on the menu also has a hotkey. Once you have activated the menu with the hotkey combination, you can type in the underlined letter of these commands without using the Alt key to execute them. For some commands, this method can be the fastest way to start them up and select options.

While working in AutoCAD, you will need to enter ample amounts of data through the keyboard, such as dimensions and construction notes, answer questions with "yes" or "no," and use the keyboard arrow keys. The keyboard will be used constantly. It may help to get into the habit of keeping the left hand on the keyboard and the right hand on the mouse—if you are right-handed—and the other way around, if you are left-handed.

The Mouse

Your mouse will most likely have two or three buttons. So far in this skill, you have used only the left mouse button, for choosing menus, commands or command options, or for holding down the button and dragging a menu, toolbar, or window. That button is the one you will be using most frequently.

While drawing, the right mouse button will be used for the following three operations:

- To bring up a menu containing options relevant to the particular step you are in at the moment

- To use in combination with the Shift key to bring up a special menu called the Cursor menu (see Skill 10, *Controlling Text in a Drawing*)

- To bring up a menu of toolbars when the pointer is on any icon of a toolbar that is presently open

If you have a three-button mouse, the third button is usually programmed to bring up the Cursor menu mentioned above, instead of using the second button with the Shift key.

The next skill will familiarize you with a few basic commands that will enable you to draw a small diagram. If you are going to take a break and want to close down AutoCAD, click File ➤ Exit and choose not to save the drawing.

Are You Experienced?

Now you can...

☑ **open a new drawing using the Start Up dialog box**

☑ **recognize the elements of the AutoCAD Graphics window**

☑ **understand how the Command window works and why it's important**

☑ **use drop-down menus**

☑ **call up and control the positioning of toolbars**

☑ **use the keyboard and mouse with AutoCAD**

SKILL 2

Basic Commands to Get Started

- ➔ Understanding coordinate systems
- ➔ Drawing your first figure
- ➔ Erasing, offsetting, filleting, extending, and trimming lines in a drawing

Now that you have taken a quick tour of the AutoCAD screen, you are ready to begin drawing. In this skill you will be introduced to the most basic commands used in drawing with AutoCAD. To get you started, I will guide you through the process of drawing a box (Figure 2.1).

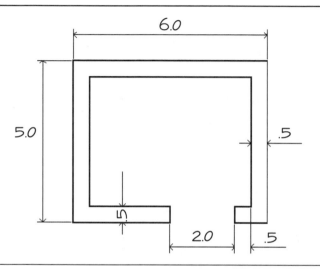

FIGURE 2.1:   The box to be drawn

You only need to use five or six commands to draw the box. First, you'll become familiar with the Line command and how to make lines a specific length. Then you'll go over the strategy for completing the box.

The Line Command

In traditional architectural drafting, lines were often drawn to extend slightly past their endpoints (Figure 2.2). This is no longer done in CAD except for special effects.

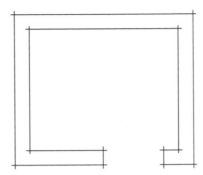

FIGURE 2.2: Box drawn with overlapping lines

The *Line command* draws a line between locations on existing lines, between geometric figures, or between two points that you can choose anywhere within the drawing area. These points can be designated by clicking them on the screen, by entering the *x* and *y* coordinates for each point in the Command window, or by entering distances and angles at the command line. After the first segment of a line is drawn, you have the option of ending the command or drawing another line segment from the end of the first one. You can continue to draw adjoining line segments for as long as you like. Let's see how it works.

1. Click File ➤ New. In the Create New Drawing dialog box, be sure English is selected, then click the Start from Scratch button and click OK to start a new drawing.

2. Be sure that the Draw and Modify toolbars have been docked on the left side of the drawing area, as in Figure 2.3. Refer to Skill 1, *Getting to Know AutoCAD*, if you need a reminder on how to bring up or move toolbars.

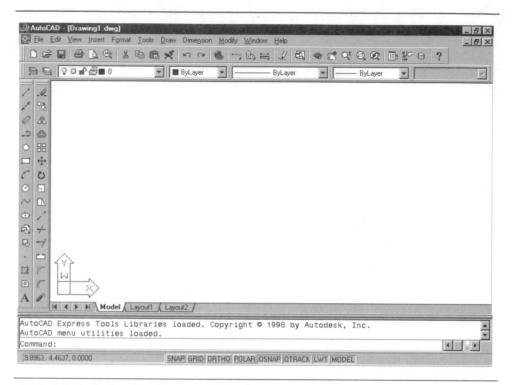

FIGURE 2.3: The Draw and Modify toolbars docked on the left side of the drawing area

3. Click the Line button at the top of the Draw toolbar.

NOTE NOTE NOTE NOTE NOTE NOTE NOTE NOTE NOTE NOTE NOTE NOTE NOTE NOTE NOTE

The Line command can also be started by picking Draw ➢ Line on the Menu bar, or by typing L and pressing the Enter key.

Look at the bottom of the Command window and see how the Command: prompt has changed.

The prompt now tells you that the Line command has been started (Command: _line) and that AutoCAD is waiting for you to designate the first point of the line (Specify first point:).

4. Move the cursor onto the drawing area and, using the left mouse button, click a random point to start a line.

5. Move the cursor away from the point you clicked and notice how a line segment appears which stretches like a rubberband from the point you just picked to the cursor. The line changes length and direction as you move the cursor.

6. Look at the Command window again and notice that the prompt has changed.

It now is telling you that AutoCAD is waiting for you to designate the next point (Specify next point or [Undo]:).

7. Continue picking points and adding lines as you move the cursor around the screen (see Figure 2.4). After the third segment is drawn, the Command window repeats the Specify next point or [Close/Undo]: prompt each time you pick another point.

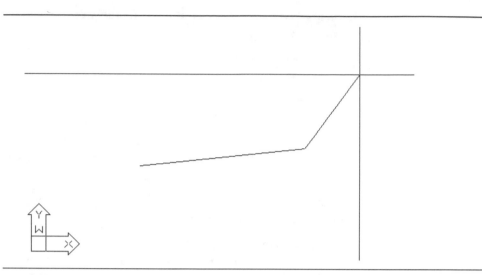

FIGURE 2.4: Drawing the second line segment

8. When you've drawn six or seven line segments, press the Enter key to end the Line command. The cursor separates from the last drawn line segment. Look at the Command window once again.

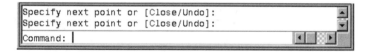

```
Specify next point or [Close/Undo]:
Specify next point or [Close/Undo]:
Command: |
```

The Command: prompt has returned to the bottom line. This tells you there is no command running.

In this exercise, you used the left mouse button to select the Line button from the Draw toolbar and also to pick several points in the drawing area to make the line segments. Then you pressed Enter (↵) on the keyboard to end the Line command.

NOTE NOTE NOTE NOTE NOTE NOTE NOTE NOTE NOTE NOTE NOTE NOTE NOTE NOTE NOTE

In the exercises that follow, the Enter symbol (↵) will be used when you are asked to press the Enter key.

Coordinates

Try using the Line command again, but instead of picking points in the drawing area with the mouse as you did before, this time enter x and y coordinates for each point from the keyboard. To see how, follow these steps:

First, you'll clear the screen using the Erase command.

1. Type **erase** ↵.

2. Type **all** ↵.

3. Press ↵.

Now start drawing lines again by following these steps:

1. Start the Line command again by clicking the Line button on the Draw toolbar.

2. Type **2,2** ↵.

3. Type **6,3** ↵.

4. Type **4,6** ↵.

5. Type **1,3** ↵.

6. Type **10,6** ↵.

7. Type **10,1** ↵.

8. Type **2,7** ↵.

9. Press ↵ again to end the command.

The lines will be similar to those you drew previously, but this time you know where each point is located relative to the 0,0 point. In the drawing area, every point has an absolute x and y coordinate. In steps 2–8 above, you entered the x and y coordinates for each point. For a new drawing, like this one, the origin (0,0 point) is in the lower-left corner of the drawing area and all points in the drawing area are positive (Figure 2.5).

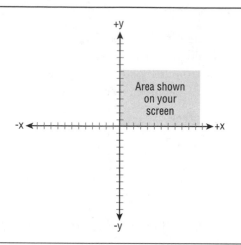

FIGURE 2.5:   The *x* and *y* coordinates on the drawing areas

Let's explore how the cursor is related to the coordinates in the drawing.

1. Move the cursor around and notice the left end of the Status bar at the bottom of the screen. This is the coordinate readout, and it displays the coordinates of the cursor's position.

2. Move the cursor as close to the lower-left corner of the drawing area as you can without it changing into an arrow. The coordinate readout should be close to 0.0000,0.0000,0.0000.

NOTE NOTE NOTE NOTE NOTE NOTE NOTE NOTE NOTE NOTE NOTE NOTE NOTE NOTE NOTE

You will see a readout for the *z* coordinate as well, but we can ignore it for now as you will be working only in two dimensions for the majority of this book. The *z* coordinate will always read as 0 until we work in three dimensions (see Appendix A, *A Look at Drawing in 3D*).

3. Move the cursor to the top-left corner of the drawing area. The readout will change to something close to 0.0000,9.0000,0.0000, indicating that the top of the screen is nine units away from the bottom.

4. Move the cursor one more time to the upper-right corner of the drawing area. The readout will still have a *y* coordinate of approximately 9.0000 and the *x* coordinate will now have a value of somewhere between 12.0000 and 16.0000, depending on the size of your monitor and how the various parts of the AutoCAD Graphics window (see Skill 1 for a recap) are laid out on your screen.

The drawing area of a new drawing is preset to be 9 units high and 12–18 units wide, with the lower-left corner of the drawing at the coordinates 0,0.

NOTE NOTE NOTE NOTE NOTE NOTE NOTE NOTE NOTE NOTE NOTE NOTE NOTE NOTE NOTE

For the moment, it doesn't matter what measure of distance these units represent. Those decisions will be addressed in Skill 3, *Setting Up a Drawing*. And don't worry about the four decimal places in the coordinate readout, which is controlled by a setting you will learn about in the next skill, as well.

Relative Coordinates

With knowledge of the coordinate system used by AutoCAD, you can draw lines of any length and in any direction you desire. Look at the box in Figure 2.1. Because you know the dimensions, you could calculate, by adding and subtracting, the absolute coordinates for each vertex and then use the Line command to draw the shape by entering these coordinates from the keyboard. But AutoCAD offers you two much easier tools for drawing this box: the relative Cartesian and relative polar coordinate systems.

When drawing lines, these systems use a set of new points based on the last point designated, rather than the 0,0 point of the drawing area. They are called "relative" coordinate systems because the coordinates used are *relative* to the last point specified. If you have the first point of a line located at the coordinate 4,6 and you want the line to extend 8 units to the right, the coordinate that is relative to the first point is 8,0 (8 units in the positive *x* direction and 0 units in the positive *y* direction), while the actual—or *absolute*—coordinate of the second point would be 12,6.

The *relative Cartesian coordinate system* uses relative *x* and *y* coordinates in just the manner shown above, while the *relative polar coordinate system* relies on a distance and an angle relative to the last point specified. You will probably favor one system over the other, but you need to know both systems because there will be times when, due to limitations created by known or unknown information, you will have no choice. A limitation of this nature will be illustrated in Skill 4, *Gaining Drawing Strategies: Part 1.*

When entering the relative coordinates, you need to enter an "at" symbol (@) before the coordinates. In the above example, the relative Cartesian coordinates would be entered as **@8,0**. The @ symbol lets AutoCAD know that the numbers following that symbol represent coordinates which are relative to the last point designated.

Relative Cartesian Coordinates

The Cartesian system of coordinates, named after philosopher René Descartes who invented the *x,y* coordinate system in the 1600s, uses a horizontal (*x*) and vertical (*y*) component to locate a point relative to the 0,0 point. The relative Cartesian system uses the same components to locate the point relative to the last point picked, so it's a way of telling AutoCAD how far left or right and up or down to extend a line or move an object from the last point picked (Figure 2.6). If the direction is to the left, the *x* coordinate will be negative. Similarly, if the direction is down, the *y* coordinate will be negative. Use this system when you know the horizontal and vertical distances from point 1 to point 2. To enter data using this system, use this form: **@*x,y*.**

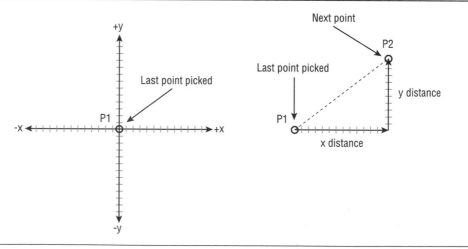

FIGURE 2.6: The relative Cartesian coordinate system

Relative Polar Coordinates

This system requires a known distance and direction from point 1 to point 2. Calculating the distance is pretty straightforward: it's always positive and is simply the distance away from point 1 that point 2 will be placed. The direction requires a convention for determining an angle. AutoCAD defines right (three o'clock) as the direction of the 0°angle, and all other directions are determined from a counter-clockwise rotation (Figure 2.7). Up is 90°, left is 180°, down is 270°, and a full circle is 360°. To let AutoCAD know that you are entering an angle and not a relative *y* coordinate, use the "less than" symbol (<) before the angle and after the distance. So in the example above, designating a point 8 units to the right of the first point, you would enter **@8<0**.

NOTE NOTE NOTE NOTE NOTE NOTE NOTE NOTE NOTE NOTE NOTE NOTE NOTE NOTE NOTE

Remember, use this method to draw a line from the first point when you know the distance and direction to its next point. For entering data using relative polar coordinates, use this form: @*distance*<angle.

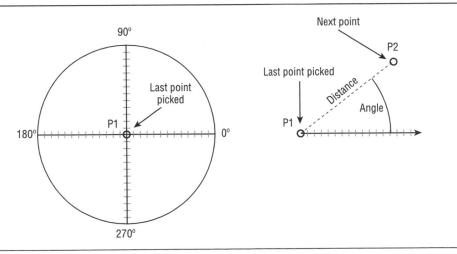

FIGURE 2.7: The relative polar coordinate system

Drawing the Box

Now that you have the basics down, the following exercises will take you through the steps to draw the four lines comprising the outline of the box using both relative coordinate systems.

Using Relative Cartesian Coordinates

To begin drawing the box, we'll start with a new drawing.

1. Click File ➤ Close. You will be prompted to save your last drawing: Click No.

2. Click File ➤ New.

3. In the Create New Drawing dialog box, click Start from Scratch, select English, then click OK.

4. Select the Line button from the top of the Draw toolbar.

5. At the `Specify First point:` prompt in the Command window, type in **3,3** ↵. This is an absolute Cartesian coordinate and will be the first point.

6. Type **@6,0** ↵.

7. Type **@0,5** ↵.

8. Type **@-6,0** ↵.

9. Type **c** ↵. The letter *c* stands for *close*. Entering this letter after drawing several lines closes the shape by making the next line segment extend from the last point specified to the first point (Figure 2.8). It also ends the Line command. Notice that in the Command window the prompt is `Command:`. This signifies that AutoCAD is ready for a new command.

Erasing Lines

To prepare to draw the box again, use the Erase command to erase the four lines you have just drawn.

1. Click Modify ➤ Erase. Notice how the cursor changes from the crosshair to a little square. This is called the *pickbox*. When you see it on the screen, it's a sign that AutoCAD is ready for you to select objects on the screen. Also, notice the Command window. It is prompting you to select objects.

2. Place the pickbox on one of the lines and click. The line changes into a dashed line. This is called *ghosting* or *highlighting*.

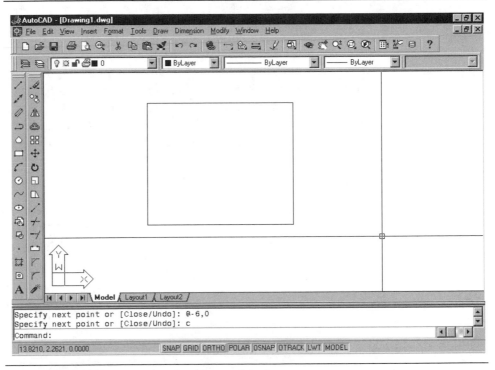

FIGURE 2.8: The first four lines of the box

3. Do the same thing with the rest of the lines.

4. Press ↵. The objects are erased and the Erase command ends.

Using Relative Polar Coordinates

Now draw the box again using the polar method by following these steps:

1. Start the Line command. (Choose the Line button from the Draw toolbar.)

2. Type in **3,3** ↵ to start the box at the same point.

3. Type **@6<0** ↵.

4. Type **@5<90** ↵.

5. Type **@6<180** ↵.

6. Type **c** ↵ to close the box and end the Line command. Your box will once again resemble the box in Figure 2.8.

You can see from this simple exercise that either method can be used to draw a simple shape. When the shapes you are drawing get more complex and the amount of available information about the shapes varies from segment to segment, there will be situations where one of the two relative coordinate systems will turn out to be more appropriate. As you start drawing the floor plan of the cabin in Skills 3 and 4, you will get more practice using these systems.

The Offset Command

The next task is to create the lines that represent the inside walls of the box. Because they are all equidistant from the lines you have already drawn, the *Offset command* is the appropriate command to use. You will offset the existing lines 0.5 units to the inside.

The Offset command has three steps:

- Setting the offset distance

- Picking the object to offset

- Indicating the offset direction

Here's how it works:

1. Be sure the prompt line in the Command window reads "`Command:`." If it doesn't, press the Esc key until it does. Then move to the menu bar and click Modify ➤ Offset, or click the Offset button on the Modify toolbar. The prompt changes to `Offset distance or Through <1.0000>:`. This is a confusing prompt.

WARNING WARNING WARNING WARNING WARNING WARNING WARNING WARNING
As important as it is to keep an eye on the Command window, some of the prompts may not make sense to you until you get used to them.

You have three choices for setting the offset distance:

- Enter a distance on the keyboard.

- Pick two points on the screen to establish the offset distance as the distance between those two picked points (the Through option).

- Accept the default offset distance of 1.0000 in the brackets (< >).

2. Enter .5 ↵ for a distance. Now you move to the second stage of the command.

**SKILL
2**

NOTE NOTE NOTE NOTE NOTE NOTE NOTE NOTE NOTE NOTE NOTE NOTE NOTE NOTE

When I say to "Enter" something, it means to type the data that follows the word *Enter* and then to press the Enter key (↵).

Note that the cursor has changed to a pickbox, and the prompt changes to say "Select object to offset or <exit>:."

3. Place the pickbox on one of the lines and click. The selected line ghosts (Figure 2.9), the cursor changes back to the crosshair, and the prompt changes to Specify points on side to offset:. AutoCAD is telling you that to determine the direction of the offset, you must specify a point on one side of the line or the other. You make the choice by picking anywhere in the drawing area, on the side of the line where you want the offset to occur.

FIGURE 2.9: The first line to be offset is selected.

4. Pick a point somewhere inside the box. The offset takes place and the new line is exactly 0.5 units to the inside of the chosen line (Figure 2.10). Notice that the pickbox comes back on. The Offset command is still running and you can offset more lines the same distance.

You have three more lines to offset.

 NOTE NOTE NOTE NOTE NOTE NOTE NOTE NOTE NOTE NOTE NOTE NOTE NOTE NOTE NOTE
You can cancel a command at any time by pressing Esc.

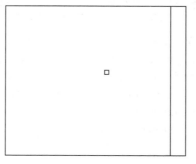

FIGURE 2.10: The first line is offset.

5. Click another line, then click inside the box again. The second line is offset.

6. Click a third line, click inside the box, then click the fourth line and click again inside the box (Figure 2.11).

 NOTE NOTE NOTE NOTE NOTE NOTE NOTE NOTE NOTE NOTE NOTE NOTE NOTE NOTE NOTE
The offset distance stays set at the last distance you specify for it—0.5, in this case—until you change it.

7. Press ↵ to end the Offset command. This command is similar to the Line command in that it keeps running until it is stopped. With Offset, after the

first offset, the prompts switch between `Select object to offset or <exit>:` and `Specify point on side to offset:` until you press ⏎ to end the command.

The inside lines are now drawn, but to complete the box, you need to clean up the intersecting corners. To handle this task efficiently, we will use a new tool called the Fillet command.

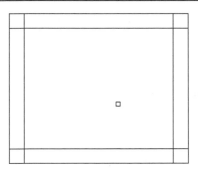

FIGURE 2.11: Four lines have been offset.

The Fillet Command

The *Fillet command* allows you to round off a corner formed by two lines. You control the radius of the curve, so if you set the curve's radius to zero, the lines will form a sharp corner. In this way you can clean up corners like the ones formed by the lines inside the box.

1. At the `Command:` prompt, click the Fillet button on the Modify toolbar.

TIP TIP TIP TIP TIP TIP TIP TIP TIP TIP TIP TIP TIP TIP TIP TIP TIP TIP TIP TIP TIP TIP TIP TIP

You can also start the Fillet command by selecting Modify ➢ Fillet from the menu bar, or by typing f ⏎.

Notice the Command window:

```
Command: _fillet
Current settings: Mode = TRIM, Radius = 0.5000
Select first object or [Polyline/Radius/Trim]:
```

The default fillet radius is 0.5 units, but you want to use a radius of 0 units.

2. Type **r** ↵ **0** ↵ to change the radius to 0. This has the effect of ending the Fillet command while setting the new radius to 0 units. Press ↵ to restart it.

 TIP TIP TIP TIP TIP TIP TIP TIP TIP TIP TIP TIP TIP TIP TIP TIP TIP TIP TIP TIP TIP TIP TIP TIP

Once a command has ended, you can restart it by pressing Enter.

3. Move the cursor—now a pickbox—to the box and click two intersecting lines as shown in Figure 2.12. The intersecting lines will both be trimmed to make a sharp corner (Figure 2.13). The Fillet command automatically ends.

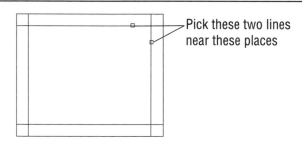

FIGURE 2.12: Pick two lines to execute the Fillet command.

4. Press ↵ to restart the command and fillet two more lines in a similar fashion.

5. Continue restarting the command and filleting the lines for each corner until all corners are cleaned up (Figure 2.14).

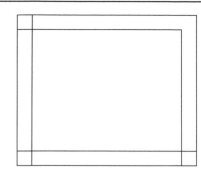

FIGURE 2.13: The first cleaned-up corner

NOTE NOTE NOTE NOTE NOTE NOTE NOTE NOTE NOTE NOTE NOTE NOTE NOTE NOTE NOTE

If you make a mistake and pick the wrong part of a line or the wrong line, press Esc to end the command and then type u ⏎. This will undo the effect of the last command.

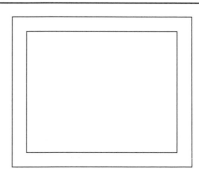

FIGURE 2.14: The box with all corners cleaned up

Used together like this, the Offset and Fillet commands are a powerful combination of tools to lay out walls on a floor plan drawing. Since these commands are so important, let's take a closer look at them to see how they work. Both commands are found on the Modify toolbar or drop-down menu, both have the option to enter a numerical value or accept the current value—for offset distance and fillet radius—and both hold that value as the default until it is changed. However, the Offset command keeps running until you stop it, and the Fillet command stops after each use and must be restarted for multiple fillets. These two commands are probably the most frequently used tools in AutoCAD. You will learn about more of their uses in later skills.

Completing the Box

The final step in completing the box (Figure 2.1) is to make an opening in the bottom wall. From the diagram, you can see that the opening is 2 units wide and set off from the right inside corner by 0.5 units. To make this opening, you will use the Offset command twice, changing the offset distance for each offset, to create marks for the opening.

Offsetting Lines to Mark an Opening

Follow these steps to establish the precise position of the opening:

1. At the Command: prompt, start the Offset command, either from the Modify toolbar or the Modify menu. Notice the Command window. The default distance is now set at 0.5, the offset distance you previously set to offset the outside lines of the box to make the inside lines. You want to use this distance again. Press ↵ to accept this preset distance.

2. Pick the inside vertical line on the right, and then pick a point to the left of this line. The line is offset to make a new line 0.5 units to its left (Figure 2.15).

3. Press ↵ to end the Offset command, then press it again to restart the command. This will allow you to reset the offset distance.

4. Enter 2 as the new offset distance and press ↵.

5. Click the new line then pick a point to the left. Press ↵ to end the Offset command (Figure 2.16).

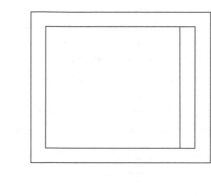

FIGURE 2.15: Offsetting the first line of the opening

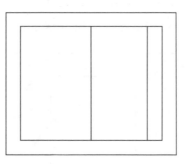

FIGURE 2.16: Offsetting the second line of the opening

You now have two new lines indicating where the opening will be. You can use these lines to form the opening using the Extend and Trim commands.

Extending Lines

The *Extend command* is used to lengthen (extend) lines to meet other lines or geometric figures (called *boundary edges*). The execution of the Extend command may be a little tricky at first until you see how it works. Once you understand it, however, it will become automatic. The command has two steps: First, you will pick the boundary edge or edges, and second, you will pick the lines you wish to extend to meet those boundary edges. After selecting the boundary edges, you must press ↵ before you begin selecting lines to extend.

1. To begin the Extend command, open the Modify menu and select Extend. Or click the Extend button on the Modify toolbar. Notice the Command window.

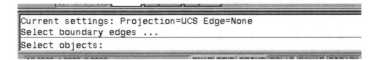

```
Current settings: Projection=UCS Edge=None
Select boundary edges ...
Select objects:
```

2. The bottom line says to "Select objects," but, in this case, you need to observe the bottom two lines of text in order to know that AutoCAD is prompting you to select boundary edges.

3. Pick the very bottom horizontal line (Figure 2.17) and press ↵.

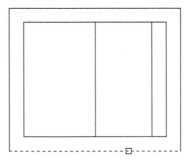

FIGURE 2.17: Selecting a line to be a boundary edge

The `Select Objects:` **prompt would be more useful if it said, "Select objects and press Enter when finished selecting objects." But it doesn't. You have to train yourself to press Enter when you are finished selecting objects for a particular step—in this case, selecting objects to serve as boundary edges—in the execution of a command, in order to get out of the selection mode and move on to the next step in the command.**

4. Pick the two new vertical lines created by the Offset command. Be sure to place the pickbox somewhere on the lower halves of these lines, or Auto-CAD will ignore your picks. The lines are extended to the boundary edge line. Press ↵ to end the Extend command (Figure 2.18).

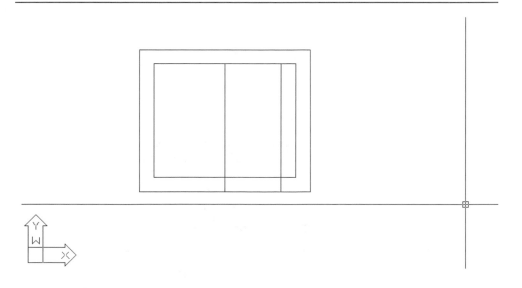

FIGURE 2.18:   The lines are extended to the boundary edge.

Trimming Lines

The final step is to trim away the horizontal lines to complete the opening. To do this, you will use the *Trim command*. As with the Extend command, there are two steps to trimming. The first one is to select reference lines—in this case, they're called *cutting edges* because they determine the edge or edges to which a line is trimmed.

1. Start the Trim command. You have three choices for doing this: Select Modify ➤ Trim from the menu bar, click the Trim button from the Modify toolbar, or type **tr** ↵. Any of these will start the Trim command.

    Notice the Command window. Similar to the Extend command, the bottom line prompts you to select objects, but the second line up tells you to select cutting edges.

2. Pick the two vertical offset lines that were just extended as your cutting edges. Then press ↵ (Figure 2.19).

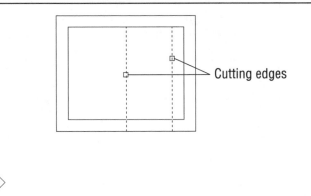

FIGURE 2.19: Lines selected to be cutting edges

3. Pick the two horizontal lines across the opening somewhere between the cutting edge lines (Figure 2.20).

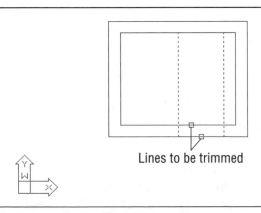

FIGURE 2.20: Lines selected to be trimmed

The opening is trimmed away (Figure 2.21).

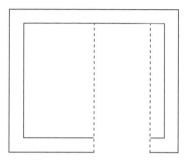

FIGURE 2.21: Wall lines are trimmed to make the opening.

NOTE NOTE NOTE NOTE NOTE NOTE NOTE NOTE NOTE NOTE NOTE NOTE NOTE NOTE NOTE

If you trim the wrong line or wrong part of a line, you can click the Undo button on the Standard toolbar. This will undo the last trim without canceling the Trim command and you can try again.

Now let's remove the extra part of our trimming guide lines.

1. Press ↵ twice—once to end the Trim command and again to restart it. This will allow you to pick new cutting edges for another trim operation.

2. Pick the two upper horizontal lines in the lower wall as your cutting edges, shown in Figure 2.22, and press ↵.

3. Pick the two vertical lines that extend above the new opening. Be sure to pick them above the opening (Figure 2.23). The lines are trimmed away and the opening is complete. Press ↵ to end the Trim command (Figure 2.24).

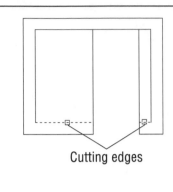

FIGURE 2.22: Lines picked to be cutting edges

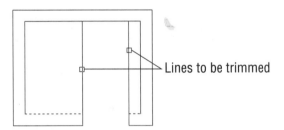

FIGURE 2.23: Lines picked to be trimmed

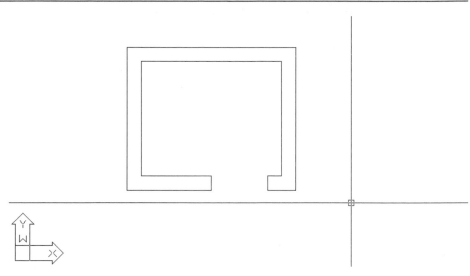

FIGURE 2.24: The completed trim

Congratulations! You have just completed the first drawing project in this book and have covered all the tools in Skill 2. As you will see in later sections of the book, these skills will be invaluable to you as you learn how to work on drawings for actual projects.

A valuable exercise at this time would be to draw this box two or three more times, until you can do it without the instructions. This will be a confidence builder and will get you ready to take on new information in the next skill, in which you will set up a drawing for a building.

The box you drew was 6 units by 5 units, but how big was it? You really don't know at this time, because the units could represent any actual distance: inches, feet, meters, miles, etc. Also, the box was positioned conveniently on the screen so you didn't have any problem viewing it. Consider the situation if you were drawing a building that was 200-feet long and 60-feet wide. The next skill to be tackled is how to set up a drawing for a project of a specific size.

You can exit AutoCAD now without saving this drawing. To do this, click File ➤ Exit. When the dialog box comes up asking if you want to save changes, click No. Or you can leave AutoCAD open and go on to the following practice section or the next skill.

If You Would Like More Practice...

Draw the following object (Figure 2.25).

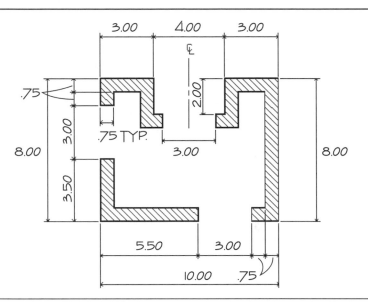

FIGURE 2.25: Practice drawing

You can use the same tools and strategy used to draw the box. Use File ➤ New to start a new drawing and click the Start from Scratch button in the Create New Drawing dialog box.

Are You Experienced?

Now you can...

- ☑ **understand the basics of coordinates**

- ☑ **discern between the two relative coordinate systems used by AutoCAD**

- ☑ **use the Line, Erase, Offset, Fillet, Extend, and Trim commands to manipulate lines in a drawing**

Setting Up a Drawing

- → Setting up drawing units
- → Using a grid
- → Zooming in and out of a drawing
- → Naming and saving a file

In Skill 2 you explored the default drawing area that is set up when a new drawing is opened. It is probably 9 units high by 12 to 16 units wide, depending upon the size of your monitor. You drew the box within this area. If you drew the additional diagram offered as a supplemental exercise, the drawing area was set up the same way.

For most of the rest of this book, you will be developing drawings for a cabin with outside wall dimensions of 25' × 16'. In this skill you will learn how to set up the drawing area to lay out the floor plan for a building of a specific size. The decimal units with which you have been drawing until now will be changed to feet and inches, and the drawing area will be transformed so that it can represent an area large enough to display the floor plan of the cabin you will be drawing. You will be introduced to some new tools that allow you to visualize the area your screen represents and to draw within a specified incremental distance. Finally, you will save this drawing to a floppy disk or to a special directory on the hard disk.

Drawing Units

When you draw lines of a precise length in AutoCAD, you will use one of five kinds of linear units. Angular units can also be one of five different types. You can select the type of units to use, or accept the default decimal units that you used in the last chapter.

When you start a new drawing using the Start from Scratch option, AutoCAD brings up a blank drawing called Drawing1.dwg with the linear and angular units set to decimal numbers. The units and other basic setup parameters applied to this new drawing are based on a prototype drawing, or drawing template, with default settings—including those for the units—which are stored with the drawing template file Acad.dwt. You can choose another template file as a prototype drawing, or you can create your own set of prototype drawings. Skill 3 will cover some of the tools for changing the basic parameters of a new drawing so you can tailor it to the cabin project. You will start by setting up new units.

1. Start up AutoCAD and, in the Startup dialog box, click the Start from Scratch button. Be sure English is selected and click OK.

2. From the Format menu, select Units. The Drawing Units dialog box appears (Figure 3.1). In the Length area, Decimal is currently selected. Similarly, in the Angle area, Decimal Degrees is the default.

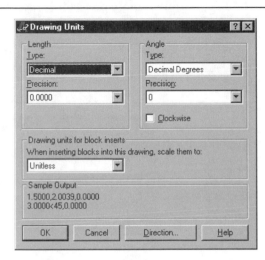

SKILL
3

FIGURE 3.1: The Drawing Units dialog box

3. In the Length area, click the arrow in the Type drop-down list and select Architectural. These units are feet and inches, which you will be using for the cabin project. Notice the two Precision drop-down lists at the bottom of the Length and Angle areas. When the linear units specification was changed from Decimal to Architectural, the number in the Precision drop-down list on the left changed from 0.0000 to 0'-0 1/16". At this level of precision, linear distances will be displayed to the nearest 1/16".

4. Select some of the other Length unit types from the list and note the way the units appear in the Sample Output area at the bottom of the dialog box. Then select Architectural again.

NOTE NOTE NOTE NOTE NOTE NOTE NOTE NOTE NOTE NOTE NOTE NOTE NOTE NOTE NOTE

Drop-down lists are lists of choices with only the selected choice displayed. When you click the arrow, the list opens. When you make another selection, the list closes and your choice is displayed. Only one choice from the list can be made at a time.

5. Click the arrow in the Precision drop-down list in the Length area. The drop-down list appears, showing the choices of precision for Architectural units (Figure 3.2). This setting controls the degree of precision to which AutoCAD will *display* a linear distance. If set to 1/16", this means that any

line that is drawn more precisely—such as a line 6'-3 1/32" long—will be displayed to the nearest 1/16" or, in the example, as 6'-3 1/16". But the line will still be 6'-3 1/32" long. If you change the precision setting to 1/32" and then use the Distance command (explained in Skill 7, *Using Blocks and Wblocking*) to measure the line, you will see that its length is 6'-3 1/32".

FIGURE 3.2: The Precision drop-down list for Architectural units

6. Click 0'-0 1/16" to maintain the precision for display of linear units at 1/16".

In the Angle area, you can see that there is a choice between Decimal Degrees and Deg/Min/Sec, among others. Most drafters find the decimal angular units the most practical, but the default precision setting is to the nearest degree. This might be too restrictive, so you should change that to the nearest hundredth of a degree.

1. Click the arrow in the Angle Precision drop-down list.

2. Click 0.00.

The Drawing Units dialog box will now indicate that, in your drawing, you plan to use Architectural units with a precision of 1/16", and Decimal angular units with a precision of 0.00 (Figure 3.3).

The Direction button at the bottom of the dialog box takes you to another dialog box that has settings to control the direction of 0 degrees. There is no need to change these from the defaults; so, if you want to take a look, open the Direction Control dialog box, note the choices, and then click OK to close it. You won't have occasion in the course of this book to change any of those settings.

FIGURE 3.3: The Drawing Units dialog box after changes

NOTE NOTE NOTE NOTE NOTE NOTE NOTE NOTE NOTE NOTE NOTE NOTE NOTE NOTE NOTE
You will have a chance to work with the Surveyor angular units later in the book, in Skill 12, *Managing External References,* **when you develop a site plan for the cabin.**

3.   Click OK in the Drawing Units dialog box to close it. When the note about Insert Units appears, click OK to close it. Notice the coordinate readout in the lower-left corner of the screen. It now reads out in feet and inches.

This tour of the Drawing Units dialog box has introduced you to the choices you have for the type of units and the degree of precision for linear and angular measurement. The next step in setting up a drawing is learning how to determine the size of a drawing.

NOTE NOTE NOTE NOTE NOTE NOTE NOTE NOTE NOTE NOTE NOTE NOTE NOTE NOTE NOTE
If you accidentally click the mouse with the cursor on a blank part of the drawing area, AutoCAD starts a rectangular window. We'll talk about these windows soon, but for now, just press the Esc key to cancel the window.

Drawing Size

As you discovered earlier, the default drawing area on the screen for a new drawing is 12 to 16–units wide and 9-units high. After changing the units to Architectural, the same drawing area is now 12 to 16–*inches* wide and 9-*inches* high. You can check this by moving the crosshair cursor around on the drawing area and looking at the coordinate readout, as you did in the previous skill.

 TIP TIP TIP TIP TIP TIP TIP TIP TIP TIP TIP TIP TIP TIP TIP TIP TIP TIP TIP TIP TIP TIP TIP TIP

When Decimal units are changed to Architectural units, one Decimal unit translates to one inch. Some industries use Decimal units to represent feet instead of inches. If their drawing's units are switched to Architectural, the drawing must be scaled up by a factor of 12 to be the accurate size.

The drawing area is defined as the part of the screen in which you draw. The distance across the drawing area can be made larger or smaller through a process known as zooming in or out. To see how this works, you'll learn about a tool called the grid that helps you to draw and to visualize the size of your drawing.

The Grid

The grid is a pattern of regularly spaced dots used as an aid to drawing. You can set the grid to be visible or invisible. The area covered by the grid depends on a setting called *drawing limits*. To learn how to manipulate the grid size, you'll make the grid visible, use the Zoom In and Zoom Out commands to vary the view of the grid and then change the area over which the grid extends by resetting the drawing limits. Before doing this, however, let's turn off the User Coordinate System icon.

1. At the Command: prompt, type **ucsicon** ↵, then type **off** ↵. The icon will disappear.

2. At the Command: prompt, move the crosshair cursor to the status bar at the bottom of the screen and click the Grid button. The button will appear to have been pushed down and dots will appear on most of the drawing area (Figure 3.4). These dots are the grid. They are preset by default to be 0.5" apart, and they extend from the 0,0 point (the Origin), out to the right, and up to the coordinate point 1'-0",0'-9". Notice that rows of grid dots run right along the left edge, top, and bottom of the drawing area; but the dots don't extend all the way to the right side. The grid dot at the 0,0 point is positioned exactly at the lower-left corner of the screen, and the one at 1'-0",0'-9" is on the top edge not too far from the upper-right corner.

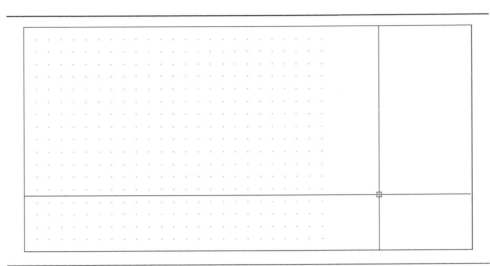

FIGURE 3.4: The AutoCAD default grid

3. For a better view of the entire grid, use the *Zoom Out* command. From the drop-down menus, select View ≻ Zoom ≻ Out. The view changes and the grid appears smaller (Figure 3.5). Move the crosshair cursor to the lower-left corner of the grid, then move it to the upper-right corner and note the coordinate readout in the lower-left of your screen. These two points should read as approximately 0'-0",0'-0" and 1'-0",0'-9" respectively.

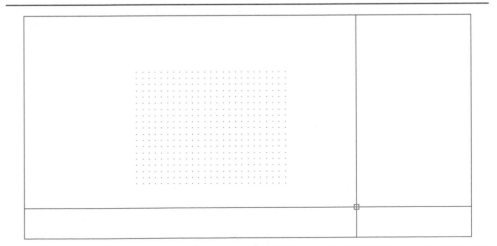

FIGURE 3.5: The grid after zooming out

4. On the status bar, next to the Grid button, click the Snap button, then move the cursor back onto the grid and look at the coordinate readout again. The cursor stops at each grid point and the readout is to the nearest half inch. Now when you place the crosshair cursor on the lower-left corner of the grid, the readout is exactly 0'-0",0'-0", and 1'-0",0'-9" for the upper-right corner. The Snap tool locks the cursor onto the grid dots, and even when the cursor is not on the grid but somewhere outside it on the drawing area, the cursor maintains the grid spacing.

5. Use the Zoom Out command two more times. The first time the grid gets even smaller. After the second use of the command, the grid may disappear, in which case you would get a message on the second line of the Command window that says, "Grid too dense to display." Once the dots get too close together, the monitor cannot display them, and AutoCAD lets you know.

6. On the same menu, use the Zoom In tool twice to bring the view of the grid back to the way it was in Figure 3.5. You are not changing the size of the grid, just the view of it. It's like switching from a wide-angle to a telephoto lens on a camera.

The grid is more of a guide than an actual boundary of your drawing. You can change a setting to force lines to be drawn only in the area covered by the grid, but this is not ordinarily done. For most purposes, you can draw anywhere on the screen. The grid merely serves as a tool for visualizing how your drawing is going to be laid out.

Because it will serve as a layout tool for this project, you need to increase the area covered by the grid from its present size of 1' × 9" to 60' × 40'. Because the drawing limits control the size of the grid, you need to change this setting.

Drawing Limits

The Drawing Limits setting records the coordinates of the lower-left and upper-right corners of the grid. The coordinates for the lower-left corner are 0,0 by default, and are usually left at that setting. You only need to change the coordinates for the upper-right corner.

1. At the Command: prompt, pick Format ➤ Drawing Limits from the drop-down menus. Notice the Command window:

```
Command: '_limits
Reset Model space limits:
Specify lower left corner or [ON/OFF] <0'-0",0'-0">:
```

The bottom command line tells you that the first step is to decide whether to change the default coordinates for the lower-left limits, which are presently set at 0,0. There is no need to change these.

2. Press ↵ to accept 0,0 for this corner. The bottom command line changes and is now allowing you to change the coordinates for the upper-right corner of the limits. This is the setting you want to change.

3. Type **60',40'** ↵. Be sure to include the foot sign (').

NOTE NOTE NOTE NOTE NOTE NOTE NOTE NOTE NOTE NOTE NOTE NOTE NOTE NOTE NOTE
AutoCAD requires that you always indicate when a distance is feet by using the foot sign ('). You do not have to use the inch sign (").

The grid now appears to extend to the top-right edge of the drawing area (Figure 3.6), but it actually extends way past the edges. It was 1-foot wide and now it's 60 times that, but the drawing area is only showing us the first foot or so. To bring the whole grid onto the screen, use the Zoom command again, but this time you will use the All option.

4. Select View ➢ Zoom ➢ All. The grid disappears, and you get the Grid Too Dense To Display message in the Command window.

FIGURE 3.6: The same view with the grid extended to 60'×40'

Remember that you found the grid spacing to be 0.5", by default. If the drawing area is giving us a view of a 60' × 40' grid with dots at 0.5", the grid is 1440 dots wide and 960-dots high. If the whole grid were to be shown on the screen, the dots would be so close together that they would only be about one pixel in size and would solidly fill the drawing area. So AutoCAD won't display them at these settings.

You need to change the spacing for the dots for two reasons: first, the spacing needs to be larger so that AutoCAD will display them; and second, for the drawing task ahead, it will be more useful to have the spacing set differently. Remember how we turned Snap on, and the cursor stopped at each dot? If you set the dot spacing to 12", you can use Grid and Snap modes to help you draw the outline of the cabin because the dimensions of the outside wall line are in even feet: 25' × 16'. Here's how:

1. At the Command: prompt, select Tools ➤ Drafting Settings from the menu bar. The Drafting Settings dialog box appears. Select the Snap and Grid tab (Figure 3.7). The settings in the Grid and Snap areas both include an X and Y Spacing setting. Notice that they are all set for a spacing of 1/2".

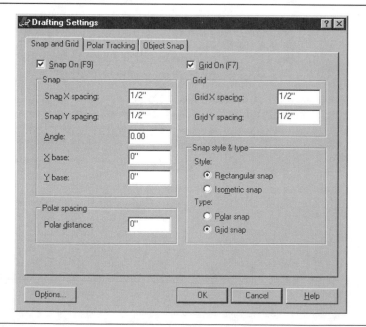

FIGURE 3.7: The Drafting Settings dialog box

2. In the Grid section, click in the Grid X Spacing text box and change it to 0. If you set the grid spacing to 0, it will then take on whatever spacing you set for the Snap X spacing text box. This is how you lock the two together.

When the X spacing reads 0, click the ½" in the Grid Y Spacing text box. It changes to match the X Spacing.

3. In the Snap section, click in the Snap X Spacing box and change the setting to 12. The inch sign is not required. Then click the Snap Y Spacing setting. It changes to automatically match the X Spacing.

4. In the Snap Type and Style area, be sure the Type is set to Grid Snap and the Style is set to Rectangular Snap.

5. Click OK. The grid is now visible (Figure 3.8). Move the cursor around on the grid—be sure Snap is on (Check the Snap button on the Status bar. It will be depressed when Snap is on.)—and notice the coordinate readout. It is displaying coordinates to the nearest foot to conform to the new grid and snap spacing.

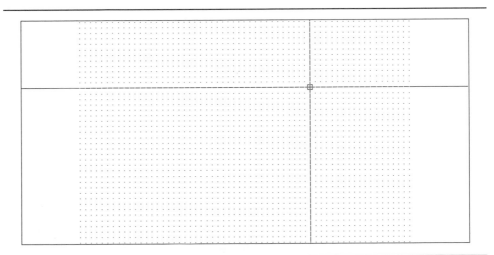

FIGURE 3.8: The new 60'×40' grid with 12" dot spacing

Drawing with Grid and Snap

Your drawing area now has the proper settings and is zoomed to a convenient magnification. You should be ready to draw the first lines of the cabin.

1. At the Command: prompt, start the Line command (Choose the Line button on the Draw toolbar.) and pick a point on the grid in the lower-left quadrant of the drawing area (Figure 3.9).

2. Hold the crosshair cursor to the right of the point just picked and look at the coordinate readout. It may be displaying relative polar coordinates from the first point picked, but it probably isn't. If it is not, try clicking once on the coordinate readout. If that doesn't work, clicking one more time will do the job, as the coordinate readout is controlled by a three-way toggle.

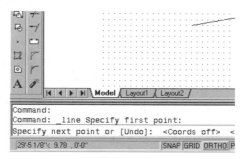

3. Now hold the crosshair cursor directly out to the right of the first point picked and look at the coordinate readout. It will be displaying a distance in even feet and should have an angle of 0.00. (Ignore the extra z coordinate.)

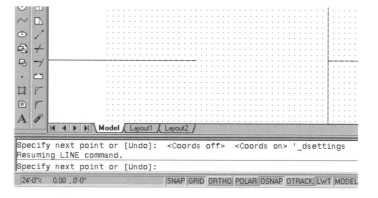

4. Continue moving the crosshair cursor left or right until the readout displays 25'-0"<0.00. At this point, click the left mouse button. The first line of the cabin wall is drawn (Figure 3.10).

5. Move the crosshair cursor directly above the last point picked to a position such that the coordinate readout displays 16'-0"<90.00, and pick that point.

6. Move the crosshair cursor directly left of the last point picked until the coordinate readout displays 25'-0"<180.00, and pick that point (Figure 3.11).

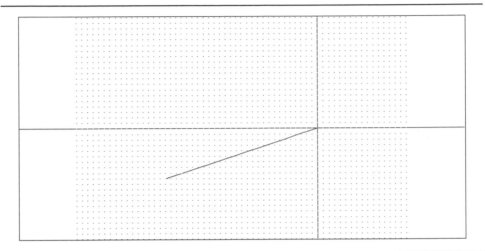

FIGURE 3.9: One point picked on the grid

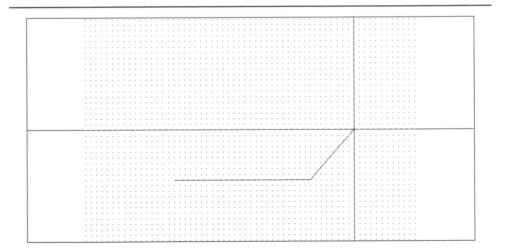

FIGURE 3.10: The first line of the cabin wall is drawn.

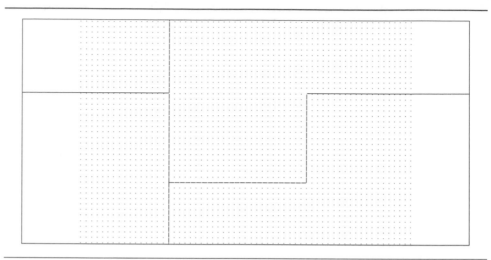

FIGURE 3.11:   Drawing the second and third wall lines

7. Finally, type **c** ↵ to close the box. This tells AutoCAD to draw a line from the last point picked to the first point picked and, in effect, closes the box. Then AutoCAD automatically ends the Line command (Figure 3.12).

This method of laying out building lines by using Snap and Grid and the coordinate readout is quite useful if the dimensions all conform to a convenient rounded-off number, like the nearest 6 inches, or as in this case, the nearest foot. It is not necessary to keep Snap and Grid set to the same spacing, as they were in this example, as long as the grid spacing is an even multiple of the snap spacing. In this project, you could have kept the snap spacing at 1' and set the grid spacing to 4'. Then you wouldn't have so many dots on the screen, and snap would have forced the crosshair cursor to stop at quarter intervals (12") between the 4-foot-spaced grid dots. This would have been a slightly more elegant way to accomplish the same thing.

The key advantage to this method over just typing in the relative coordinates— as was done with the box in Skill 2—is that you avoid having to type in the numbers. You should, however, assess whether the layout you need to draw has characteristics that lend themselves to using grid, snap, and the coordinate readout area; or whether just typing in the relative coordinates would be more efficient. As you get more comfortable with AutoCAD, you will see that this is the sort of question that comes up often: which way is the most efficient? This happy dilemma is inevitable in an application with enough tools to give you many strategic choices. In Skills 4 and 5: *Gaining Drawing Strategies Part I & II*, you will learn about other techniques for drawing rectangles.

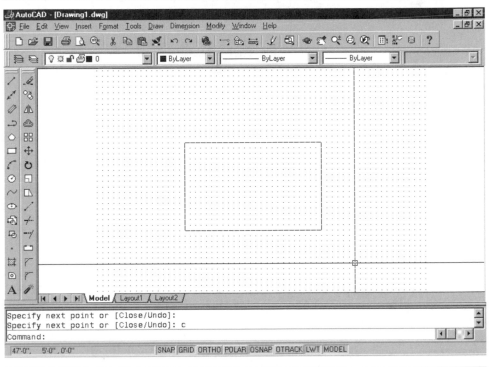

FIGURE 3.12: The completed outside wall lines

Saving Your Work

Like all Windows-compatible applications, when you save a file for the first time by clicking File ➤ Save, you are given the opportunity to designate a name for the file and a directory or folder to store it in. Normally you use Windows Explorer to designate file and directory information before you start a new drawing; but for the cabin project, you will do that now, after the drawing has been started.

I recommend that you create a special folder called something like TrainingData, for storing the files you will generate as you work your way through this book. This will keep them separate from project work already on your computer, and you will always know where to save or find a training drawing. To save your drawing, follow these steps. While in AutoCAD:

1. Click the Save button on the Standard toolbar or select File ➤ Save. The Save Drawing As dialog box comes up.

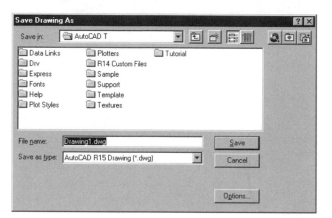

NOTE NOTE NOTE NOTE NOTE NOTE NOTE NOTE NOTE NOTE NOTE NOTE NOTE NOTE NOTE
The actual directories and files may be different on your computer.

2. In the Save In drop-down list, designate the drive where you wish to save the drawing. If you are saving it on the hard drive or server, navigate to the directory in which you want to place the new Training Data folder.

3. Click the Create New Folder button at the top of the dialog box.

4. Enter **Training Data** (or whatever name you wish to give the new folder) ↵.

5. Double click the new folder to open it.

6. In the File Name box, change the name from the default name (Drawing1.dwg) to Cabin03. You're not required to enter the .dwg extension in this case.

NOTE NOTE NOTE NOTE NOTE NOTE NOTE NOTE NOTE NOTE NOTE NOTE NOTE NOTE NOTE
From now on, when you are directed to save the drawing, you should save it as Cabinx, **with _x_ indicating the number of the skill. This way, you will know where in the book to look for review, if necessary. Multiple saves within a skill should be called** Cabinxa, Cabinxb, **etc.**

7. Click Save. It is now safe to exit AutoCad.

8. If you want to shut AutoCAD down at this time, click File ➤ Exit. Otherwise, keep your drawing up and read on.

The tools covered in this skill will be your key to starting up a new drawing from scratch and getting it ready for a specific project.

NOTE NOTE NOTE NOTE NOTE NOTE NOTE NOTE NOTE NOTE NOTE NOTE NOTE NOTE NOTE

When starting a new drawing, you have the options of selecting a template file as a prototype, or using an Advanced or Quick Wizard, in addition to the Start from Scratch option that we are using in this book. For more information on the template files or wizards, see *Mastering AutoCAD 2000*, by George Omura (Sybex, 1999)

SKILL
3

The next skill will focus on adding to the drawing and modifying commands you learned as part of Skill 2 and will develop strategies for solving problems that occur in the development of a floor plan.

Are You Experienced?

Now you can...

☑ set up linear and angular units for a new drawing

☑ make the grid visible and modify its coverage

☑ use the Zoom In and Zoom Out features

☑ activate the Snap mode and change the snap and grid spacing

☑ use the Zoom All function to fit the grid on the drawing area

☑ draw lines using Grid, Snap, and the coordinate readout

☑ create a new folder on your hard drive from within AutoCAD

☑ name and save your file

Gaining Drawing Strategies: Part 1

- ➔ Making interior walls
- ➔ Zooming in on an area using various zoom tools
- ➔ Making doors and swings
- ➔ Using Object Snaps
- ➔ Using the Copy and Mirror commands

Assuming that you have worked your way through the first three skills, you have now successfully drawn a box (Skill 2) as well as the outer wall lines of the cabin (Skill 3). From here on, you will develop a floor plan for the cabin and, ultimately, elevations (views of the front, back, and sides of the building that show how the building will look if you're standing facing it). Elevations will be drawn in Skill 8, *Generating Elevations*. The focus in Skill 4 is on gaining a feel for the strategy of drawing in AutoCAD, and on how to solve drawing problems that may come up in the course of laying out the floor plan. Working your way through this skill, your activities will include making the walls, cutting doorway openings, and drawing the doors (Figure 4.1). In Skill 5, *Gaining Drawing Strategies: Part 2*, you will add steps and a balcony, and place fixtures and appliances in the bathroom and kitchen.

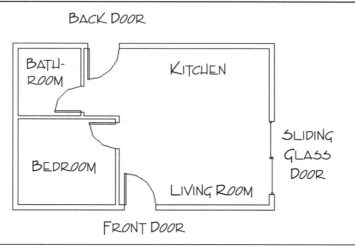

FIGURE 4.1:   The basic floor plan of the cabin

Each of the exercises in this skill will present opportunities to practice using commands you already know from previous skills and to learn a few new ones. The most important goal is to begin to use strategic thinking as you develop methods for creating new objects in the floor plan.

Laying Out the Walls

For most floor plans, the walls come first. The first lesson of this skill is to understand that you will not be putting very many new lines in the drawing, at least not as many as you might expect. Most new objects in this skill will be created from items already in your drawing. In fact, no new lines will be drawn to make walls. All new walls will be generated from the four exterior wall lines you drew in the last skill.

You will need to create an inside wall line for the exterior walls (because the wall has thickness) and then make the three new interior walls (Figure 4.2). The wall thickness will be 4" for interior walls and 6" for exterior walls, as exterior walls have an additional layer or two of weather protection, such as shingles or stucco. Finally, you will need to cut five openings in these walls (interior and exterior) for the doorways.

SKILL
4

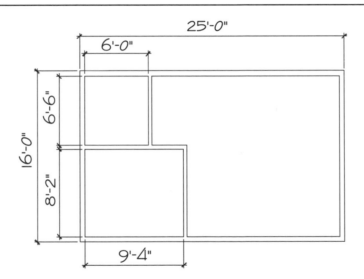

FIGURE 4.2: The wall dimensions

TIP TIP TIP TIP TIP TIP TIP TIP TIP TIP TIP TIP TIP TIP TIP TIP TIP TIP TIP TIP TIP TIP TIP TIP

All the commands used for this exercise have been presented in Skills 2 and 3, so feel free to glance back to these chapters if you find you need a refresher.

The Exterior Wall Lines

The first step is to offset the existing four wall lines to the inside to make the inside wall lines for the exterior walls. Then you will need to fillet them to clean up their corners, just like you did for the box in Skill 2.

TIP TIP TIP TIP TIP TIP TIP TIP TIP TIP TIP TIP TIP TIP TIP TIP TIP TIP TIP TIP TIP TIP TIP TIP

Buildings are usually—but not always—dimensioned to the outside edge of exterior walls and to the centerline of interior walls. Wood frame buildings are dimensioned to the outside edges of their frames, and to the centerlines of the interior walls.

1. If AutoCAD is already running, select File ➤ Open. Open the folder you have designated as your training folder and select your cabin drawing. (You named it Cabin03.dwg at the end of Skill 3.) Then click Open. If you are starting up AutoCAD, the Startup dialog box will appear. Be sure the Open a Drawing button is selected, then look for the Cabin03 drawing in the Select a File box. This box keeps a list of the most recently opened .dwg files. Highlight your .dwg file and click OK. If you don't find your file in the list, click the Browse button. The Select File dialog box will open. Find and open your training folder, select your drawing file, and click Open. The drawing should consist of four lines making a rectangle (Figure 4.3).

2. On the status bar, click the Grid and Snap buttons to turn them off. Then start the Offset command by clicking the Offset button on the Modify toolbar.

NOTE NOTE NOTE NOTE NOTE NOTE NOTE NOTE NOTE NOTE NOTE NOTE NOTE NOTE NOTE

You can also start the Offset command by typing o ↵, or selecting Modify ➤ Offset from the drop-down menus.

3. At the Offset distance: prompt, type **6** ↵.

NOTE NOTE NOTE NOTE NOTE NOTE NOTE NOTE NOTE NOTE NOTE NOTE NOTE NOTE NOTE

Remember: You do not have to enter the inch sign ("), but you are required to enter the foot sign (').

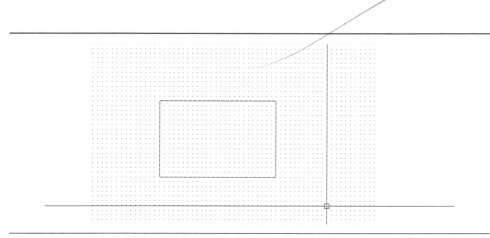

FIGURE 4.3: The cabin as you left it in Skill 3

4. At the Select object to offset: prompt, click one of the four lines.

5. Click in a blank area inside the rectangle. The first line is offset 6" to the inside (Figure 4.4). The Offset command is still running and the Select object to offset: prompt is still in effect.

FIGURE 4.4: The first line is offset.

6. Select another outside wall line and click in a blank area on the inside again. Continue doing this until you have offset all four outside wall lines to the inside at the set distance of 6". Then press ↵ to end the Offset command (Figure 4.5). Now you will clean up the corners with the Fillet command.

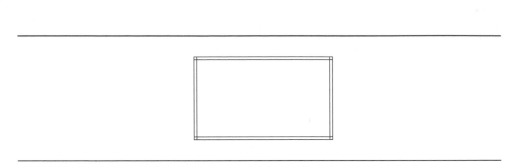

FIGURE 4.5:   All four lines are now offset 6" to the inside.

7.   Start the Fillet command by clicking the Fillet button on the Modify toolbar.

NOTE NOTE NOTE NOTE NOTE NOTE NOTE NOTE NOTE NOTE NOTE NOTE NOTE NOTE

Look at the Command window to see whether or not the radius is set to 0. If it is, go on to step 8. Otherwise, type r ↵ then type 0 ↵ to set the Fillet radius to 0. The Fillet command will end after a new radius is set. Press ↵ one more time to restart the Fillet command.

8.   Click any two lines that form an inside corner. Be sure to click the part of the lines you want to remain after the fillet is completed. (Refer to Skill 2 to review how the Fillet command is used in a similar situation.) Both of the two lines will be trimmed to make an inside corner (Figure 4.6). The Fillet command automatically ends after each fillet.

9.   Press ↵ to restart the Fillet command.

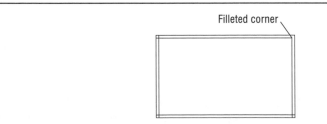

Filleted corner

FIGURE 4.6:   The first corner is filleted.

TIP TIP TIP TIP TIP TIP TIP TIP TIP TIP TIP TIP TIP TIP TIP TIP TIP TIP TIP TIP TIP TIP TIP
You can restart the most recently used command by pressing ↵ at the Command: **prompt.**

10. Pick two more lines to fillet, then press ↵ to restart the Fillet command. Continue doing this until all four corners have been cleaned up (Figure 4.7). After the last fillet, the Fillet command will end automatically.

FIGURE 4.7: The four inside corners have been cleaned up.

NOTE NOTE NOTE NOTE NOTE NOTE NOTE NOTE NOTE NOTE NOTE NOTE NOTE NOTE NOTE
This procedure was identical to the one you performed in Skill 2 on the box.

CHARACTERISTICS THAT OFFSET AND FILLET HAVE IN COMMON

- Both are found on the Modify toolbar and on the Modify drop-down menu.
- Both have a default distance setting—offset distance and fillet radius—that can be accepted or reset.
- Both require you to select object(s).

CHARACTERISTICS THAT ARE DIFFERENT IN OFFSET AND FILLET

- You select one object with Offset and two with Fillet.
- Offset keeps running until you stop it. Fillet ends after the radius is changed and after each fillet operation, so Fillet needs to be restarted to be used again.

You will find several uses for Offset and Fillet in the subsequent sections of this skill and throughout the book.

The Interior Walls

Create the interior wall lines by offsetting the exterior wall lines.

1. At the Command: prompt, start the Offset command by typing **o** ↵ (the letter *o*, not the number *0*) or by selecting Offset from the Modify toolbar.

2. At the Offset distance: prompt, type **9'4** ↵. Leave no space between the foot sign (') and the *4*.

NOTE NOTE NOTE NOTE NOTE NOTE NOTE NOTE NOTE NOTE NOTE NOTE NOTE NOTE NOTE

AutoCAD requires that you enter a distance containing feet and inches in a particular format: no space between the foot sign (') and the inches, and a hyphen (-) between the inches and the fraction. So if you were entering a distance of 6'-4 3/4", you would type 6'4-3/4. The measurement will be displayed in the normal way, like 6'-4 3/4", but it must be entered in the format that has no spaces.

3. Click the inside line of the left exterior wall (Figure 4.8).

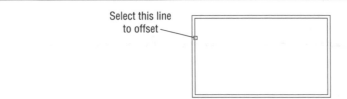

Select this line to offset

FIGURE 4.8: Selecting the wall line to offset

4. Click in a blank area to the right of the selected line. The line is offset 9'-4" to the right.

5. Press ⏎ twice. The Offset command is now restarted, and you can reset the offset distance.

TIP TIP TIP TIP TIP TIP TIP TIP TIP TIP TIP TIP TIP TIP TIP TIP TIP TIP TIP TIP TIP TIP TIP

In the Offset command, your opportunity to change the offset distance comes right after you start the command. So if the Offset command is already running, and you need to change the offset distance, you need to stop and then restart the command. This is easily done by pressing ⏎ twice.

6. Type **4** ⏎ to reset the offset distance.

7. Click the new line that was just offset, and then click in a blank area to the right of that line. You have created a vertical interior wall (Figure 4.9). Press ⏎ twice to stop and restart the Offset command.

8. Type **6.5'**⏎. This sets the distance for offsetting the next wall.

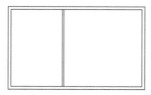

FIGURE 4.9: The first interior wall

NOTE NOTE NOTE NOTE NOTE NOTE NOTE NOTE NOTE NOTE NOTE NOTE NOTE NOTE NOTE

With Architectural units set, you can still enter distances in decimal form for feet and inches, and AutoCAD will translate them into their appropriate form. So 6'6" can be entered as 6.5' and 4 1/2" can be entered as 4.5 without the inch sign. Remember, when entering figures, the inch sign (") can be left off, but the foot sign (') must be included.

9. Pick a point on the inside, upper exterior wall line (Figure 4.10).

SKILL
4

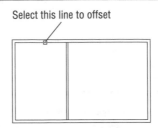

FIGURE 4.10: Selecting another wall line to offset

10. Click in a blank area below the line selected. The inside exterior wall line is offset to make a new interior wall line. Press ↵ twice to stop and restart the Offset command.

11. Type **4** ↵. Click the new line and click again below it. A second wall line is made, and you now have two interior walls. Press ↵ to end the Offset command.

These interior wall lines form the bedroom and one side of the bathroom. Their intersections with each other and with the exterior walls need to be cleaned up. If you take the time to do this now, it will be easier to make the last interior wall and, thereby, complete the bathroom.

Cleaning Up Wall Lines

Earlier, you used the Fillet command to clean up the inside corners of the exterior walls. You can use that command again to clean up some of the interior walls, but you will have to use the Trim command to do the rest of them. You'll see why as you progress through the next set of steps.

1. It will be easier to pick the wall lines if the drawing is made larger on the screen. Type **z** ↵, then type **e** ↵. Press ↵, then type **.6x** ↵. The drawing is bigger. You've just used two options of the Zoom command: First, you zoomed to *Extents* to fill the screen with your drawing. Then you zoomed to a scale (.6x) to make the drawing 0.6 the size it had been after zooming to Extents. This is a change in magnification on the view only, as the drawing is still 25-feet long by 16-feet wide.

2. Pick the Fillet button from the Modify toolbar to start the Fillet command and, after checking the Command window to be sure that the radius is still

set to 0, click two of the wall lines as shown in Figure 4.11a. The lines will be filleted, and the results will look like Figure 4.11b.

3. Press ↵ to restart the Fillet command. Select the two lines as shown in Figure 4.12a. The results are shown in Figure 4.12b.

The two new interior walls are now the right length, but you will have to clean up the area where they form T intersections with the exterior walls. The Fillet command won't work in T intersections because too much of one of the wall lines gets trimmed away. You'll have to use the Trim command in T intersection cases. The Fillet command does a specific kind of trim and is easy and quick to execute, but its uses are limited (for the most part) to single intersections between two lines.

TIP TIP TIP TIP TIP TIP TIP TIP TIP TIP TIP TIP TIP TIP TIP TIP TIP TIP TIP TIP TIP TIP TIP TIP

The best rule for choosing between Fillet and Trim is the following: If you need to clean up a single intersection between two lines, use the Fillet command. For other cases, use the Trim command.

SKILL
4

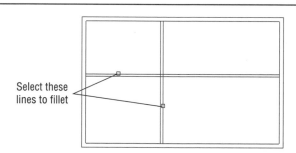

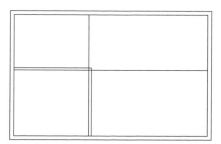

FIGURE 4.11: Selecting the first two lines to fillet (a), and the result of the fillet (b)

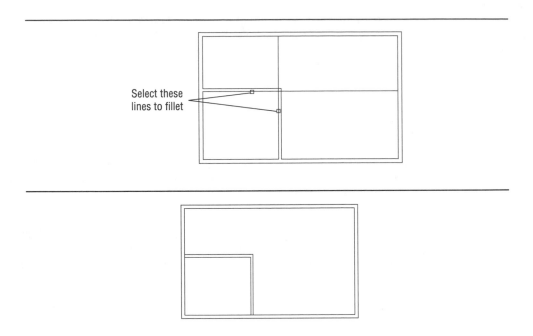

Select these
lines to fillet

FIGURE 4.12: Selecting the second two lines to fillet (a), and the result of the second fillet (b)

Using the Zoom Command

To do this trim, you need to have a closer view of the T intersections. Use the Zoom command to get a better look.

1. Type **z** ↲. Then move the crosshair cursor to a point slightly above and to the left of the upper T intersection (Figure 4.13) and click in a blank area outside the floor plan.

2. Move the cursor down and to the right, and notice a rectangle with solid lines being drawn. Keep moving the cursor down and to the right until the rectangle encloses the upper T intersection (Figure 4.14a). When the rectangle fully encloses the T intersection, click again. The view changes to a

closer view of the intersection of the interior and exterior wall (Figure 4.14b). The rectangle you've just created is called a *zoom window*. The part of the drawing enclosed by the zoom window becomes the view on the screen. This is one of several zoom options for changing the magnification of the view. Other zoom options are introduced later in this skill and throughout the book.

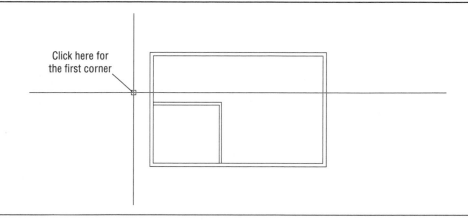

Click here for
the first corner

FIGURE 4.13: Positioning the cursor for the first click of the Zoom command

NOTE NOTE NOTE NOTE NOTE NOTE NOTE NOTE NOTE NOTE NOTE NOTE NOTE NOTE NOTE
When you start the Zoom command by typing z ↵ and then pick a point on the screen, a zoom window begins.

3. On the Modify toolbar, click the Trim button. In the Command window, notice the second and third lines of text. You are being prompted to select cutting edges, or objects to use as limits for the lines you want to trim.

4. Select the two interior wall lines and press ↵. The prompt changes, now asking you to select the lines to be trimmed.

SKILL
▼4

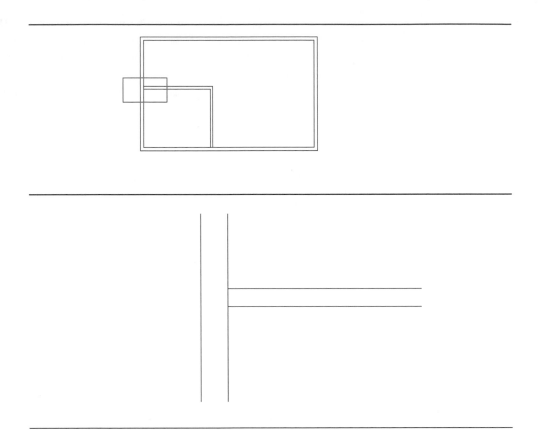

FIGURE 4.14: Using the Zoom Window option: positioning the rectangle (a), and the new view after the Zoom command (b)

5. Select the inside exterior wall line at the T intersection, between the two intersections with the interior wall lines that you have just picked as cutting edges (Figure 4.15a). The exterior wall line is trimmed at the T intersection (Figure 4.15b). Press ↵ to end the Trim command.

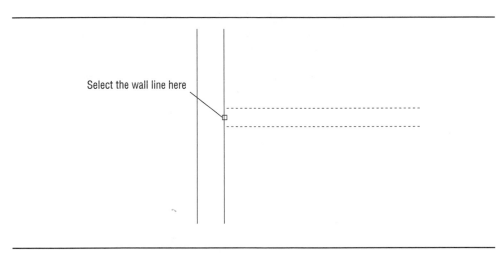

Select the wall line here

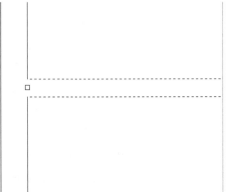

FIGURE 4.15: Selecting a line to be trimmed (a), and the result of the Trim command (b)

TIP TIP TIP TIP TIP TIP TIP TIP TIP TIP TIP TIP TIP TIP TIP TIP TIP TIP TIP TIP TIP TIP TIP

In the Trim command, when picking lines to be trimmed, click the part of the line that needs to be trimmed away. In the Fillet command, select the part of the line that you want to keep.

6. Return to a view of the whole drawing by typing **z** ↵, then **p** ↵. This is the Zoom command's Previous option, which restores the view that was active before the last use of the Zoom command (Figure 4.16).

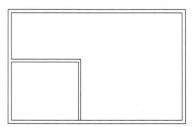

FIGURE 4.16: The result of the Zoom Previous command

7. Repeat this procedure to trim the lower T intersection. Follow these steps:

   A. Type **z** ↵ and click two points to make a rectangular zoom window around the intersection.

   B. Start the Trim command by choosing Modify ➤ Trim, select the interior walls as cutting edges, and press ↵.

   C. Select the inside exterior wall line between the cutting edges.

   D. Press ↵ to end the Trim command.

   E. Zoom previous by typing **z** ↵ **p** ↵.

Figure 4.17 shows the results.

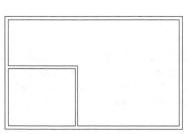

FIGURE 4.17: The second trim is completed.

You need to create one more interior wall to complete the bathroom.

Finishing the Interior Walls

You will use the same method to create the last bathroom wall that you used to make the first two interior walls. Briefly, this is how it's done:

1. Offset the upper-inside line of the left exterior wall 6' to the right, then offset this new line 4" to the right.

2. Use the zoom window to zoom into the bathroom area.

3. Use the Trim command to trim away the short portion of the intersected wall lines between the two new wall lines.

4. Use Zoom previous to restore the full view.

The results should look like Figure 4.18. You used Offset, Fillet, Trim, and a couple of Zooms to create the interior walls. The next task is to create five doorway openings in these walls. If you need to end the drawing session before completing the chapter, click File ➤ Save As, then change the name of this drawing to Cabin04a.dwg and click Save. Then you can exit AutoCAD.

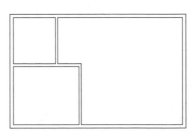

FIGURE 4.18: The completed interior walls

Cutting Wall Openings

Of the five doorway openings needed, there are two on the interior and three on the exterior walls (Figure 4.19). Four of them will be for swinging doors, and one will be for a sliding glass door.

SKILL
4

The procedure used to make each doorway opening is the same one that you used to create the opening for the box in Skill 2. First, you establish the location of the *jambs*, or sides, of an opening. One jamb for each swinging door opening will be located 6" away from an inside wall corner. This allows the door to be positioned next to a wall and out of the way when swung open. When the jambs are established, you will trim away the wall lines between the edges. The commands used in this exercise are Offset, Extend, and Trim. You'll make openings for the 3'-0" exterior doorways first.

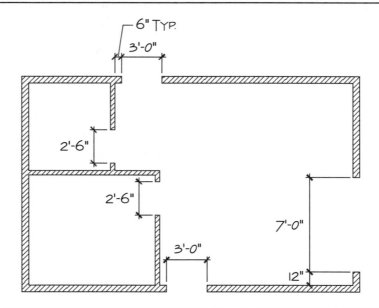

FIGURE 4.19: The drawing with doorway openings

The Exterior Openings

These openings are on the front and back walls of the cabin and have one side set 6" in from an inside corner.

1. Click the Offset button on the Modify toolbar to start the Offset command, then type **6** ↵ to set the distance.

2. Click one of the two lines indicated in Figure 4.20, then click in a blank area to the right of the line that you selected. Now do the same thing to the second wall line. You have to offset one line at a time because of the way that the Offset command works.

3. End and restart the Offset command by typing ↵ twice, then type **3'**↵ to set a new offset distance and offset the new lines to the right (Figure 4.21). Next, you will need to extend these four new lines through the external walls to make the jamb lines.

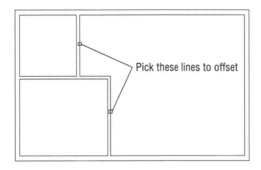

FIGURE 4.20: Lines to offset for 3'-0" openings

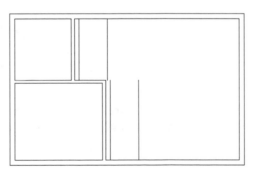

FIGURE 4.21: Offset lines for 3'-0" openings

4. Be sure to end the Offset command by pressing ↵, then type **ex** ↵ to start the Extend command. Extend is used here exactly as it was used in Skill 2.

Select the upper- and lower-horizontal outside, external wall lines as boundary edges for the Extend command, and press ↵.

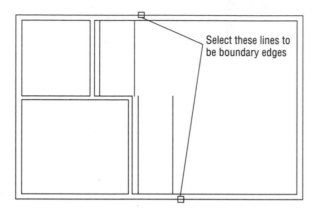

Select these lines to be boundary edges

5. Click the four lines to extend them. The lines are extended through the external walls to make the jambs (Figure 4.22). End the Extend command by pressing ↵.

TIP TIP TIP TIP TIP TIP TIP TIP TIP TIP TIP TIP TIP TIP TIP TIP TIP TIP TIP TIP TIP TIP TIP

The lines to be extended must be picked on the half of them nearest the boundary's edge, or they will be extended to the opposite boundary edge.

To complete the openings, first trim away the excess part of the jamb lines and then trim away the wall lines between the jamb lines. Use the Trim command the same way you used it in Skill 2, but this time do a compound trim to clean up the wall and jamb lines in one cycle of the command.

6. Type **tr** ↵ to start the Trim command and select the three lines at each opening as shown in Figure 4.23. Then press ↵ to tell AutoCAD you are finished selecting objects to serve as cutting edges.

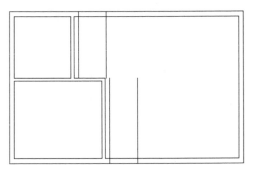

FIGURE 4.22: The lines after being extended through the external walls

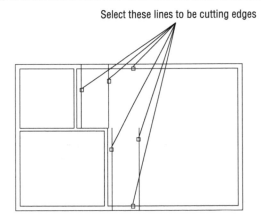

FIGURE 4.23: Selecting the cutting edges

7.   Pick the jamb lines—the lines you just extended to the outside exterior walls—and the four wall lines between the jamb lines. Each time you pick a line, it is trimmed. Press ↵ to end the command. Your drawing should look like Figure 4.24.

TIP TIP TIP TIP TIP TIP TIP TIP TIP TIP TIP TIP TIP TIP TIP TIP TIP TIP TIP TIP TIP TIP TIP

When picking lines to be trimmed, remember to pick the lines on the portion to be trimmed away.

The two interior openings can be constructed using the same procedure.

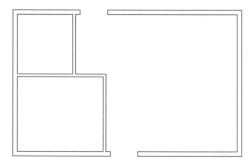

FIGURE 4.24:   The finished 3'-0" openings

The Interior Openings

These doorways are 2'-6" wide and also have one jamb set in 6" from the nearest inside corner. Figure 4.25 shows the three stages of fabricating these openings. Refer to the previous section on making openings for step-by-step instructions.

Construct the 7–foot–0–inch exterior opening using the same commands and technique.

The 7'-0" Opening

Notice the opening on the right side of the building has one jamb set 12" in from the inside corner. This will be the sliding glass door.

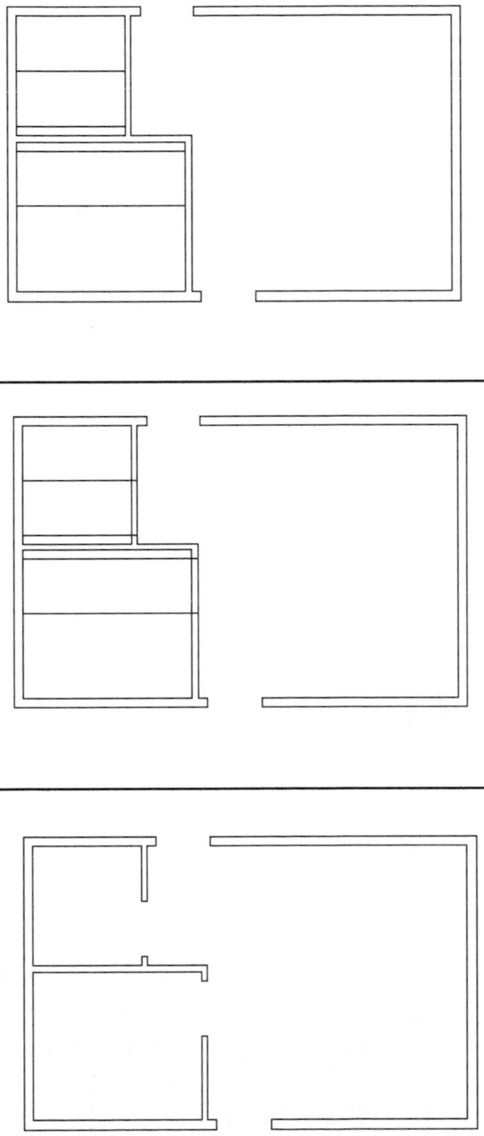

FIGURE 4.25: Creating the interior openings: the offset lines that locate the jamb lines (a), the extended lines that form the jamb lines (b), and the completed openings after trimming (c)

You've done this before, so here's a summary of the steps:

1. Offset a wall line 12".

2. Offset the new line 7'-0".

3. Extend both new lines through the wall.

4. Trim the new lines and the wall lines to complete the opening.

Save this drawing now as Cabin04b.dwg. This completes the openings. The results should look like Figure 4.26.

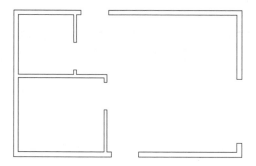

FIGURE 4.26: The completed doorway openings

As you gain more control over the commands you used here, you will be able to anticipate how much of a task can be done for each use of a command. Each opening required offsetting, extending, and trimming. You constructed these openings by drawing two at a time except for the last one, thereby using each of the three commands three times. It is possible to do all the openings using each command only once. In this way, you would do all the offsetting, then all the extending, and finally, all the trimming. In cutting these openings, however, the arrangement of the offset lines determined how many cycles of the Trim command were most efficient to use. If lines being trimmed and used as cutting edges cross each other, the trimming gets complicated. For these five openings, the most efficient procedure was to use each command twice. In Skill 8, when you draw the elevations, you'll get a chance to work with more complex multiple trims.

Now that the openings are complete, doors and door swings can be placed in their appropriate doorways. In doing this, you'll be introduced to two new objects and a few new commands, and there will be an opportunity to use the Offset and Trim commands in new, strategic ways.

Creating Doors

In a floor plan, doors are usually indicated by a rectangle for the door and an arc showing the path of the door swing. The door's position varies, but it's most often shown at 90° from the closed position (Figure 4.27). The best rule I have come across is to display them in such a way that others working with your floor plan will be able to see how far, and in what direction, the door will swing open.

FIGURE 4.27: Possible ways to illustrate doors

The cabin has five openings, four of which need swinging doors that open 90°. The fifth is a sliding glass door. Drawing the sliding glass door will require a different approach.

Drawing Swinging Doors

The swinging doors are of two widths: 3' for exterior and 2'-6" for interior (refer to Figure 4.1). In general, doorway openings leading to the outside are wider than the interior doors, with bathroom and closet doors usually being the most narrow. For the cabin, we'll use two sizes of swinging doors. You will draw one door of each size, and then just copy these to the other openings as required. Start with the front door at the bottom of the floor plan. To get a closer view of the front door opening, use the Zoom Window command.

1. Before you start drawing, check the Status Bar at the bottom of the screen and make sure only the Model button at the far right is depressed. All other

buttons should be in the Off position—that is, up. If any are depressed, click them once to turn them off.

2. Click Tools ➤ Drafting Settings to bring up the Drafting Settings dialog. Then click the Object Snap tab to activate it, if it's not already on top.

Be sure all checkboxes are unchecked. If any boxes have checks in them, click once to uncheck them. Then click OK to close the dialog box.

3. At the Command: prompt, move the cursor to the Standard toolbar and click the Zoom Window button. This has the same effect as typing **z** ↵, used earlier in this skill.

4. Pick two points to form a window around the front doorway opening, as shown in Figure 4.28a. The view changes, and you now have a close-up view of the opening (Figure 4.28b). You'll draw the door in a closed position and then rotate it open.

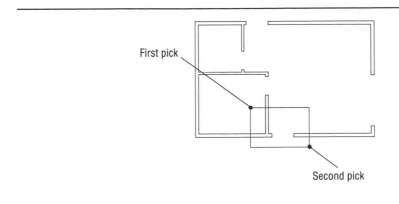

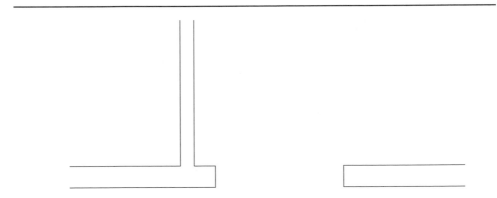

FIGURE 4.28: Forming a zoom window at the front door opening (a), and the results (b)

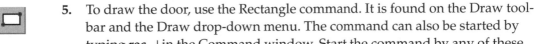

5. To draw the door, use the Rectangle command. It is found on the Draw tool-bar and the Draw drop-down menu. The command can also be started by typing **rec** ↵ in the Command window. Start the command by any of these means.

Notice the Command window prompt. There are several options in brackets, but option `Specify first corner point` (before the brackets) is the default and is the one you want. The rectangle is formed like the zoom window—by picking two points to represent opposite corners of the rectangle. In its closed position, the door will fit exactly between the jambs, with its upper corners coinciding with the upper endpoints of the jambs. To make the first corner of the rectangle coincide with the upper endpoint of the left jamb exactly, you will use an Object Snap to assist you. *Object Snaps* (or *Osnaps*) allow you to pick specific points on objects like endpoints, midpoints, the center of a circle, etc.

6. Move the cursor onto the Temporary Tracking Point button on the Standard toolbar and hold down the left mouse button. The Object Snap flyout opens and you see all the Object Snap tools (Figure 4.29).

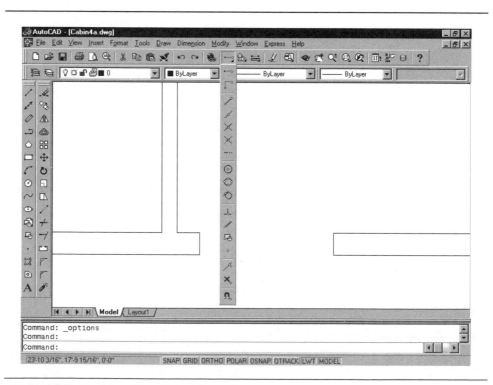

FIGURE 4.29: The Object Snap flyout

7. Holding the left mouse button down, drag the cursor down the column to the Endpoint button, and release the mouse button. The prompt line now says, "_endp of." This is a signal to you that the Endpoint Object Snap has been activated.

8. Move the cursor near the upper end of the left jamb line. When the cursor gets very close to a line, a colored square appears at the nearest endpoint. This shows you which endpoint in the drawing is closest to the position of the crosshair cursor at that moment.

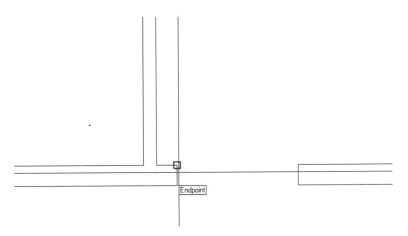

9. Move the cursor until the square is positioned on the upper end of the left jamb line, as shown above, and then click that point. The first corner of the rectangle now is located at that point. Move the cursor to the right and slightly down to see the rectangle being formed (Figure 4.30a). To locate the opposite corner, let's use the relative Cartesian coordinates discussed in Skill 2.

10. When the Command window shows the `Specify other corner point:` prompt, type **@3',-1.5** ↵ in the command line. The rectangle is drawn across the opening, creating a door in a closed position (Figure 4.30b). The door now needs to be rotated around its hinge point to an opened position.

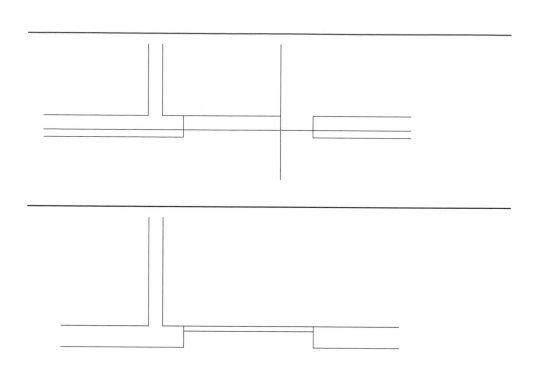

FIGURE 4.30: The rectangle after picking the first corner (a), and the completed door in a closed position (b)

NOTE NOTE NOTE NOTE NOTE NOTE NOTE NOTE NOTE NOTE NOTE NOTE NOTE NOTE NOTE NOTE

You could have used the Rectangle command to lay out the first four wall lines of the cabin in Skill 3. Then you could have offset all four lines in one step to complete the exterior walls, and the corners would have been automatically filleted. It would have been faster than the method we used, but a rectangle's lines are all one object. In order to offset them to make the interior walls, they would have to be separated into individual lines using the Explode command.

Rotating the Door

This will be a 90° rotation in the counter-clockwise direction, making it a rotation of +90. You'll use the *Rotate command* to rotate the door. This command can be found on the Modify drop-down menu or on the Modify toolbar. Typing **ro** ⏎ can also start it.

 NOTE NOTE NOTE NOTE NOTE NOTE NOTE NOTE NOTE NOTE NOTE NOTE NOTE NOTE NOTE

By default, counter-clockwise rotations are positive and clockwise rotations are negative.

1. Pick the Rotate button from the Modify toolbar. You'll see a prompt to select objects. Click the door and press ⏎.

 NOTE NOTE NOTE NOTE NOTE NOTE NOTE NOTE NOTE NOTE NOTE NOTE NOTE NOTE NOTE

Note that when you select the door, one pick selects all four lines. Rectangles are made of a special line called a *Polyline* that connects all segments into one object. You will learn more about them in Skill 10, *Controlling Text in a Drawing*.

SKILL
4

You will be prompted for a base point. You need to indicate a point around which the door will be rotated. To keep the door placed correctly, pick the hinge point for the base point.

2. Return to the Standard toolbar and select the Endpoint Osnap button. Endpoint Osnap has replaced the Tracking button because it was the last Osnap button selected from the flyout toolbar.

3. Move the cursor near the upper-left corner of the door. When the colored square is displayed at that corner, left-click to locate the base point.

4. Check the status bar to be sure the Ortho button is not depressed. If it is, click it to turn Ortho off. When the Ortho button is on, the cursor is forced to move in a vertical or horizontal direction. This is very useful at times; but, in this instance, such a restriction would keep you from being able to see the door rotate. You'll learn more about Ortho in Skill 5, *Gaining Drawing Strategies: Part 2*.

5. Move the cursor away from the hinge point and see how the door rotates as the cursor moves (Figure 4.31a). If the door swings properly, you are reassured that you correctly selected the base point. The prompt reads Specify rotation angle or [reference], asking you to enter an angle.

6. Type **90** ⏎. The door is rotated 90° to an open position (Figure 4.31b).

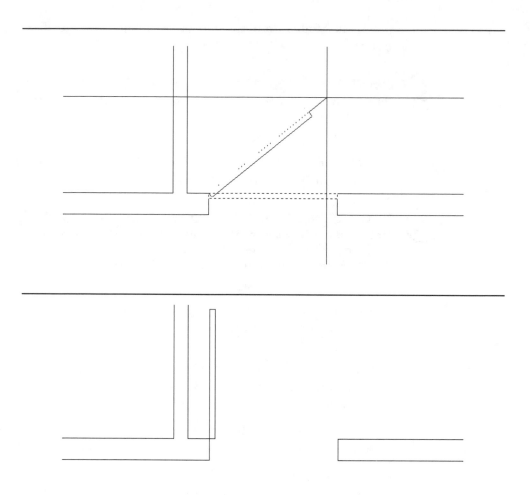

FIGURE 4.31: The door rotating with movement of the cursor (a), and the door after the 90° rotation

To finish this door, you need to add the door's swing. You'll use the Arc command for this.

Drawing the Door Swing

The *swing* shows the path that the outer edge of a door takes when it swings from closed to fully open. Including a swing with the door in a floor plan helps to resolve clearance issues. The swings are drawn with the *Arc command*, in this case using the Endpoint Osnap. When you are learning AutoCAD, it is best to start the Arc command from the Draw menu, because this displays all the Arc options. An abbreviated version of the command can be started from the Draw toolbar, or by typing **a** ↵.

1. From the Draw menu, select Arc. The Arc menu is displayed. An arc for this door swing needs to be drawn from the upper end of the right jamb line through a rotation of 90°. The center point of the arc is the hinge point of the door.

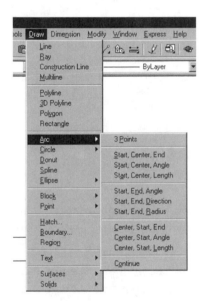

SKILL
4

TIP TIP TIP TIP TIP TIP TIP TIP TIP TIP TIP TIP TIP TIP TIP TIP TIP TIP TIP TIP TIP TIP

The position and size of an arc can be specified by a combination of its components, some of which are starting point, ending point, angle, center point, and radius. The Arc command gives you eleven options, each of which uses three components. With a little study of the geometric information available to you on the drawing, you can choose the option that best fits the situation. In this case, the arc needs to be drawn from the upper end of the right jamb line through a rotation of 90°, and the center point of the arc is the hinge point of the door. Thus, you know the start point, the center point, and the angle.

2. From the Arc menu, select Start, Center, Angle. The command prompt now reads: `_arc Specify start point of arc or [CEnter]:`. The default option is `Specify start point of arc`. There is also the option to start with the center point, but you would have to type **c** ↵ before picking a point to be the center point.

3. Activate the Endpoint Osnap and pick the upper endpoint of the right jamb line.

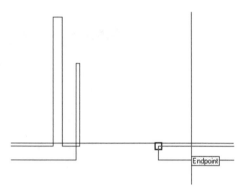

The prompt changes to read: `Specify second point of arc or [CEnter/ENd]: _c Specify center point of arc`.

This may be confusing at first. The prompt shows you three options to choose: Second Point, Center and End. (Center and End are in brackets.) Because you have previously chosen the Start, Center, Angle option, AutoCAD automatically chooses Center for you. That is the last part of the prompt.

4. Activate the Endpoint Osnap again and select the hinge point. The arc is now visible, and its endpoint follows the cursor's movement (Figure 4.32a). The prompt displays a different set of options, then ends the Included angle option.

5. Type **90** ↵. The arc is completed and the Arc command ends (Figure 4.32b).

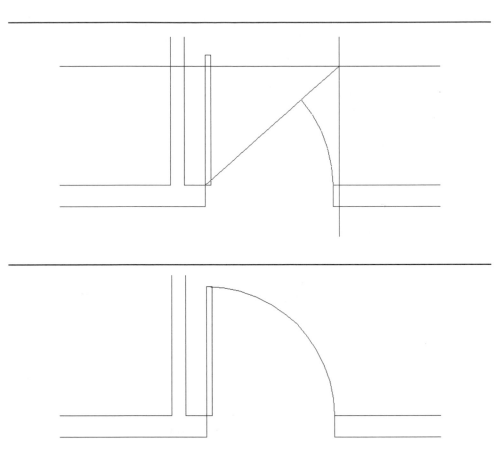

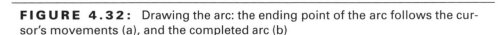

FIGURE 4.32: Drawing the arc: the ending point of the arc follows the cursor's movements (a), and the completed arc (b)

The front door is completed. Since the back door is the same size, you can save time by copying this door to the other opening. Next, let's see how to do that.

Copying Objects

The *Copy command* makes a copy of the objects you select. This copy can be located either by a point you pick or by relative coordinates that you enter from the keyboard. For AutoCAD to position these copied objects, you must designate two points: a base point, which serves as a point of reference for where the copy

SKILL
4

move starts; and then a second point, which serves as the ending point for the Copy command. The copy is moved the same distance and direction from its original that the second point is moved from the first point. When you know the actual distance and direction to move the copy, the base point isn't critical because you will specify the second point with relative polar or Cartesian coordinates. But in this situation, you don't know the exact distance or angle to move a copy of the front door to the back door opening, so you need to choose a base point for the copy carefully.

In copying this new door and its swing to the back door opening of the cabin, you need to find a point somewhere on the existing door or swing that can be located precisely on a point at the back door opening. There are two points like this to choose from: the hinge point or the start point of the door swing. Let's use the hinge point. You usually know where the hinge point of the new door belongs, so this is easier to locate than the start point of the arc.

The Copy command can be started in three ways: from the drop-down menus, by picking Modify ➤ Copy; from the Modify toolbar, by clicking the Copy button; or from the keyboard, by typing **cp**↵.

1. Select the Copy button on the Modify toolbar. The prompt asks you to select objects to copy. Pick the door and swing, then press ↵. The prompt reads "Specify base point or displacement, or [Multiple]:." Activate the Endpoint Osnap and pick the hinge point. A copy of the door and swing is attached to the crosshair cursor at the hinge point (Figure 4.33). The prompt changes to Specify second point of displacement or <use first point of displacement>:. You need to pick where the hinge point of the copied door will be located at the back door opening. To do this, you need to change the view back to what it was before you zoomed into the doorway opening.

2. From the Standard toolbar, click the Zoom Previous button. The full view of the cabin is restored. Move the crosshair cursor with the door in tow up to the vicinity of the back door opening. The back door should swing to the inside and be against the wall when open, so the hinge point for this opening will be at the lower end of the left jamb line.

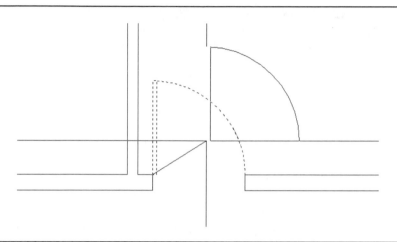

FIGURE 4.33: The copy of the door and swing attached to the crosshair cursor

3. Activate the Endpoint Osnap and pick the lower end of the left jamb line on the back door opening. The copy of the door and swing is placed in the opening (Figure 4.34) and, by looking at the Command window, you can see that the Copy command has ended.

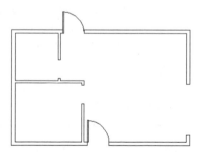

FIGURE 4.34: The door is copied to the back door opening.

TIP TIP TIP TIP TIP TIP TIP TIP TIP TIP TIP TIP TIP TIP TIP TIP TIP TIP TIP TIP TIP TIP TIP

The Copy command ends when you pick or specify the second point of the move, unless you're copying the same object to multiple places. You'll do that in Skill 5 when you draw the stovetop.

The door is oriented the wrong way, but you'll fix that next.

When you copy doors from one opening to another, often the orientation may not match. The best strategy is to use the hinge point as a point of reference and place it where it needs to go, as you have just done. Then flip and/or rotate the door so that it sits and swings the right way. The flipping of an object is known as *mirroring*.

NOTE NOTE NOTE NOTE NOTE NOTE NOTE NOTE NOTE NOTE NOTE NOTE NOTE NOTE NOTE

Take note that you were able to use the Zoom command while you were in the middle of using the Copy command. Most of the display commands—Zoom, Pan, etc.—can be used in this way. This is called using a command *transparently*.

Mirroring Objects

You have located the door in the opening, but it needs to be flipped so that it swings to the inside of the cabin. To do this, we'll use the *Mirror command*.

The Mirror command allows you to flip objects around an axis called the *mirror line*. You define this imaginary line by designating two points to be the endpoints of the line. Strategic selection of the mirror line ensures the accuracy of the mirroring action, so it's critical to visualize where the proper line lies. Sometimes you will have to draw a guideline in order to designate one or both of the endpoints.

1. Choose the Zoom Window icon from the Standard toolbar and create a window around the back door and its opening.

2. Pick the Mirror button on the Modify toolbar. (This command can also be found on the Modify drop-down menu or can be started by typing **mi** ↵.) Select the back door and swing, and press ↵. The prompt line changes to read "Specify first point of mirror line:."

3. Activate the Endpoint Osnap, then pick the hinge point of the door. The prompt changes to read "Specify second point of mirror line:", and you will see the mirrored image of the door and the swing moving as you move the cursor around the drawing area. You are rotating the mirror line about the hinge point as you move the cursor. As the mirror line moves, the location of the mirrored image moves (Figure 4.35).

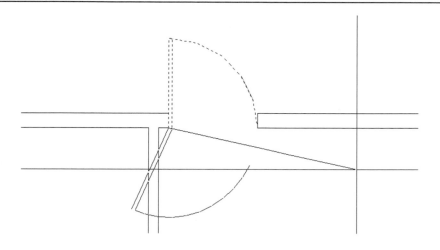

FIGURE 4.35: The mirror image moves as the mirror line moves.

4. Hold the crosshair cursor directly to the right of the first point picked, along the inside wall line. The mirror image appears to be where you want the door to be.

5. Activate the Endpoint Osnap again and pick the lower end of the right jamb line. The mirror image disappears and the prompt changes to read "Delete source objects? [Yes/No] <N>:." You have two choices. You can keep both doors by pressing ↵ and accepting the default (No). Or you can discard the original one by typing **y** (for yes) in the command line and pressing ↵.

6. Type **y** ↵. The flipped door is displayed and the original one is deleted (Figure 4.36). The Mirror command ends. Like the Copy command, the Mirror command ends automatically after one mirroring operation.

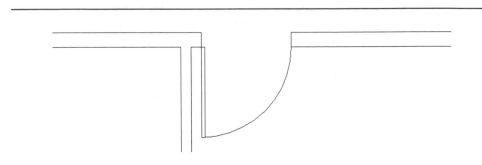

FIGURE 4.36: The mirrored door and swing

It may take some practice to become proficient at visualizing and designating the mirror line, but once you are used to it, you will have learned a very powerful tool. Because many building layouts have some symmetry to them, wise use of the Mirror command can save you a significant amount of drawing time.

You have two more swinging doors to place in the floor plan.

Finishing the Swinging Doors

You cannot copy the existing doors and swings to the interior openings because the sizes don't conform, but you can use the same procedure to draw one door and swing, and then copy it to the other opening.

NOTE NOTE NOTE NOTE NOTE NOTE NOTE NOTE NOTE NOTE NOTE NOTE NOTE NOTE
We could have used the Stretch command to lengthen the door, but it's an advanced Modify command, and won't be introduced until Skill 9, *Working with Hatches and Fills*. Besides, the arc would have to be modified to a larger radius. It turns out to be easier to draw another door and swing to a different size.

1. Click the Zoom Previous button on the Standard toolbar. Then click the Zoom Window button right next to the Zoom Previous button, and make a zoom window to magnify the view of the interior door openings. Be sure to make the zoom window large enough to leave some room for the new doors to be drawn (Figure 4.37).

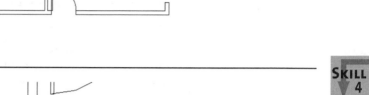

FIGURE 4.37: A zoom window in the interior door opening area (a), and the results of the zoom (b)

2. Follow the same procedure to draw the door and swing in the lower opening. Here is a summary of the steps:

   A. Use the Rectangle command and Endpoint Osnap to draw the door from the hinge point to a point @1.5,-2'6.

   B. Rotate the door around the hinge point to an open position. You will have to use a rotation angle of –90°.

C. Use the Start, Center, Angle option of the Arc command to draw the door swing, starting at the upper-left corner of the door, and using Endpoint Osnap for the two picks.

NOTE NOTE NOTE NOTE NOTE NOTE NOTE NOTE NOTE NOTE NOTE NOTE NOTE NOTE NOTE

The Start, Center, Angle option—as well as a few others—of the Arc command requires that you choose the start point for the arc in such a way that the arc is drawn in a counter-clockwise direction. If you progress in a clockwise direction, use a negative number for the angle.

3. Use the Copy command to copy this door and swing to the other interior opening. The base point will be the hinge point, and the second point will be the left end of the lower jamb line in the upper opening. Use the Endpoint Osnap for both picks.

4. Use the Mirror command to flip this copy of the door and swing up. The mirror line will be different from the one used for the back door because for this one, the door and its swing must flip in a direction parallel to the opening, while the geometrical arrangement at the back opening required that the door and its swing be flipped across the opening. For this opening, the mirror line is the lower jamb line itself, so pick each end of this line (using Endpoint Osnap) to establish the mirror line.

5. Use the Zoom Previous button to see the four swinging doors in place (Figure 4.38).

The last door to draw is the sliding glass door. This kind of door requires an entirely different strategy, but you'll use commands familiar to you by now.

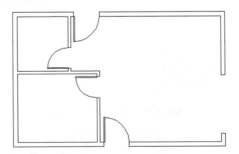

FIGURE 4.38: The four swinging doors in place

Drawing a Sliding Glass Door

Sliding glass doors are usually drawn to show their glass panels within the door frames.

To draw the sliding door, you will apply the Line, Offset, and Trim commands to the 7-foot opening you made earlier.

1. Pick the Zoom Window button on the Standard toolbar and make a zoom window closely around the 7-foot opening. In making the zoom window, pick one point just above and to the left of the upper doorjamb and below and to the right of the lower jamb. This will make the opening as large as possible while including everything you will need in the view (Figure 4.39).

FIGURE 4.39: The view when zoomed in as close as possible to the 7-foot opening

2. You will be using several Osnaps for this procedure, so it will be convenient to have the Osnap Flyout toolbar more immediately available. Here's how.

    A. From the View menu, pick Toolbars. The Toolbars dialog box appears.

B. Scroll down the list and click in the box next to Object Snap. The Object Snap toolbar will appear.

C. Click the Close button of the Toolbars dialog box.

D. Put the cursor on the colored title bar of the Object Snap toolbar, and, holding down the left mouse button, drag the toolbar to the right side of the drawing area. Dock it there by releasing the mouse button (Figure 4.40). Now all Object Snaps can easily be selected as needed.

Object Snap toolbar docked

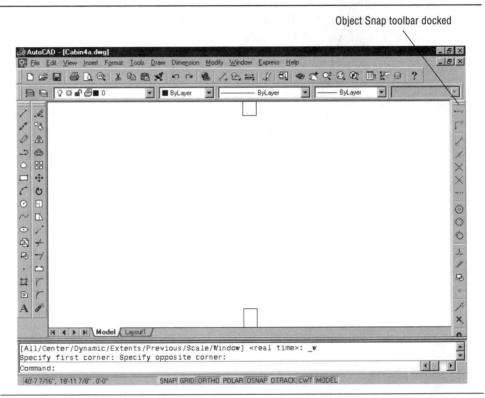

FIGURE 4.40: The Object Snap toolbar docked to the right of the drawing area

3. Offset each jamb line 2" into the doorway opening (Figure 4.41).

FIGURE 4.41: Jamb lines offset 2" into the doorway opening

4. Type **l** ⏎ to start the Line command. Pick the Midpoint Osnap button from the Object Snap toolbar, then place the cursor near the midpoint of the upper doorjamb line. Notice how a colored triangle appears when your cursor gets in the vicinity of the midpoint. Each Osnap has a symbol with a distinctive shape. When the triangle appears at the midpoint of the jamb line, left-click. Click the Midpoint Osnap button again, move the cursor to the bottom jamb line, and, when the triangle appears at that midpoint, click again. Press ⏎ to end the Line command.

5. Start the Offset command and type **1.5** ⏎ to set the offset distance. Pick the newly drawn line, then pick a point anywhere to the right side. Then, while the Offset command is still running, pick the original line again and pick another point in a blank area somewhere to the left side of the doorway opening (Figure 4.42). Press ⏎ to end the Offset command.

FIGURE 4.42: Offset vertical line between jambs

NOTE NOTE NOTE NOTE NOTE NOTE NOTE NOTE NOTE NOTE NOTE NOTE NOTE NOTE NOTE

A line *offset* from itself, that is, a copy of the selected line, is automatically made at a perpendicular specified distance from the selected line.

6. Click the Ortho button on the Status bar. Make sure Ortho is activated. Type l ↵ to start the Line command. Click the Midpoint Osnap button and then move the cursor near the midpoint of the left vertical line. When the colored triangle appears at the midpoint of this left-most line, click. Hold the cursor out directly to the right of the point you just selected to draw a horizontal line through the three vertical lines. When the cursor is about two feet to the right of the three vertical lines, pick a point to set the endpoint of this guideline. Press ↵ to end the Line command (Figure 4.43).

7. Type o ↵ to start the Offset command. Type 1 ↵ to set the offset distance. Pick this new line, and then pick a point in a blank area anywhere above the line. Pick the original line again and then pick anywhere below it. The new line has been offset 1" above and below itself (Figure 4.44). Now you have placed all the lines necessary to create the sliding glass door frames in the opening. You still need to trim some of these lines back and erase others. Press ↵ to end the Offset command.

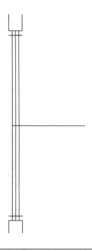

FIGURE 4.43: Horizontal guideline drawn through vertical lines

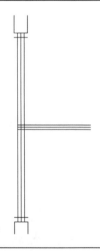

FIGURE 4.44: Offset horizontal guideline

8. Start the Trim command by typing **tr** ↵. When you are prompted to select cutting edges, pick the two horizontal lines that were just created with the Offset command. Then press ↵.

9. Now trim the two outside vertical lines by picking them as shown in Figure 4.45a. The result is shown in Figure 4.45b.

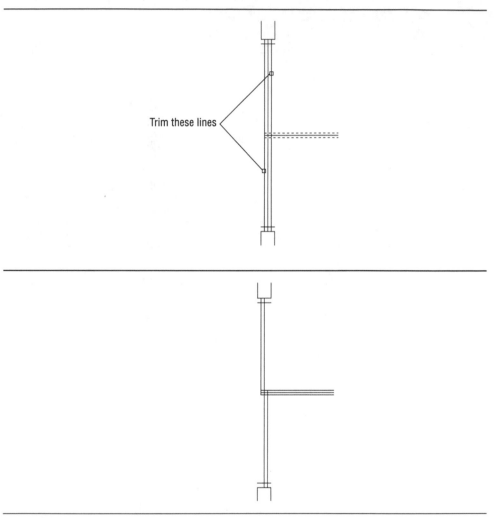

Trim these lines

FIGURE 4.45: Picking the vertical lines to trim (a), and the result (b)

10. Press ↵ twice to stop and restart the Trim command. When you are prompted to select cutting edges, use a special window called a *crossing window* to select all the lines visible in the drawing. A crossing window will select everything within the window or crossing it. Here's how to do it:

 A. Pick a point above and to the right of the opening.

 B. Move the cursor to a point below and to the left of the opening, forming a window with dashed lines (Figure 4.46).

 C. Pick that point. Everything inside the rectangle or crossing an edge of it is selected.

 D. Press ↵.

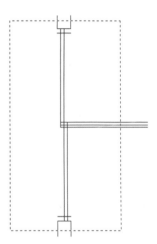

FIGURE 4.46: The crossing window for selecting cutting edges

11. To trim the lines, pick them at the points noted in Figure 4.47a. When you finish trimming, the opening should look like Figure 4.47b. Be sure to press ↵ to end the Trim command.

NOTE NOTE NOTE NOTE NOTE NOTE NOTE NOTE NOTE NOTE NOTE NOTE NOTE NOTE NOTE
If all lines don't trim the way you expect them to, you may have to change the
setting for the Edgemode variable. This is easy to do. Cancel the trim operation
and undo any trims you've made to the sliding glass door. Type edgemode ↵,
then type 0 ↵. Now start the trim command and continue trimming.

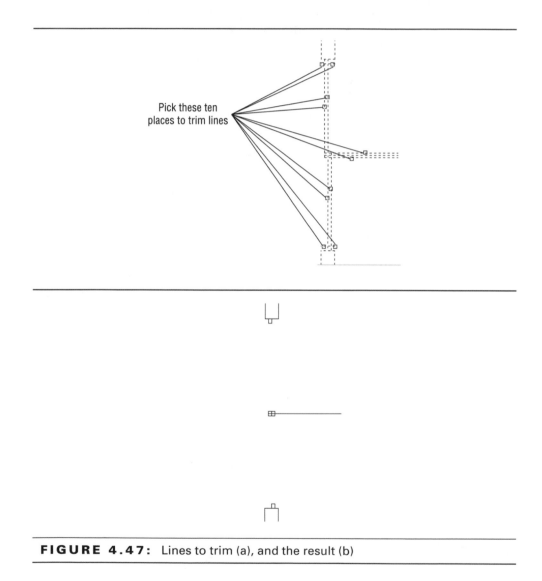

Pick these ten
places to trim lines

FIGURE 4.47: Lines to trim (a), and the result (b)

12. Start the Erase command and erase the remaining horizontal guideline.

    To finish the sliding glass doors, you need to draw in two lines to represent the glass panes for each door panel. Each pane of glass is centered inside its frame, so the line representing the pane will run between the midpoints of the inside edge of each frame section.

13. Type l ↵ to start the Line command and pick the Midpoint button on the Object Snap toolbar.

14. For each of the two sliding door frames, put the cursor near the midpoint of the inside line of the frame section nearest the jamb. When the colored triangle appears there, click. Then select the Perpendicular Osnap button from the Object Snap toolbar and move the cursor to the other frame section of that door panel. When you get near the horizontal line that represents both the inside edge of one frame section and the back edge of the frame section next to it, the colored Perpendicular Osnap symbol will appear on that line. When it does, select that point.

15. Press ↵ to end the Line command.

16. Press ↵ to restart the Line command and repeat the procedure described in step 14 for the other door panel, being sure to start the line at the frame section nearest the other jamb. The finished opening should look like Figure 4.48a.

17. Use the Zoom Previous button to see the full floor plan with all doors (Figure 4.48b).

18. Save this drawing as Cabin04b.

This completes the doors for the floor plan. The focus here has been on walls and doors, and the strategies for drawing them. As a result, you now have a basic floor plan for the cabin, and you will continue to develop this plan in the next skill.

SKILL 4

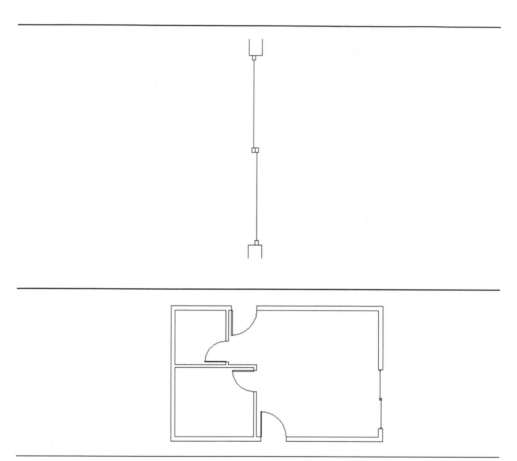

FIGURE 4.48: The finished sliding glass doors (a), and the floor plan with all doors finished

By working with the tools and strategies in this skill, you now should have an idea of an approach to drawing many objects. In the next skill, you will continue in this same vein, learning a few new commands and strategies as you add steps, a balcony, a kitchen, and a bathroom to the floor plan.

If you would like to practice the skills you have learned so far, a practice drawing is included at the end of this skill. It is an addition connected to the cabin by a sidewalk, and consists of a remodeled two-car garage in which one car slot has been converted into a storage area and an office (Figure 4.49). Use the same commands and strategies you have been using up to now to draw this layout adjacent to the cabin. Save this exercise as Cabin04b-addon.dwg.

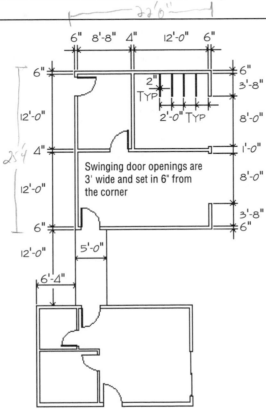

FIGURE 4.49: The Garage Addition

Are You Experienced?

Now you can . . .

- ☑ offset exterior walls to make interior walls
- ☑ zoom in on an area with a zoom window and zoom back out with the Zoom Previous command
- ☑ use the Rectangle and Arc commands to make a door
- ☑ use the Endpoint, Midpoint, and Perpendicular Object Snap modes
- ☑ use the crossing window selection tool
- ☑ use the Copy and Mirror commands to place an already existing door and swing in another opening
- ☑ use the Offset and Trim commands to make a sliding glass door

SKILL 5

Skill 5: Gaining Drawing Strategies: Part 2

- ⊙ Using Object Snaps
- ⊙ Zooming with Realtime and Pan
- ⊙ Copying and moving objects
- ⊙ Creating circles and ellipses

Developing a drawing strategy begins with determining the best way to start, or when to start, a command. AutoCAD provides several ways to start most of the commands you will be using. You have seen how the Offset, Fillet, Trim, and Extend commands can be found on either the Modify toolbar or Modify drop-down menu. They can also be started by typing in the first letter or two of the command, then pressing Enter.

TIP TIP TIP TIP TIP TIP TIP TIP TIP TIP TIP TIP TIP TIP TIP TIP TIP TIP TIP TIP TIP TIP TIP TIP

For a quick recap, to start the Offset and Fillet commands, enter o or f, respectively. To execute the Trim command, enter tr, and to execute the Extend command, enter ex. Remember also that the drop-down menus may be activated by holding down the Alt Key while pressing the hotkey—the letter that is underlined in the menu name. For example, to open the Modify drop-down menu, enter Alt+m.

The choice of which method to use will be determined, to an extent, by what you are doing at the time, as well as by your command of the keyboard. When using the abbreviations, keyboard entry is generally the fastest method; but if your hand is already on the mouse, and the Modify toolbar is docked on the screen, selecting commands from the toolbar may be faster.

There are also usually several drawing strategies that can be used in any particular situation to accomplish the same goal. For example, in the last skill, you could have used the Line command to draw the doors, instead of using the Rectangle command. Or the openings could have been made by copying the jamb lines from one completed opening to another. One of the key elements for efficient drafting on the computer is to be able to observe what objects currently in your drawing can serve as aids in accomplishing your next task. In the previous skill, we used the outer wall lines to create the rest of the wall lines, including the doorjambs, thereby avoiding drawing any new lines. As you get more familiar with the commands and techniques for computer drafting, you will start looking more carefully at the geometry of your drawing to see what help it can offer you.

In this chapter, you will be introduced to several new commands and, through the step-by-step instructions, be shown some alternate methods for accomplishing tasks similar to those you have previously completed. In this skill, you will add front and back steps, thresholds, a balcony, and kitchen and bath fixtures to the floor plan of the cabin (Figure 5.1). In each of these tasks, the focus will be on noticing what is already in the drawing that can make your job easier.

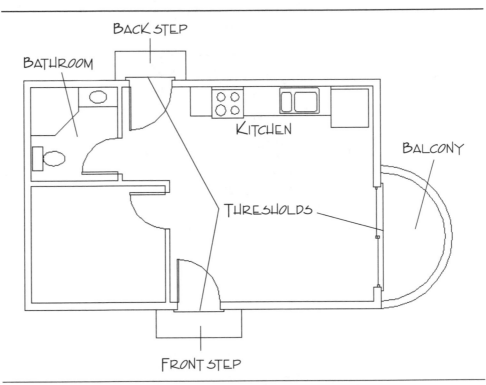

FIGURE 5.1: The cabin with front and back steps, thresholds, balcony, kitchen, and bathroom

Drawing the Steps and Thresholds

The steps and thresholds are each drawn with three simple lines. The trick is to see what part of the drawing can be effectively used to generate and position those lines. Use a width of 2' for the front and back step, and lengths of 6' and 5', respectively. The three thresholds extend 2" beyond the outside wall line and run 3" past either jamb line (Figure 5.2).

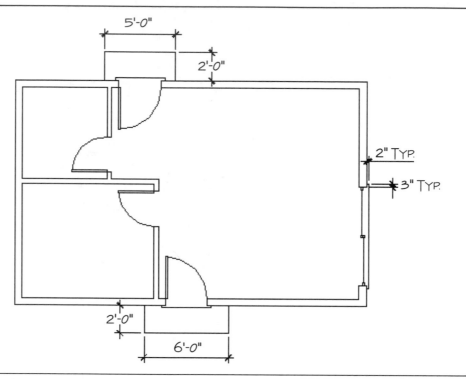

FIGURE 5.2: The steps and thresholds with their dimensions

These are simple shapes to draw, but you will learn a few new techniques as you create them.

The Front Step

As you can see in Figure 5.2, the front step is 2-feet wide and 6-feet long. Because you know the width of the doorway opening, you can determine how far past the opening the step extends, assuming it to be symmetrical. A line can then be drawn from the endpoint of one of the jamb lines, down 2', then offset the proper distance left and right to create the sides of the step. Here's how it's done:

1. With AutoCAD running, bring up your cabin drawing (last saved as Cabin04b) and use the Zoom command options to achieve a view similar to Figure 5.3. The Object Snap toolbar may be docked on the right side of the drawing area. If not, you can either bring it up and dock it or just use the Object Snap flyout. This is activated by holding down the left mouse

button when the cursor is on the Tracking button on the Standard toolbar. The cursor menu also has the Object Snaps on it. You can open this menu by holding down the Shift key and clicking the right mouse button. If you're using an Intellimouse or have a mouse with three buttons, you can activate the cursor menu by clicking the Intellimouse wheel or clicking the third mouse button.

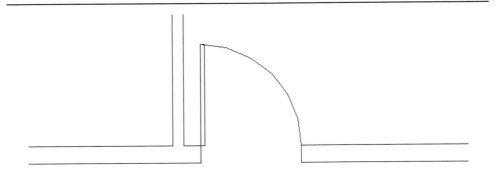

FIGURE 5.3:   Zoomed into the front opening

2. Start the Line command, activate the Endpoint Osnap, and pick a point at the lower end of the left jamb line.

3. Click the Ortho button on the status bar at the bottom of the screen to turn on Ortho mode (if it's not already on). Hold the crosshair cursor so that it is directly below the first point picked. Do not pick a point yet (Figure 5.4).

4. Type **2'** ↵. A vertical line is drawn that is 2-feet long. When the line command is running and the crosshair cursor is held away from the last point picked in a particular direction, you can enter a distance, and the line will be drawn to the desired length in the direction of the crosshair cursor. Because you want the line to be vertical, Ortho assisted you by forcing the line to be drawn in the vertical direction. This is called the *Direct Entry* method of entering distances.

NOTE NOTE NOTE NOTE NOTE NOTE NOTE NOTE NOTE NOTE NOTE NOTE NOTE NOTE NOTE

When Ortho mode is on, lines you draw are forced to be horizontal or vertical.

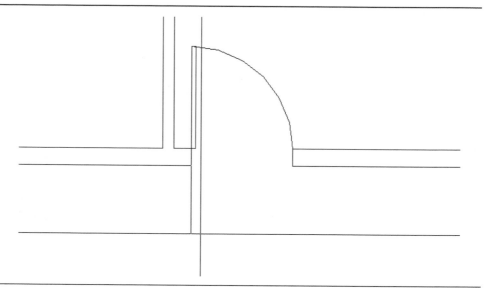

FIGURE 5.4: Line command running with Ortho on

5. Press ↵ to end the Line command. Type **o** ↵ to start the Offset command. Type **1'6** ↵ for an offset distance and offset this line to the left.

6. Press ↵ twice to stop and restart Offset. Type **6'**↵ and offset this new line to the right (Figure 5.5). Press ↵ to end the Offset command.

7. Erase the original line and draw a line from the lower endpoints of these two new lines to represent the front edge of the step. Use Endpoint Osnap for each point picked. Press ↵ to end the Line command. Your drawing should look like Figure 5.6.

8. Zoom previous to view the entire floor plan.

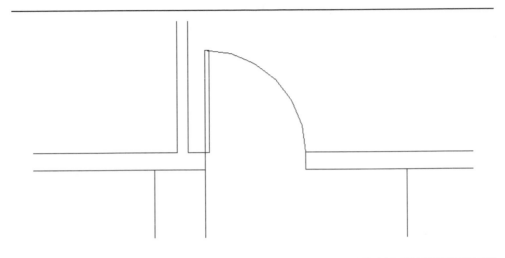

FIGURE 5.5: The sides of the front step after offsetting

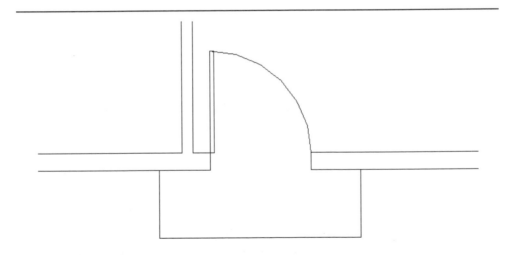

FIGURE 5.6: The completed front step

The strategy here was to recognize that a line drawn from the jamb line could be used to determine the location of the sides of the step. The new technique of using the Ortho mode to draw showed you a quick method for entering distances when the lines are horizontal or vertical. For the back step, you'll build on this by adding the From Osnap drawing aid to your bag of tools.

The Back Step

The method used on the front step can be applied here as well. The situation is identical: you will be working with the same geometry in the drawing and will accomplish the same thing. This time, however, you'll use From Osnap to locate the side of the step. Remember that the step in the back is 5-feet wide.

1. Zoom into the back step area. Start the Line command and pick the Snap From button on the Object Snap toolbar.

   The prompt line in the Command window will read: "`_line Specify first point: _from Base point:`." This is actually four prompts grouped together:

   - `_line` signifies the starting of the Line command.
   - `Specify first point:` is the first prompt for the Line command.
   - `_from` signifies that the From Osnap has been selected.
   - `Base point:` is the first prompt for the From Osnap option.

   The From Osnap option enables you to pick a point at a specified distance from a known point. In this case, because the step is 5-feet long, we want to begin the side of the step 1' to the left of the doorway opening. So the Base point that AutoCAD is prompting you for is the starting point from which you will measure the one-foot distance—in this case, it is the upper end of the left jamb line.

2. Pick the Endpoint Osnap and pick the upper end of the left jamb line. The prompt line now has `_endp of <Offset>:` added to it. This is actually two more prompts:

   - `_endp` signifies that the Endpoint Osnap was selected.
   - `<Offset>:` is the second prompt for the From Osnap option. It means that you now need to enter the relative coordinates that describe the distance and direction from the last point picked to the point that you want to start the line at. In other words, you need to tell AutoCAD how far away and in what direction the beginning of the line will be from the point you just picked—in this case, it's 1' to the left.

3. Type **@-12,0** ↵. A line begins 1' to the left of the opening on the outside wall line (Figure 5.7). Make sure that Ortho is still on. Hold the crosshair

cursor directly above the beginning of the line and type **2'** ↵. The side of the step is drawn using the Direct Entry technique with Ortho.

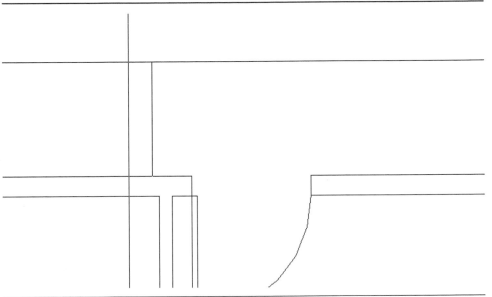

FIGURE 5.7: Starting a line for the side of the step

4. Hold the crosshair cursor directly to the right from the last point, then type **5'** ↵. The front edge of the step is drawn. You used Direct Entry with Ortho again, and didn't have to enter either the relative polar, or Cartesian coordinates.

5. Pick Perpendicular Osnap from the Object Snap toolbar and move the cursor to the outside wall line (Figure 5.8). When the perpendicular icon appears on the wall line, click the mouse button. The right edge of the step is drawn and the back step is complete. Press ↵ to end the Line command.

6. Zoom previous to view the completed back step with the whole floor plan.

The From Osnap is a welcome new tool to AutoCAD users. It will be used a few more times in the book. When you combine it with the technique of using Ortho to help enter distances, as you have for the back step, you will be surprised at how quickly you can lay out orthogonal walls in a floor plan. The Ortho technique, used by itself, powerfully facilitates drawing the footprint of a building. When you work through the next section, you'll get to practice using the From Osnap once more, then you'll learn about another Osnap tool—tracking.

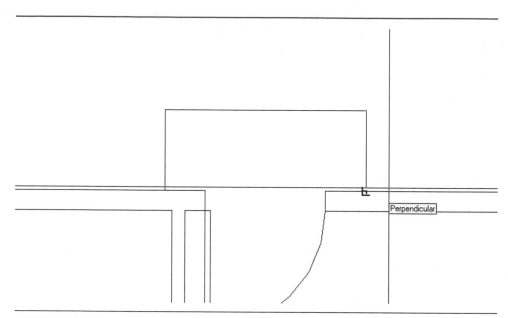

FIGURE 5.8: Completing the back step with the Perpendicular Osnap

You now have to do the thresholds for the three external openings.

The Thresholds

Thresholds generally are used on doorway openings where the level changes from one side of the opening to the other. This usually occurs at entrances that open from or to the outside. Though quite different in shape, each threshold for the cabin has the same geometry as the steps. The lip of each threshold is offset 2" from the outside wall, and each edge runs 3" past the doorjamb (refer to Figure 5.2). You'll use the From Osnap to draw the threshold for the 7-foot opening. Then you'll learn another, more efficient technique for drawing the thresholds for the front and back doorway openings.

To draw the threshold for the 7-foot opening:

1. Zoom into the 7-foot opening.

2. Use the Line command, From and Endpoint Osnaps, and relative polar coordinates to start the first line.

3. Draw all three lines for the threshold using the Ortho tool and the Direct Entry method for distances. (You learned the distances when drawing the front and back steps. Calculate the length of the threshold by adding the

length of the opening to two times the distance that the threshold edge runs past the jamb: 7' + 2(3")=7'-6".)

NOTE NOTE NOTE NOTE NOTE NOTE NOTE NOTE NOTE NOTE NOTE NOTE NOTE NOTE

Direct Entry is a method used to specify distances for line segments. In this method, you use the crosshair to indicate the direction for the next segment and type in the distance without using either the relative polar, or Cartesian coordinates. This technique is primarily used with Ortho to draw line segments that are horizontal or vertical. It saves time because there is less data to type in.

4. When finished, Zoom previous to view the finished threshold with the rest of the drawing.

Now you will use a feature called Tracking to draw the other two thresholds. You can use Tracking, just as you used From Osnap, to establish the first point of a line at a specified distance and direction from a known point in the drawing. The advantage of using Tracking is that you can use the Direct Entry method for distances instead of entering the relative coordinates, as is required with From Osnap.

SKILL
5

1. Zoom into a close view of the front door opening.

2. Start the Line command and pick the Temporary Tracking Point button on the Osnap toolbar.

3. Pick the Endpoint Osnap button on the Osnap toolbar.

4. Move the cursor to a point near the lower end of the left jamb line and, when the Endpoint Osnap symbol appears at that location, click to set a tracking point. A small cross will appear at the point you picked to let you know that the point is a tracking point. Also, a small *x* will move with the cursor along the tracking path.

5. Move the cursor directly to the left of the tracking point, near the exterior wall line. A dotted line and a tooltip will appear (Figure 5.9a).

6. While the dotted line and Track Point tooltip are visible, type **3** ↵. Then move the crosshair cursor a short distance down the screen to verify that the line has begun 3" to the left of the doorjamb (Figure 5.9b).

7. Be sure Ortho is on. Then, while holding the crosshair cursor below the first point of the line, type **2** ↵.

8. Hold the crosshair cursor to the right of this last point, then type **3'6** ↵.

9. Pick the Perpendicular Osnap tool and click the exterior wall line. The front door threshold is now complete (Figure 5.9c).

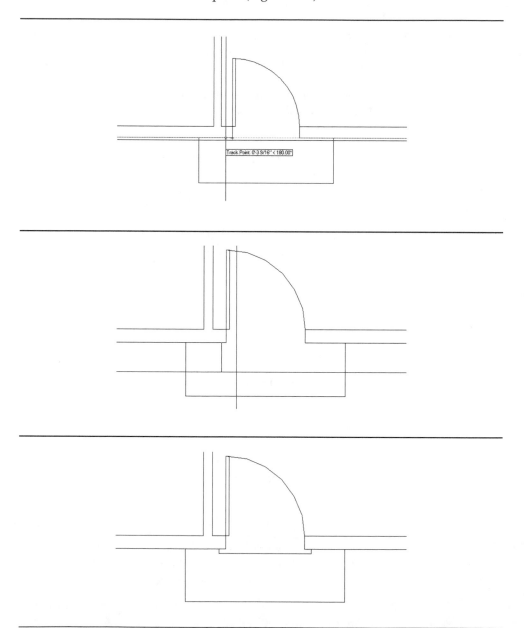

FIGURE 5.9: The tracking path and Track Point tooltip (a), the first threshold line is started (b), and the completed threshold (c).

10. Using the Zoom commands you already know, change your view to the back door area and follow the same procedure to draw the back door threshold. Then zoom out to a full view of the cabin.

Tracking is a very powerful tool for drawing that can be used in several ways. We will use it again later in this skill to illustrate a few more of its features.

The Balcony: Drawing Circles

A glance at Figure 5.1 will tell you that the balcony is made up of two semi-circles. There are several ways that these could be drawn, but you will form them from a circle. Often the easiest way to draw an arc is to draw a circle that contains the arc segment, then to trim the circle back.

1. Select Draw ➤ Circle and look at the Circle menu for a moment.

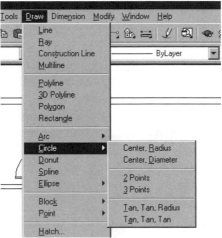

There are six options for constructing a circle. Two of the options require you to specify a point to be the center of the circle and to enter a radius or a diameter. The next two options are used when you know two or three points that the circle must intersect. And, finally, the last two options use tangents and a radius, or just tangents, to form a circle.

2. The balcony has a radius of 5', so select the Center, Radius option. The Command window will prompt you to specify a point to be the center of the circle. The actual center for the balcony will be 5' above the lower-right corner of the outside wall line; but, for this exercise, we will draw the circle in the living room and then move it into position later.

3. Pick a point in the middle of the largest room of the cabin. The center is established, and, as you move the cursor, the circle changes size and becomes attached to the crosshair cursor (Figure 5.10). You could pick a point to establish the radius; but, in this case, you know exactly what you want the radius to be.

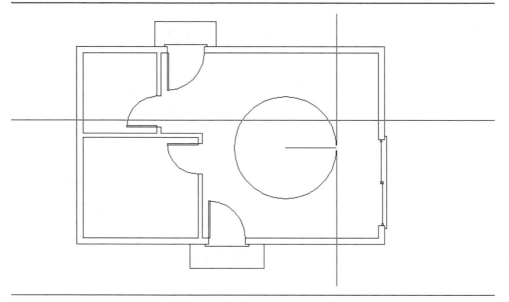

FIGURE 5.10: The circle attached to the crosshair cursor

4. Type **5'** ↵. The circle is drawn, and the command ends.

5. Select the Move button on the Modify toolbar. The cursor changes to a pick-box. Select the circle and press ↵.

6. On the Object Snap toolbar or flyout, pick the Quadrant button. Select the circle somewhere near its bottom extremity (Figure 5.11a). An image of the circle is attached to the crosshair cursor. Turn Ortho off by clicking the Ortho button on the status bar.

7. Move the crosshair cursor around to see that the lowest point on the circle is attached at the crosshair (Figure 5.11b). This point on the circle needs to be placed at the lower-right corner of the outside wall line.

8. Select Endpoint Osnap, then pick the lower-right corner of the cabin. The circle is positioned correctly for the balcony (Figure 5.11c). Now you can use the existing wall lines to trim the circle into a semi-circle.

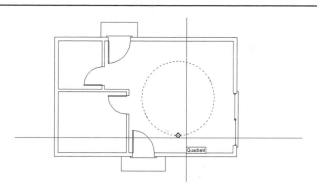

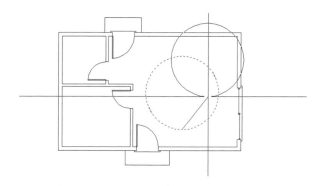

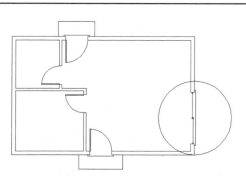

FIGURE 5.11: Selecting the base point with Quadrant Osnap (a), the circle attached to the crosshair cursor at lowest point (b), and the circle positioned for the balcony (c)

9. Zoom into the area of the balcony and start the Trim command.

10. Select the two outside wall lines on the far right, as shown in Figure 5.12, then press ↵.

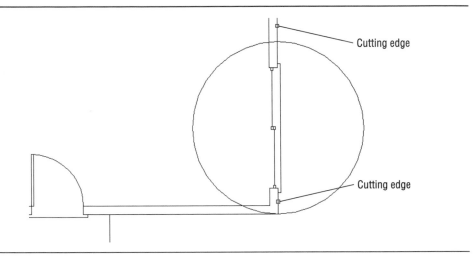

Cutting edge

Cutting edge

FIGURE 5.12: Selecting wall lines to be cutting edges

11. Select the portion of the circle that is inside the cabin. The circle is trimmed into a semi-circle. Press ↵ to end the Trim command.

12. Start the Offset command, set the distance for 6", and offset the semi-circle to the inside. Press ↵ to end the Offset command. The balcony is complete. Zoom previous to view the floor plan with the completed balcony. Save the drawing as Cabin05a.dwg (Figure 5.13).

As mentioned at the beginning of this section, there are several techniques for drawing the balcony. The one you used gave you the opportunity to use the Move command and the Quadrant Osnap, and allowed you to see how using the lowest quadrant snap point on the circle is an easy way to locate the balcony on the building. No entry of relative coordinates was required.

In the next section, you will continue to develop drawing strategies as you focus on creating a counter and fixtures to comprise a kitchen.

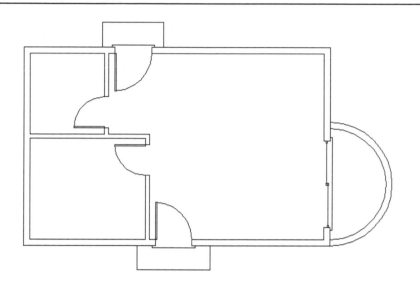

FIGURE 5.13: The floor plan with the balcony completed

Laying Out the Kitchen

The kitchen for the cabin will have a stove, a refrigerator, and a counter with a sink (Figure 5.14). The refrigerator is set 2" away from the back wall. Approaching this drawing task, your goal is to think about the easiest and fastest way to complete it. The first step in deciding on an efficient approach is to ascertain what information you have about the various parts, and what geometry in the drawing will be able to assist you. The basic dimensions are given here, and you will get more detailed information about the sink and stove as we progress through the exercise.

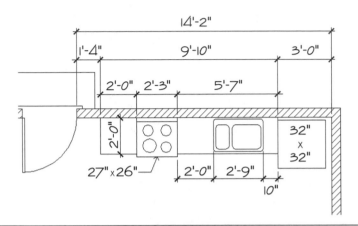

FIGURE 5.14: The general layout of the kitchen

The Counter

Although the counter is in two pieces, you will draw it as one piece and then cut out a section for the stove. Try two ways to draw the counter to see which method is more efficient.

Using Tracking and Direct Entry with Ortho

1. Use a zoom window to zoom your view so it is about the same magnification as Figure 5.15.

2. Start the Line command. Activate the Temporary Tracking Point Osnap and click Endpoint Osnap. Then pick the lower end of the right back doorjamb line. A small cross is placed on the point you pick.

3. Hold the crosshair cursor directly to the right of that point. When the Track Point tooltip and the dotted-line tracking path appear, type **1'4** ↵. The line for the left side of the counter is begun.

4. Turn Ortho back on. Then hold the crosshair cursor directly below the first point of the line and type **2'** ↵. Hold the crosshair cursor to the right and type **9'10** ↵ (Figure 5.15). Select Perpendicular Osnap and pick the inside wall line again. Press ↵ to end the Line command. The counter is drawn.

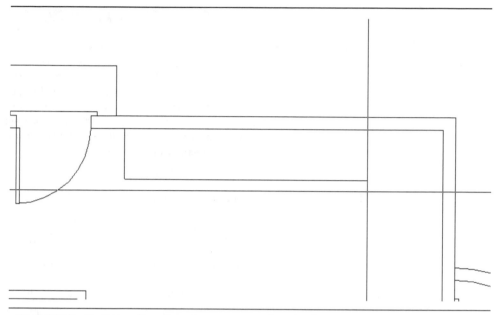

FIGURE 5.15: Drawing the counter using the Direct Entry technique

Using Offset and Fillet

To do the same thing using the Offset command, you'll need to undo the effects of the previous command. Since all lines were drawn in one cycle of the Line command, one use of the U command will undo the entire counter.

1. Click the Undo button on the Standard toolbar. The counter you just drew should disappear. If you ended the Line command while drawing the counter and had to restart it before you finished, you may have to click the Undo button more than once. If you undo too much, click the Redo button, just to the right of the Undo button. The Redo command will only undo the effect of one undo. So, if you undo one step too many, you can still get the last undone step back. But, undoing more than one step has the effect of deleting work permanently; your work will then have to be redrawn.

WARNING WARNING WARNING WARNING WARNING WARNING WARNING WARNING
AutoCAD has two Undo commands, and they operate quite differently. When you click the Undo button on the Standard toolbar, you are using the U command. It can also be started by typing u ↵. The U command works like the undo command for Windows-compatible applications by undoing the results of commands one step at a time. The Undo command in AutoCAD has many options and is started by typing undo ↵. This is used when you want to undo everything you've done since you last saved your drawing, or back to a point in your drawing session that you marked earlier. Be careful when you use the Undo command, as you could easily lose a lot of your work.

Now draw the counter again, this time using the Offset and Fillet commands.

2. Offset the right inside wall line 3' to the left. Then offset this new line 9'-10" to the left. Finally, offset the upper inside wall line 2' down (Figure 5.16).

3. Use the Fillet command with a radius of zero to clean up the two corners.

You can decide which of the two methods is more practical for you. Both are powerful techniques for laying out orthogonal patterns of lines for walls, counters, and other objects.

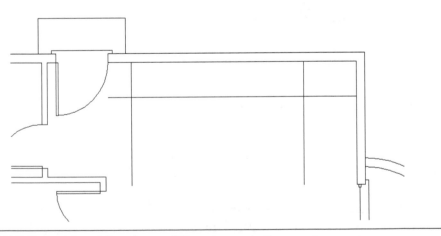

FIGURE 5.16: Offsetting wall lines to create the counter

The Stove and Refrigerator

The stove and refrigerator are simple rectangles. Use the Temporary Tracking Point Osnap to locate the first corner of each shape.

1. For the refrigerator, select the Rectangle button on the Draw toolbar, then select the Temporary Tracking Point Osnap option. Use Endpoint Osnap to select a base point at the upper end of the right side of the counter. Then hold the cursor directly below that point. When the dotted tracking path and the Track Point tooltip appear, type **2** ↵. This starts the rectangle 2" away from the back wall, along the side of the counter. To specify the opposite corner of the rectangle, type **@32,-32** ↵.

2. For the stove, right-click the mouse. A menu pops up next to the crosshair cursor. Click Repeat Rectangle. Use the same technique that was used in step 1, but pick the upper end of the left side of the counter as the tracking point. Hold the cursor directly to the right of that point and type **1'6** ↵. Then type **@27,-26** to complete the rectangle.

3. Use the Trim command to trim away the front edge of the counter at the stove (Figure 5.17).

NOTE NOTE NOTE NOTE NOTE NOTE NOTE NOTE NOTE NOTE NOTE NOTE NOTE NOTE NOTE
Because the stove rectangle is drawn as a *polyline*—that is, one unique entity—you only need to select it once for all sides of the rectangle to be cutting edges.

**SKILL
5**

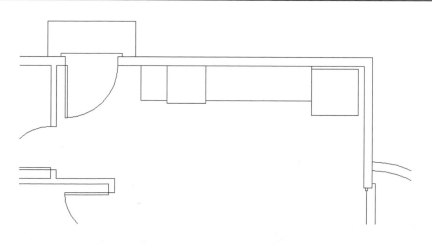

FIGURE 5.17: The stove and refrigerator made with rectangles

Completing the Stove

The stove needs a little more detail. You will need to add circles to represent the burners and to add a line off the back to indicate the control panel (Figure 5.18). The burners are located by their centers.

1. Zoom into a closer view of the stove using the zoom window. You need to draw a line along the back of the stove that is 2.5" in from the wall line. Offsetting seems like the right command to use.

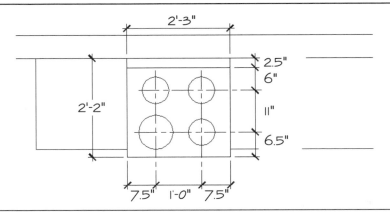

FIGURE 5.18: The details of the stove

2. Offset the wall line down 2.5", then trim it back to the sides of the stove (Figure 5.19).

WARNING WARNING WARNING WARNING WARNING WARNING WARNING WARNING

When you pick the wall line to offset it, choose a location on the wall line on either side of the stove, but not where the back of the stove coincides with the wall. You don't want to offset a line of the stove because it was made using the Rectangle command and is therefore a polyline. When any side of a polyline is offset, all sides are offset and all corners are filleted automatically. This would be an inconvenience in this situation because only one line needs to be offset. When you draw the sink, you'll learn a technique for selecting the line you want when two or more lines overlap or coincide.

3. The next step is to lay out guidelines to locate the centers of the burners. Offset the line you created for the control panel in Step 2 down 6". Then offset this new line down 11". Next you need vertical guidelines. Use tracking to draw the first guideline.

4. Start the Line command and pick Temporary Tracking Point Osnap and then Endpoint Osnap. Then pick the upper-left corner of the stove.

5. With Ortho on, hold the cursor directly to the right of this point. When the dotted tracking path and the Track Point tooltip appear, type **7.5** ↵. The first guideline is started.

6. Hold the crosshair cursor below the first point of the guideline and pick a point just below the stove. Press ↵ to end the Line command.

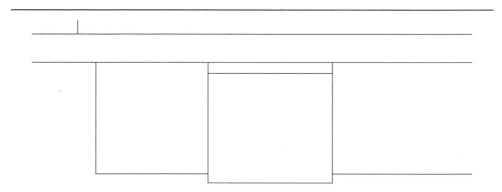

FIGURE 5.19: The stove with the control panel drawn

7. Offset this line 12" to the right (Figure 5.20). The guidelines are set in place.

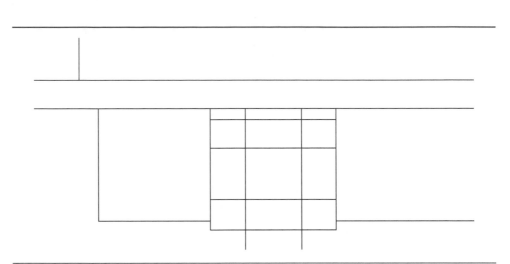

FIGURE 5.20: The guidelines for the centers of the burner circles

The next step is to draw a circle for one burner, copy it to the other three burner locations, and then change the radius of the left front burner.

1. Using Intersection Osnap and the Circle command, draw a circle with its center at the lower-left intersection of the guidelines, and a radius of 3.5".

2. Start the Copy command. Select the circle and then press ↵.

3. Type **m** ↵. This starts the Multiple option. Pick Intersection Osnap. Select the intersection of the guidelines at the center of the circle as a base point. Press ↵.

4. Select Intersection Osnap again and pick the intersection of guidelines above the first circle (Figure 5.21). Select Intersection Osnap again and pick one of the intersections on the right side. Then select Intersection Osnap one more time and pick the fourth intersection of guidelines. Press ↵ to end the Multiple Copy command. The burners are in place. Now you need to change the size of the lower left burner.

5. Pick the lower left burner. Five colored boxes will appear on the circle and its center. These are called *Grips*.

6. Pick the Properties button near the right end of the Standard Toolbar. The Properties dialog box comes up on the left part of the screen (Figure 5.22). Notice the drop-down list at the top of the Properties dialog box. This tells you the currently selected object is a circle.

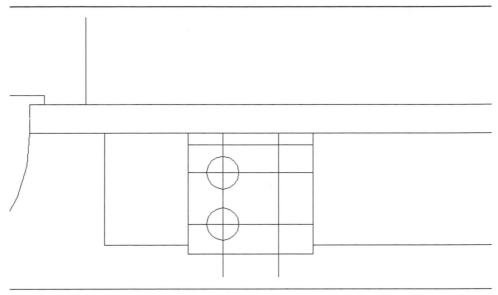

FIGURE 5.21: The first burner is copied.

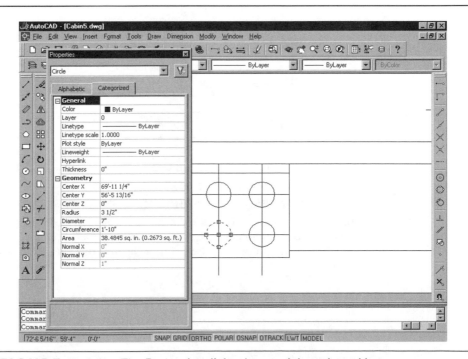

FIGURE 5.22: The Properties dialog box and the selected burner

7. Be sure that the Categorized tab below the drop-down list is selected (i.e., in front). If it is not, click the tab to bring it forward. Now move down the categorized list of properties and click Radius.

8. Highlight the 3½" radius setting. Change it to 4½" and press ↵. The burner in the drawing is enlarged.

9. Click the X in the upper-right corner of the Properties dialog box to close it. Then press the Esc key twice to turn off the five Grips that were on the circle.

10. Erase the guidelines and the stove is completed (Figure 5.23). Zoom previous to see the whole kitchen with the completed stove.

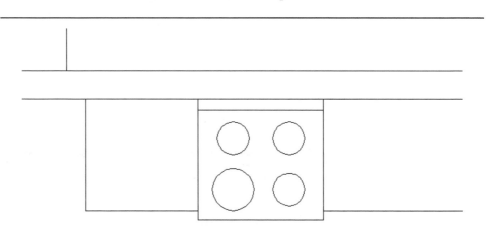

FIGURE 5.23: The completed stove

With the stove finished, the final task in the kitchen is to draw the sink.

NOTE NOTE NOTE NOTE NOTE NOTE NOTE NOTE NOTE NOTE NOTE NOTE NOTE NOTE NOTE

The Properties dialog box is an important tool for working with objects in the drawing. You will be learning more about it in *Skill 6: Using Layers to Organize Your Drawing*; and you will be using it throughout the rest of the book.

The Kitchen Sink

The sink you will draw is a double sink, with one basin larger than the other (Figure 5.24). You will use Offset, Fillet, and Trim to create it from the counter and wall lines.

1. Zoom into the sink area, keeping the edges of the refrigerator and stove in view. Offset the wall line 1" down and the front edge of the counter 1.5" up.

2. Offset the right side of the counter 10" to the left. When you pick this line to offset, hold down the Ctrl key as you pick the line. Then release the Ctrl key. If the refrigerator ghosts, pick the line again. The selected line will switch to the one representing the edge of the counter. When the counter edge is selected, press ↵, then complete the offset. This technique allows you to select a line that may coincide with another line.

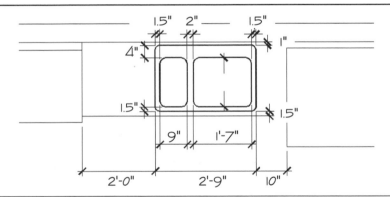

FIGURE 5.24: The sink with dimensions

3. Offset this new line 2'-9" to the left. This forms the outside edge of the sink (Figure 5.25a).

4. Fillet the corners of this rectangle to clean them up, using a radius of zero.

5. Offset the left side, bottom, and right side of the sink 1.5" to the inside. Offset the top side 4" to the inside. Then offset the new line on the left 9" to the right, and then again, 2" further to the right. This forms the basis of the inside sink lines (Figure 5.25b).

6. Trim away the horizontal top and bottom inside sink lines between the two middle vertical sink lines. Then fillet the four corners of each sink with a 2-inch radius to clean them up.

7. Fillet all outside sink corners with a 1.5-inch radius. This will finish the sink (Figure 5.25c). Zoom previous to view the whole kitchen with the completed sink.

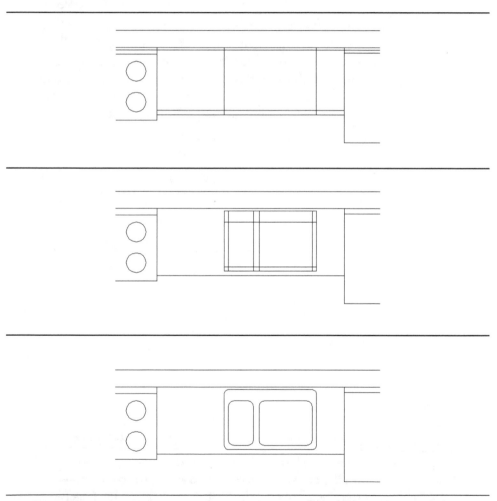

FIGURE 5.25: The offset lines to form the outside edge of the sink (a), the offset lines to form the inside edges of the sink (b), and the finished sink (c)

This completes the kitchen area. Very few new lines were drawn to accomplish this task because most of them were created by offsetting existing lines, then trimming or filleting them. Keep this in mind as you move on to the bathroom.

Constructing the Bathroom

The bathroom has three fixtures: sink, shower, and toilet (Figure 5.26). In drawing these fixtures, you will be using a few Object Snaps over and over again. You can set one or more of the Osnap choices to be continually running until you turn them off. That way, you won't have to pick them each time.

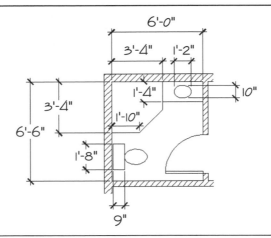

FIGURE 5.26: The bathroom fixtures with dimensions

Setting Running Object Snaps

You will set only two Osnaps to run continually for now, until you get used to how they work.

1. Select Tools ➤ Drafting Settings. The Drafting Settings dialog box comes up. Notice the three tabs at the top. Be sure the Object Snap tab is on top. If it's not, click it.

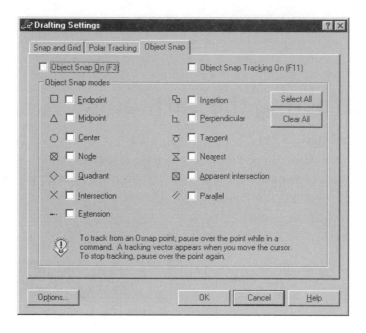

The 13 Osnap options are listed with a checkbox, and their symbol to the checkbox's left. Each Osnap option has a different symbol, which appears in the drawing when a particular Osnap is selected and the cursor is near a point where that Osnap can be used. You can check any number of Osnaps to be running at a time.

NOTE NOTE NOTE NOTE NOTE NOTE NOTE NOTE NOTE NOTE NOTE NOTE NOTE NOTE NOTE

The symbols or icons that appear on an object when an Osnap is active and when you move the cursor near the object are called *Autosnaps*. They're quite helpful, and you can choose a different color for them if you wish. If you're using a dark background in the drawing area, use a bright color, like yellow. For a white background, try blue.

2.   In the lower-left corner of the Drafting Settings dialog box, click Options. In the Options dialog box, click the Drafting tab at the top. Then, on the left side in the AutoSnap Settings area, open the AutoSnap Marker Color drop-down list and select a color. While you're in this area, make sure the Marker, Magnet, and Display AutoSnap Tooltip checkboxes are selected. Also make sure that the Display AutoSnap Aperture Box is unchecked. Then click OK.

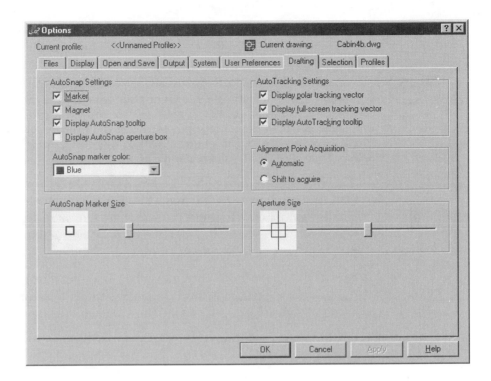

SKILL
▼ 5

3. Back in the Object Snap tab of the Drafting Settings dialog box, click in the checkboxes next to Endpoint and Midpoint. Then, above the list and to the left, click the checkbox next to Object Snap On (F3). Click OK to close the dialog box. These Osnaps will now be active any time you are prompted to select a point on the drawing.

NOTE NOTE NOTE NOTE NOTE NOTE NOTE NOTE NOTE NOTE NOTE NOTE NOTE NOTE NOTE
Osnap is a nickname for Object Snap. The two terms are used interchangeably.

Now you are ready to begin drawing the three fixtures for the bathroom. The shower determines the placement of the other two, so you will start there.

Drawing a Shower Unit

You will start the shower unit with a rectangle, then trim away one corner.

1. Zoom to Extents. Then use the Zoom window to view the bathroom close-up. Start the Rectangle command. For the first point, move the cursor to the upper-left inside corner of the room. Notice the square that appears at the corner. This is the Autosnap symbol for the Endpoint Osnap. As soon as it

appears on the endpoint you want to snap to, click the left mouse button. The first corner of the rectangle is placed. For the second point, type **@40,-40** ↵.

TIP TIP TIP TIP TIP TIP TIP TIP TIP TIP TIP TIP TIP TIP TIP TIP TIP TIP TIP TIP TIP TIP TIP TIP TIP

If you don't get the rectangle you want after entering the relative coordinates for the second corner, check this setting: Pick Tools ➤ Options. Then click the Preferences tab. In the upper-right corner of the Priority for Coordinate Data Entry area, be sure that the button next to Keyboard Entry Except Scripts is active. Then click OK. Try the rectangle again.

2. Start the Line command and move the cursor to the bottom line of the rectangle. Notice how a triangle, the Midpoint Autosnap symbol, appears when you get near the midpoint of the line. When you see the triangle on the midpoint you want, click it.

3. Be sure that Ortho is off. Then move the cursor near the midpoint of the right side of the rectangle until you see the triangle appear at the midpoint location (Figure 5.27). Click again. Press ↵ to end the Line command.

4. Use this line as a cutting edge and trim away the lower-right corner of the shower rectangle. Pess ↵ to stop the Trim command. This completes the shower.

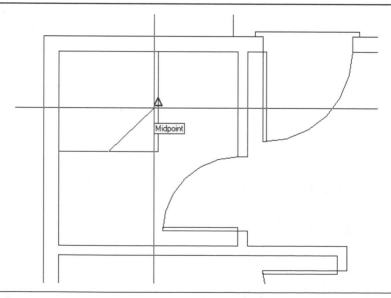

FIGURE 5.27: Using Midpoint Osnap to complete a line across the corner of the shower

Next, draw the sink to the right of the shower.

The Bathroom Sink

You will offset a line and draw an ellipse for this fixture, while practicing the Temporary Tracking Point Osnap option in the process. The Endpoint and Midpoint Osnaps are still running.

1. Zoom into the sink area with a zoom window. Offset the top inside wall line down 16". Then use the shower wall as a cutting edge and trim the line back.

2. Click the Ellipse button on the Draw toolbar. Type **c** ↵ to select the Center option.

3. Click the Temporary Tracking Point Osnap button and then click the newly offset line near its midpoint. This establishes a tracking point (small cross).

   When you have Osnaps running continually, you can still use an Osnap that is not running. Just click the Osnap button you want to use, and the running Osnaps will be suspended for the next pick. In this case, the Temporary Tracking Point Osnap first requires you to pick a base point. After selecting Temporary Tracking Point, the running Osnaps (Endpoint and Midpoint) are restored, and you can use Midpoint Osnap to locate the base point.

4. Move the crosshair cursor directly above the tracking point. When the dotted tracking path and the Track Point tooltip appear, type **8** ↵ to locate the center of the counter. The Command window will prompt you for the location of the ends of two perpendicular axes. You will start with the left/right axis and enter the distance using Direct Entry and Ortho, as you did for the steps earlier in the skill.

5. Turn Ortho on. Then hold the crosshair cursor directly to the right of the center point. Type **7** ↵. Hold the crosshair cursor directly above the center and type **5** ↵. The ellipse is constructed, and the sink fixture is complete (Figure 5.28). Leave the view on your screen as it is for a moment.

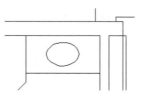

FIGURE 5.28: The completed sink fixture

Drawing the toilet will be the final task in this chapter. You will use the Ellipse command again, along with the Rectangle command. You will also be introduced to a couple of new display options.

Positioning a Toilet

The toilet consists of a rectangle and an ellipse centered between the shower and the wall. The tank is offset 1" from the back wall, and is 9"x20". The seat measures 18" in one direction and 1' in the other.

1. On the Standard toolbar, click the Pan Realtime button. The cursor changes to a small hand when you return it to the drawing area. Position it in the lower-left corner of the drawing area with the view still zoomed in on the sink.

2. Hold down the left mouse button and drag the hand up and to the right. When the toilet area comes into view, release the mouse button. The drawing slides along with the movement of the cursor. If necessary, do this again until you have the toilet area centered in the drawing area.

3. Go back to the Standard toolbar and click the Zoom Realtime button. Back on the drawing, the cursor changes to a magnifying glass with a plus and minus sign.

4. Position the Zoom Realtime cursor near the top of the drawing and hold down the left mouse button. Drag the cursor down and watch the view being zoomed out in real time. Move the cursor up, still holding the mouse button down. Position the cursor in such a way that you have a good view of the toilet area, then release the mouse button. Press Esc to exit the Zoom Realtime command.

NOTE NOTE NOTE NOTE NOTE NOTE NOTE NOTE NOTE NOTE NOTE NOTE NOTE NOTE

With Zoom Realtime, moving the cursor to the left or right has no effect on the view. The magnification is controlled solely by the up-and-down motion.

These zooming options are convenient tools for adjusting the view of your drawing. Move on to the toilet. You need to find a way to position the toilet accurately, centering it between the wall and shower. The midpoint of the left wall line won't be useful because the wall line runs behind the shower. You will have to construct a guideline.

Skill
5

1. With the Rectangle command, draw the toilet tank a few inches to the right of the wall, not touching any lines. (See Figure 5.26 for the dimensions.) Then offset the left wall line 1" to the right to make a guide line. Use the shower as a cutting edge and trim this guideline down to the shower (Figure 5.29a).

2. Start the Move command and select the tank, then press ↵.

3. For the base point, move the cursor to the middle of the left side of the tank. When you see the triangle at the midpoint, click the left mouse button.

4. For the second point, move the cursor onto the guide line. When it gets closer to the midpoint than the endpoint, the triangle will appear at the midpoint. At this point, click the left mouse button. The rectangle is accurately positioned 1" from the left wall and centered between the shower and lower wall (Figure 5.29b).

5. Erase the guide line.

6. Start the Ellipse command. The Command window displays a default prompt of `Specify axis endpoint of ellipse or [Arc/Center]:`. Using the Specify Axis endpoint option, you can define the first axis from one end of the ellipse to the other. This will help you here.

7. Move the cursor near the midpoint of the right side of the tank and, when the triangle shows up there, click. This starts the ellipse.

8. With Ortho on, hold the crosshair cursor out to the right of the rectangle and type **1'6** ↵. The first axis is positioned. Now as you move the crosshair cursor, you will see that a line starts at the center of the ellipse, and the cursor's movement controls the size of the other axis (Figure 5.29c). To designate the second axis, you need to enter the distance from the center of the axis to the end of it, or half the overall length of the axis.

9. Hold the crosshair cursor directly above the center point and type **6** ↵. The ellipse is complete, and the toilet is finished.

10. Select Tools ➤ Drafting Settings from the drop-down menus. In the dialog box, be sure the Object Snap tab is in front, then click the Clear All button. This turns off all running Osnaps. Click OK to close the dialog box.

11. Before you save this drawing, use the Pan Realtime and Zoom Realtime commands to zoom out and pan your drawing until the whole floor plan fills the drawing area, except for a thin border around the outside of the plan (Figure 5.30). Save this drawing as `Cabin05b`.

The bath is complete, and you now have a fairly complete floor plan for the cabin. In accomplishing the drawing tasks for Skill 5, you have been exposed to several new commands and techniques that will add to those introduced in Skill 4. Combined, you now have a set of tools for drawing that will take you a long way towards being able to lay out a floor plan of any size.

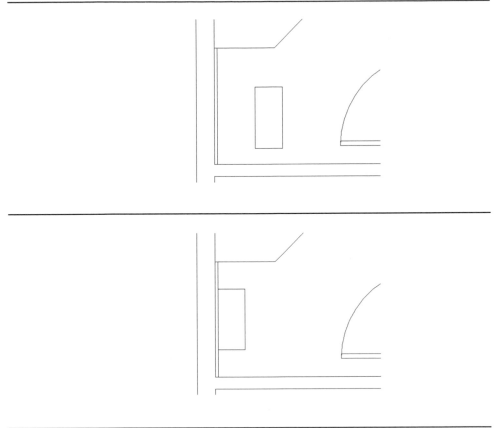

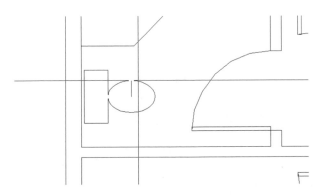

FIGURE 5.29: The toilet tank with an offset guide line (a), the tank correctly positioned (b), and the cursor controlling the size of the second axis for the toilet seat (c)

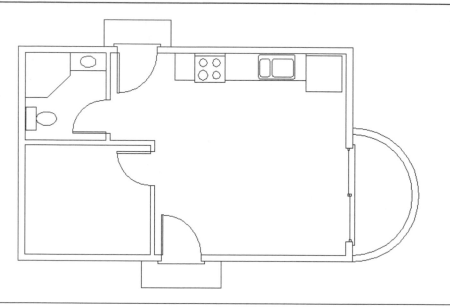

FIGURE 5.30: The completed floor plan zoomed and panned to fill the screen

As is true for almost any computer skill, the key to mastery is practice. Redrawing the entire cabin may seem like a daunting task at this point because you may be thinking about how long it took you to get here. But if you try it all again, you will find that it will take you about half the time as it did the first time, and if you do it a third time, half that time again. Once you understand the techniques used and how the commands work, feel free to experiment with alternative techniques to accomplish tasks and other options on the commands. If you have a specific project in mind you would like to draw in AutoCAD, so much the better—try it out.

Skills 1 through 5 fill out the basic level of skills in AutoCAD that allow you to draw on the computer approximately like you would with pencil and vellum, though you may already be seeing some of the advantages CAD offers over traditional board drafting. Beginning with the next skill, you will be introduced to concepts of AutoCAD that do not have a counterpart in board drafting. These features will take you to a new level of knowledge and skill, and you will start to get an idea of what sets computer drafting apart.

Are You Experienced?

Now you can...

- ☑ use From Osnap to start a line at a specified distance and direction from a known point
- ☑ use the Temporary Tracking Point Osnap to create and use tracking points
- ☑ use Quadrant and Intersection Osnaps
- ☑ set up and use running Object Snaps
- ☑ move around the drawing area with Realtime Zoom and Pan
- ☑ use the Circle and Ellipse commands
- ☑ move and duplicate objects with the Move and Copy Multiple commands
- ☑ use a circle and the Trim command to make a semi-circle arc
- ☑ use guide lines to locate the center of circles for a stove top

SKILL
5

Using Layers to Organize Your Drawing

- ➔ Creating new layers
- ➔ Assigning a color and linetype to layers
- ➔ Moving existing objects onto a new layer
- ➔ Freezing and thawing layers
- ➔ Working with linetypes

In pre-computer days, drafters used a set of transparent overlays on the drafting table. They were sheets that stacked on top of one another, and the drafters could see through several at a time. Specific kinds of information were drawn on each overlay, all related spatially so that several overlays might all be drawn to the same floor plan. Each overlay had small holes punched into it near the corners so the drafter could position it onto buttons, called registration points, which were taped to the drawing board. Because all overlays had holes punched at the same locations with respect to the drawing, information on the set of overlays was kept in alignment.

To help you organize your drawing, AutoCAD provides you with an amazing tool, called *layers*, which is a computerized metaphor for the transparent overlays, only much more powerful and flexible. In manual drafting, you could use only four or five overlays at a time before the information on the bottom overlay became unreadable. In AutoCAD, you are not limited in the number of layers that you can use. You can have hundreds of layers, and complex CAD drawings often do.

Layers as an Organization Tool

To understand what layers are and why they are so useful, think again about the transparent overlay sheets used in hand drafting. Each overlay is designed to be printed. The bottom sheet may be a basic floor plan. To create an overlay sheet for a structural drawing, the drafter traces over the lines of the floor plan that they need in the overlay, then adds new information pertinent to that sheet. For the next overlay, the same thing is done again. Each sheet, then, contains some information in common, in addition to data unique to that sheet.

In AutoCAD, using layers will allow you to generate all the sheets for a set of overlays from one file (Figure 6.1). Nothing needs to be drawn twice or traced. The wall layout will be on one layer and the roof lines on another. Doors will be on a third. The visibility of layers can be controlled so that all objects residing on a layer can be made temporarily invisible. This feature provides you with the means to put all information keyed to a particular floor plan in one .dwg file and, from that drawing, to produce a series of derived drawings, such as the foundation plan, the second floor plan, the reflected ceiling plan, and the roof plan, by making different combinations of layers visible for each drawing. When you make a print, you decide which of the layers will be visible in the print. Consequently, in a set of drawings, each sheet based on the floor plan will display a unique combination of layers, all of which are in one file.

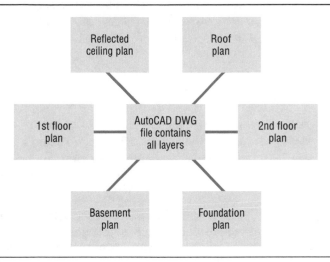

FIGURE 6.1: Diagram of several drawings coming from one file

Layers, as an organization tool, allow you to classify the various objects in a computerized drawing—lines, arcs, circles, etc.—according to the component of the building they represent, such as doors, walls, and windows. Each layer is assigned a color, and all objects placed on the layer take on that assigned color. This allows you to easily distinguish between objects that represent separate components of the building (Figure 6.2). And you can quickly tell what layer a given object, or group of objects, is on.

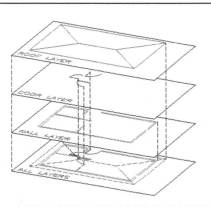

FIGURE 6.2: Separate layers combined to make a drawing

The procedure for achieving this level of organization is to set up the new layers, and then move existing objects onto them. Following that, you will learn how to create new objects on a specific layer.

Setting Up Layers

All AutoCAD drawings have one layer in common—the 0 layer. The 0 layer is the default layer in all new drawings; so if you don't add any new layers on a drawing, everything you create in that drawing will be on the 0 layer. Everything you have drawn so far in the cabin drawing has been drawn on the 0 layer.

NOTE NOTE NOTE NOTE NOTE NOTE NOTE NOTE NOTE NOTE NOTE NOTE NOTE NOTE NOTE

A good way to think about objects and layers is the analogy of people and countries: Just as all persons must reside in some country, so must all objects be on some layer.

All objects in AutoCAD are assigned a layer. In this book, I will refer to objects assigned to a particular layer as "being on" that layer. Objects get placed on a layer in two ways: either they are moved to the layer, or they are created on the layer in the first place. You will learn to do both in this chapter. But first you need to learn how to set up layers. To see how this is done, you will create seven new layers for your cabin drawing—Walls, Doors, Steps, Balcony, Fixtures, Headers, and Roof—then move the existing objects in your drawing onto the first five of these layers. After that, you will create new objects on the Header and Roof layers. Let's begin by creating a few new layers.

1. If you have taken a break and shut down your system, bring up AutoCAD and open Cabin05b.dwg. The Object Properties toolbar, just above the drawing area on your screen, contains buttons and drop-down lists for controlling layers, linetypes, colors, and other layer properties. The layer controls are on the left end of the toolbar.

Layer controls

2. Click the Layers button on the Object Properties toolbar. It's the second button from the left. The Layer Properties Manager dialog box is displayed (Figure 6.3). Notice the large open area in the middle of the dialog box with

the 0 layer listed at the top. This is called the Layer List box. All of the layers in a drawing are listed here along with their status and characteristics. For Cabin5b, there is only one layer so far.

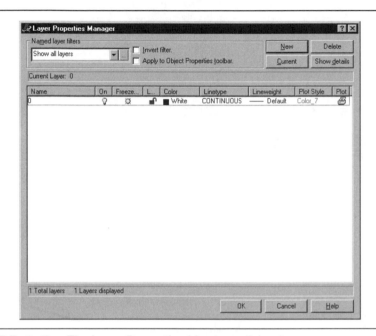

FIGURE 6.3: The Layer Properties Manager dialog box

SKILL
6

The Layer Properties Manager Dialog Box

Besides the Layer List box, there is also a drop-down list, titled Named Layer Filters, and several command buttons in the dialog box. Before setting up new layers, look for a moment at the Layer List box.

The Layer List Box

The Layer List box lists all the layers in the drawing along with each layer's properties and modes.

Each layer has four properties: Color, Linetype, Lineweight, and Plot Style. Look at the 0 layer row in the list and notice the square and the word "White" in the color column. The square is black (or white if you have a black background for your drawing area), but the name of the color is called White whether the square is black or white. Continuous is in the Linetype column. This tells us that the 0 layer has been assigned the color White (black or white) and the Continuous linetype by default.

The three columns to the left of the Color column are titled On, Freeze, and Lock. They have picture icons in the 0 layer row. These columns represent some of the status modes of the layer and control whether objects on a layer are visible or can be changed. The visibility status of a layer will be discussed later in this skill. The columns to the right of the Linetype column—Lineweight, Plot Style, and Plot—will be discussed in *Skill 14: Printing an AutoCAD Drawing*.

Creating New Layers and Assigning Colors

Let's create a few new layers, name them, and assign them colors.

1. In the upper-right corner of the dialog box, click New. A new layer called Layer1 appears in the list. The layer's name is highlighted, which means that it can be renamed by entering another name now.

2. Type **Walls** ↵. Layer1 changes to Walls. Walls should still be highlighted (Figure 6.4).

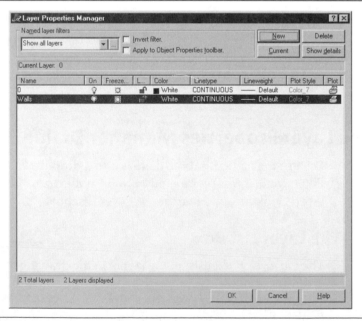

FIGURE 6.4: The Layer Properties Manager dialog box with a new layer named Walls

3. Click the word White in the Color column for the Walls row. The Select Color dialog box comes up (Figure 6.5). There are four areas of color choices. In the Standard Colors area, click the cyan (turquoise) square. In the Color text box, under the Full Color Palette, white has changed to cyan, and the square just to the right has taken on the color cyan.

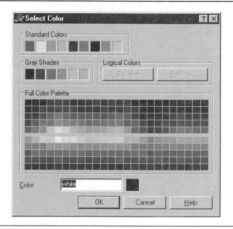

FIGURE 6.5: The Select Color dialog box

4. Click OK. The Select Color dialog box disappears. Now, in the Layer List box of the Layer Properties Manager dialog box, you can see that the color square for the Walls layer has changed to cyan.

As you saw in the Select Color dialog box, there are nine standard colors; six gray shades; two logical colors; and a full color palette, containing as many colors as your video card and driver can support, up to 256. Most computers running AutoCAD 14 will support 256 colors. With one color as the background, that leaves 255 colors for you to choose from. Colors 1–7, all in the Standard Colors palette, have names. Those numbered 8–255 have numbers only. Color number 7 is named white, but will actually be black if you are using a white background color.

When you assign the color cyan to the Walls layer and place all objects representing walls on that layer, all wall objects will be cyan. In this way, you will be able to easily distinguish which objects in your drawing represent walls. Most offices have a standard they follow for organizing layers by name, color, and linetype. The American Institute of Architects publishes their Layering Standards, which are often adapted by architecture firms and customized to fit their specific needs. With the cabin drawing, you will start out developing a basic set of layers. Once you learn how to manage this set, tackling more complex layering systems will come naturally.

As you create your new list of layers and assign them colors, notice how each color looks in your drawing. Some are easier to see on a screen with a light background, and others do better against a dark background. In this book, I will be assigning colors that work well with a black background. If your system has a white background, you may want to use darker colors, which can be found on the Full Color Palette in the middle of the Select Color dialog box.

So let's continue creating new layers and assigning them colors. You'll master this procedure as you add a new layer or two in each skill throughout the rest of the book.

1. In the Layer Properties Manager dialog box, click New.

2. Type **Doors** ↵ to change the name of the layer.

3. Pick the color square in the Doors row. When the Select Color dialog box comes up, click the red square in the Standard Colors area. Then click OK.

4. Repeat these steps, creating each of the following layers with their assigned colors. Pick the colors from the Standard Colors area of the Select Color dialog box.

Layer Name	Color
Steps	9 (Light Gray)
Balcony	Green
Fixtures	Magenta
Headers	Yellow
Roof	Blue

TIP TIP TIP TIP TIP TIP TIP TIP TIP TIP TIP TIP TIP TIP TIP TIP TIP TIP TIP TIP TIP TIP

The color Blue may or may not read well on a black background. If you don't like the way it looks, try picking a lighter shade of blue from the Full Color Palette in the Select Color dialog box.

When finished, the layer list should have eight layers listed with their assigned colors in the color squares of each row (Figure 6.6). All layers are assigned the Continuous linetype by default. This is convenient since most building components are represented in the floor plan by continuous lines, but the roof—because of its position above the walls—needs to be represented by a dashed line. So you need to assign a Dashed linetype to the Roof layer.

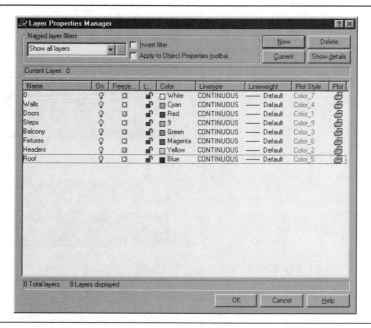

FIGURE 6.6: The Layer List box, in the Layer Properties Manager dialog box, with the seven new layers and the 0 layer

NOTE NOTE NOTE NOTE NOTE NOTE NOTE NOTE NOTE NOTE NOTE NOTE NOTE NOTE NOTE

In more complex drawings, you may need to have several layers for variations of the same building components, such as Existing Walls to Remain, Walls to Be Demolished, and New Walls. Once you acquire the skills presented here, you will have no difficulty progressing to a more complex layering system.

Assigning Linetypes to Layers

When you assigned a color to a layer, all colors supported by your system were available to choose from. Not so with linetypes. Each new drawing has only one linetype loaded into it by default (the Continuous linetype). You must load in any other linetypes you need from an outside file.

1. In the Layer Properties Manager dialog box, click Continuous in the row for the Roof layer. The Select Linetype dialog box comes up (Figure 6.7). In the Loaded linetypes list, only Continuous is displayed. No other linetypes have been loaded into this drawing.

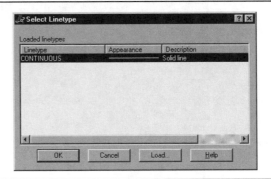

FIGURE 6.7: The Select Linetype dialog box

2. Click Load. The Load or Reload Linetypes dialog box comes up. In the Available Linetypes list, there are 45 linetypes listed. They fall into three groups. The first 14 linetypes are in the Acad_iso family (International Standards Organization). Below these are eight families of three linetypes each, mixed with seven special linetypes that contain graphic symbols. Scroll down the list to where the Dashed, Dashed2, and Dashedx2 linetypes are located (Figure 6.8). Notice how, in this family, the dashed lines are different sizes.

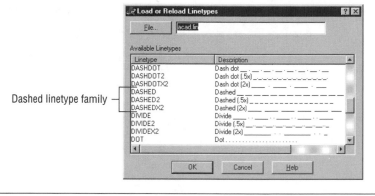

Dashed linetype family ⎯

FIGURE 6.8: The list scrolled to the three Dashed linetypes

3. Click the word Dashed in the left-hand column, then click OK. You are
    returned to the Select Linetype dialog box. In the Select Linetype dialog box,
    the Dashed linetype has been added to the Linetypes list under Continuous
    (Figure 6.9). Click Dashed to highlight it and click OK. In the Layer Proper-
    ties Manager dialog box, the Roof layer has been assigned the Dashed line-
    type (Figure 6.10).

SKILL
6

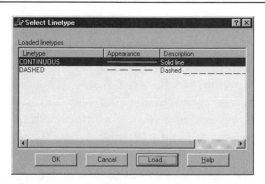

FIGURE 6.9: The Select Linetype dialog box with the Dashed linetype loaded

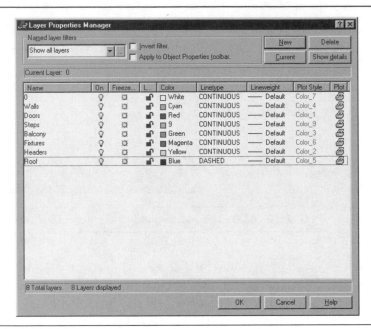

FIGURE 6.10: The Layer Properties Manager dialog box with the Roof layer assigned the Dashed linetype

The eight families of three linetypes each are the standard AutoCAD linetypes. The Dashed line family, like the others, has one basic linetype and two that are multiples of it: one has dashes twice the size (called Dashed×2), and one has dashes one half the size (called Dashed2). (See Figure 6.8.) Therefore, you have an assortment of different sizes of one style of linetype. This will be helpful for distinguishing between building components, such as foundation walls and beams, which, in addition to roof lines, may also need dashed lines.

Now is a good time to look at what it means for a layer to be current.

The Current Layer as a Drawing Tool

Notice the Current button in the top-right corner of the Layer Property Manager dialog box. On the left side, just above the Layer List box, is the name of the current layer, in this case, 0.

At any one time, there is always one—and only one— layer that is set to be the current layer. When a layer is current, all objects you draw will be on that layer and take on the properties assigned to it. Because the 0 layer is current, all objects currently in your drawing are on the 0 layer and have the linetype and color that are specified by default for the 0 layer: Continuous and White (or Black), respectively. If you make the Walls layer current, any new lines you draw will be Cyan and Continuous. If the Roof layer is current, any new lines will be Blue and Dashed.

1.   Click the Walls layer in the Layer List box to highlight it. Then click Current. The Walls layer replaces 0 layer as the current layer.

2.   Click OK at the bottom of the Layer Properties Manager dialog box. The dialog box closes, and you are returned to your drawing.

3.   Look at the Layer Control drop-down list on the Object Properties toolbar. Most of the symbols you saw in the Layer List box, in the Layer Properties Manager dialog box, are on this drop-down list. The Walls layer is the visible entry on the list and has a cyan square (the color you assigned to the Walls layer earlier). The layer visible in this list when it is closed is the current layer.

4.   Now look at your drawing. Nothing has changed because the objects in the drawing are still on the 0 layer.

You need to move the objects in the drawing onto their proper layers. To do this, you'll use the Layer Control drop-down list on the Object Properties toolbar to assign each object to one of the new layers.

Assigning Objects to Layers

When assigning existing objects in the drawing to new layers, our strategy will be to begin by selecting all the objects that belong on the same layer and that are easiest to select. Then you'll reassign them to their new layer, using the Layer Control drop-down list. Then we'll move to a set of objects that belong on a different layer and are slightly more difficult to select, and so on.

1.   In the drawing, pick the two arcs of the balcony. Small squares, called Grips, appear on the arcs to signal that they have been selected (Figure 6.11). Notice also that in the Layer Control drop-down list, the layer being displayed now is the 0 layer rather than Walls, the current layer. When objects are selected with no command running, the Layer Control drop-down list displays the layer that the selected objects are currently assigned to. If selected

objects are on more than one layer, the Layer Control drop-down list goes blank.

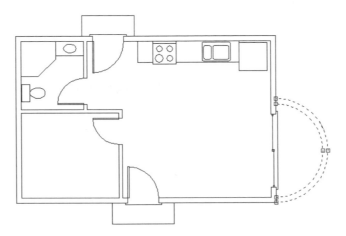

FIGURE 6.11: The balcony arcs, selected and displaying their grips

2. Click the Layer Control drop-down list to open it (Figure 6.12).

3. Click the Balcony layer. The list closes. The Balcony layer is displayed in the Layer Control drop-down list. The balcony arcs have been moved to the Balcony layer and are now green.

4. Press Esc twice to remove the grips. The current layer, Walls, returns to the Layer Control drop-down list.

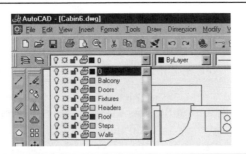

FIGURE 6.12: The opened Layer Control drop-down list

When a color and a linetype are assigned to a layer, objects on that layer take on the Bylayer color and linetype. This means their color and linetype are controlled "by the layer" the objects are on.

This is the process you need to go through for each layer, so that the new layers can receive objects that are currently on the 0 layer. This time, move the threshold and steps to the Steps layer. You will select the threshold and steps by using a selection window.

Selecting Objects with Windows

AutoCAD provides many tools for selecting objects in your drawing. Two of the most powerful are the crossing and regular selection windows. The size and location of these selection windows are determined by picking points on your drawing to be opposite corners of a rectangle that will serve as the window. The regular window selects any objects completely enclosed by the window. The crossing window selects objects that are completely enclosed by, or cross through an edge of, the window. The crossing window is represented by dashed lines, and the regular window is represented by solid lines.

By default, AutoCAD is set up so that whenever there is no command running and the prompt in the Command window is Command:, you can pick objects one at a time or start a regular or crossing window. If you pick an object, it is selected and its grips are displayed. If you select a blank area of the drawing, a selection window is started. If you then move the cursor to the right of the point just picked, a regular window is started. If you move the cursor to the left, a crossing window is started. You'll use three crossing windows to select the thresholds and the front and back steps.

1. Zoom into the sliding glass door area.

2. Hold the crosshair cursor above and to the right of the upper-right corner of the balcony threshold—still inside the balcony wall—as shown in Figure 6.13a. Click that point, then move the cursor down and to the left until you have made a tall, thin crossing window that completely encloses the right edge of the threshold, and is crossed on its left edge by the short horizontal connecting lines, as shown in Figure 6.13b. Then click again.

SKILL
6

Click in the Layer Control drop-down list to open it, then click the Steps layer. The balcony threshold is now on the Steps layer.

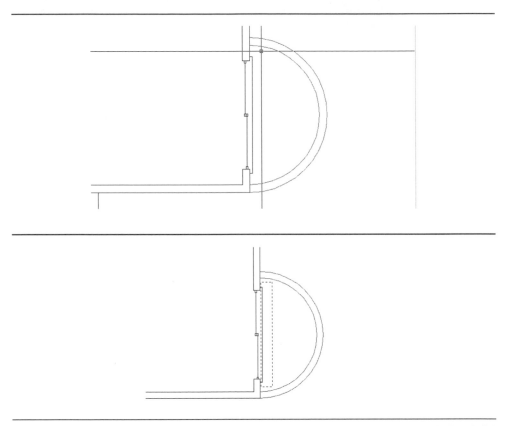

FIGURE 6.13: Starting the crossing selection window (a), and completing it (b)

3. Zoom previous to return to a view of the entire drawing. Make two regular windows to select the front and back steps and their thresholds. Be sure your first pick starts a window at the left and finishes to the right of each step, so the window completely encloses the horizontal and vertical lines

that make up each step and threshold. Figure 6.14 illustrates the two regular selection windows and the points to pick to create them. Once selected, the objects display their grips. For lines, grips appear at each endpoint and at the midpoint of each segment. In this case, some of the grips overlap.

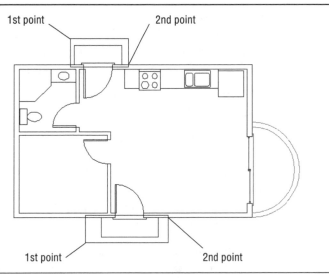

FIGURE 6.14: The two regular selection windows used to select the front and back steps and thresholds

4. Click the Layer Control drop-down list, then click the Steps layer. The front and back steps and their thresholds are now on the Steps layer.

5. Press the Esc key twice to remove the grips.

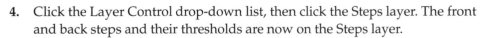

NOTE NOTE NOTE NOTE NOTE NOTE NOTE NOTE NOTE NOTE NOTE NOTE NOTE NOTE NOTE

Grips have other uses than signaling that an object has been selected. You'll learn about some of these other uses as we progress through the skills.

Selecting the Doors and Swings

To accomplish this task, you can use a crossing window to select the objects. Let's examine this task closely to learn more valuable skills about how to select objects.

1. Place the crosshair cursor in a clear space below and to the right of the back door, then pick that point. This starts the selection window. Move the cursor up and to the left until the crossing window crosses the back door and swing, but does not cross the wall line, as in Figure 6.15a.

2. When you have the crossing window positioned correctly, click in a clear space again. This selects the back door and its swing.

3. Move to the bathroom and position the crosshair cursor in the clear space directly above the swing. When the crosshair is positioned, click in a clear space. Then move the cursor down and to the left until the window you are creating crosses the bathroom door and swing, without crossing any wall lines (Figure 6.15b). Then click in a clear space again. The bathroom door and swing are selected.

4 Continue this procedure to select the other two doors and their swings. For the bedroom door, start the crossing window directly below the door swing. For the front door, start a crossing window above and to the right of the door. Figure 6.15c shows the two crossing windows that will select the bedroom and front doors.

5. Open the Layer Control drop-down list and select the Doors layer. Then press Esc twice to remove the Grips. The swinging doors are now red and on the Doors layer.

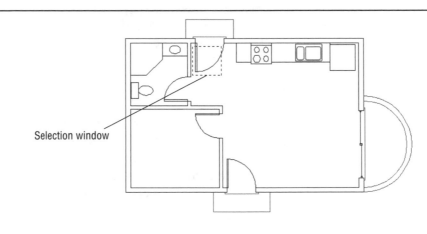

Selection window

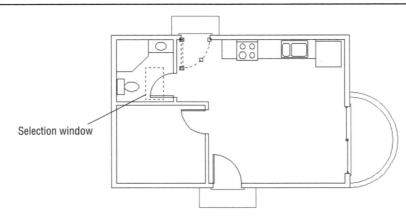

Selection window

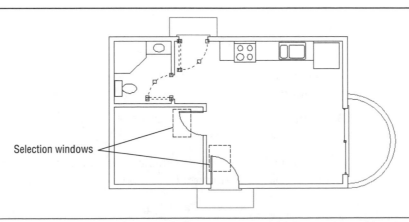

Selection windows

FIGURE 6.15: Using a crossing window to select the doors and swings: the back door (a), the bathroom door (b), and the bedroom and front doors (c)

For the sliding glass door, it will not be easy to create a crossing window from left to right because it may be difficult to position the pickbox between the threshold lines and the sliding door. In this situation, use a regular window to select the objects.

1. Zoom into the sliding glass door area. Pick a point to the left of the balcony opening, just above the upper jamb line. Move the crosshair down and to the right until the right edge of the window sits inside the wall but to the right of the sliding glass window frames. When your window is positioned as in Figure 6.16, click. The entire sliding glass door assembly will be selected, but not the jambs, walls, threshold, or balcony. Many grips appear: there are 13 lines making up the sliding glass door and each one has three grips. Many overlap.

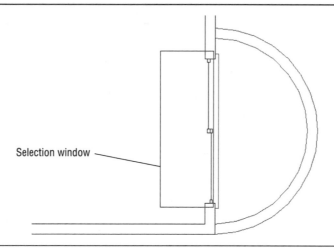

Selection window

FIGURE 6.16: Using a Regular Selection Window to select the sliding glass door

2. Open the Layer Control drop-down list and select the Doors layer. Back in your drawing, the doors are the color Red and are on the Doors layer.

3. Press Esc twice to remove the grips, then Zoom previous. You will have a full view of the floor plan.

The next task is to move the kitchen and bathroom counters and fixtures onto the Fixtures layer. In doing this, you'll learn how to undo parts of selections.

Selecting the Kitchen and Bathroom Fixtures

As you select objects in the Cabin drawing to move onto their prescribed layers, you are using various tools to select a group of objects and gradually learning how to build a *selection set*. After a group of objects has been selected, an editing operation can be performed on them as a whole. It will often happen that, as you build up a selection set, you will find it easier to select more objects than the amount you want to be in the selection set, and then to remove the unwanted ones before performing the intended modification. You'll see how this is done when you select the kitchen and bathroom fixtures.

1. Pick a point in the kitchen area just below the refrigerator to start a crossing window.

2. Move the cursor to the left and up until the upper-left corner of the crossing window is to the left of the left edge of the counter, and inside the back wall, as in Figure 6.17a. When you have it right, click that point. The entire kitchen counter area and the back wall line are selected.

3. Now move over to the bathroom and pick a point in the middle of the bathroom sink, being careful to not touch any lines with the crosshair cursor.

4. Move the crosshair cursor down and to the left until the lower-left corner of the crossing window is in the middle of the toilet tank (Figure 6.17b). When you have it positioned this way, click that point. All the bathroom fixtures and the door swing are selected.

5. Hold down the Shift key, then pick the selected door swing in the bathroom and the back wall line in the kitchen. As you pick them, their lines become solid again, letting you know that they have been de-selected or removed from the selection set, but their grips remain (Figure 6.17c). Be sure to pick the back wall line in the kitchen where it doesn't coincide with the stove.

6. Release the Shift key. Open the Layer Control drop-down list and select the Fixtures layer. The fixtures are now on the Fixtures layer and are magenta in color.

7. Press the Esc key twice to remove the grips.

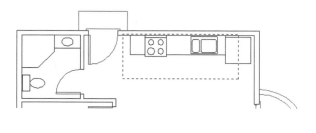

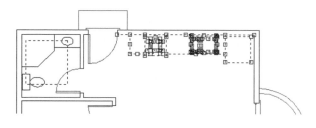

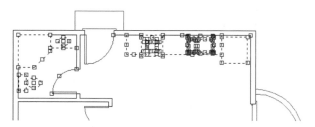

FIGURE 6.17: A crossing window to select the kitchen objects (a), another crossing window to select the bathroom objects (b), and the completed selection set after removing the door swing and back wall line (c)

The last objects to move onto a new layer are the wall lines. As the drawing is now, it will not be easy to select the wall lines because there are so many other objects in the drawing that are in the way. However, these other objects are now on their own layers while the wall lines are still on the 0 layer. If you make all of your layers temporarily invisible except for the 0 and Walls layers, selection of the wall lines will be easy.

Freezing and Turning Off Layers

Layers can be made invisible either by freezing them or turning them off. These two procedures operate the same way and do about the same thing. The difference between freezing and turning a layer off is technical and beyond the scope of this book; but, in general, freezing layers has the effect of minimizing the amount of time needed by AutoCAD to make the geometrical calculations for a drawing. So, for our purposes, freezing is preferable to turning layers off. We will freeze all the layers except the 0 layer and the Walls layer. Then we will move the wall lines onto the Walls layer.

1. Click the Layers button on the Object Properties toolbar. The Layer Properties Manager dialog box comes up. Notice that the 0 layer is still first in the list, and the other layers have been reorganized alphabetically (Figure 6.18a). Layers beginning with numbers are listed first in numerical order. Following them, the rest of the layers are listed alphabetically.

2. Click the Balcony layer to highlight it. Then hold down the Shift key and click the Walls layer. All layers have been selected except the 0 layer.

3. Move the arrow cursor over to the Freeze column, which has yellow suns as symbols for each layer row.

4. Click one of the suns of the selected layers. A warning box comes on and tells you that you cannot freeze the current layer, which at the moment is Walls, in your drawing. Click OK to close this box. The sun symbols have all changed to snowflakes except the ones for the 0 layer and the Walls layer (Figure 6.18b).

SKILL
6

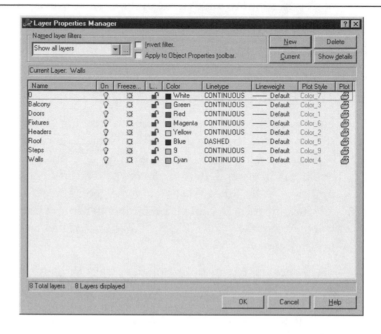

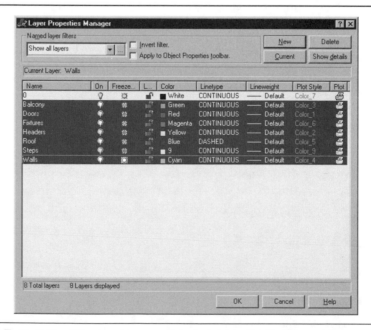

FIGURE 6.18: The layers, now listed alphabetically (a), and the newly frozen layers signified by snowflakes (b)

5. Click OK. All objects in your drawing are invisible except the wall lines (Figure 6.19). The wall lines are still on the 0 layer.

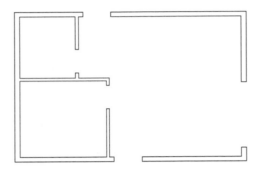

FIGURE 6.19: The floor plan with all layers frozen except the Walls and 0 layer

SKILL
6

6. Make a regular selection window around the cabin wall lines: click in the upper-left corner of the drawing area, above and to the left of any lines. Then click in the lower-right corner in the same way. All the wall lines are selected, and grips appear on all of them.

7. Open the Layer Control drop-down list, then click the Walls layer. The walls move to the Walls layer and are now cyan. Press Esc twice to remove the grips.

8. Click the Layers button on the Object Properties toolbar. In the Layer Properties Manager dialog box, click the Balcony layer. Then hold down the Shift key and click the Steps layer. All layers are highlighted except the 0 layer and the Walls layer.

9. Click one of the snowflakes in the Freeze column. All snowflakes become suns. Click OK. Back in your drawing, all objects are now visible (*thawed*) and on their correct layers (Figure 6.20).

10. Save this drawing in your training folder as Cabin06a.

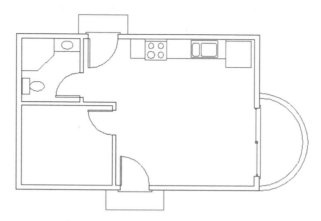

FIGURE 6.20: The floor plan with all layers visible and all objects on their correct layer

Two of your layers, Roof and Header, still have no objects on them because these components haven't been drawn yet. We'll draw the headers now.

Drawing the Headers

Most door and window openings do not extend to the ceiling. The portion of the wall above the opening and below the ceiling is the *header*. The term comes from the name of the beam inside the wall that spans across the opening. In a floor plan, wall lines usually stop at the door and window openings, but you need lines across the gap between jamb lines to show that an opening does not extend to the ceiling, hence, the header.

To draw the headers you need to make the Header layer current—as you've seen above—you can use the Layer Properties Manager dialog box. But there is a shortcut—the Layer Control drop-down list, which you have just been using to move objects from one layer to another.

1. Click anywhere on the drop-down list or on the down-arrow button on the right end. The drop-down list opens, displaying a list of the layers in your drawing. If you have more than 10 layers, a scroll bar becomes operational, giving you access to all of the layers.

2. Click the Headers layer. The drop-down list closes. Header is now in the box; this tells you that the Header layer has replaced Walls as the current layer.

3. Click Tools ➤ Drafting Settings. Then click the Object Snap tab if it's not already on top. Click in the checkbox next to Endpoint to place a checkmark in the box. Be sure Object Snap On is checked, then click OK.

4. The doors and steps may be in your way. Click the Layer drop-down list. When the list of layers appears, click the sun icons for the Doors and Steps layers to freeze them. Then click Header at the top of the list. The drop-down list closes, the Header layer is still current. The doors, steps, and thresholds have temporarily disappeared.

   You need to draw two parallel lines across each of the five openings, from the endpoint of one jamb line to the corresponding endpoint of the jamb on the opposite side of the opening.

5. Type l ↵ to start the Line command. Move the cursor, with its target box, near the upper end of the left jamb for the back door until the blue square appears at the upper endpoint of the jamb line, then click.

6. Move the cursor to the upper end of the right jamb and do the same thing as you did in the previous step.

7. Right-click once. A menu appears near your cursor.

8. Click Enter on the menu, then right-click again. Another menu appears at the cursor.

9. Click Repeat Line on the menu.

10. Move to the lower endpoint of the right jamb line for the back door and—with the same technique used in Steps 5 through 9—draw the lower header line across the opening. The results are shown in Figure 6.21a.

    Keep using the same procedure to draw the rest of the header lines for the remaining four doorway openings. Use a *click, click, right-click, click, right-click, click* pattern on your mouse that repeats for each header line. Here's the pattern:

    A. Click one of the jamb corners.

    B. Click the opposite jamb corner.

    C. Right-click. A small menu comes up.

    D. Click Enter to end the line command.

    E. Right click again. Another small menu comes up.

    F. Click Repeat Line.

    G. Click one of the Jamb corners.

    H. And so on.

    When you're finished, the floor plan will look like Figure 6.21b.

11. Thaw the Doors and Steps layers.

NOTE NOTE NOTE NOTE NOTE NOTE NOTE NOTE NOTE NOTE NOTE NOTE NOTE NOTE

These menus that appear are called right-click menus, short-cut menus, or context menus. They contain frequently used tools. The specific tools on a menu will vary depending on what you're doing when you right-click. It was not terribly efficient to use them to draw in the header lines, but it was a good way to introduce them to you. It's also a method of drawing without using the keyboard.

The Layer drop-down list box is a shortcut that allows you to quickly pick a different layer to be the current layer and to freeze or thaw individual layers. To create new layers, or to freeze many layers at a time, use the Layer Properties Manager dialog box, accessed by clicking the Layers button on the Object Properties toolbar. You'll learn another tool for changing the current layer as you draw the roof lines.

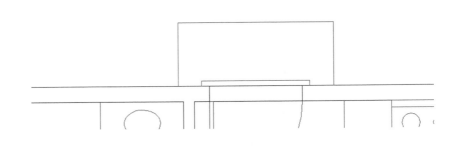

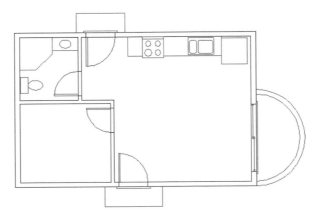

FIGURE 6.21: The header lines drawn for the back door opening (a), and for the rest of the doorway openings (b)

Drawing the Roof

Before starting to draw the roof lines, refer to Figure 6.22 and note the lines representing different parts of the roof:

- Four *eaves lines* around the perimeter of the building, representing the lowest edge of the roof

- One *ridgeline*, representing the peak of the roof

- Four *hip lines*, connecting the endpoints of the eaves line to an endpoint of the ridgeline

The roof for the cabin is called a *hip roof* because the end panels slope down to the eaves just as the middle panels do. The intersections of the sloping roof planes form the hip lines. We'll start with the eaves.

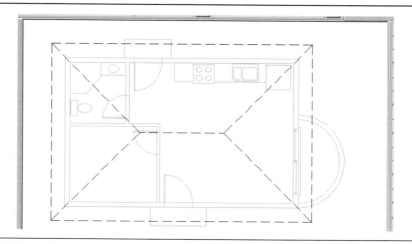

FIGURE 6.22:   The floor plan with the roof lines

Creating the Eaves

Because the roof cantilevers beyond the exterior walls the same distance on all sides of the building, we can generate the eaves lines by offsetting the outside wall lines.

1.   Type **o** ↵ to start the Offset command. Then type **1'-6"**↵ to set the offset distance. Pick the left outside wall lines and then pick a point to the left of that line to offset it to the outside.

2.   Move to another side of the building and pick one of the outside wall lines on that side and offset it to the outside.

3. Repeat this for the other two sides of the building until you have offset one outside wall line to the outside of the building on each side of the cabin (Figure 6.23). Press ↵ to end the Offset command. Be sure you have only one line offset on each side of the building. If you offset two lines on one side, erase one.

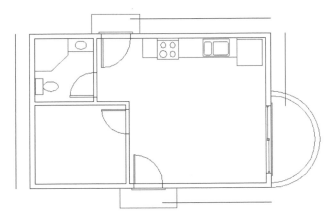

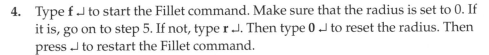

FIGURE 6.23: One outside wall line is offset to each side of the building.

4. Type **f** ↵ to start the Fillet command. Make sure that the radius is set to 0. If it is, go on to step 5. If not, type **r** ↵. Then type **0** ↵ to reset the radius. Then press ↵ to restart the Fillet command.

5. Click any two of these newly offset lines that are on adjacent sides of the building. Click the half of the line nearest the corner that the two selected lines will meet (Figure 6.24a). The lines extend to meet each other and form a corner (Figure 6.24b). The Fillet command ends.

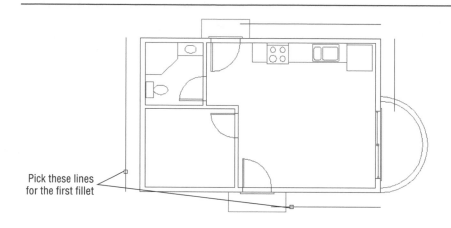

Pick these lines
for the first fillet

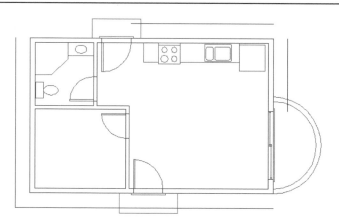

FIGURE 6.24: Picking lines to fillet one of the eaves corners (a), and the result (b)

6. Press ↵ to restart the Fillet command. Pick two more adjacent lines that will meet at another corner.

7. Start the Fillet command again and keep picking pairs of lines until all the corners are filleted and the result is a rectangle that represents the eaves of the roof surrounding the building, offset 1'-6" from the outside exterior walls (Figure 6.25).

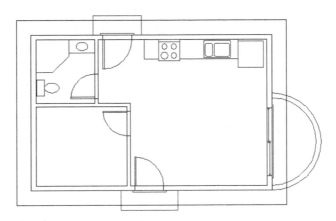

FIGURE 6.25: The eaves lines after filleting

Because the eaves lines were offset from wall lines, they are on the Walls layer. You need to move them onto the Roof layer. Then you'll make the Roof layer current so when you draw the hip lines and the ridgeline, they will be on the Roof layer.

1. Select the four eaves lines, then click the Layer Control drop-down list on the Object Properties toolbar.

2. Click Roof. The eaves lines are now on the Roof layer.

3. Press Esc twice to remove the grips.

The eaves lines are still solid lines, even though the Roof layer has been assigned a dashed linetype. Actually, the lines are dashed, but the dashes are so small the monitor can't display them.

Setting a Linetype Scale Factor

By default, the dashes are set up to be ½-inch long with ¼-inch spaces. This is the right size for a drawing that is close to actual size on your screen, like the box you drew in Skill 2. But for something the size of your cabin, you must increase the linetype scale to make the dashes large enough to see. If the dashes were 1-foot long with 6-inch spaces, they would at least be visible, though possibly not exactly the right size. To make such a change in the dash size, ask what you must multiply ½" by to get 12". The answer is 24—so that's your scale factor. AutoCAD stores a Linetype Scale Factor setting that controls the size of the dashes and spaces of non-continuous linetypes. The default is 1.00, which gives you the ½-inch dash, so we need to change it to 24.00.

1. Type **ltscale** ↵. The prompt in the Command window reads New scale factor <1.0000>:.

2. Type **24** ↵ to set the linetype scale factor to 24. Your drawing changes, and you can see the dashes (Figure 6.26). If you are not satisfied with the dash size, restart the Ltscale command and increase the scale factor for a longer dash or decrease it for a shorter one. This linetype scale factor is a global one, meaning it affects every non-continuous line in the drawing. There is also an individual scale factor for linetypes. You'll see that after you finish the roof.

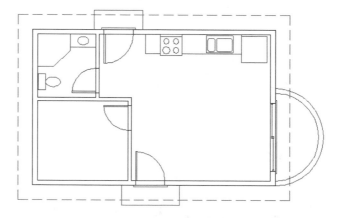

FIGURE 6.26: The eaves lines on the roof layer with visible dashes

Drawing the Hip and Ridgelines

Next, you'll draw two of the diagonal hip roof lines, then use the Mirror command to create the other two. To do this, you need to assign the Roof layer to be the current layer. Because you have moved the lines you just offset to the Roof layer, you can use the Make Object's Layer Current button to make the Roof layer current.

1. Click the Make Object's Layer Current button on the left end of the Object Properties toolbar. You will get the `Select object whose layer will become current:` prompt.

2. Pick one of the dashed eaves lines. The Roof layer replaces Header in the Layer drop-down list, telling you the Roof layer is now the current layer. Look at the Linetypes drop-down list on the Object Properties toolbar. A dashed line with the name ByLayer appears there. ByLayer tells you that the current linetype is going to be whatever linetype has been assigned to the current layer. In the case of the Roof layer, the assigned linetype is dashed. You will read more about ByLayer at the end of this chapter.

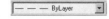

3. The Endpoint Osnap should still be running. How can you tell? Type **os** ↵. The Osnap tab on the Drafting Settings dialog box comes up and you can easily see which Osnaps are checked. First, be sure Object Snap On is checked. Then, if Endpoint is checked, click the Polar Tracking tab. Otherwise, click in the checkbox next to Endpoint and then click the Polar Tracking tab (Figure 6.27).

4. At the top, click in the Polar Tracking On (F10) checkbox to turn Polar Tracking on.

5. In the Polar Angle Settings area, open the Increment Angle drop-down list and select 45.

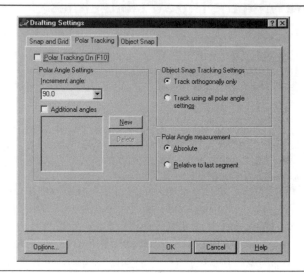

FIGURE 6.27: The Polar Tracking tab on the Drafting Settings dialog box

6. Click OK to close the Drafting Settings dialog box.

7. Start the Line command by typing **l** ↵. Move the crosshair cursor to the lower-left corner of the rectangle representing the roof until the square appears on the corner, then click. A line is started.

8. Be sure Ortho is off. Move the crosshair cursor up and to the right at a 45° angle from the lower-left corner of the roof. When the angle of the line being drawn approaches 45°, a tracking path and a Polar tooltip will appear, along with a small *x* near the crosshair cursor (Figure 6.28a).

9. While the tracking path is visible, type **15'** ↵↵. The first hip line is drawn (Figure 6.28b).

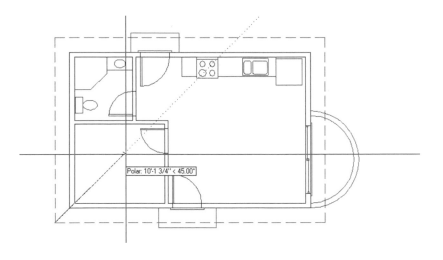

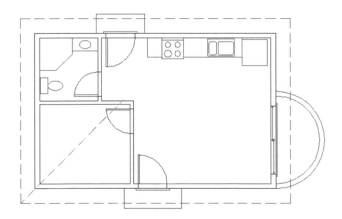

FIGURE 6.28: The 45° tracking path for the first hip line of the roof (a), and the completed first hip line (b)

Use the same procedure to draw another hip line from the upper-left corner of the roof. Here's a summary of the steps:

1. Restart the line command and start a line at the upper-left corner of the roof.

2. Hold the crosshair cursor down and to the right at an angle of approximately 45° until the Polar tracking path with its tooltip appears. (The tooltip will confirm that the actual angle is 315°.)

3. Type **15'** ↵ ↵. The second hip line is completed.

The two hip lines need to be filleted together at their intersection, but the bedroom door is in the way.

1. Open the Layer Control drop-down list and freeze the Door layer. Then click the Roof layer in the list to close the list.

2. Type **f** ↵ to start the Fillet command. The radius should still be set to zero. Click the two diagonal lines at a place that is close to, and on the left side of, their intersection. The lines are filleted together (Figure 6.29a). Now you need to mirror these two diagonal lines to the right side of the roof.

3. Type **mi** ↵ to start the Mirror command. At the prompt to select objects, select the two diagonal lines, then press ↵. Pick the Midpoint Osnap button and place the cursor on the horizontal eaves line above the cabin. When the triangle appears at the midpoint of the eaves line, click.

4. Turn Ortho on. Then move the crosshair cursor down into the living room, keeping it directly below the point just picked, and click in a clear space. Press ↵ when asked whether to delete old objects. The diagonal lines from the left are mirrored to the right (Figure 6.29b). The Mirror command automatically ends. To finish the roof, we'll draw in the ridgeline.

5. Type **l** ↵ to start the Line command. Endpoint Osnap is still running. Pick the two intersections of the diagonal lines, then press ↵. Open the Layer Control drop-down list and click the snowflake for the Doors layer to turn it into a sun. Then click the roof layer to close the drop-down list. This completes the ridgeline and finishes the roof (Figure 6.30). Save this drawing as Cabin06b.

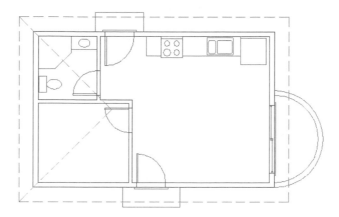

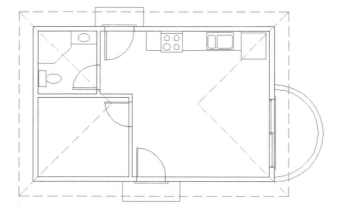

FIGURE 6.29: The first two hip lines are filleted together (a), and the two hip lines are mirrored to the right (b).

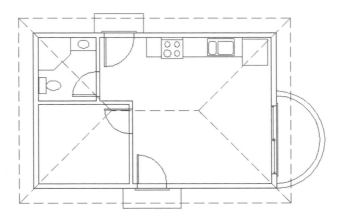

FIGURE 6.30: The completed roof

By drawing the roof lines, you have completed the exercises for this chapter. The cabin floor plan is almost complete. In the next skill, you will complete the floor plan by placing windows in the external walls using a new grouping tool called the block. The rest of this chapter contains a short discussion on color and linetypes, and how they work with layers and objects.

Color, Linetypes, and Layers

First, look at the colors in your drawing. If the background of your drawing area is white, notice which colors are the easiest to read. For most monitors, the yellow, light gray, and cyan are somewhat faded out; while the blue, green, red, and magenta are read very easily. If the drawing area background is black, the blue is sometimes too dark to read easily, but the rest of the colors usually read very well. This is one reason why most people prefer the black, or at least a dark, background color. The other consideration is the lighting in your work area. Bright work areas usually make it difficult to read monitors easily; and, with a dark background, you will often get sharp contrast between the screen and your surroundings, and get distracting reflections on the screen. Eyestrain can result. Darkening your work area will usually mollify these effects.

Assigning a Color or Linetype to an Object

While you have been taught to assign colors and linetypes to layers, in order to control the way objects on those layers appear, colors and linetypes can be individually assigned to objects and made to be current in the drawing.

If an object is assigned a color that is different from the color assigned to the object's layer, that object will be a different color from the rest of the objects on the layer. The same thing is true for linetypes. There may be an occasion where it makes sense to do this, especially for linetypes; but that would be the rare exception, rather than the rule. Changing the color of an object could result in confusion. If you do need to make such a change, you would first select the object, then open the Color Control drop-down list on the Object Properties toolbar. (It's just to the right of the Layer Control drop-down list, which you have just been using.) Click the color you want to assign to the selected object. The list will close and the selected objects will take on the color you've picked. Press the Esc key twice to remove the grips, and the modification is complete. The danger in making this kind of change is that if the color of an object is changed from the color assigned to the whole layer, you won't be able to tell which layer the object belongs to as easily. If the new color matches that of another layer, you may mistake the object for being on that layer.

SKILL 6

Making a Color or Linetype Current

If you look at the Object Properties toolbar for a moment, you will see, to the right of the Layer Control drop-down lists, more drop-down lists. The first two are the Color and the Linetype Controls. These tools allow you to set a color or linetype to be current. When this is done, each object subsequently created will be assigned the current linetype and/or color, regardless of which linetype and color have been assigned to the current layer. If, for example, the Doors layer was set to be the current layer, and the dashed linetype and green color were also assigned to be current, any lines drawn would be dashed and green, but still on the Doors layer. This is not a good way to set up the system of layers, linetypes, and colors because of the obvious confusion it would create in your drawing; but beginners often accidentally do this without knowing what they've done.

The best way to keep all this straight is to keep the current linetype and color set to ByLayer, as it is by default. When you do this, colors and linetypes are controlled by the layers, and objects take on the color and linetype of the layers they are on. If this configuration is accidentally disturbed and objects are created with the wrong color or linetype, you can correct the situation without too much trouble. First, reset the current color and linetype to ByLayer by using the Color Control and Linetype Control drop-down lists on the Object Properties toolbar. Then use the Properties button to change the linetype or color of the problem objects to ByLayer. They will then take on the color and linetype of the layer to which they have been assigned.

Assigning an Individual Linetype Scale Factor

Although the Ltscale command sets a linetype scale factor for all non-continuous lines in the drawing, you can adjust the dash and space sizes for individual lines by using the Properties button to change the current linetype scale. If you want to change the dash and space size for the ridgeline of the roof to make them larger, follow these steps:

1. Click the Properties button on the Standard toolbar.

2. Select the ridgeline. Grips will appear.

3. In the Properties dialog box, click Linetype Scale. Highlight the current scale of 1.0000 and type **3** ↵.

4. Close the Properties dialog box and press Esc twice to remove the grips. The dashes and spaces of the ridgeline are three times larger than those for the rest of the roof lines. All non-continuous lines that are drawn from now on will be affected by this Linetype scale setting.

5. Click the Properties button and use the same procedure to change the current linetype scale factor for the ridgeline back to 1.

NOTE NOTE NOTE NOTE NOTE NOTE NOTE NOTE NOTE NOTE NOTE NOTE NOTE NOTE NOTE

When Linetype Scale in the Properties dialog box is set to a number other than 1.000, this has an effect on any currently selected non-continuous lines, as well as on any non-continuous lines that are subsequently drawn.

This tool allows you to get subtle variations in the size of dashes and spaces for individual, non-continuous lines. But remember that a line that has an individual linetype scale factor is also controlled by the global linetype scale factor. The actual size of the dashes and spaces for a particular line is a result of the two linetype scale factors working together. This additional flexibility requires you to keep careful track of the variations you are making.

Are You Experienced?

Now you can . . .

- ☑ create new layers and assign them a color and linetype
- ☑ load a new linetype into your current drawing file
- ☑ move existing objects onto a new layer
- ☑ freeze and thaw layers
- ☑ make a layer current and create objects on the current layer
- ☑ reset the linetype scale factor to make non-continuous lines visible
- ☑ use Polar Tracking to draw a diagonal line
- ☑ use the individual linetype scale factor to adjust the size of one dashed line

SKILL
6

Using Blocks and Wblocking

- ⊕ **Creating and inserting blocks**
- ⊕ **Using the Wblock command**
- ⊕ **Detecting blocks in a drawing**
- ⊕ **Using point filters and blips**

Computer drafting gains a significant portion of its efficiency from features that allow you to group a collection of objects into one object, and to repeatedly use this new object in your current drawing as well as export it to other drawings. AutoCAD calls the grouped objects a *block*, and calls the process of moving blocks outside your current drawing *wblocking*.

These features allow you to:

- Create a block in your current drawing.

- Repeatedly place copies of the block in precise locations in your drawing.

- Save a copy of the block on the hard disk as a drawing file.

- Insert a copy of this new drawing file into a different drawing.

In general, objects best suited to becoming part of a block are the components of your building that are repeatedly used in the drawing, such as doors, windows and fixtures, or drawing symbols, like a North arrow or labels for a section cut line (Figure 7.1). In your cabin drawing, you will convert the doors with swings into blocks. Then you will create a new block that you will use to create the windows in the drawing.

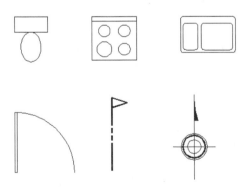

FIGURE 7.1:   Examples of blocks often used in drawings

Making a Block for a Door

When making a block, you will create a *block definition* that will consist of:

- The block name
- An insertion point to help place the block in the drawing
- The objects to be grouped into the block

You will specify each of these in the course of using the Block command. When the command is completed, the block definition is stored with the drawing file. You can insert the object (as a block) back into the drawing using the Insert command.

Before you create a block, you must consider the layers on which the objects to be blocked reside. When objects on the 0 layer are grouped into a block, they will take on the color and linetype of the layer that is current when the block is inserted. Objects on other layers retain the properties of their original layers, regardless of which color or linetype has been assigned to the current layer. This characteristic distinguishes the 0 layer from all other layers.

As you define a block, you must decide which—if any—of the objects to be included in the block will need to be on the 0 layer before they are blocked. If a block is always going to be on the same layer, the objects making up the block can remain on that layer. On the other hand, if a block may be inserted on several layers, the objects in the block will need to be moved to the 0 layer before the block definition is created, so as to avoid confusion of colors and linetypes.

As you learn to make blocks for the doors, you will also see how layers work in the process of creating block definitions. We'll create a block for the exterior doors first, using the front door, and call it door3_0 to distinguish it from the smaller interior door. For the insertion point, you will need to assign a point on or near the door that will facilitate its placement as a block in your drawing. The hinge point will make the best insertion point.

For this skill, the Endpoint Osnap should be running most of the time. To be sure it is running, follow these steps:

1. Click Tools ➤ Drafting Settings
2. Click the Object Snap tab.

SKILL
7

3. Be sure the checkbox next to Endpoint is marked. Also, be sure Object Snap On is checked.

4. Then click OK.

Now you are ready to create blocks.

1. If you are continuing on from the last skill, go on to step 2. If you are starting up a new session, start AutoCAD. In the Start Up dialog box, click Open a Drawing. In the Select a File list, highlight `Cabin06b` and click OK. If this `.dwg` file is not in the list, use the Browse button to find and select the file.

2. The Roof layer should be visible in the Layers drop-down list on the Object Properties toolbar. Click the list to open it, then click Doors to make the Doors layer current. The list will close. Click the drop-down list again and this time click the sun icons for the Roof and Header layers to freeze them. Then click the Doors layer to close the list. The Doors layer is now current, and the Headers and Roof are no longer visible in the drawing (Figure 7.2).

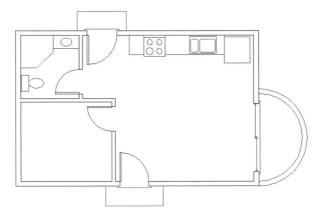

FIGURE 7.2: The floor plan with the Headers and Roof layers frozen

3. Click the Make Block button on the Draw toolbar. (The Block command can also be started by picking Draw ➤ Block ➤ Make, or by typing **b** ↵.) The Block

Definition dialog box comes up (Figure 7.3). Notice the flashing cursor in the text box next to Name. Type **door3_0**.

4. Click the Pick Point button in the Base Point area. The dialog box momentarily disappears, and you are returned to your drawing.

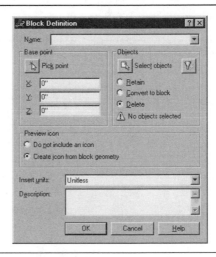

FIGURE 7.3: The Block Definition dialog box

5. You need to zoom into the front door area. In your drawing, click the Zoom Window button on the Standard toolbar and make a window around the front door area. The area in the window will fill the screen.

6. Move the cursor to the front door area and position it near the hinge point of the door. When the square appears on the hinge point (Figure 7.4a), click. This selects the insertion point for the door, and the Block Definition dialog box returns.

7. Click the Select Objects button in the Objects area. You are returned to the drawing again. The cursor changes to a pickbox, and the Command window displays the `Select objects:` prompt.

8. Select the door and swing, then press ↵. You are returned to the Block Definition dialog box. At the bottom of the Objects area, the count of selected objects is displayed. Just above that, there are three radio buttons. Click Retain if it's not already selected. Click OK, and the dialog box disappears.

9. Erase the door and swing by typing **e** ↵, picking the door and swing, and then pressing ↵. The door and swing are erased (Figure 7.4b).

You have now created a block definition, called door3_0. Block definitions are stored electronically with the drawing file. You need to insert the door3__0 block (known formally as a *block reference*) into the front door opening to replace the door and swing that were just erased.

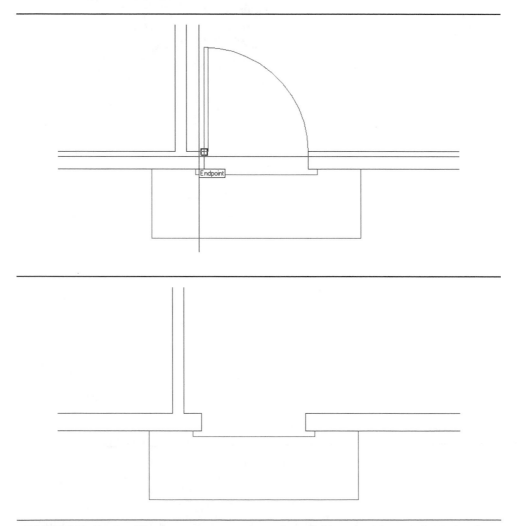

FIGURE 7.4: The front door opening when picking the hinge point to be the insertion point (a), and after creating the door3_0 block and erasing the door and swing (b)

> TIP TIP TIP TIP TIP TIP TIP TIP TIP TIP TIP TIP TIP TIP TIP TIP TIP TIP TIP TIP TIP TIP
>
> The "buttons" you have been clicking in this skill are also referred to as "icons" and "tools." When they are in dialog boxes or on the Status Bar, they actually look like buttons to push that have icons on them. When they are on the toolbars, they look like icons, i.e. little pictures. But when you move the Pointer Arrow cursor onto one, it takes on the appearance of a button with an icon on it. All three terms—"button," "icon," and "tool"—will be used interchangeably in this book.

Inserting the Door Block

You will use the Insert command to place the door3_0 block back into the drawing.

1. On the Draw toolbar, click the Insert Block button. (The Insert command can also be started by selecting Insert ➤ Block, or by typing i ↵.) The Insert dialog box comes up (Figure 7.5). At the top, the Name drop-down list contains the names of the blocks in the drawing. In this case, there is only one so far—door3_0—so it is on top. Below the Name list, there are three areas with the Specify On-screen option. These are used for the insertion procedure.

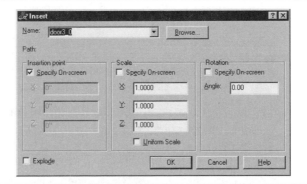

FIGURE 7.5: The Insert dialog box

SKILL 7

2. Be sure the Specify On-screen option is checked for all three areas.

3. Click OK. You are returned to your drawing and the door3_0 block is now attached to the cursor, with the hinge point coinciding with the intersection of the crosshairs (Figure 7.6). The Command window reads "Specify insertion point:."

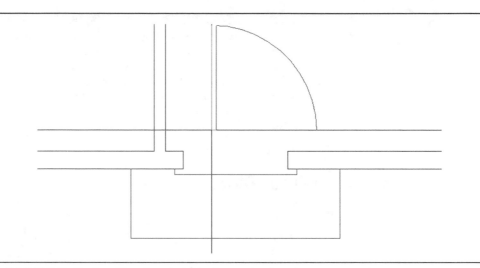

FIGURE 7.6: The door3_0 block attached to the cursor

4. With Endpoint Osnap running, move the cursor towards the upper end of the left jamb line in the front door opening. When a colored square appears at the jamb-line upper endpoint, click. The insertion point has been positioned, and the Command window now displays an additional prompt: Enter X scale factor, specify opposite corner, or [corner/XYZ]<1>:.

5. Press ↵ to accept the default of 1 for the X scale factor. The prompt changes to: Y scale factor <use X scale factor> :.

6. Press ↵ again to accept the default for this option. Be sure Ortho is off. The door3_0 block comes into view, and you can see that its insertion point has been placed at the upper end of the left jamb line, and that the block rotates as you move the cursor (Figure 7.7a). Another prompt comes up: Specify rotation angle <0>:. Press ↵ again to accept the default of 0. The door3_0 block is placed in the drawing (Figure 7.7b).

Each time a block is inserted, you have the option of specifying the following on-screen or in the Insert dialog box:

*   The location of the insertion point of the block

*   The X and Y scale factors

*   The Z factor in the dialog box (used in 3-D drawings only)

*   A rotation angle

When blocks are inserted, they can be stretched or flipped horizontally (the X scale factor) or vertically (the Y scale factor), or they can be rotated from their original orientation. Because the door3_0 block was created from the door and swing that occupied the front door opening, and the size was the same, inserting this block back into the front door opening required no rotation, so we followed the defaults. When you insert the same block into the back door opening, you will have to change the Y scale factor, because the door will be flipped vertically.

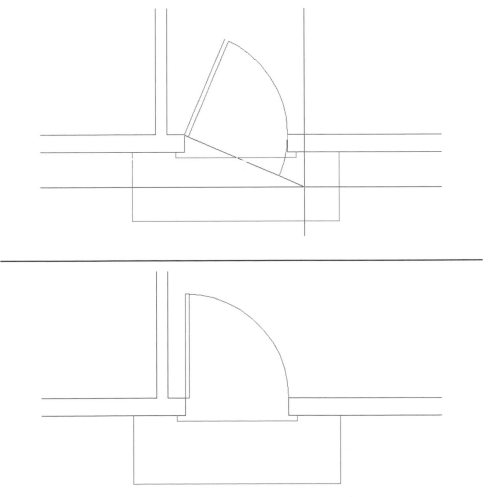

FIGURE 7.7: The rotation option (a), and the final placement (b)

Inserting a Block While Flipping It

The *X* scale factor controls the horizontal size and orientation. The *Y* scale factor mimics the *X* scale factor unless you change it. For the next insertion, you will make such a change.

1. Click the Zoom Previous button on the Standard toolbar to zoom back out to a full view of the floor plan.

2. Click the Zoom Window button and make a window around the back door area, including plenty of room inside and outside the opening so that you can see the door3_0 block as it is being inserted. You will be zoomed into a close view of the back door (Figure 7.8).

3. Use the Erase command to erase the door and swing from the back door opening.

4. Click Insert ➤ Block. In the Insert dialog box, door3_0 should still be in the Name drop-down list.

5. Click OK. You are returned to your drawing, and the door3_0 block is attached to the cursor.

6. Move the cursor to the lower end of the left jamb line. When the colored square appears at that endpoint (Figure 7.9a), click. The insertion point has been placed and the prompt reads "Enter X scale factor, specify opposite corner, or [corner/XYZ]<1>:."

7. Press ↵ to accept the default *X* scale factor of 1. The prompt changes to read "Specify Y scale factor <use X scale factor:." In order to flip the door down to the inside of the cabin, you need to give the *Y* scale factor a value of -1.

8. Type **-1** ↵. Then press ↵ again to accept the default rotation angle of 0°. The Insert command ends, and the door3_0 block is placed in the back door opening (Figure 7.9b). Figure 7.9b will look exactly like Figure 7.8.

NOTE NOTE NOTE NOTE NOTE NOTE NOTE NOTE NOTE NOTE NOTE NOTE NOTE NOTE NOTE

Nothing has changed about the geometry of the door, but it is now a different kind of object. Before it was a rectangle and an arc, now it's a block reference made up of a rectangle and an arc.

9. Click the Zoom Previous button on the Object Properties toolbar to zoom back out to a full view of the floor plan.

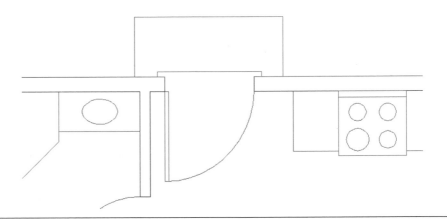

FIGURE 7.8: The result of the zoom

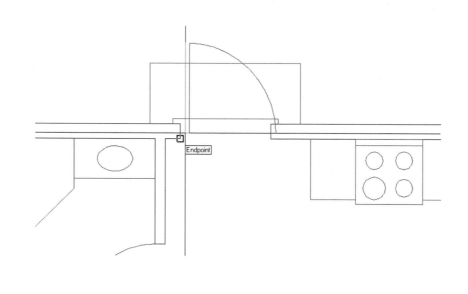

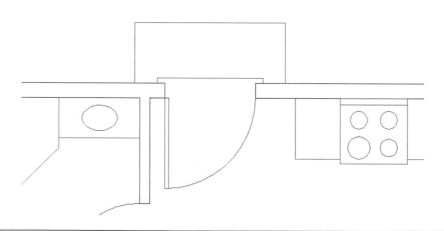

FIGURE 7.9: Placing the door3_0 insertion point (a), and the block after insertion (b)

NOTE NOTE NOTE NOTE NOTE NOTE NOTE NOTE NOTE NOTE NOTE NOTE NOTE NOTE
When inserting a block, giving a value of -1 to the *X* or *Y* scale factor has the effect of flipping the block, much like the Mirror command did in Skill 4 when you first drew the doors. Because you can flip or rotate the door3_0 block as it is inserted, it can be used to place a door and swing in any 3-foot-0-inch opening, regardless of its orientation.

Doors are traditionally sorted into four categories, which are determined by which side the hinges and doorknob are on and by which way the door swings open. To be able to use one door block for all openings of the same size, you need to know:

- How the door and swing in the block is oriented
- Where the hinge point is to be in the next opening
- How the block has to be flipped and/or rotated during the insertion process to properly fit in the next doorway opening

Blocking and Inserting the Interior Doors

Because the interior doors are smaller, you will need to make a new block for them. We could insert the door3_0 block with a ⅚ scale factor, but the door thickness would also be reduced by the same factor, and we don't want that.

1. Click the Zoom Window button on the Standard toolbar. Pick two points to define a window that encloses both the bathroom and bedroom doors (Figure 7.10a). The view will change to a close up view of the area enclosed in your window (Figure 7.10b).

2. Repeat a procedure similar to the one you used to make a block out of the front door and swing to make a block out of the bathroom door and swing. Here is a summary of the steps:

   A. Start the Block command (type **b** ↵).

   B. In the dialog box, type **door2_6** to name the new block. Don't press ↵.

   C. Click the Pick Point button and pick the hinge point of the bathroom door.

   D. Click the Select Objects button and pick the door and swing. Then press ↵.

   E. In the Objects area, select the radio button for Convert to Block.

   F. Click OK. This time the door and swing remain, but they have been converted into a block.

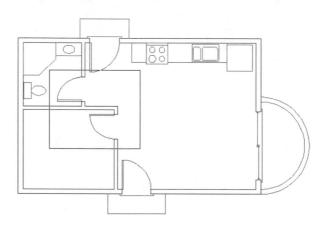

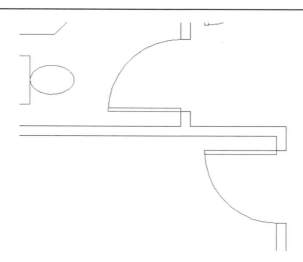

FIGURE 7.10: Creating a zoom window (a), and the result (b)

NOTE NOTE NOTE NOTE NOTE NOTE NOTE NOTE NOTE NOTE NOTE NOTE NOTE NOTE NOTE

The three radio buttons in the Objects area of the Block Definition dialog box represent the options you have for objects transformed into a block: *Retain*—the objects remain as unblocked; *Convert to Block*—the objects become a block reference; and *Delete*—the objects are automatically erased after the block has been defined.

3. Start the Insert command and insert the door2_6 block into the bedroom doorway opening. Here's a summary of the steps:

    A. Press ⏎ to restart the Insert command.

    B. Click OK.

    C. Pick the left end of the upper jamb line.

    D. Erase the bedroom door and swing, then accept the default of 1 for the X scale factor.

    E. Type **-1** ⏎ to give the Y scale factor a value of -1.

    F. Press ⏎ to accept the default rotation of 0.

    G. Zoom previous to view the full floor plan (Figure 7.11).

This view looks the same as the view you started with at the beginning of this skill. Blocks look the same as other objects and can't be detected by viewing only. Their usefulness comes from our being able to use them over and over again in a drawing or many drawings, and in the fact that the block is a grouping of two or more (and sometimes many more) objects together into a single object. The next section will go into how you can detect a block.

Finding Blocks in a Drawing

There are three ways of detecting blocks in a drawing: with grips, with the List command, or with the Properties button. Each method is detailed below.

SKILL
7

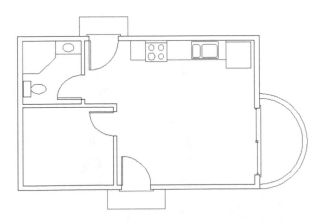

FIGURE 7.11: The floor plan with all swinging doors converted into blocks

Using Grips to Detect a Block

1. At the Command: prompt, click one of the door swings. The door and swing ghost and a colored square appears at the hinge point. Grips appear on objects that are selected when no command is started. We'll look at grips in more detail in Skill 11, *Dimensioning a Drawing*.

2. Press Esc twice to clear the grips.

TIP TIP TIP TIP TIP TIP TIP TIP TIP TIP TIP TIP TIP TIP TIP TIP TIP TIP TIP TIP TIP TIP TIP TIP

Selecting an object with no command started is a quick way to see if it is a block. When an object that is not a block is selected in the above manner, grips appear at strategic places. But if you select a block, by default, only one grip appears and it's always located at the block's insertion point.

You may need to know more about a block than just whether or not something is one. If that is the case, you will need to use the List command.

Using the List Command to Detect a Block

1. Move the cursor to the Distance button on the Standard toolbar and hold down the mouse button. The Inquiry flyout appears.

2. Move the cursor down the flyout to the List button, then release the mouse button. The List command is started, and you are prompted to select objects.

3. Click the bedroom door block, then press ↵. The AutoCAD Text Window temporarily covers the drawing (Figure 7.12). In the text window, you can see the words BLOCK REFERENCE Layer: DOORS, followed by eight lines of text. These nine lines describe the block you selected.

NOTE NOTE NOTE NOTE NOTE NOTE NOTE NOTE NOTE NOTE NOTE NOTE NOTE NOTE NOTE

Each time you use the List command and select an object, the text screen will display information that is tailored to the kind of object selected.

Some of the information stored here about the selected object is:

-   What the object is (Block Reference)
-   The layer the object is on (Doors layer)
-   The name of the block (door2_6)
-   The coordinates of the insertion point in the drawing

- The X and Y scale factors
- The rotation angle

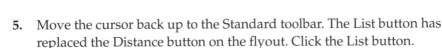

```
AutoCAD Text Window - Cabin6b                              _ □ ×
Edit
Specify rotation angle <0>:

Command: '_zoom

Specify corner of window, enter a scale factor (nX or nXP), or
[All/Center/Dynamic/Extents/Previous/Scale/Window] <real time>: _p
Command:
Command:
Command: _list
Select objects: 1 found

Select objects:
                    BLOCK REFERENCE  Layer: "Doors"
                            Space: Model space
                   Handle = 164
                   "door3_0"
              at point, X=   20'-4"  Y=   29'-6"  Z=    0'-0"
                X scale factor    1.0000
                Y scale factor   -1.0000
           rotation angle   0.00
                Z scale factor    1.0000

Command: |
```

FIGURE 7.12: The AutoCAD text window

4. Press F2. The drawing area returns.

NOTE NOTE NOTE NOTE NOTE NOTE NOTE NOTE NOTE NOTE NOTE NOTE NOTE NOTE NOTE
The F2 key toggles the text screen on and off.

SKILL
7

5. Move the cursor back up to the Standard toolbar. The List button has replaced the Distance button on the flyout. Click the List button.

6. At the `Select objects:` prompt, click one of the arcs that represent the balcony, then click one of the wall lines and press ↵.

7. The text screen comes up again, and you see information about the arc that you selected, followed by information about the selected wall line.

8. Press F2, then slowly press it a few more times. As you switch back and forth between the text screen and the drawing, notice that the last three lines on the text screen are the three lines of text in the Command window of the drawing (Figure 7.13). The Command window is displaying a strip of text from the text screen, usually the last three lines.

9. Press F2 to display the drawing.

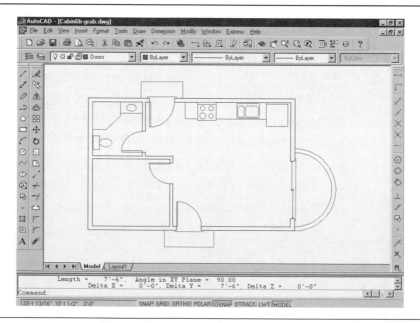

FIGURE 7.13: Toggling between the text window (a), and the drawing with its Command window (b)

Using the Properties Dialog Box to Detect a Block

The Properties button on the Standard Properties toolbar was used in the last skill to change the individual linetype scale for the ridgeline of the roof. It can also be a tool for investigating objects in your drawing. When the Properties command is started, and only one object is selected, the Properties dialog box will display data specific to the selected object.

1. Click the Properties button on the Object Properties toolbar. The Properties dialog box appears. If the Categorized tab is not on top, click it.

2. Click one of the door blocks. The data displayed in the dialog box is similar to that displayed when you used the List Command, but in slightly different form (Figure 7.14). At the top of the dialog box, a drop-down list displays the type of object selected—in this case, a Block Reference.

NOTE NOTE NOTE NOTE NOTE NOTE NOTE NOTE NOTE NOTE NOTE NOTE NOTE NOTE

Block insertion **means the same thing as block reference, and they are both casually called blocks.**

3. Close the Properties dialog box by clicking the X in the upper-right corner, then press Esc twice.

If you are ever working on a drawing that you did not draw, these tools for finding out about objects will be invaluable. The next exercise on working with blocks will involve the placement of windows in the walls of the cabin.

SKILL
7

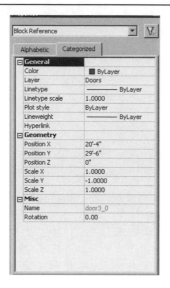

FIGURE 7.14: The Properties dialog box

Creating a Window Block

The windows in the cabin floor plan can all be created from one block, even though there are four different sizes (Figure 7.15). You'll create a window block, then we'll go from room to room to insert the block into the walls.

1. Click the Layers list on the Object Properties toolbar to open the drop-down list and click the 0 layer in the list to make it current.

2. Zoom into a section of wall where there are no jamb lines or intersections with other walls, by clicking the Zoom Window button on the Standard toolbar and picking two points to be opposite corners of the zoom window (Figure 7.16). Because the widths of the windows in the cabin are multiples of 12", a block made from a 12-inch–wide window can be inserted for each window, and an *X* scale factor can be applied to the block to make it the right width. The first step is to draw a 12-inch–wide window inside the wall lines.

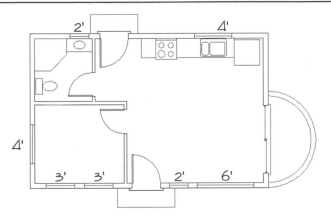

FIGURE 7.15: The cabin windows in the floor plan

3. Start the Line command by typing l ↵, then pick the Nearest Osnap button from the Object Snap toolbar or the Osnap flyout on the Standard toolbar. The Nearest Osnap will allow you to start a line on one of the wall lines. It finds the point on the wall line nearest to the point you pick.

4. Move the cursor to the upper wall line, a little to the left of the center of the screen and, with the hourglass symbol still displayed, click. A line begins.

5. Click the Perpendicular Osnap on the Object Snap toolbar, then move the cursor to the lower wall line. A colored perpendicular icon will appear directly below the point you previously picked. When it is displayed, click. The line is drawn between the wall lines. Press ↵ to end the Line command.

6. Start the Offset command by typing o ↵. Type **12** ↵ to set the offset distance to 12". Pick the line you just drew, then pick a point to the right of that line. The line is offset 12" to the right. Press ↵ to end the Offset command.

7. Start the Line command again by typing l ↵. Then pick the Midpoint Osnap button from the Object Snap toolbar. Click the line you first drew, and a line will begin at its midpoint. Select the Midpoint Osnap button again and click the line that was just offset. Press ↵ to end the Line command. Your drawing should look like Figure 7.17.

SKILL
7

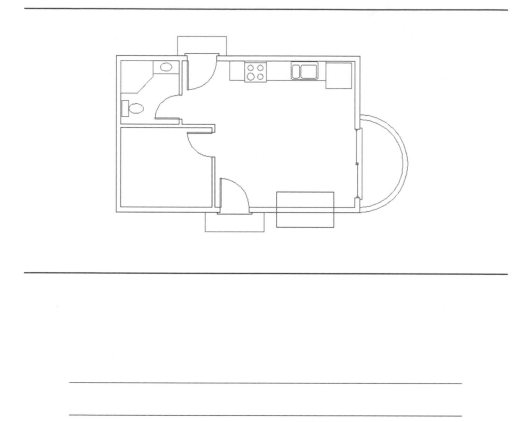

FIGURE 7.16: Making a zoom window (a), to zoom into a section of straight length of wall (b)

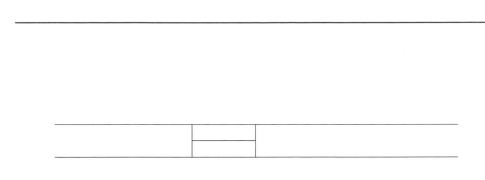

FIGURE 7.17: Completed lines for the window block

The three lines you've drawn will make up a window block. They represent the two jamb lines and the glass (usually called *glazing*). When inserted, by varying the X scale factor from 2 to 6, you will be able to create windows 2-, 3-, 4-, and 6-feet wide.

Before you create the block, you need to decide the best place for the insertion point. For the doors, you chose the hinge point because you always know where it will be in the drawing. Locating a similar strategic point for the window is a little more difficult, but certainly possible. We know the insertion point can't be on the horizontal line representing the glazing, because it will always rest in the middle of the wall, and there is no guideline in the drawing for the middle of the wall. Windows are usually dimensioned to the midpoint of the glazing line rather than to either jamb line, so we don't want the insertion point to be at the endpoint of a jamb line. The insertion point will need to be positioned on a wall line but also lined up with the midpoint of the glazing line.

To locate this point, draw a guideline from the midpoint of the glazing line straight to one of the wall lines.

1. Press ↵ to restart the Line command. Pick the Midpoint Osnap button and click the glazing line.

2. Pick the Perpendicular Osnap button and click the bottom wall line. A guideline is drawn from the midpoint of the glazing line that is perpendicular to the lower wall line (Figure 7.18). The lower endpoint of this line is the location of the window block insertion point. Press ↵ to end the Line command. Now you are ready to define the window block.

SKILL
7

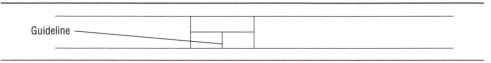

FIGURE 7.18: The guideline is completed.

3. Type **b** ↵ to start the Block command. In the dialog box, type **win-1** for the block name. Then click the Pick Point button.

4. Back in the drawing, with Endpoint Osnap running, move the cursor to the lower end of the guideline you just drew. When the colored square appears at that location, click.

5. In the dialog box, click the Select Objects button.

6. Back in the drawing, select the two jamb lines and the glazing line, but do not select the guideline whose endpoint locates the insertion point. Press ↵.

7. Back in the dialog box, click the radio button next to Delete. Then click OK. The win-1 block has been defined, and the 12-inch window has been erased.

8. Erase the guideline with the Erase command.

9. Zoom previous to zoom out to a view of the whole floor plan.

This completes the definition of the block that will represent the windows. The next task is to insert the win-1 block where the windows will be located.

Inserting the Window Block

Several factors come into play when deciding where to locate windows in a floor plan:

- The structure of the building
- The appearance of windows from outside the building
- The appearance of windows from inside a room
- The location of fixtures that may interfere with placement
- The sun angle and climate considerations

For this exercise, we will work on the windows for each room, starting with the bedroom.

Rotating a Block during Insertion

The bedroom has windows on two walls: two 3-foot windows centered in the front wall 12" apart, and one 4-foot window centered in the left wall (Figure 7.19). You'll make the 4-foot window first.

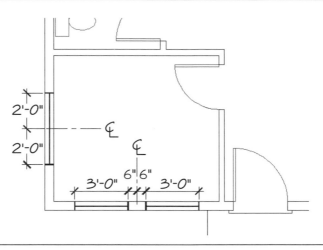

FIGURE 7.19: The bedroom windows

1. Use a zoom window to zoom into a view of the bedroom similar to that of Figure 7.19.

2. Create a new layer by clicking the Layer button and then clicking the New button in the Layer Properties Manager dialog box. Layer1 will appear and be highlighted. Type **Windows** ↵ to rename Layer1.

3. Click the color square in the Windows row. When the Select Color dialog box comes up, White will be highlighted in the Color text box. Type **30** ↵ to change the color to a bright orange. (If you don't have 256 colors available, choose any color.) The Select Color dialog box will close.

4. With Windows still highlighted in the Layers Properties Manager dialog box, click the Current button to make the Windows layer current. Then click OK. You are returned to your drawing, and Windows is the current layer.

5. Type **i** ↵ to start the Insert command. Open the Name drop-down list in the Insert dialog box. In the list of blocks, click win-1. Be sure all three of the Specify On-Screen checkboxes are selected, then click OK.

6. In your drawing, the 12-inch window block is attached to the cursor at the insertion point (Figure 7.20). Note that it is still in the same horizontal orientation that it was in when you defined the block. To fit into the left wall, you will need to rotate it as you insert it.

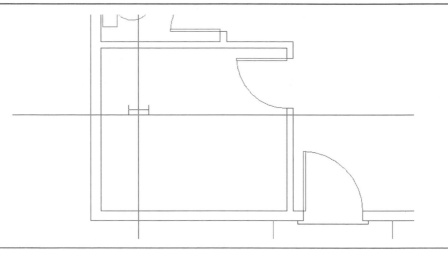

FIGURE 7.20: The win-1 block attached to the cursor

7. Pick Midpoint Osnap from the Object Snap toolbar. Move the cursor to the left inside wall line. When a colored triangle appears at the midpoint of that wall line, click.

8. You will be prompted for an *X* scale factor. This is a 4-foot window, so type **4** ↵. For the *Y* scale factor, type **1** ↵.

NOTE NOTE NOTE NOTE NOTE NOTE NOTE NOTE NOTE NOTE NOTE NOTE NOTE NOTE NOTE

The *Y* scale factor will be 1 for all the win-1 blocks because all walls that have windows are 6-inches wide—the same width as the win-1 block.

9. You are prompted for the rotation angle. Turn Ortho off if it's on. The window block is now 4-feet wide and rotates with movement of the cursor. Move the cursor so that it's directly to the right of the insertion point (Figure 7.21a). This will show you how the window will be positioned if the rotation stays at the 0-degree default. Obviously, you don't want this.

10. Move the cursor so that it is directly above the insertion point. This shows what position a 90-degree rotation will result in (Figure 7.21b). The window fits nicely into the wall here.

11.   Type **90** ↵. The win-1 block is placed in the left wall. The Insert command ends (Figure 7.21c).

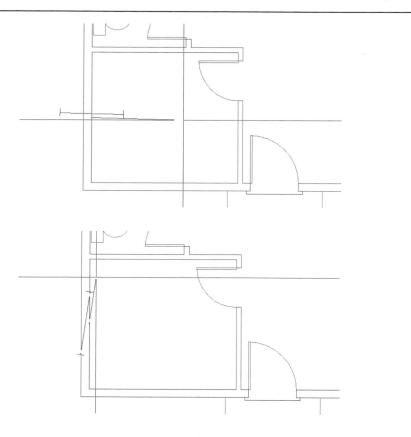

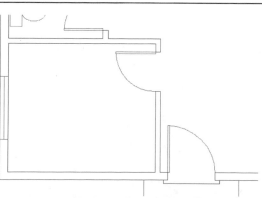

FIGURE 7.21:   Rotating the win-1 block 0° (a), 90° (b), and the final position (c)

Using Guidelines When Inserting a Block

The pair of windows in the front wall of the bedroom are 3-feet wide, 12" apart, and centered horizontally in the bedroom wall. You can use a guideline to locate the insertion points for these two windows.

1. Type l ↵ to start the Line command and pick Midpoint Osnap from the Object Snap toolbar. Locate the cursor with its target box on the inside, horizontal exterior wall line. When the colored triangle appears at the midpoint of this line, click. A line starts.

2. Click the Ortho button on the status bar to turn Ortho on, then pick a point a few feet below the first point of the line. Press ↵ to end the Line command. This establishes a guideline at the center of the wall. The insertion points for each window will be at its center. The distance between the center of the wall and the insertion point will be half the width of the window, plus half the distance between the windows—or 2'.

3. Offset the line that you just drew 2' to the right and left (Figure 7.22). Now you have established the locations for the insertion points of the win-1 blocks, and you are ready to insert them.

4. Select the Insert button on the Draw toolbar to start the Insert command. In the Insert dialog box, the win-1 block will still be displayed in the Name drop-down list because it was the last block inserted. Click OK.

5. Back in the drawing, the win-1 block is again attached to the cursor. To locate the insertion point, you can choose the upper endpoint of one of the outer guidelines, or the intersection of this guideline with the exterior outside wall line. Which one would be better? The second choice requires no rotation of the block, so it's easier and faster to use that intersection.

6. Pick the Intersection Osnap button from the Object Snap toolbar and position the cursor on the outside wall (Figure 7.23a). A colored x appears with three dots to its right, along with a tooltip that says "Extended Intersection."

Click. Now hold the crosshair cursor on the lower portion of the left-most offset guideline, again without touching any other lines. The x will appear, this time at the intersection of this guideline with the outside wall line, and without the three dots. The tooltip now says "Intersection" (Figure 7.23b). Click again. The insertion point is set at the intersection of the guideline and the outside wall line.

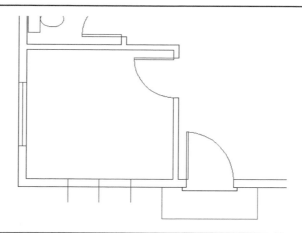

FIGURE 7.22: Guidelines for the pair of window blocks

7. Type **3** ↵ for the X scale factor, then type **1** ↵ for the Y scale factor. At the rotation angle prompt, press ↵ to accept the default of 0°. The 3-foot window on the left is inserted in the front wall.

8. Repeat this procedure for the other 3-foot window.

9. Erase the three guidelines.

SKILL
7

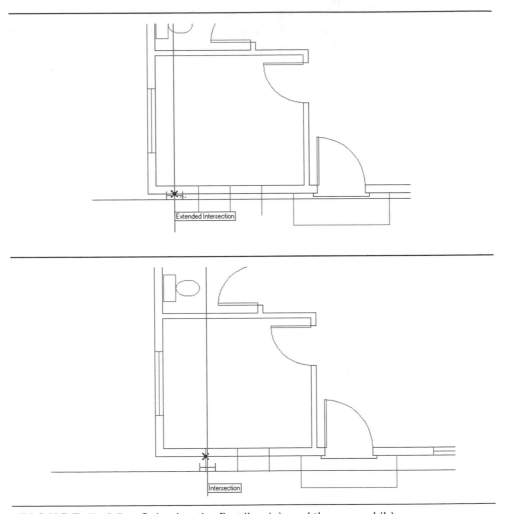

FIGURE 7.23: Selecting the first line (a), and the second (b)

Because you chose the lower of the two wall lines to locate the insertion point on, the block needed no rotation. When finished, the bedroom will look like Figure 7.24.

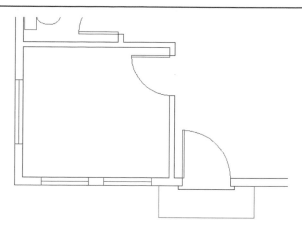

FIGURE 7.24: The bedroom with all windows inserted

Using Point Filters to Insert a Block

The next room to work on is the bathroom. In this room, there is one small window over the sink.

1. Click the Pan button on the Standard toolbar. The cursor changes to a hand.

2. Position the hand on the wall between the bedroom and bathroom, then hold down the left mouse button and drag the drawing down. When the bathroom is in the middle of the drawing area, release the mouse button. Press Esc or ↵ to cancel the Pan command. You want one 2-foot window in the bathroom, centered over the sink. This time you'll insert the block without the use of guidelines. Endpoint Osnap should be running.

3. Start the Insert command (type **i** ↵), be sure win-1 is in the Name dropdown list, and check that all Specify On-screen checkboxes are marked. Then click OK and, at the Specify insertion point: prompt, type .x ↵ to start point filters. *Point filters* allow you to locate a point by picking two

SKILL

7

points: one having the x coordinate you want, and the other having the y coordinate you want. If this sounds confusing, it will become clearer once you use the feature.

4. Select the Midpoint Osnap and position the crosshair cursor on the line representing the front edge of the sink counter. A colored triangle will appear at the midpoint of that line (Figure 7.25a). When it does, click—you have selected the x coordinate. Now the prompt in the Command window reads "(need YZ):." This means that AutoCAD wants you to specify the y coordinate. (We'll ignore the z coordinate.) You can do this in two ways: type in a relative coordinate based on the previously specified x coordinate, or pick a point in the drawing that has the value that you need for the y coordinate. We'll use the second option.

5. The Endpoint Osnap is running. Move the cursor to the upper-left corner of the counter top. This corner has the y coordinate that you want because it is on the inside wall line. When the colored square appears on the corner (Figure 7.25b), click. The insertion point has been placed on the inside wall line, centered over the sink.

6. At the X scale factor prompt, Type **2** ↵. Then, at the Y scale factor prompt, type **1** ↵. Press ↵ again to accept the default rotation angle of 0°. The 2-foot window is inserted into the wall behind the sink (Figure 7.26). Press Esc to cancel Pan Realtime.

NOTE NOTE NOTE NOTE NOTE NOTE NOTE NOTE NOTE NOTE NOTE NOTE NOTE NOTE NOTE

Note that no mark is left at the insertion point location on the wall. You have to wait until the insertion process is over to see if everything has been done correctly. When I walk you through the next insertion, you'll learn how to change a setting so that AutoCAD will leave a mark.

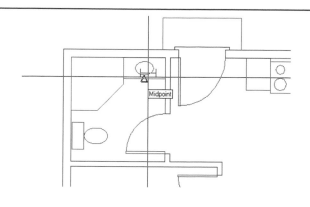

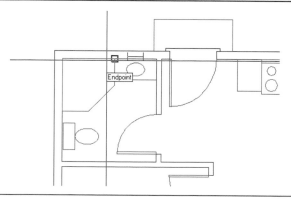

FIGURE 7.25: Using point filters to select a point to get the x coordinate (a), and the y coordinate (b)

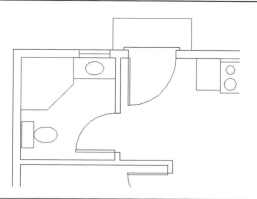

FIGURE 7.26: The 2-foot window after insertion

Using Blips to Help in Inserting Blocks

You're over half way done with the windows—just three remain to be inserted: one in the kitchen and two in the living room.

1. Click the Pan button on the Standard toolbar. Then position the hand cursor on the back door swing. Hold down the left mouse button and drag the drawing over to the left until the kitchen is in the middle of the drawing area. Release the mouse button. Then press the Esc key or ↵ to cancel the Real Time Pan.

2. Type **blipmode** ↵, then type **on** ↵. Blipmode feature is activated.

3. You need to insert a 4-foot window in the back wall, centered behind the sink (see Figure 7.15). Start the Insert command. Click OK when the Insert dialog box comes up. The win-1 block appears on the cursor.

4. At the Specify insertion point: prompt, type **.x** ↵ to activate the point filters. You need to pick the midpoint of the back or front edge of the sink. Since the front edge is more accessible, select that one.

5. Select the Midpoint Osnap and put the target box on the front edge of the sink. When the colored triangle appears on the front edge, click. A small + is placed at the midpoint of the front edge of the sink (Figure 7.27a). This is called a *blip* or a *blipmark*.

6. Position the target box on the inside wall line of the back wall where it's not touching any other lines. Because Endpoint Osnap is running, a colored square should show up at one of the endpoints of this wall line. When it does, click. The + is placed at the endpoint of the wall line and at a position on the wall line directly behind the midpoint of the sink's back edge (Figure 7.27b). This assures you that the point filters successfully set the insertion point exactly where you need it.

7. Type **4** ↵ for the X scale factor. Then type **1** ↵ for the Y scale factor. For the rotation angle, press ↵ again to accept the default angle of 0°. The window is placed in the back wall, centered behind the sink (Figure 7.28).

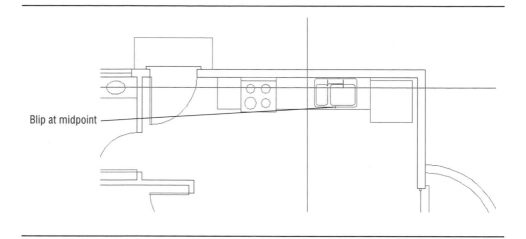

Blip at midpoint

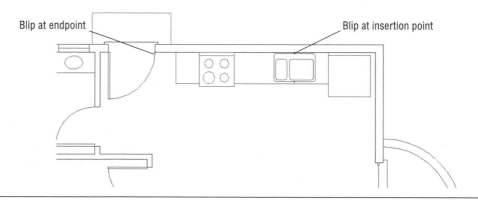

Blip at endpoint

Blip at insertion point

FIGURE 7.27: A blip marks the midpoint of the front edge of the sink (a), and the resulting insertion point location (b)

When Blipmode is on, a + is placed wherever you pick a point in the drawing area, whether you are drawing or selecting objects. These are temporary markers and are not saved with the drawing file, nor do they show up in prints. As they accumulate, you can delete them by typing **r** ↵ at the Command: prompt, or by picking View ➤ Redraw. Using blips is up to you—some people find them irritating and would rather not see them. Others find them useful because they are a record of what you've done, as you just saw when placing an insertion point. Leave them visible for the rest of the skill and see how you feel about them.

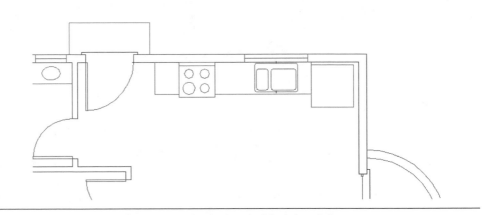

FIGURE 7.28: The inserted window behind the sink

Finishing the Windows

The last two windows to insert are both in the front wall of the living room. You will use skills you've already worked with to place them.

1. Use the Pan command to move the drawing down to the front wall of the living room. One window is 6-feet wide. Its right jamb is 12" to the left of the inside corner of the wall. The other one is a circular window, 2-feet in diameter, positioned halfway between the 6-foot window jamb and the front doorjamb (Figure 7.29).

2. Start the Insert command and click OK in the Insert dialog box to select the win-1 block.

3. Select the Temporary Tracking Point Osnap button. Then, with Endpoint Osnap running, pick the lower-right inside corner of the cabin. The insertion point will be positioned to the left of this corner at a distance of 12" in, plus half the width of the 6-foot window—or 4' from the corner.

4. Hold the crosshair cursor directly to the left of the point just picked. When the tracking path and tooltip appear, type **4'** ↵. This sets the insertion point 4' to the left of the corner, on the inside wall line. A blip appears there.

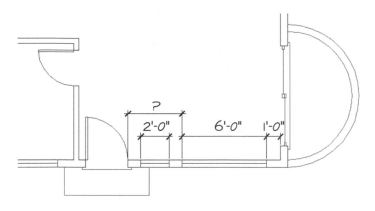

FIGURE 7.29: The windows in the front wall of the living room

5. For the scale factors, type **6** ↵, then type **1** ↵.

6. For the rotation angle, turn Ortho off if it's not already off. Hold the cursor directly to the right of the insertion point to see the position of the window at 0-degree rotation. Then hold the cursor directly above the insertion point to see how a 90-degree rotation would look. Finally, hold the cursor directly to the left for a view of the effect of a 180-degree rotation. The 180-degree view is the one you want.

7. Type **180** ↵. The 6-foot window is placed in the front wall.

SKILL
7

Finally, you need to locate the 2-foot circular window halfway between the left jamb of the 6-foot window and the right jamb of the front door opening. Use the Distance command to find out the distance between the two jambs. Then offset one of the jambs half that distance to establish the location of the insertion point on the wall lines. Of the two jamb lines, you must offset the doorjamb because the window jamb is part of the window block and can't be offset.

1. Type **di** ↵ to start the Distance command. With Endpoint Osnap running, pick the upper end of the front doorjamb, then pick the upper end of the left window jamb. In the Command window, the distance is displayed as 3'-10". You need to offset the doorjamb half that distance to locate the insertion point for the 2-foot window.

2. Start the Offset command, then type **1'-11** ↵ to set the offset distance.

3. Pick the doorjamb and type **non** ↵. Then pick a point to the right of the doorjamb. Press ↵ to end the Offset command.

TIP TIP TIP TIP TIP TIP TIP TIP TIP TIP TIP TIP TIP TIP TIP TIP TIP TIP TIP TIP TIP TIP TIP TIP

Typing non ↵ (none) cancels any running Osnaps for one pick.

4. Start the Insert command. Click OK to accept the win-1 block. Pick the bottom endpoint of the offset jamb line to establish the insertion point.

5. Type **2** ↵ for the X scale factor. Type **1** ↵ for the Y scale factor.

6. For the rotation angle, press ↵ to accept the default of 0°. The last window is inserted in the front wall, and the Insert command ends. Erase the offset jamb line (Figure 7.30).

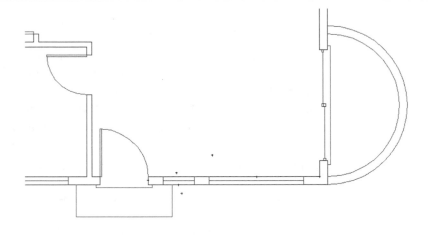

FIGURE 7.30: The two windows inserted in the front wall of the living room

NOTE NOTE NOTE NOTE NOTE NOTE NOTE NOTE NOTE NOTE NOTE NOTE NOTE NOTE NOTE

Notice how the blips have been appearing on and near the wall as you've been working.

7. Type **r** ↵ to use the Redraw command to refresh the screen. The blips disappear.

8. Type **z ↵ e ↵** to zoom out to the Extents view of the drawing. This changes the view to include all the visible lines. The view fills the drawing area.

NOTE NOTE NOTE NOTE NOTE NOTE NOTE NOTE NOTE NOTE NOTE NOTE NOTE NOTE

Zooming to *Extents* is one of the zoom options, and is the bottom button of the Zoom flyout on the Standard toolbar.

9. Type **z ↵ .85x ↵** to zoom out a little from the Extents view, so all objects are set in slightly from the edge of the drawing area (Figure 7.31).

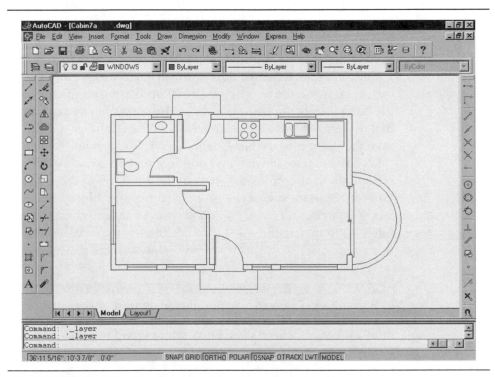

FIGURE 7.31: Zooming to .85x after zooming to Extents

10. Save this drawing as Cabin07a.

You have inserted seven windows into the floor plan, each of them generated from the win-1 block. You created the win-1 block on the 0 layer and then made the Windows layer current, so each window block reference took on the characteristics of the Windows layer when it was inserted.

Blocks can be ungrouped by using the *Explode command*. Exploding a block has the effect of reducing the block to the objects that make it up. For the win-1 block, exploding it would reduce it to three lines, all on the 0 layer. If you exploded one of the door blocks, it would be reduced to a rectangle and an arc, with both objects on the Doors layer because these components of the door block were on the Doors layer when the block was defined.

Revising a Block

If you need to revise a block that has already been inserted several times, you will need to modify one of the block references that was inserted with the same X and Y scale factors. All the windows were inserted using different X and Y scale factors, so to revise the win-1 block, we'll need to insert that block one more time, this time using uniform scale factors. Then you can make changes to the objects that make up the win-1 block reference. When finished with the changes, you can save the changes to the block definition. This redefines the block.

Let's say that the client who's building the cabin finds out that double glazing is required in all windows. You want the windows to show two lines for the glass. You cannot make such a change in each window block because blocks can't be modified in this way, and you don't want to have to change seven windows separately. If you revise the win-1 block definition, the changes you make in one block reference will be made in all seven windows.

NOTE NOTE NOTE NOTE NOTE NOTE NOTE NOTE NOTE NOTE NOTE NOTE NOTE NOTE NOTE

Blocks can be moved, rotated, copied, erased, scaled, and exploded; but they can't be trimmed, extended, offset, or filleted; and you can't erase or move part of a block. All objects in a block are grouped together and behave as if they were one object.

1. Start the Insert command and click OK to accept the win-1 block to be inserted.

2. Pick a point in the middle of the living room. This establishes the insertion point location.

3. Press ↵ three times to accept the defaults for *X* and *Y* scale factors and the rotation angle. The win-1 block is inserted in the living room (Figure 7.32).

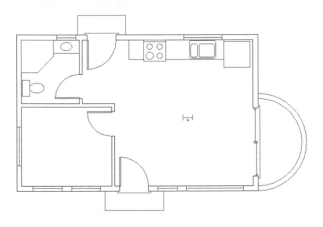

FIGURE 7.32: The win-1 block inserted into the living room

4. Zoom into a closer view of the window, then click Modify ➤ In-place Xref and Block Edit ➤ Edit reference.

5. Select the new block reference in the middle of the living room. The Reference Edit dialog box comes up. The win-1 block is identified and a preview is displayed.

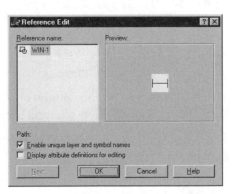

6. Click OK. You are prompted to select nested objects.

7. Select the glazing line in the win-1 block, then press ↵. The glazing line turns white (or black) and the Refedit toolbar appears.

8. Use the Offset command to offset the glazing line 0.5" up and down. Then erase the original horizontal line (Figure 7.33). This window block now has double glazing.

9. On the right side of the Refedit toolbar, click the right-most button, whose tooltip says "Save back changes to reference."

10. An AutoCAD warning window appears. Click OK. The glazing lines change back to orange. The block definition has been revised.

11. Erase this block reference—we don't need it any more.

12. Zoom previous to view the entire drawing. All windows in the cabin now have double glazing.

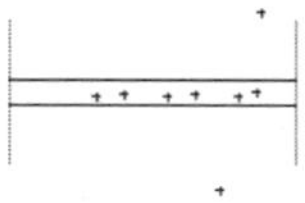

FIGURE 7.33: The result of the modifications to the win-1 block

13. Zoom into a closer look at the bedroom in order to view some of the modified window block references (Figure 7.34).

14. This is a good time to turn off the blips if you find them more of a nuisance than an aid. To turn them off, type **blipmode** ↵, then type **off** ↵.

15. Zoom previous to a view of the entire floor plan. Save this drawing as Cabin07b.

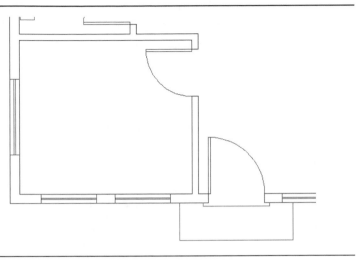

FIGURE 7.34: Zooming in to see the revised window blocks with double glazing

Wblocking

Blocks can be copied out of one drawing and inserted into another one. This feature allows blocks generated during the course of one job to be used in future jobs. Usually a folder is set up on the hard drive to contain these blocks. This folder is often called a *Symbols Library* and may have sub-folders for kitchen fixtures, bathroom fixtures, doors, etc. You'll create a Symbols folder below. Sets of standard, pre-drawn blocks are often purchased from software vendors and loaded into your Symbols Library.

When a block is copied from a drawing to a Symbols Library, the Wblock command is used, and two things happen to the copy of the block as it leaves the drawing: It is unblocked, and it is made into a .dwg file. So blocks stored in the Symbols Library are actually little drawing files. When they are inserted into another drawing, they get reblocked in the insertion process.

To see how this works, you will wblock the win-1 block out of your cabin drawing. Then you will insert it into another drawing.

1. Minimize AutoCAD and open Windows Explorer. Find the training folder where your cabin drawings are stored and highlight the folder. Create a

sub-folder in this directory called Symbols. Close Windows Explorer and restore AutoCAD.

2. Type **wblock** ↵ to start the Wblock command. The Write Block dialog box comes up (Figure 7.35). There is a Source area on top and a Destination area on the bottom of this dialog box.

3. In the Source area, click the radio button next to Block. Then open the drop-down list and select win-1.

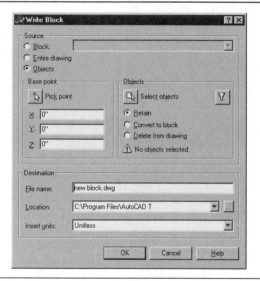

FIGURE 7.35: The Write Block dialog box

4. In the Destination area, click the ... (browse) button to the right of the Location drop-down list. Negotiate your way to your Training Data folder, then highlight the new Symbols sub-folder.

5. Click OK. Then, in the Write Block dialog box, click OK again.

6. If you want to see if it's there, minimize AutoCAD and open up Windows Explorer or File Manager. Find and open the Symbols folder. There should be a Win-1.dwg in the folder. Close Windows Explorer and restore AutoCAD.

Next you need to create a new drawing and put a couple of wall lines in it so you can insert this new Win-1 drawing.

Inserting a .*Dwg* File into Another .*Dwg* File

If you need more help setting up a new drawing than the following steps provide, refer to Skill 3. For a reminder on how to change layer properties, review Skill 6.

1. Click the New button on the Standard toolbar. Click the Start from Scratch button, then click OK. A new, blank drawing comes up.

2. Click Format ➤ Units. In the Length area, open the Type drop-down list and select Architectural for the units. Click OK. When an AutoCAD alert dialog box appears, click OK to close it.

3. Click the Layers button and create two new layers: Walls and Windows. Leave the Windows layer in its default color and make the Walls layer blue.

4. With the Walls layer highlighted, click the Current button to make the Walls layer current. Click OK to return to the drawing.

5. Start the Rectangle command. For the first corner, type **0,0** ↵. For the other corner, type **25',15'** ↵.

6. Zoom to Extents. Then use the Zoom Realtime button to zoom out just enough to create a border of blank space around the rectangle.

7. Use the Offset command to offset this rectangle 6" to the inside (Figure 7.36).

8. Use the Layers drop-down list to make the Windows layer current.

9. Pick the Insert command from the Draw menu. In the Insert dialog box, click the Browse button.

10. In the Select Drawing File dialog box, find and open the Symbols directory, highlight Win-1.dwg, and click Open.

11. In the Insert dialog box, win-1 will be displayed in the Name drop-down list. Win-1.dwg will be displayed, along with its directory path, below the Name drop-down list. Place a mark in the Specify On-screen checkbox in the Scale area. Then click OK.

12. In your drawing, pick the Midpoint Osnap and pick the bottom outside wall line. Type **6** ↵, then type **1** ↵. The win-1 block is inserted in the wall (Figure 7.37). Save this drawing in your Training Data folder as Cabin-test.

SKILL
7

FIGURE 7.36: The rectangle after Zoom Realtime and Offsetting

FIGURE 7.37: The *Win-1.dwg* file is inserted into the new drawing.

You have completed the basic procedure for using a block that is created in one drawing in another drawing. It will help to practice this routine. Make a couple of openings in the Cabin-test drawing and repeat the steps for one or two of the door blocks. You won't have to create a new directory for the symbols this time. Here is an outline of the procedure:

1. Explode the two rectangles. (Pick the Explode button on the Modify toolbar.)

2. Create openings, then save Cabin-test.

3. Switch to Cabin07b. (Open the Window menu and pick Cabin07b.)

TIP TIP TIP TIP TIP TIP TIP TIP TIP TIP TIP TIP TIP TIP TIP TIP TIP TIP TIP TIP TIP TIP TIP TIP

Like most Windows-based programs, AutoCAD 2000 can have multiple drawing files open in a session. When you open the Window menu, the bottom of the menu contains a list of AutoCAD files currently open. Click the file you want.

4. Start the Wblock command. (Type **wblock** ↵.)

5. Click the Block radio button, then open the drop-down list and select door3_0.

6. Be sure that the Symbols folder is selected in the Location drop-down list in the Destination area. Then click OK.

7. Open the Window menu and select Cabin-test.

8. Create a new layer called Doors. Assign it the color red and make it current. Start the Insert command.

9. Click the Browse button. Find and open the Symbols folder and select the .dwg file named after the block (door3_0.dwg). Then click Open.

10. In the Insert dialog box, be sure all Specify On-screen checkboxes are marked, then click OK.

11. Place the insertion point and respond to the scale factor and rotation prompts.

If you want to practice creating blocks, open the Cabin07b drawing and make blocks out of any of the fixtures in the bathroom or kitchen. Try to decide on the best location to use for the insertion point of each fixture. Then insert them back into the Cabin07b drawing in their original locations. You can also wblock any of these new blocks into the Symbols folder. Then insert them as .dwg files into the Cabin-test drawing.

This skill has outlined the procedure for setting up and using blocks. Blocks follow a set of complex rules, some of which are beyond the scope of this book. For a more in-depth discussion on blocks, refer to *Mastering AutoCAD 2000* by George Omura (Sybex, 1999).

Are You Experienced?

Now you can...

☑ **create blocks out of existing objects in your drawing**

☑ **insert blocks into your drawing**

☑ **vary the size and rotation of blocks as they are inserted**

☑ **detect blocks in a drawing**

☑ **use point filters to locate an insertion point**

☑ **control the visibility of blips in your drawing**

☑ **revise a block**

☑ **use the Wblock command to put blocks in a Symbols folder**

☑ **insert blocks from the Symbols folder into a drawing**

Generating Elevations

- ⊖ **Drawing an exterior elevation from a floor plan**
- ⊖ **Using grips to copy objects**
- ⊖ **Setting up, naming, and saving a User Coordinate System and a new view**
- ⊖ **Transferring height lines from one elevation to another**
- ⊖ **Moving and rotating elevations**

Now that you have created all the building components that will be in the floor plan, it's a good time to draw the exterior elevations. *Elevations* are horizontal views of the building, as if you were standing facing the building, instead of looking down at it, as you do in the floor plan. The elevations view shows you how windows and doors fit into the walls, and gives you an idea of how the building will look from the outside. In most design projects, at least four exterior elevations are included in the drawings: front, back, and one from each side. We'll go over how to create the front elevation first. Then we'll discuss some of the considerations necessary to complete the other ones, and you will have the chance to draw these on your own. Finally, we will look at how interior elevations are set up. They are similar to exterior elevations, but are usually of individual walls on the inside of a building to show how objects, such as doors, windows, cabinets, shelves, and finishes, will look in and on the walls.

Drawing the Front Elevation

The front elevation is drawn using techniques very similar to those used on the traditional drafting board. You will draw the front elevation view of the cabin directly below the floor plan by dropping lines down from key points on the floor plan and intersecting them with horizontal lines representing the heights of the corresponding components in the elevation. Those heights are shown in Figure 8.1.

1. Open Cabin07b.

2. Create a new layer called F-elev. Assign it color 42 and make it current. Here's a summary of the steps to do this:

   A. Click the Layers button, then click New.

   B. Type in the new layer's name (F-elev) and press ↵.

   C. Click the colored square for the F-elev layer. Type **42** ↵.

   D. Click Current, then click OK.

3. Thaw the Roof and Headers layers. Then offset the bottom horizontal roof line 24' down. The offset line will be off the screen.

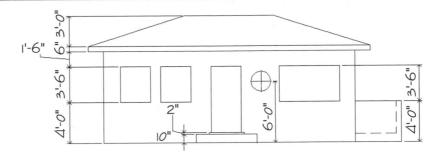

FIGURE 8.1: The front elevation with heights of components

4. Click the Zoom Extents button on the Zoom flyout toolbar.

5. Use Realtime Zoom to zoom out just enough to bring the offset roof line up off the bottom edge of the drawing area.

6. Erase this offset line. Your drawing should look like Figure 8.2.

FIGURE 8.2: The floor plan with space below it for the front elevation

Setting Up Lines for the Heights

You need to establish a base line to represent the ground. Then you can offset the other height lines from the base line or from other height lines.

1. With Ortho on, draw a horizontal ground line across the bottom of the screen using the Line command. Be sure the line extends on the left to a few feet beyond points directly below the outside edge of the roof, and on the right to directly below the balcony (Figure 8.3).

FIGURE 8.3: The floor plan with the ground line

2. Offset the ground line 10" up to mark the height of the step. Then offset this new line 2" up to mark the top of the threshold.

3. Move back to the ground line and offset it 4' up to mark the top of the balcony wall and the bottom of the windows.

4. Offset the bottom line for the windows 3'-6" up to mark the top of the door and windows.

5. Offset the top line for the windows and door 1'-6" up to mark the soffit of the roof.

A roof *soffit* is the underside of the roof overhang that extends from the outside edge of the roof, back to the wall.

6. Offset the soffit line 6" up to mark the lower edge of the roof's top surface.

7. Offset this lower edge of the roof's top surface 3' up to mark the roof's ridge (Figure 8.4).

8. Press ↵ to end the Offset command.

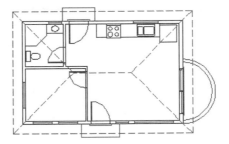

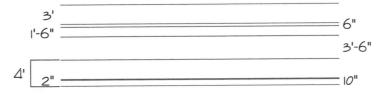

FIGURE 8.4: The horizontal height lines for the elevation in place

Each of these lines represents the height of one or more components of the cabin. Now you will drop lines down from the points in the floor plan that coincide with components that will be visible in the front elevation. The front elevation will consist of the balcony, front step, front door and windows, front corners of the exterior walls, and parts of the roof.

Using Grips to Copy Lines

In the following steps, you will learn how to use grips to copy the dropped lines.

1. Be sure your Endpoint Osnap is running and make sure Ortho is on. Start a line from the lower-left corner of the walls of the building. Pick Perpendicular Osnap and click the ground line. Press ↵ to end the Line command (Figure 8.5a).

2. At the Command: prompt, select the line you just drew. The line is selected and small squares appear on the line's midpoint and endpoints (Figure 8.5b). These are grips.

3. Click the grip on the upper endpoint. The grip changes color, and the prompt changes to Specify stretch point or [Base point/Copy/Undo/eXit]:. This is the *Stretch command* activated by grips. Any time you activate a grip, the Stretch command starts. You can press the space bar to bring up another command.

NOTE NOTE NOTE NOTE NOTE NOTE NOTE NOTE NOTE NOTE NOTE NOTE NOTE NOTE NOTE

The *Stretch command* is a modifying tool that you use to lengthen or shorten lines and other objects. You'll have a chance to use it in Skill 9: *Working with Hatches and Fills.*

4. Press the space bar once. This begins cycling you through the five commands that you can use grips with: Stretch, Move, Rotate, Scale, and Mirror. The prompt changes to Specify move point or [Base point/Copy/Undo/eXit]:. This is the *Move command* activated by grips. You'll use the Move command with its Copy option to copy the line you just selected.

5. Type c ↵ to select the Copy option of the Move command.

NOTE NOTE NOTE NOTE NOTE NOTE NOTE NOTE NOTE NOTE NOTE NOTE NOTE NOTE NOTE

Each of the commands that work with grips has a Copy option, which keeps the original object as is while you modify the copy. You can copy with grips in several ways that are not possible with the regular Copy command.

6. Select the lower-right corner of the building. The line is copied to this corner.

7. Select the Quadrant Osnap and click the right extremity of the outside wall line of the balcony. Another line is copied, this time to the balcony. It does not extend to the ground line because it was directly copied and therefore is the same length as the other two lines. You will extend it later.

8. Type x ↵ to end the Move command. Press Esc twice to remove the grips. Your drawing will resemble Figure 8.5c.

In Skill 7, you saw how grips could be used to detect whether an object is a block or not, but they actually serve a larger function. The grips feature is a tool for editing objects quickly, using one or more of the following five commands: Stretch, Move, Rotate, Scale, or Mirror. These commands operate a little differently when using grips than when using them normally. There are a few more things the commands can do with the help of grips. Each command has a Copy option; so, for example, if you rotate an object with grips, you have the option of having the original object stay unchanged while you make multiple copies of the object in various angles of rotation. This can't be done using the Rotate command in the normal way, nor by using the regular Copy command.

The steps to use grips are summarized as follows:

1. Click an object you wish to modify when no commands have been started.

2. Click the grip that will be the base point for the command's execution.

3. Watch the prompt and cycle through the five commands by pressing the space bar. (You can also right-click at this point and choose any of the five commands from the menu that comes up on the drawing area.)

4. When the command you need comes up, execute the necessary option.

5. Type x ↵ when finished.

6. Press Esc twice to remove the grips.

SKILL
8

The key to being able to use grips efficiently is knowing which Grip to select to start the process. This requires a good understanding of the workings of the five commands that work with grips.

This book will not cover grips in much depth, but will introduce you to the basics. You will get a chance to use the Move command with grips in this skill, and we will use grips again when we get to Skill 11, *Dimensioning a Drawing*.

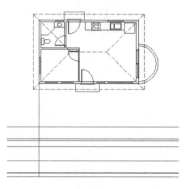

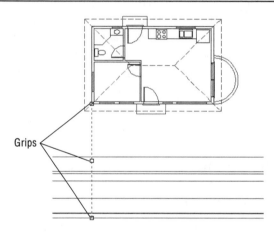

Grips

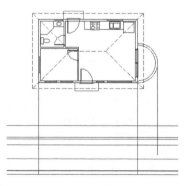

FIGURE 8.5: Dropping a line from the floor plan to the elevation (a), the dropped line with grips (b), and the copied lines (c)

Trimming Lines in the Elevation

The next task is to trim the appropriate lines in the elevation, but first you need to extend the line dropped from the balcony down to the ground line.

1. Start the Extend command. Select the ground line. Press ↵. Pick the line dropped from the balcony anywhere on its bottom half. Press ↵ to end the Extend command.

2. Start the Trim command. Select the soffit line for a cutting edge for the two building lines, then press ↵. The two lines to be trimmed are the ones that were dropped from the corners of the building. Pick them anywhere between the soffit line and the floor plan. The lines are trimmed (Figure 8.6).

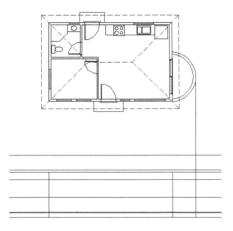

FIGURE 8.6: The building corner lines after being trimmed to the soffit line

3. Press ↵ twice to stop and restart the Trim command. You need to trim a horizontal height line and a vertical dropped line for the balcony. To select cutting edges, pick the line dropped from the balcony and the horizontal height line that represents the top of the balcony wall and the bottom of the windows (Figure 8.7a). The lines ghost (change to lines with small dashes) after they've been selected. Press ↵.

4. To trim the lines properly, click the line dropped from the balcony anywhere above the balcony in the elevation. To trim the horizontal line representing the top of the balcony wall, pick this line anywhere to the right of the line dropped from the balcony (Figure 8.7b). The lines are trimmed (Figure 8.7c). Press ↵ to end the Trim command.

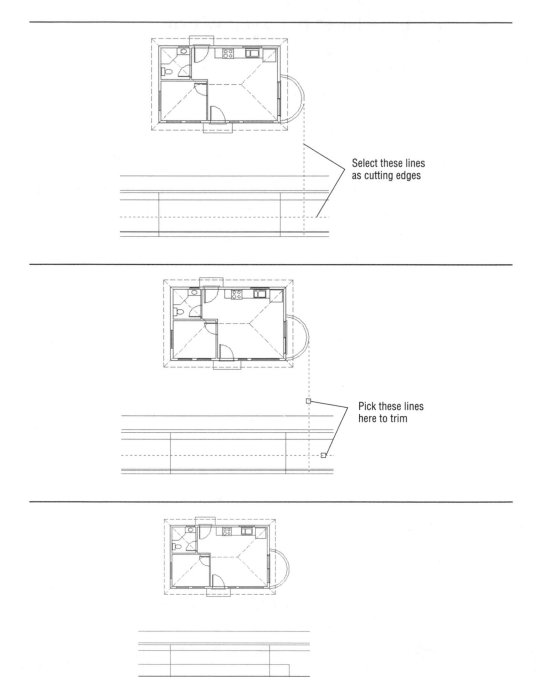

Select these lines
as cutting edges

Pick these lines
here to trim

FIGURE 8.7: Trimming the balcony lines: selecting cutting edges (a), picking lines to be trimmed (b), and the result (c)

This is the basic process for generating an elevation: Drop lines down from the floor plan and trim the lines that need to be trimmed. The trick is to learn to see the picture you want somewhere in all the crossed lines and then be able to perform the Trim command accurately to trim the appropriate lines away.

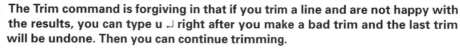

TIP TIP TIP TIP TIP TIP TIP TIP TIP TIP TIP TIP TIP TIP TIP TIP TIP TIP TIP TIP TIP TIP TIP

The Trim command is forgiving in that if you trim a line and are not happy with the results, you can type u ↵ right after you make a bad trim and the last trim will be undone. Then you can continue trimming.

We'll try the process a couple more times. First we'll make the roof.

Drawing the Roof in Elevation

To draw the roof in elevation, follow these steps:

1. Use the Line command with Ortho on and Endpoint Osnap running to start a line from the right endpoint of the ridgeline of the roof and draw it straight down past the soffit line (Figure 8.8a). End the Line command.

TIP TIP TIP TIP TIP TIP TIP TIP TIP TIP TIP TIP TIP TIP TIP TIP TIP TIP TIP TIP TIP TIP TIP

If you have trouble selecting a second point of the line in step 1 without snapping it to the endpoint of a line, try clicking the Snap to None Osnap button on the Object Snap toolbar before you pick the line. This will turn off any running Osnaps—in this case, Endpoint—for the next pick.

2. Click this line to activate grips. Select the grip at its upper endpoint. Press the space bar once to access the Move command.

3. Type c ↵ and then click the lower-right and lower-left corners of the roof, and the left endpoint of the ridgeline. This will copy the dropped line to these three locations (Figure 8.8b).

4. Type x ↵ to end the Move command, then press Esc twice to remove the grips.

5. Start the Trim command and select the two lines dropped from the ridgeline. Press ↵.

SKILL
8

6. In the elevation, pick the ridgeline to the left and right of these dropped lines (Figure 8.9a). The ridgeline is trimmed back to its correct length (Figure 8.9b). Press ↵.

7. Erase the two dropped lines that were just used as cutting edges.

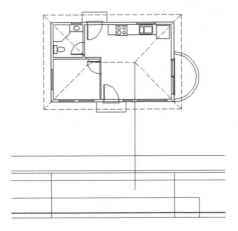

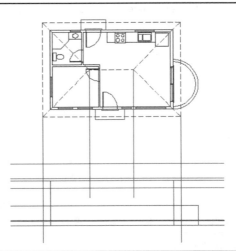

FIGURE 8.8: Dropping a line from the roof (a), and copying this line (b)

8. Type **tr** ↵ to restart the Trim command. Select the two lines dropped from the corners of the roof, the horizontal soffit line, and the line 6" above the soffit line to be cutting edges—four lines in all. Press ↵.

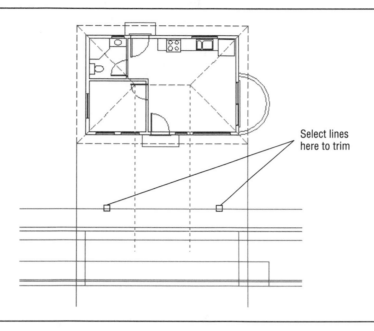

Select lines
here to trim

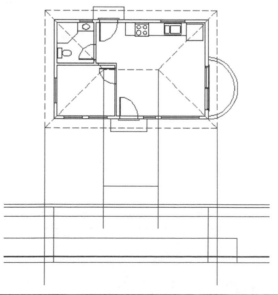

FIGURE 8.9: Selecting the lines to trim (a), and the result (b)

9. To do the trim, click the dropped lines above and below the two horizontal cutting edges, then click the two selected horizontal lines to the left and right of the dropped lines—eight picks in all (Figure 8.10a). Press ↵. The roof edge is complete (Figure 8.10b).

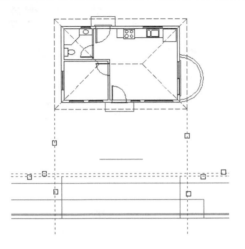

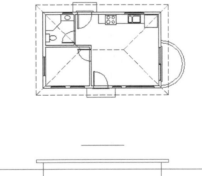

FIGURE 8.10: Trimming the lines to form the roof edge (a), and the result (b)

10. Use the Line command to draw the two hip lines from the roof edge to the ridgeline. Zoom in to do this if you need to, then zoom previous when you're finished to view the completed front elevation of the roof (Figure 8.11).

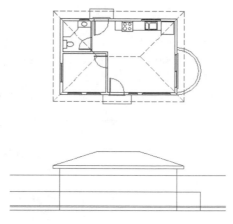

FIGURE 8.11: The completed roof in elevation

Putting in the Door, Step, and Windows

To finish the front elevation, all we need to put in are the front door, windows, front step and threshold, and a few finishing touches. We'll do the door and all of the windows, except the round one, in one cycle. We'll save the step and threshold for later.

1. Use Zoom Window to zoom into as close a view as possible, while still seeing as much of the drawing as you need to. You need to see the entire elevation, the front wall of the floor plan, and the lower half of the balcony, so make your zoom window large enough to enclose just those elements (Figure 8.12a).

2. With Ortho on, use Endpoint and Perpendicular Osnaps to draw a line from the left end of the left-most window in the front wall of the floor plan to the ground line.

3. Click the upper grip on this line at the Command: prompt to activate it. Follow the same process as you did in steps 2 and 3 of the "Drawing the Roof

SKILL
8

in Elevation" section to copy this line to (a) each end of each window in the front wall, except the 2-foot circular one to the right of the front door, and (b) each edge of the front door opening.

4. Type **x** ↵ to end the Move command. Press Esc twice to remove the grips (Figure 8.12b).

Before we begin trimming all these lines, study the floor plan and elevation for a minute and try to visualize the three windows and the door in the middle of all the crossing lines.
We'll trim a few at a time, working from the top down.

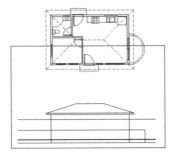

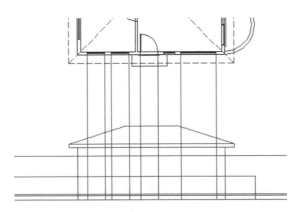

FIGURE 8.12: The window for zooming in closer (a), and dropping a line from a window and copying it to the edges of the windows and the front door

5. Start the Trim command. For cutting edges, select the horizontal line representing the top of the windows and doors, and the eight lines you just dropped from the floor plan. Press ↵.

6. To trim, pick the horizontal line at each segment between the windows and the door and near the endpoints of the line (five places). Then pick each selected dropped line above the tops of the windows and door (eight places). This makes 13 places to pick. Then press ↵. The results of the trim are shown in Figure 8.13.

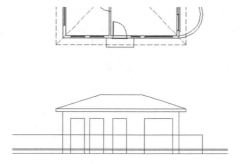

FIGURE 8.13: Trimming the top of the door and windows

Moving down, trim the lines that form the bottom of the windows.

7. Start the Trim command. Select as cutting edges (a) the horizontal line representing the bottom of the window and the top of the balcony wall, (b) the six vertical lines forming the sides of the windows, and (c) the vertical line representing the right edge of the front wall. Press ↵.

8. To trim, pick the horizontal line (a) at each segment between the windows (two picks), (b) between the right edge of the 6-foot window and the right edge of the building (one pick), and (c) where it extends to the left of the left-most window (one pick). Then pick the vertical lines that extend below the bottoms of the windows (six picks). This will be a total of 10 picks. Then press ↵. The results of the trim are shown in Figure 8.14.

TIP TIP TIP TIP TIP TIP TIP TIP TIP TIP TIP TIP TIP TIP TIP TIP TIP TIP TIP TIP TIP TIP TIP

It will be helpful if you zoom into a closer view of the Front Elevation when you are picking lines to trim. After step 8, zoom previous.

SKILL
8

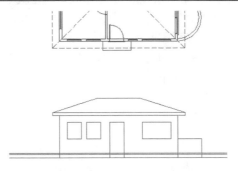

FIGURE 8.14: Trimming the bottom of the windows

Now we will draw the step and threshold, the bottom of the door, and the balcony floor.

1. Be sure Ortho is on. Drop a line down from the left corner of the threshold to a point past the ground line. Use grips to copy this line to the other corner of the threshold and to the two corners of the step (Figure 8.15a).

2. Zoom into a close view of the step and threshold. Use the Trim command to trim away the lines so that the result looks like Figure 8.15b. You'll probably have to stop and restart the command a couple of times in order to make all the trims you need. Here's one way to do it, in summarized form:

   A. Create the step first. For cutting edges, select the two lower horizontal lines and the two outer vertical lines. To trim, pick each of these lines (except the ground line) in two places above and below, or to the left and right of, the step.

   B. Trim the two inside vertical lines up to the top horizontal line.

   C. Create the threshold. For cutting edges, select the four lines that form the outside edges of the threshold. To trim, pick each of these lines (except the line that forms the top of the step) in two places above and below, or to the left and right of, the threshold.

3. When finished, zoom previous to a view of the front elevation and the bottom of the floor plan.

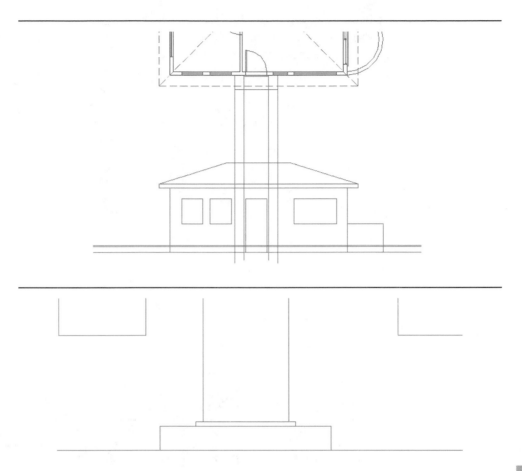

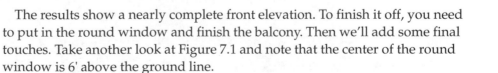

FIGURE 8.15: Dropped and copied lines for the step and threshold (a), and the finished step and threshold (b)

The results show a nearly complete front elevation. To finish it off, you need to put in the round window and finish the balcony. Then we'll add some final touches. Take another look at Figure 7.1 and note that the center of the round window is 6' above the ground line.

1. Offset the ground line 6' up.

2. Start the line command, then click the Snap to Insert button on the object Snap toolbar. Click the 2-foot window in the floor plan to start a line at the

insertion point of this block reference. With Ortho on, draw the line down through the newly offset line. Then draw a circle, using the intersection of these two lines as the center, and give it a 12-inch radius.

3. Start the Trim command and select the circle as a cutting edge, then press ↵.

4. Pick the intersecting lines passing through the circle in four places outside of the circle. The round window is finished (Figure 8.16).

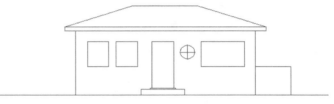

FIGURE 8.16: The completed round window

5. Make a zoom window only around the front elevation.

6. Offset the vertical line representing the balcony's right edge 6" to the left. Then offset the ground line up 10". These lines will serve as the balcony's floor and inside wall.

7. Fillet these two lines at their intersection with a radius of zero. Then trim the balcony floor line back to the right wall line of the cabin.

8. Select these two new lines. Click the Properties button.

9. In the Properties dialog box, click Linetype. Then open the linetype list and click Dashed. Close the Properties dialog and press the Esc key twice. The lines are changed to dashed lines to indicate that they are hidden in the elevation (Figure 8.17).

10. Zoom previous twice to a view of the completed front elevation with the entire floor plan. Save this drawing as Cabin08a.

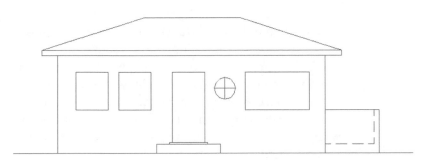

FIGURE 8.17: The completed balcony

Finishing Touches

You have gotten all the information you can from the floor plan to help you with the front elevation. You may, however, want to add some detail to enhance the appearance of the elevation.

1. Try zooming in and adding detail to the windows and door, and placing an extra step leading to the front step. Figure 8.18 shows an example. Yours can be different.

2. Zoom previous to a full view of your drawing when finished.

3. Save this drawing as Cabin08b.

SKILL
8

FIGURE 8.18: The Front Elevation with detail added

Generating the Other Elevations

In a full set of construction drawings for a building—drawings to be used by contractors to build the building—there will be an elevation for each side of the building. In traditional drafting, the elevations are usually drawn on separate sheets. This would require transferring measurements from one drawing to another by taping drawings next to drawings, turning the floor plan around to orient it to each elevation, and several other cumbersome techniques. You actually do about the same thing on the computer; but it is much easier to move the drawing around, and you can quickly borrow parts from one elevation that can be used in another.

Making the Rear Elevation

Because the rear elevation shares components and sizes with the front elevation, you can mirror the front elevation to the rear of the building and then make the necessary changes.

1. Open up Cabin08a. You need to change the view to include space above the floor plan for the rear elevation.

2. Use Realtime Pan to move the floor plan to the middle of the screen. Then use Realtime Zoom to zoom the view out enough to include the front elevation.

3. Start the Mirror command. Use a window to select the front elevation and press ↵.

4. Be sure Ortho is turned on. For the mirror line, select the Midpoint Osnap and pick the right edge line of the roof in the floor plan.

5. Hold the crosshair cursor directly to the right of the point you just picked (Figure 8.19a) and pick another point. At the Delete source objects? [Yes/No]<N> prompt, press ↵ to accept the default of No. The front elevation is mirrored to the rear of the cabin (Figure 8.19b). You can now make the necessary changes to the rear elevation so that it correctly describes the rear of the cabin. But you may find it easier to work if the view is right-side up.

6. Click View ➤ Display ➤ UCS Icon ➤ On to make the User Coordinate System icon visible. (We turned it off in Skill 5.) Take a look at the icon for a moment. The two arrows in the icon show the positive X and Y directions

and the *W* means that the current user coordinate system is the *World Coordinate System*, which is the default system for all AutoCAD drawings. The orientation of the icon can be changed.

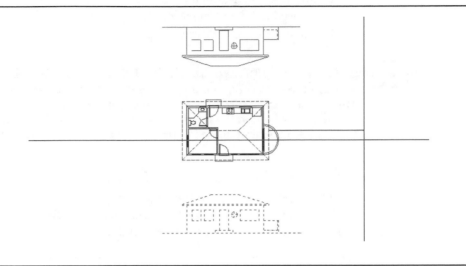

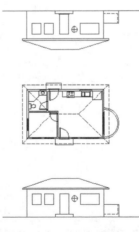

FIGURE 8.19: Specifying a mirror line (a), and the result (b)

7. Type **ucs ↵ z ↵ 180 ↵**. This will rotate the icon to an upside-down position. The *W* disappears, meaning that we are no longer using the default coordinate system.

8. Type **plan** ↵ to activate the *Plan Command*. At the Enter an option [Current ucs/Ucs/World]<Current>: prompt, press ↵. The entire drawing is rotated 180°. And the mirrored front elevation, which will eventually be the back elevation, is now right-side-up. Note that the UCS icon is now oriented the way it used to be, but the *W* in the icon is gone. This signals that the current UCS is no longer the World UCS.

NOTE NOTE NOTE NOTE NOTE NOTE NOTE NOTE NOTE NOTE NOTE NOTE NOTE NOTE NOTE

You used the UCS command to reorient the UCS icon relative to the drawing. Then you used the *current* option of the Plan command to reorient the drawing on the screen so that the positive *X* and *Y* directions of the current user coordinate system are directed to the right and upwards, respectively.

9. Use Realtime Zoom to zoom out enough to bring the outermost lines of the drawing slightly in from the edge of the drawing area. Then use Zoom Window to zoom in so that the floor plan and mirrored elevation fill the screen (Figure 8.20). Now you can work on the rear elevation.

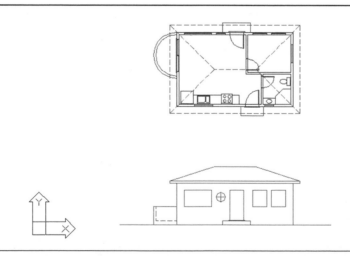

FIGURE 8.20:   The cabin drawing rotated 180° and zoomed in

Revising the Rear Elevation

A brief inspection will tell us that the roof, balcony, and building wall lines need no changes. The windows and step need revisions, as do the door and threshold:

• The round window and one of the 3-foot windows need to be deleted.

- The two remaining windows need resizing and repositioning.
- The door, threshold, and step need repositioning.
- The step needs resizing.

These tasks can be accomplished quickly by using commands with which you are now familiar.

1. Erase the round window and one of the 3-foot windows.

2. Erase the sides of the remaining windows (Figure 8.21a).

3. Drop lines down from the jambs of the two windows in the back wall of the floor plan, past the bottoms of the windows in elevation (Figure 8.21b).

4. Extend the horizontal window lines that need to meet the dropped lines, and trim all lines that need to be trimmed.

5. Use a similar strategy to relocate and resize the step. The door and threshold can be moved into position by using point filters or by dropping a guideline. Use zoom window and zoom previous as needed. The finished rear elevation looks like Figure 8.21c.

6. You need to save the User Coordinate System (UCS) you used to work on this elevation so that you can quickly return to it in the future, from the World coordinate system, or any other coordinate system you may be in. Type **ucs** ↵ **s** ↵. For the UCS name, type **rear_elev** ↵. This will allow you to recall it if you need to work on this elevation again.

NOTE NOTE NOTE NOTE NOTE NOTE NOTE NOTE NOTE NOTE NOTE NOTE NOTE NOTE NOTE

You can save any UCS in this way. The World coordinate system is a permanent part of all drawings, so it never needs saving.

SKILL
8

7. You also can save the view to be able to quickly recall it. Click View ➤ Named Views. The View Control dialog box comes up. (You can also start the View command by typing **v** ↵.)

8. Click New. The New View dialog box appears.

9. In the New Name text box, type **rear_elev**. Select the Current Display radio button and click OK. Back in the View Control dialog box, **rear_elev** appears in the list of views. Click OK again. Now you can restore the drawing to its original orientation with the front elevation below the floor plan and right-side-up.

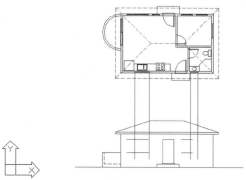

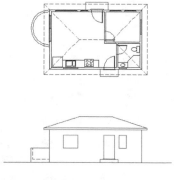

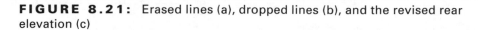

FIGURE 8.21:   Erased lines (a), dropped lines (b), and the revised rear elevation (c)

Any view of your drawing can be named and saved, then recalled later. When you have done this, you can quickly restore a previously used view of your drawing.

10. Type **ucs** ↵ ↵. This sets the original and default UCS—called the *World UCS*—as the current UCS. Now you need to re-orient the drawing to the plan view in the World UCS.

11. Type **plan** ↵ ↵. This zooms to extents and displays a plan view of the drawing with the *X* and *Y* positive directions in their default orientation.

We created a new UCS as a tool to flip the drawing upside down without changing its orientation with respect to the World Coordinate System. You'll get a chance to use UCSs in another way in Appendix A: *A Look at Drawing in 3D*. But for now, we'll use it again to create the right and left elevations.

Making the Left and Right Elevations

The left and right elevations can be generated using techniques similar to those you have been using for the front and back elevations. You need to be able to transfer the heights of building components from the front elevation to one of the side elevations. There are several ways of doing this: One is almost identical to the traditional, hand-drafting procedure. We'll use this method to create the right elevation.

1. Use Realtime Zoom to zoom out slightly, then zoom into a view of the floor plan and front elevation. Pan the drawing so that the floor plan and front elevation are on the left part of the drawing area. You need to transfer the height data from the front elevation to the right elevation. To insure that the right elevation is the same distance from the floor plan as the front elevation, we'll use a 45-degree line that extends down and to the right from the right-most and lower-most lines in the floor plan.

2. Turn Polar Tracking on and be sure it's set to 45°. Also make sure that the Otrack button on the Status bar is toggled on. Turn Ortho off. Then set the Quadrant and Endpoint Osnaps to running.

3. Start the Line command. Move the crosshair cursor to the right edge of the outside arc of the balcony in the floor plan. Hold it there for a moment. A cross will appear at the Quadrant point. (Don't click yet.)

4. Turn Ortho off. Move the crosshair cursor to the lower-right corner of the step and hold it there until a cross appears at that point. (Don't click yet.)

5. Now move the crosshair cursor to a point directly to the right of the corner of the step and directly under the right quadrant point of the balcony (Figure 8.22a). Vertical and horizontal tracking lines appear and intersect where the crosshair cursor is positioned, and a small x appears at the intersection. A tracking tooltip will also appear.

6. When all this has happened, click. A line is started at this point.

7. Move the crosshair cursor down, away from this point, and to the right at a negative 45-degree angle (or a positive 315-degree angle). When the 45-degree polar tracking path appears, type **35'** ↵. Press ↵ again. The diagonal reference line is completed (Figure 8.22b).

8. Turn off Quadrant as a running Osnap and turn Ortho on. Draw a line from the right endpoint of the roof ridge in the front elevation to the right, almost to the right edge of the drawing area. Press ↵.

9. Copy this line to the endpoint of each object that has a height that needs to be transferred to the right elevation (Figure 8.23a). Use the zooming tools if you need to get a closer view, and don't worry about transferring the height line for the threshold.

10. Start the Trim command and select the 45-degree line as a cutting edge. Press ↵. You'll use a selection fence to select the height lines to trim.

11. Be sure Ortho is off, then type **f** ↵. Click the Snap to None Osnap button and pick a point below the ground line and to the right of the 45-degree line. Click the Snap to None button again. Then move the crosshair cursor up and to the left until a dashed line appears to the right of, and approximately parallel to, the 45-degree line and crosses all of the height lines (Figure 8.23b). Then pick a point.

12. Press ↵. All lines are trimmed (Figure 8.23c). Press ↵ to end the Trim command. If you zoomed in to perform this operation, zoom previous now.

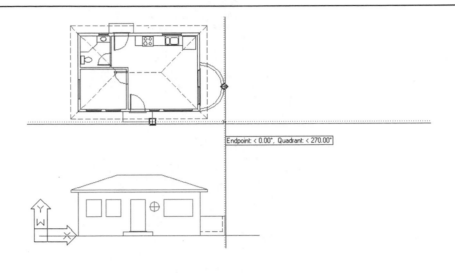

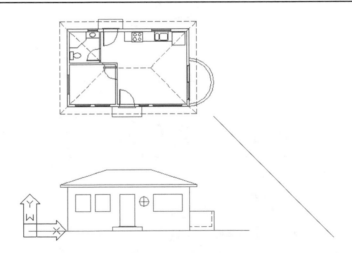

FIGURE 8.22: Starting a diagonal reference line with tracking points (a), and the completed diagonal line (b)

NOTE NOTE NOTE NOTE NOTE NOTE NOTE NOTE NOTE NOTE NOTE NOTE NOTE NOTE

The *selection fence* is a line of one or more segments that you draw across objects to select them. It is similar to the lines of a crossing window in that any objects crossed by the fence line segments are selected.

SKILL
8

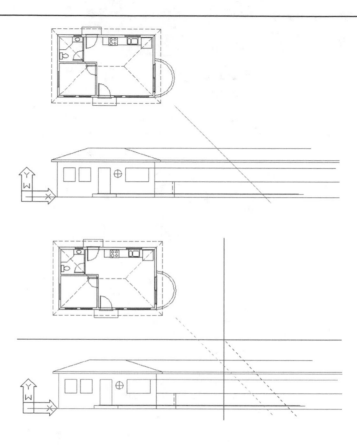

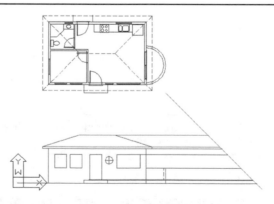

FIGURE 8.23: Creating the horizontal height lines (a), using a fence to select height lines to trim (b), and the trimmed height lines (c)

13. Use Realtime Zoom to zoom out a little. Use the Mirror command to mirror the height lines around the diagonal transfer line (Figure 8.24a).

14. With Ortho on, draw a horizontal line from the upper-right corner of the back step in the floor plan to the right edge of the screen. Then extend the mirrored height lines to this new line (Figure 8.24b). This transfers the height lines "around the corner" where they can now be used to construct the right elevation.

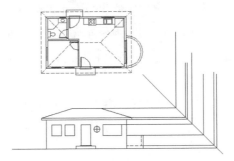

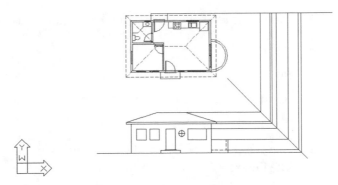

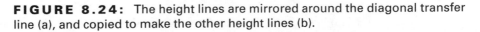

FIGURE 8.24: The height lines are mirrored around the diagonal transfer line (a), and copied to make the other height lines (b).

SKILL
8

TIP TIP TIP TIP TIP TIP TIP TIP TIP TIP TIP TIP TIP TIP TIP TIP TIP TIP TIP TIP TIP TIP

If you're working on a small monitor, you may have to do some extra zooming in and out that isn't mentioned in these steps.

The rest of the process for creating the right elevation is straightforward and uses routines you have just learned. Here's a summary of the steps:

1. Set up a new UCS for the right elevation. (Type **ucs** ↵ **z** ↵ **90** ↵.) Use the Plan command to rotate the drawing to the current UCS.

2. Drop lines from the floor plan across the height lines in the right elevation.

3. Trim these lines as required and add any necessary lines.

4. Erase the original height lines from the front elevation, and the diagonal transfer line.

5. Name and save the UCS and view.

The left elevation can be created from a mirrored image of the right elevation. Here are the steps:

1. Mirror the right elevation to the opposite side.

2. Set up a UCS for the left elevation. Use Plan to rotate the drawing to the current UCS.

3. Revise the elevation to match the left side of the cabin.

4. Name and save the UCS and view.

When you have completed all elevations:

1. Return to the World Coordinate System.

2. Call up the Plan view.

3. Zoom out slightly for a full view of all elevations. The drawing will look like Figure 8.25a.

4. Save the drawing as Cabin08c.

Once an elevation has been drawn, it may be rotated to the same orientation as the front elevation and moved to another area of the drawing. The four elevations for the cabin could all be displayed next to each other as in Figure 8.25b.

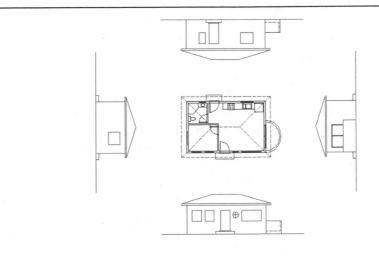

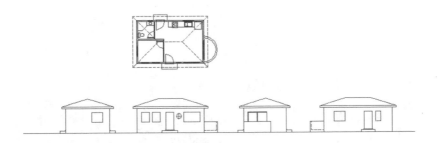

FIGURE 8.25: The finished elevations (a), and the elevations in line (b)

Drawing Scale Considerations

This last view brings up several questions: How will these drawings best fit on a
page? How many pages will it take to illustrate these drawings? What size sheet
should be used? At what scale will the drawing be printed? In traditional hand
drafting, the first line could not be drawn without answers to some of these questions. You have completed a great deal of the drawing on the computer without

having to make decisions about scale and sheet size because in AutoCAD you draw in real-world scale or full-scale. This means that when you tell AutoCAD to draw a 10-foot line, it draws it 10-feet long. If you inquire how long the line is, AutoCAD will tell you that it is 10-feet long. Your current view of the line may be to a certain scale, but that changes every time you zoom in or out. The line is stored in the computer as 10-feet long.

Decisions about scale need to be made when you are choosing the sheet size, putting text and dimensions on the drawing, or using hatch patterns and non-continuous linetypes. Since we have a dashed linetype in the drawing, we had to make a choice about scale in Skill 6, when we assigned a linetype scale factor of 24 to the drawing. That number was chosen because when the drawing consisted of only the floor plan and the view was zoomed as large as possible while still having all objects visible, the scale of the drawing at was about 1/2" = 1'-0". That scale has a true ratio of 1:24, or a scale factor of 24. We will get further into scale factors and true ratios of scales in the next skill.

If you look at your Cabin08c drawing with all elevations visible on the screen, the dashes in the dashed lines look like they may be too small, so you may need to increase the linetype scale factor. Don't worry about that now. Beginning with Skill 9, and right on through the end of the book, we will need to make decisions about scale each step of the way.

Interior Elevations

Interior elevations are constructed using the same techniques you have learned for the exterior elevations. Lines are dropped from a floor plan through offset height lines and then trimmed away. Interior elevations usually include fixtures and built-in cabinets and shelves, and are used to show finishes. Each elevation will consist of one wall and may include a side view of items on an adjacent wall if the item extends into the corner. Not all walls are shown in elevation—usually just the ones that require special treatment or illustrate special building components. You might use one elevation to show a wall that has a window and to describe how the window is treated or finished, then assume that all other windows in the building will be treated in the same way unless noted otherwise. A few examples of interior wall elevations are shown in Figure 8.26. Try to identify which walls of the cabin each one represents.

For some practice with interior elevations, try drawing one or two elevations, using Figure 8.26 as a guide. You can measure the heights and sizes of various fixtures in your own home or office as a guide. Save what you draw as Cabin8d.

In the next skill, you will learn how to use hatch patterns and fills to enhance floor plans and elevations.

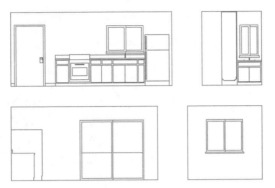

FIGURE 8.26: Samples of interior elevations of the cabin

Are You Experienced?

Now you can ...

- ☑ draw an exterior elevation from a floor plan
- ☑ use grips to copy objects
- ☑ add detail to an elevation
- ☑ set up, name, and save a User Coordinate System and a new view
- ☑ transfer height lines from one elevation to another
- ☑ move and rotate elevations

Working with Hatches and Fills

- ⊖ Creating a predefined hatch pattern and applying it to a drawing
- ⊖ Setting up and applying user-defined hatch patterns
- ⊖ Modifying the scale and shape of a hatch pattern
- ⊖ Specifying the origin of a hatch pattern
- ⊖ Filling an enclosed area with a solid color

Hatches can be abstract patterns of lines, or they can resemble the building material that covers a surface. To give texture to an AutoCAD drawing, a drafter will hatch in areas or fill them in with a solid color. Solid *fills* in a drawing can give a shaded effect when printed using a half-screen, resulting in a look quite different from the solid appearance in the AutoCAD drawing on the screen.

In a floor plan, the inside of full-height walls are often hatched or filled to distinguish them from low walls. Wooden or tile floors can be hatched to a parquet or tile pattern. In a site plan, hatches are used to distinguish between areas with different ground covers, such as grass, gravel, or concrete. When working with elevations, almost any surface can be hatched to show shading and shadows, and realistic hatch patterns can be used to illustrate surface materials, such as concrete, stucco, or shingles. Hatches and fills are widely used in details as a tool to aid in clear communication.

For the purposes of learning how to hatch and fill areas, you will start with some of the visible surfaces in the front elevation. Then you will move to the floor plan and hatch the floors, and put hatch patterns and fills in the walls. The *Hatch command* will be used for all hatching and filling. It is a complex command with many options.

A key part of a hatch pattern is the boundary of the pattern. The area being hatched is defined through a complex procedure in which AutoCAD searches the drawing for lines or objects to serve as the hatch boundary.

Hatching the Front Elevation

Hatches and fills generally need to be on their own layers so they can be frozen without making other objects also invisible. We will begin the exercise by creating new layers for the hatches and assigning colors to them.

1. Open the Cabin08a drawing. It should contain the floor plan and front elevation only. Turn off any running Object Snaps and turn off the UCS icon.

2. Set up three new layers as follows:

Layer Name	Color
Hatch-elev-brown	42
Hatch-elev-gray	Light gray (8)
Hatch-elev-black	Black (White) (7)

3. Make the Hatch-elev-gray layer current. Now, any new objects we create will be assigned to this layer.

4. Start the Hatch command. You can select the Hatch button from the Draw toolbar, pick Draw ➤ Hatch, or type **h** ↵. The Boundary Hatch dialog box comes up (Figure 9.1). You will use this dialog box to choose a pattern, set up the pattern's properties, and determine the method of specifying the boundary of the area to be hatched. The Quick tab should be active. If it's not, click the tab. Predefined and ANSI31 should be displayed on the Type and Pattern drop-down lists, respectively. If not, open the lists and select these options.

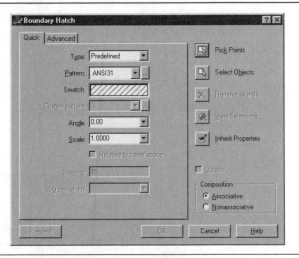

FIGURE 9.1: The Boundary Hatch dialog box

5. Move to the right of the Pattern drop-down list and click the Browse button. The Hatch Pattern Palette dialog box comes up (Figure 9.2). Of the four tabs, ANSI will be active and the ANSI31 pattern will be highlighted.

6. Click the Other Predefined tab. Find the AR-RROOF pattern and click it, then click OK. Back in the Boundary Hatch dialog box, note that AR-RROOF has replaced ANSI31 in the Pattern drop-down list. A new pattern is displayed in the Swatch preview box, which is below the Pattern drop-down list (Figure 9.3). The Scale and Angle settings can be changed in their drop-down lists, which are below the Swatch preview box. In the Angle drop-down list, the preset angle of 0.00 is fine; but you need to adjust the Scale setting.

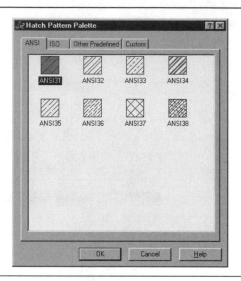

FIGURE 9.2: The Hatch Pattern Palette dialog box

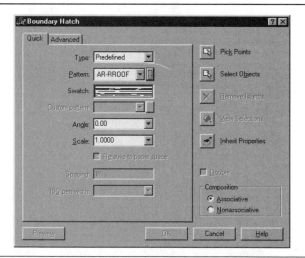

FIGURE 9.3: The Boundary Hatch dialog box with the AR-RROOF pattern chosen

7. In the Scale drop-down list, delete 1.0000 and type **6**. The scale is now displayed as 6.000, which means 1:6.

The Scale drop-down list contains preset scale factors that range from 0.2500 to 2.0000. To set the scale to 6.0000, you have to type it in. Once you do that, however, 6.0000 is added to the drop-down list.

8. Move to the upper-right corner of the dialog box and click the Pick Points button. You will return to the drawing.

9. In the elevation view, click in the middle of the roof area. The lines that form the boundary of the roof area ghost, forming an outline of the area to be hatched (Figure 9.4).

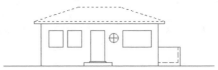

FIGURE 9.4: The roof's boundary is selected.

10. Press ↵. You are returned to the Boundary Hatch dialog box. Click the Preview button in the lower-left corner. In the preview drawing, take a look at how the hatch will appear, then right-click to return to the Boundary Hatch dialog box.

11. Click OK. You are returned to the drawing. The hatch is now placed in the roof area (Figure 9.5).

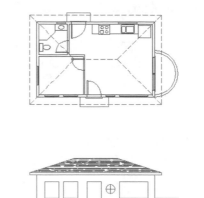

FIGURE 9.5: The finished hatch pattern in the roof area

12. Zoom into a view of just the front elevation. Note how the appearance of the hatch pattern changes with the new view.

Looking at Hatch Patterns

Let's take a short tour through the available patterns.

1. Type **h** ↵.

2. In the Boundary Hatch dialog box, be sure that the Quick tab is active. Then click the Browse button that is next to the Pattern drop-down list. The Hatch Pattern Palette dialog box comes up.

3. Make the Other Predefined tab active if it is not already. Look at the list of hatch pattern names. There are 11 names beginning with *AR-*, including the one that we just used. These patterns have been designed to look like architectural and building materials, hence the AR prefix. In addition to the roof pattern we just used, there are several masonry wall patterns, a couple of floor patterns, and one pattern for concrete, shakes, and sand.

4. Scroll down the list and observe the other non-AR patterns. They are geometrical patterns, some of which represent various materials by convention.

5. Click the ANSI tab and take a look at a few of the ANSI patterns. These are abstract line patterns developed by the American National Standards Institute and are widely used by public and private offices in the United States.

6. Click the ISO tab. These are also abstract line patterns developed by another organization—the International Standards Organization. The Custom tab will be empty unless custom hatch patterns have been loaded into AutoCAD.

7. Click Cancel in the Hatch Pattern Palette dialog box. Click Cancel again to close the Boundary Hatch dialog box.

As you work with hatch patterns, you will need to adjust the scale factor for each pattern so the patterns will have an appropriate appearance when the drawing is printed. The AR patterns are drawn to be used with the scale factor set approximately to the default of one-to-one (displayed as 1.0000), and should only need minor adjustment. However, the pattern you just chose for the roof is an AR pattern, and its scale factor needed to be changed to 6.0000. The AR-RROOF pattern is somewhat anomalous compared to the rest of the AR patterns and requires this unusually large adjustment.

TIP TIP TIP TIP TIP TIP TIP TIP TIP TIP TIP TIP TIP TIP TIP TIP TIP TIP TIP TIP TIP TIP TIP

When using one of the AR patterns, leave the scale factor at 1.0000 until you preview the hatch; then you can make changes. This rule also applies to the 14 ISO patterns displayed on the ISO tab of the Hatch Pattern Palette.

For the rest of the patterns, you will need to assign a scale factor that imitates the true ratio of the scale at which you expect to print the drawing. The table below gives the true ratios of some of the standard scales used in architecture and construction.

TABLE 9.1: Standard Scales and Their Corresponding Ratios

Scale	True Scale Factor
1"=1'-0"	12
1/2"=1'-0"	24
1/4"=1'-0"	48
1/8"=1'-0"	96
1/16"=1'-0"	192

SKILL
9

Some confusion arises from the fact that the scale is traditionally written by mixing inches with feet in the expression. For example, the third scale in the table, commonly called "quarter inch scale," shows that a quarter inch equals one foot. A True Ratio of this scale would have to express the relationship using the same units, as in 1/4"=12". Simplifying this expression to have no fractions, you would translate it to say 1"=48". This is how you arrive at the True Scale Factor of 48, or True Ratio of 1:48.

As you continue through the skill, take special note of the various scale factors used for different hatch patterns.

Hatching the Rest of the Front Elevation

You will apply hatches to the foundation, front door, and front wall. Then we'll work with some special effects.

Using a Concrete Hatch on the Foundation

For the foundation hatch, you'll work on the same layer.

1. To represent the top of the foundation, draw lines from the upper-left and upper-right corners of the step to the edges of the building (Figure 9.6a).

2. Start the Hatch command. Then click the Browse button next to the Pattern drop-down list in the Boundary Hatch dialog box.

3. Activate the Other Predefined tab. Find and select the AR-CONC pattern and click OK.

4. Open the Scale drop-down list and select 1.0000.

5. Click Pick Points. Then, in the drawing, click once in each rectangle representing the foundation. The borders of these areas will ghost. Press ↵.

6. Click Preview, right-click, and then click OK. The concrete hatch pattern is applied to the foundation surfaces (Figure 9.6b).

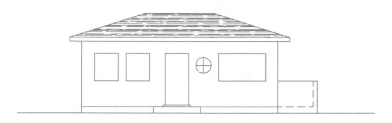

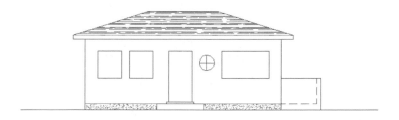

FIGURE 9.6: The front elevation with foundation lines drawn (a), and the resulting hatches in place (b)

NOTE NOTE NOTE NOTE NOTE NOTE NOTE NOTE NOTE NOTE NOTE NOTE NOTE NOTE NOTE

After you select the Pick Points button in the Boundary Hatch dialog box, pick a point in the area to be hatched, and AutoCAD finds the boundary of that area and displays it in ghosted form.

Hatching the Front Door and Wall

For the front door, we'll use a standard hatch pattern: ANSI31. This is the default pattern when you first use the Hatch command, but now the default pattern is the last one used.

1. Start the Hatch command and select the Browse button.

2. Activate the ANSI tab. Select ANSI31 and click OK.

3. In the Scale text box, type **18**. Then click Pick Points.

4. Click in the middle of the door. The edges of the door and door sill ghost. Press ↵.

5. Click Preview, right-click, then click OK. The door is hatched (Figure 9.7).

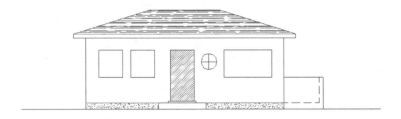

FIGURE 9.7: Hatching the door

6. Change the current layer to Hatch-elev-brown.

7. Start the Hatch command and go through the same process to apply a hatch to the wall. This time you will use the AR-RSHKE pattern, which looks like wooden shingles (often called shakes). Here is a summary of the steps:

   A. Click the Browse button.

   B. Activate the Other Predefined tab, select the AR-RSHKE pattern, and click OK.

   C. Set the Scale to **1** and click Pick Points.

   D. Pick anywhere on the front wall that's not inside a window.

   E. Press ↵. Click Preview, right-click, then click OK.

The wall is hatched (Figure 9.8).

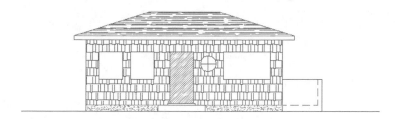

FIGURE 9.8: The hatching of the front wall is completed.

Using a Solid Fill Hatch

The windows will be hatched with a solid fill. It operates the same way as the other hatches you have been using, except that you don't have a choice of scale or angle.

1. Make Hatch-elev-black the current layer.

2. Start the Hatch command. Then click the Browse button. Make sure the Other Predefined tab is active and select the first pattern: SOLID. Click OK. Back in the Hatch Boundary dialog box, note that the text boxes for Scale and Angle are not available. These don't apply to solid fills.

3. Click Pick Points. In the drawing, select a point in the middle of each of the four windows. The round window will have to be clicked in four times because of the mullions (the separators between the panes). Press ↵.

4. Click Preview, right-click, then click OK. The windows have a solid black (or white) fill (Figure 9.9).

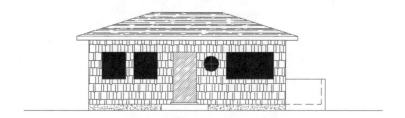

FIGURE 9.9: The windows with a solid fill hatch

Special Effects

To finish the Front Elevation, you will learn how to show shading and work a little with a curved surface.

Applying Shading to a Surface

When shaded surfaces are illustrated on an exterior elevation, they give a three-dimensional quality to the surface. We'll put some additional hatching at the top portion of the wall to illustrate the shading caused by the roof overhang.

You need to hatch the top 2'-6" of the wall with the same hatch that was put on the front door. To determine the boundary line of the hatch, you need to freeze the layer that has the shake pattern. Then you will create a guideline to serve as the lower boundary of the hatch.

1. Be sure the Hatch-elev-black layer is still current. Then freeze the Hatch-elev-brown layer.

2. Offset the soffit line of the roof down 2'-6" (Figure 9.10a).

3. Start the Hatch command. In the Boundary Hatch dialog box, click the Inherit Properties button. You are returned to the drawing. The cursor is now a pick box accompanied by a paintbrush, telling you that AutoCAD is in Select Hatch Mode.

4. Pick the hatch pattern on the door. The command window will display the name, scale, and rotation of the hatch pattern you picked. Now, the prompt is `Select internal point:`.

5. Pick a point on the wall above the offset line but not inside the door or windows. Click the door above the offset line. The boundary lines ghost (Figure 9.10b). Press ↵.

6. In the Boundary Hatch dialog box, change the scale from 18 to 16. Click Preview, press ↵, and click OK. The pattern is applied to the upper part of the wall.

7. Thaw the Hatch-elev-brown layer and erase the offset guideline. The drawing will look like Figure 9.10c.

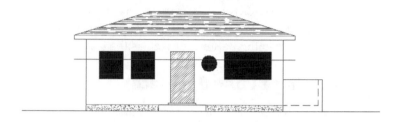

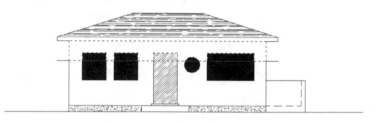

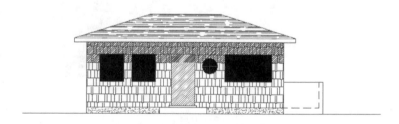

FIGURE 9.10: Applying a hatch to a shaded area: drawing a guideline (a), finding the hatch boundary (b), and the resulting effect (c)

SKILL
9

You erased the offset guideline because there is no edge on the wall at the bottom of the shaded area. And you used the Inherit Properties button to set up a hatch pattern exactly like one that was already existing in the drawing. You can also use the List command on hatch patterns to find out the name, scale, and rotation of an existing pattern, as well as the layer the hatch is on.

Indicating a Curved Surface

The curved outside wall of the balcony appears as a rectangle in the front elevation. We need to use a pattern that will increase in density in the X direction as we move around the curve. Vertical straight lines will do this job if we space them properly. We'll use the floor plan to help us to do that.

1. Make the Hatch-elev-brown current. Use Realtime Zoom to zoom the view out until you can see the balcony in the floor plan.

2. Use the Line command with Quadrant Osnap to start a line from the right extremity of the outside balcony wall. Use Endpoint Osnap to end the line at the top-right corner of the balcony in the elevation (Figure 9.11).

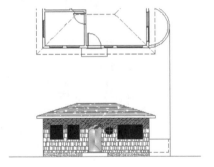

FIGURE 9.11: A line is dropped from the balcony in the floor plan to the elevation.

3. Freeze the Headers, Roof, and Steps layers. Use Zoom Window to zoom into the lower half of the balcony in the floor plan. Set Endpoint snap to be running, then use Center Osnap to draw a line from the center point of the balcony arc, down to the lower-right corner of the building (Figure 9.12a).

4. At the Command: prompt, click the Array button on the Modify toolbar.

5. Select the line you just drew, then press ↵.

6. At the `Enter the type of array [Rectangular/Polar] <R>:` prompt, type **p** ↵.

7. At the `Specify center point of array:` prompt, click the upper end-point of the line that you have selected.

8. When the `Enter the number of items in the array:` prompt appears, type **10** ↵.

9. At the `Specify angle to fill (+=360, -=cw) <360>:` prompt, type **90** ↵.

10. When asked whether to rotate arrayed objects, press ↵ to accept the default of Yes. The line is arrayed around the lower half of the balcony (Figure 9.12b).

11. Set Endpoint Osnap to running. Then use grips again to copy/move the dropped line to the endpoint of each line that was just arrayed. Here is a summary of the steps:

    A. Click the dropped line to activate grips.

    B. Click the grip on the upper endpoint.

    C. Press the space bar once. This switches the active command from the default Stretch command to the Move command.

    D. Type **c** ↵. This activates the Copy options for the Move command.

    E. Click each spoke line (like the spoke of a wheel) near its outer end-point, but before the point where the spoke line crosses the inside bal-cony arc. Don't copy the line to the vertical spoke line you first drew.

    F. Type **x** ↵, then press Esc twice.

    The results will look like Figure 9.13a.

12. Erase all the spoke lines and the original dropped line (Figure 9.13b).

13. Thaw the Headers, Roof, and Steps layers. Zoom previous, then zoom in close to the elevation of the balcony.

SKILL
▼ 9

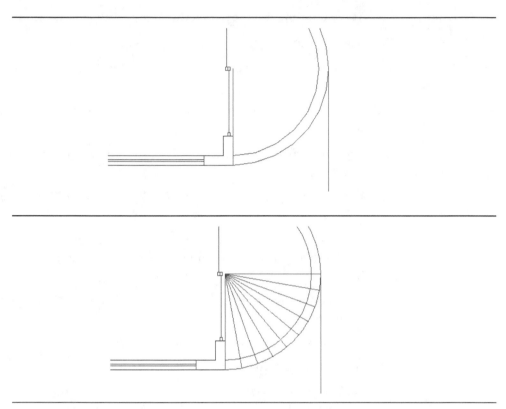

FIGURE 9.12: The line drawn from the center of the balcony (a), and the results of the polar array, (b)

14. Erase the two dashed lines that represent the floor and inside wall of the balcony. Extend the five dropped lines, which don't yet reach down to the ground line, until they do. Trim all the dropped lines to the top line of the balcony and the ground line (Figure 9.14).

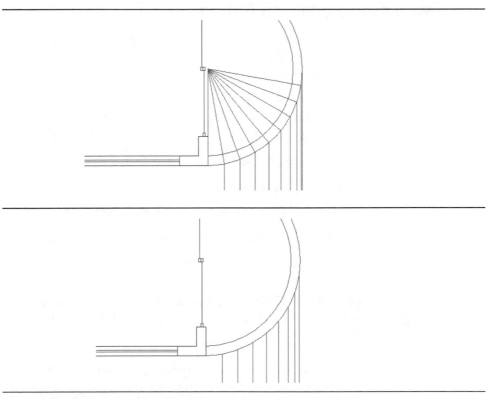

FIGURE 9.13: The drop line is copied to the ends of the spoke lines (a), and the spoke lines and first dropped line are erased (b).

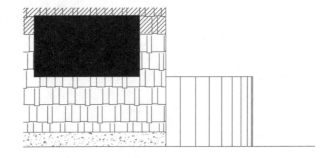

FIGURE 9.14: The balcony in elevation after erasing, extending, and trimming lines

Modifying a Hatch Pattern

You won't know for sure if the hatch patterns will look right until you print the drawing, but you can at least see how they look together now that you've finished hatching the elevation.

1. Zoom previous and use Realtime Pan to have both the floor plan and elevation on the screen (Figure 9.15a). The roof hatch could be a little denser. You can use the *Modify Hatch command* to change the hatch scale.

2. Click Modify ➢ Hatch.

3. Select the roof hatch pattern.

4. In the Hatch Edit dialog box, change the scale from 6.000 to 4.000.

5. Click OK. The roof hatch pattern is denser now (Figure 9.15b).

6. Save this drawing as Cabin09a.

NOTE NOTE NOTE NOTE NOTE NOTE NOTE NOTE NOTE NOTE NOTE NOTE NOTE NOTE

You can use the Modify Hatch command to change the pattern, scale, or angle of an existing hatch.

If you worked on putting more detail in the front elevation in Skill 8, and saved this as Cabin08b, you can go through the exercise again with that drawing. Then you can see how more detail and hatch patterns enhance the way the elevations appear. Figure 9.16 shows the front elevation with hatch patterns and more detail in the door and windows. If you have the time to do any hatching on this drawing, save your work as Cabin09b.

FIGURE 9.15: Full view of the drawing with the hatching completed for the front elevation (a), and the same view with the roof hatch modified (b)

FIGURE 9.16:   Cabin09b with the front elevation hatched

Using Hatches in the Floor Plan

In the floor plan, hatches can be used to fill in the walls or to indicate various kinds of floor surfaces. We'll start with the floors.

Hatching the Floors

So far you have used only predefined hatch patterns—the 72 patterns that come with AutoCAD. There is also a *user-defined pattern*, which is a series of parallel lines that can be set at any spacing and angle. If you want to illustrate square floor tile, the user-defined pattern also has a Double option, which uses two sets of parallel lines, one perpendicular to the other, resulting in a tiled effect.

The User-Defined Hatch Pattern

You'll use the user-defined pattern for a couple of rooms, then return to the pre-defined patterns.

1.   With Cabin09a open, zoom into the floor plan and be sure the Headers and Doors layers are thawed and visible. The header lines can be used to help form a boundary line across an entryway to a room and to keep the hatch pattern from extending to another room.

2.   With the floor plan in full view, zoom into the bathroom and freeze the Roof layer. Even if the roof lines are dashed, they will still form a boundary to a hatch.

3. Create a new layer called Hatch-plan-floor. Assign it color 142 and make it current. (If you only have 16 colors, choose any color.)

4. Type **h** ↵ to start the Hatch command. Be sure the Quick tab is active.

5. Open the Type drop-down list and select User-defined. The list closes and User-defined replaces Predefined as the current Pattern Type. The Pattern and Scale drop-down lists are not available, but the Spacing text box is.

6. In the Spacing text box, change 1" to 9". Click in the checkbox next to Double to activate it. Then click Pick Points.

7. Back in the drawing, be sure no Osnaps are running. Then click a point in the bathroom floor, not touching the fixture lines or the door. Click the floor between the door swing and the door, being careful to not touch the door. Press ↵.

8. Click Preview. The tiled hatch pattern should fill the bathroom floor and stop at the header, while not going onto the door or fixtures. If the tile pattern looks OK, press ↵. Then click OK (Figure 9.17).

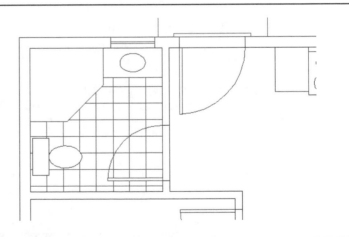

FIGURE 9.17: The tiled hatch pattern in place

Note that in the User-defined pattern, there is no scale factor to worry about. You simply set the distance between lines in the Spacing text box.

WARNING WARNING WARNING WARNING WARNING WARNING WARNING WARNING

If you can't get the Hatch command to hatch the desired area, some of the lines serving as the hatch boundary may not have been drawn accurately. This may prevent AutoCAD from being able to find the boundary that you intend to use. Zoom into the areas where objects meet and check to see that they really do meet where they should.

Controlling the Origin of the Hatch Pattern

Often a designer will want to lay out the tile pattern such that the pattern is centered in the room. To do this, the tiles are set to start in the center of the room and move out to the edges, where they are cut to fit. We'll use the *Snapbase* setting to set this up in the bedroom.

1. Use Realtime Pan to slide the drawing up until the bedroom occupies the screen. Use Realtime Zoom to zoom out if you need to.

2. Draw a diagonal line from one corner of the room to the opposite corner (Figure 9.18a). Use Endpoint Osnap to be accurate.

3. Type **snapbase** ↵. Activate Midpoint Osnap and select the diagonal line. This sets the origin of any subsequently created hatch patterns to be at the center of the room.

4. Erase the diagonal line and start the Hatch command. The User-defined Pattern Type is still current and the spacing is set to 9".

5. Change the spacing to 12". Be sure Double is still checked, then click Pick Points.

6. In the drawing, pick a point anywhere in the middle of the bedroom and between the door swing and the door, similar to what you did in the bathroom. Press ↵.

7. Click Preview. Inspect the drawing to see if the hatch looks all right, then press ↵. Click OK. The hatch of 12-inch tiles is placed in the bedroom (Figure 9.18b). Note how the pattern is centered left-to-right and top-to-bottom.

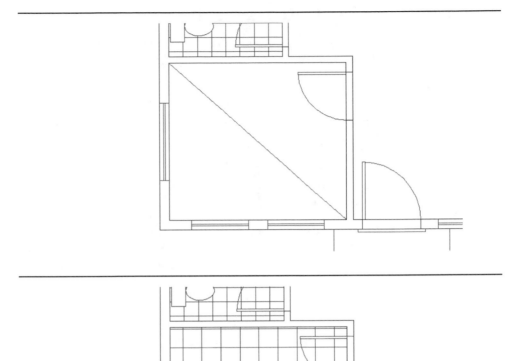

FIGURE 9.18: Hatching the bedroom: the diagonal line (a), and the finished, centered hatch (b)

The default setting for Snapbase is 0,0 or the origin of the drawing. Each time you change this setting, all subsequent hatch patterns will use the new setting as their origin. For most hatches, the origin isn't important, but if you need to control the location of tiles or specific points of other hatch patterns, you can reset the Snapbase setting before you create the hatch.

Finishing the Hatches for the Floors

To finish hatching the floors, you'll use a parquet pattern—from the set of predefined patterns—in the living room and kitchen, and another user-defined pattern on the balcony.

1. Use Realtime Pan and Zoom to re-adjust the view so that it includes the living room, kitchen, and balcony.

2. Start the Hatch command and set the current Pattern Type to Predefined.

3. Use the Browse button and activate the Other Predefined tab. Select the AR-PARQ1 pattern. Set the scale to **1** and be sure the angle is set to zero. Then click Pick Points.

4. Pick anywhere in the living room. Then pick in between each of the door swings and doors for the front and back doors. Check the ghosted boundary line to be sure that it follows the outline of the floor. Press ↵.

5. Click Preview. The squares look a little small.

6. Press ↵. Reset the scale to **1.33**.

7. Click Preview again. This looks better. Press ↵ and click OK. The parquet pattern is placed in the living room and kitchen (Figure 9.19).

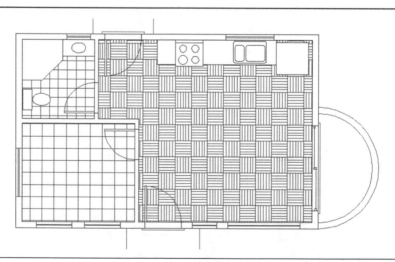

FIGURE 9.19: The parquet hatch in the living room and kitchen

8. Type **snapbase** ↵. Pick Midpoint Osnap and select the threshold line that extends across the sliding glass door opening.

9. Restart the Hatch command and set user-defined to be the pattern type.

10. Click the checkmark in the Double checkbox to uncheck it. Set the spacing to 0'6". Click Pick Points.

11. Click anywhere on the balcony floor. Press ↵.

12. Click Preview. Then press ↵ and click OK. The balcony floor is hatched with parallel lines that are 6" apart (Figure 9.20).

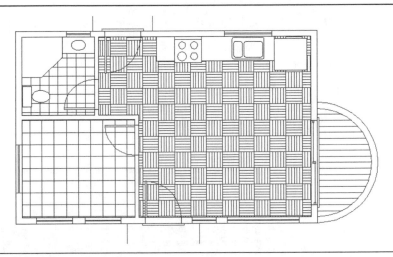

FIGURE 9.20: The user-defined hatch on the balcony floor

With the floors complete, the only components left to hatch are the walls.

Hatching the Walls in the Floor Plan

A solid fill is often used for full-height walls but not for low walls. The interior and exterior walls of the cabin are all full-height and will be hatched with a solid fill. Then you'll use a regular predefined pattern for the low balcony wall.

1. Zoom and pan to a full view of the floor plan.

2. Create a new layer called Hatch-plan-wall. Assign it the same color that you are using for the Walls layer and make this new layer current.

3. Start the Hatch command. Set the type to Predefined. Open the Pattern drop-down list and select the Solid pattern from the list.

4. Click Pick Points. In the drawing, pick in the 10 areas inside the wall and between the door and window jamb lines. Then press ↵.

5. Click Preview Hatch and look at the drawing. The fill will look a little odd because the blue boundaries of the wall line are ghosted. Check to be sure all 10 areas in the wall are properly filled, then press ↵.

6. Click OK. The walls now have a solid fill.

7. Restart the Hatch command and click Pattern.

8. Select ANSI31 for the pattern and enter a scale of **24**.

9. Select Pick Points and pick a point between the two balcony arcs. Then press ↵.

10. Click Preview, click Continue, and then click Apply. A diagonal crosshatch pattern is placed on the balcony wall (Figure 9.21).

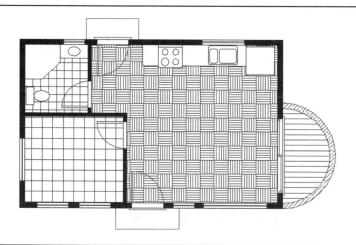

FIGURE 9.21: The hatched balcony wall

This completes the exercises for setting up and placing hatch patterns.

Modifying the Shape of Hatch Patterns

The final exercise in this chapter will be a demonstration of how hatches are *associative*. This characteristic means that a hatch pattern will automatically update when you modify the part of a drawing that is serving as the *boundary* for the pattern. You will be changing the current drawing, so before you begin making those changes, save the drawing as it is.

1. Zoom out and pan to get the floor plan and front elevation in the view. Thaw the Roof layer.

2. Save this drawing as Cabin09c. You'll use the Stretch command to modify this drawing.

3. Click the Stretch button on the Modify toolbar.

4. Pick a point above and to the right of the ridge of the roof in elevation. Drag a window down and to the left until a crossing selection window encloses the ridgeline of the roof (Figure 9.22a). Click to complete the window. Then press ↵ to finish the selection process.

5. For the base point, pick a point in the blank area to the right of the elevation.

6. Be sure Ortho is on. Hold the cursor directly above the point you picked and type **3'** ↵. The roof is now steeper and the hatch pattern has expanded to fill the new roof area (Figure 9.22b).

7. Save this drawing as Cabin09d.

Hatches are a necessary part of many drawings. You have seen a few of the possibilities AutoCAD offers for using them in plans and elevations. For a more in-depth treatment on how they can be created and controlled, see *Mastering AutoCAD 2000* by George Omura (Sybex, 1999).

SKILL
9

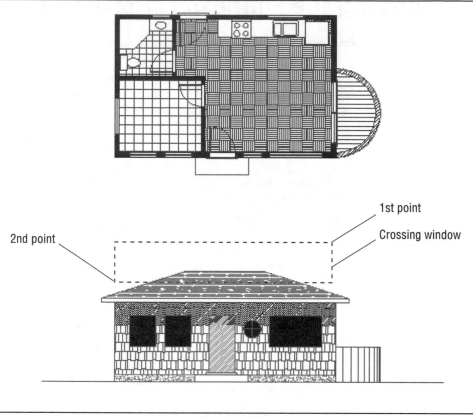

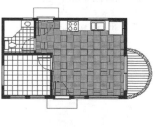

FIGURE 9.22: The crossing selection window (a), and the modified roof (b)

Are You Experienced?

Now you can ...

- ☑ create a predefined hatch pattern and apply it to a drawing
- ☑ set up and apply user-defined hatch patterns
- ☑ create a polar array of a line
- ☑ use lines to indicate a curved surface
- ☑ modify the scale of a hatch pattern
- ☑ modify the shape of a hatch pattern
- ☑ control the origin of a hatch pattern

SKILL
9

Controlling Text in a Drawing

- ➔ Setting up text styles
- ➔ Placing labels and titles of views in the drawing
- ➔ Modifying text in a drawing
- ➔ Working with grid lines
- ➔ Managing several lines of text

You will have many uses for text in your drawings. Titles of views, notes, and dimensions are a few of the components of a drawing that require text, with each of these uses possibly requiring a different height, orientation, and style of lettering. In order to control the text in your drawing, you will need to learn how to do three basic operations:

- Determine how the text will look by setting up text styles.

- Specify where the text will be located and enter it into the drawing.

- Modify the text already in your drawing.

AutoCAD offers two types of text objects: single line and multiline text. Single line text makes a distinct object of each line of text whether the line is one letter or many words. This type of text is useful for titles of drawings, titles of views within a drawing, room labels, and short notes. Dimensions and longer notes are done with multiline text. AutoCAD treats a whole body of multiline text as one object, whether the text consists of one letter or many paragraphs.

The two types of text share the same text styles, but each have their own command for placing text in the drawing. When you modify text, you can use the same commands for either type of text, but the commands operate differently for multiline than for single line text. Dimension text is handled slightly differently from other text and will be covered in Skill 11, *Dimensioning a Drawing*.

We will progress through this skill by first looking at the process of setting up text styles. Then we will start placing and modifying single line text in the cabin drawing. Finally we'll have a look at the methods of controlling multiline text.

Setting Up Text Styles

In AutoCAD, a text style consists of a combination of a style name, text font, height, width factor, oblique angle, and a few mostly static settings. These text style properties will be specified with the help of a dialog box that comes up when you start the *Style command*. You will begin by setting up two text styles—one for labeling the rooms in the floor plan and the other for putting titles on the two views. You will need a new layer for text.

1. Open the Cabin09c drawing.

2. Create a new layer named Text1. Assign it a color and make it current.

3. Freeze the Hatch-plan-floor and Hatch-plan-wall layers. Be sure all other layers are thawed. Your drawing should look like Figure 10.1.

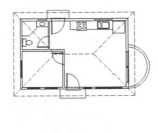

FIGURE 10.1: The Cabin09c drawing with the Hatch-plan-floor and Hatch-plan-wall layers frozen

Text and Drawing Scale

Before you set up text styles for this drawing, you have to determine how high the text letters need to be. To make this determination, you first need to decide the scale at which the final drawing will be printed.

In traditional drafting, you could ignore the drawing scale and set the actual height that each kind of text needed to be. This was possible because, while the drawing was drawn to a scale, the text didn't have to conform to that scale and was drawn full size. In the cabin drawing, the drawing is actual size, but the text has to be much larger than actual size because both the drawing and its text will be scaled down by the same factor in the process of printing the drawing. (You will learn about an alternate way of handling text height in Skill 13, *Using Layouts to Set Up a Print.)*

We will use a final scale of this drawing of ⅛"=1'-0". This scale has a true ratio of 1:96 and a scale factor of 96 (see Table 9.1 in Skill 9, *Working with Hatches and Fills*). If you want the room label text to be ⅛-inch high when you print the drawing at ⅛-inch scale, multiply ⅛" by the scale factor of 96 to get 12" for the text height. You can check that calculated text height by studying the floor plan for a moment and noting the sizes of the building components represented in the drawing. You can estimate that the room label text should be about half as high as the front step is wide, or 1-foot high.

SKILL
10

Defining a Text Style for Room Labels

Now that you have a good idea of the text height you need, it's time to define a new text style. Each new AutoCAD .dwg file comes with one predefined text style named Standard. You will add two more.

1. Type **st** ↵ or select Format ➤ Text Style. This starts the Style command and brings up the Text Style dialog box (Figure 10.2). In the Style Name area, you will see the default Standard text style.

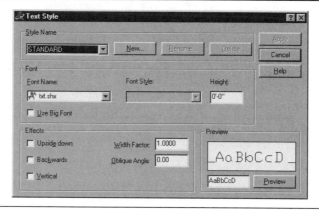

FIGURE 10.2: The Text Style dialog box, where text styles are set up

NOTE NOTE NOTE NOTE NOTE NOTE NOTE NOTE NOTE NOTE NOTE NOTE NOTE NOTE
By default, all .dwg **files have the Standard text style as the current text style.**

2. Click New. The New Text Style dialog box comes up. There is a Style Name text box with Style1 in it, highlighted. When you enter a new style name, it will replace Style 1.

3. Type **Label** ↵. The New Text Style dialog box closes and, in the Text style dialog box, Label appears in the Style Names drop-down list. You have created a new text style named Label. It has settings identical to those of the Standard text style, and it is now the current text style. Now you will change some of the settings for this new style.

4. Move down to the Font area and click the Font Names drop-down list to open it. A list of fonts appears; the number of choices depends on what software is installed on your computer.

5. Scroll through the list until you find romans.shx, then click on it. The list closes, and, in the Font Name text box, the romans.shx font replaces the txt.shx font that was previously there. In the Preview area in the lower-right corner, a sample of the romans.shx font replaces that of the txt.shx font.

NOTE NOTE NOTE NOTE NOTE NOTE NOTE NOTE NOTE NOTE NOTE NOTE NOTE NOTE NOTE

A font is a collection of text characters and symbols that all follow a characteristic style of design and proportion.

6. Press the Tab key to jump to the next text box. The Height setting is highlighted at the default of 0'0".

7. Type **12**, then press Tab again. A height of 1'-0" replaces the default height.

8. You won't need to change any of the other parameters that define the new Text Style. They can all stay at their default settings.

9. Click Apply in the upper-right corner of the dialog box. The Label text style is saved with the current drawing, and becomes the current text style.

NOTE NOTE NOTE NOTE NOTE NOTE NOTE NOTE NOTE NOTE NOTE NOTE NOTE NOTE NOTE

The current text style is similar to the current layer. All text created while a text style is current will follow the parameters or settings of this text style.

When you define a new text style, you first name the new style. This has the effect of making a copy of the current text style settings, giving them the new name and making the new text style current. Then you change the settings for this new style and save the changes by clicking Apply.

Defining a Second Text Style

Before you close the dialog box, define another text style.

1. Click New.

SKILL
10

2. In the New Text Style dialog box, type **Title** and click OK. A new text style called Title has been created and is now the current text style. Its font, height, and other settings are a copy of the Label text style. Now you will make changes to these settings to define the Title text style.

3. Click the current font, romans.shx. The drop-down list of fonts opens. Scroll up one font and click romand.shx. The list closes and romand.shx is displayed as the chosen font.

4. Tab once to move to the Height text box and type **18,** then Tab once more. The height is converted to 1'-6".

TIP TIP TIP TIP TIP TIP TIP TIP TIP TIP TIP TIP TIP TIP TIP TIP TIP TIP TIP TIP TIP TIP
If you press ↵ after typing in the height, the new style is automatically applied, meaning saved and made to be the current text style. Don't do this if you need to change other settings for the style.

5. Click Apply, then click Close.

As you will soon see, the romans.shx font is a very simple font, often used for notes in a drawing. The romand.shx font is very similar, although it is boldface. More complex fonts are used for titles of drawing sheets and other larger text.

Of the many fonts available in AutoCAD, you will only use a few of them for your drawings. Some are set up for foreign languages or mapping symbols. Others would appear out of place on architectural or technical drawings. Later on in the chapter, you'll have a chance to experiment with the available fonts.

Look back at Figure 10.2 for a moment, and note that the Standard text style has a height of 0'-0". When the current text style has a height set to 0, you can make the text any height and are prompted to enter a height each time you begin to place text in the drawing.

Now that you have two new text styles, you can start working with single line text.

Using Single Line Text

Your first task is to put titles in for the floor plan and front elevation, using the new Title text style.

Placing Titles of Views in the Drawing

The titles need to be centered approximately under each view. If we establish a vertical guideline through the middle of the drawing, we can use it to position the text.

1. Pan the drawing up to create a little more room under the front elevation.

2. With Ortho on, drop a line from the midpoint of the ridgeline in the floor plan, down through the front elevation, to a point near the bottom of the screen.

3. Offset the bottom line of the front step in the floor plan down 4'.

4. Type **dt** ↵ or pick Draw ➤ Text ➤ Single Line Text. This will start the *Dtext command*—the command used for single line text.

5. The bottom line of text in the Command window reads, "`Specify start·
    point of text or [Justify/Style]:`." The line above it displays the name of the current text style and the style's height setting. The bottom line is the actual prompt, with three options. By default, the Justification point is set to the lower-left corner of the text. You need to change it to the middle of the text to be able to center it on the guideline.

6. Type **j** ↵. All the possible justification points appear in the prompt.

7. Type **c** ↵ to choose Center as the justification.

8. Hold down the Shift key and click the right mouse button. A menu of Osnap options appears on the screen next to where the cursor had just been positioned.

SKILL
▼10

9. Click Intersection on the menu and pick the intersection of the guideline and the offset line.

NOTE NOTE NOTE NOTE NOTE NOTE NOTE NOTE NOTE NOTE NOTE NOTE NOTE NOTE NOTE

The Osnap Cursor menu (Shift+right-click) contains all the Object Snap options; an Osnap Settings option, which opens the Osnap Settings dialog box to allow you to set running Osnaps; and a Point Filters menu.

10. For the rotation, press ↵ to accept the default angle of 0°. An "I" cursor will be positioned at the intersection (Figure 10.3).

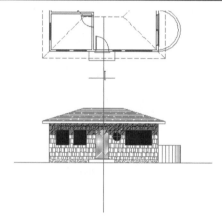

FIGURE 10.3: The text cursor sits on the guidelines.

11. With Caps Lock on, type **floor plan** ↵. The text is at the intersection as you type it (but not centered yet), and the cursor jumps down to allow you to type another line (Figure 10.4a).

12. Press ↵ again to end the Dtext command. The text is centered relative to the vertical guideline and sits on the offset line (Figure 10.4b).

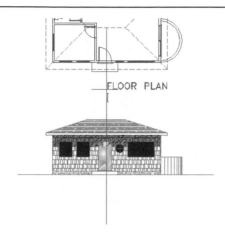

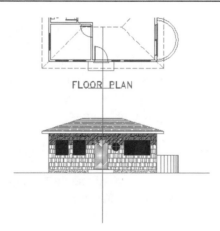

FIGURE 10.4: The first line of text is entered (a), and placed (b).

13. Offset the ground line of the elevation down 4'. Start the Dtext command
    again and repeat steps 4–12 above, this time entering **front elevation** (again
    with Caps Lock on). When finished, erase the offset lines and the guideline.
    Your drawing will look like Figure 10.5.

SKILL
10

FLOOR PLAN

FRONT ELEVATION

FIGURE 10.5: The drawing with the titles complete

You specified a location for the text in two steps: First, you set the justification point of each line of text to be centered horizontally; then you used the Intersection Osnap to position the justification point at the intersection of the two guidelines. We will discuss justification in more depth a little later in this chapter.

Next you will move to the interior of the cabin floor plan and place the room labels in their respective rooms.

Placing Room Labels in the Floor Plan

Text for the room labels will use the Label text style, so you need to make that style current before you start placing text. You can accomplish this from within the Dtext command by using the *Style option*.

1. Pan the drawing down and zoom into the floor plan. Turn off any running Osnaps.

2. Type **dt** ↵ to start the Dtext command. At the prompt, type **s** ↵ to choose the Style option. The prompt reads "Enter style name or [?] <Title>:."

3. Type **?** ↵ ↵ to see a list of defined text styles. In the text screen, you see Label, Standard, and Title listed along with information about the parameters of each style (Figure 10.6). At the bottom of the text screen you can see the Dtext prompt again.

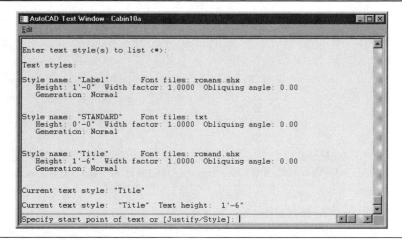

FIGURE 10.6: The text screen listing the defined text styles

4. Type **s** ↵ again. Then type **label** ↵ to make Label the current text style.

5. Press F2 to close the text screen and return to the drawing.

6. Pick a point in the kitchen a couple of feet below and to the left of the oven.

7. Press ↵ at the Rotation prompt. The text cursor appears at the point you picked.

8. With Caps Lock on, type **kitchen** ↵ **living room** ↵ **bedroom** ↵ **bath** ↵ ↵. The Dtext command ends. You will have four lines of text in the kitchen and living room area (Figure 10.7).

SKILL
10

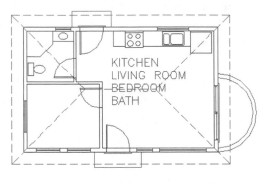

KITCHEN
LIVING ROOM
BEDROOM
BATH

FLOOR PLAN

FIGURE 10.7: The four room labels placed in the cabin

For this text, you used the default Left justification, and each line of text was positioned directly below the previous line at a spacing set by AutoCAD. In many cases it is more efficient to type in a list of words or phrases first, and then move the text to its appropriate location. That's what we are doing for this text.

Moving Text

We will "eyeball" the final position of this text because it doesn't have to be exactly centered or lined up precisely with anything—it should just sit in the rooms in such a way that it is easily readable.

1. Start the Move command and pick anywhere on the text that says, "BATH." Then press ⏎.

2. Move the cursor to a place near the middle of the BATH text and pick that point. The BATH text is attached to the cursor (Figure 10.8a).

3. Be sure that Ortho, Polar, Osnap, and Otrack are turned off. Move the cursor to the bathroom and click a location to place the word in such a way that the letters—while they may be on top of the door swing and the roof line—don't touch any fixtures or walls (Figure 10.8b). The Move command automatically ends when you complete a move.

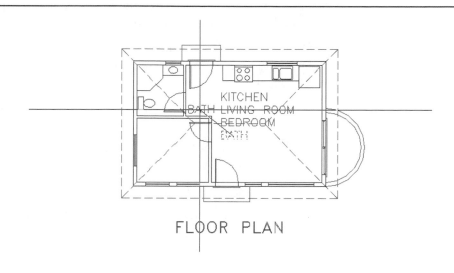

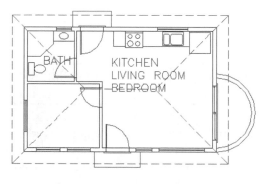

FIGURE 10.8: Moving the BATH text (a), and the new location (b)

4. Press ↵ to restart the Move command. Select the BEDROOM text and press ↵.

5. Pick a point in the middle of the selected text.

SKILL
10

6. Pick a point in the bedroom so that the BEDROOM text is positioned approximately at the center of the bedroom and crossing only the roof line.

7. Repeat this process to move the LIVING ROOM and KITCHEN text into their appropriate locations (Figure 10.9). You may not have to move the KITCHEN text.

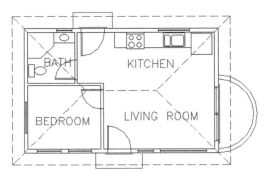

FLOOR PLAN

FIGURE 10.9: The BEDROOM, LIVING ROOM, and KITCHEN text moved to their positions

As you have seen, text is easily moved around the drawing. Often, however, you will be unable to position it without it sitting on top of a line or other object. In the cabin, three of the room labels are crossing the roof line, and BATH is crossing a door swing. You need to erase parts of these lines around the text. To do this, you'll use the Break command.

Breaking Lines

The *Break command* separates a line into two lines. When working with text that is sitting on a line, you will usually want a gap left between the lines after the break. You can start the Break command in three ways.

1. Be sure no Osnaps are running, then click the Break button on the Modify toolbar, pick Modify ➤ Break, or type **br** ↵. Each of these actions starts the Break command.

2. Move the cursor near the roof line that crosses through the LIVING ROOM text. Place the pickbox on the roof line just above the text and click. The line ghosts. The cursor changes to the crosshair cursor.

3. Put the crosshair cursor on the roof line just below the text and pick that point. The line is broken around the text and the Break command ends.

4. Press ↵ to restart the Break command and do the same operation on the roof line that crosses the BEDROOM text.

5. Press ↵ again and break the roof line around the BATH text. The arc representing the door swing is part of the door2_6 block and, as such, cannot be broken. You must explode the block to be able to break the arc.

6. Select the Explode button on the Modify toolbar and select the bathroom door. Then press ↵. The door2_6 block is exploded.

7. Zoom in closer to the bathroom. Start the Break command and pick two points on the arc to break it around the BATH text. Zoom previous to get a full view of the floor plan (Figure 10.10).

FLOOR PLAN

FIGURE 10.10: Lines are broken around the room labels.

You should use your own judgement to determine how far away from the text a line has to be broken back. You have to strike a balance between making the text easier to read and keeping what the broken line represents clear. In the bathroom, you were directed to keep the text away from any fixtures because if any lines of the fixtures had to be broken to accommodate the text, this might have made it difficult for a viewer to recognize that those lines represent a shower or a toilet.

NOTE NOTE NOTE NOTE NOTE NOTE NOTE NOTE NOTE NOTE NOTE NOTE NOTE NOTE NOTE

When you selected the line to break here, the point where you picked the line became the beginning of the break. If the point where the break needs to start is at the intersection of two lines, you must select the line to be broken somewhere else than at a break point. Otherwise, AutoCAD won't know which line you want to break. In that case, after selecting the line to break, type f ↵. You will be prompted to pick the first point of the break, and the command continues.

The Break command can also be used to break a line into two segments without leaving a gap. You might want to do this to place one part of a line on a different layer from the rest of the line. To break the line this way, after specifying the first point of the break, type @ ↵. This will force the second break point to be at the same place as the first one. If you're using Osnaps, you can snap to the same point twice to accomplish this.

NOTE NOTE NOTE NOTE NOTE NOTE NOTE NOTE NOTE NOTE NOTE NOTE NOTE NOTE NOTE

When you create a gap in a line for text, the line will have a gap in it even when the text layer is frozen. This will be a problem for the bath door swing and the roof line. We'll attend to it in the last few skills of the book.

Using Text in a Grid

AutoCAD provides a grid of dots, which you worked with in Skill 3. It is a tool for visualizing the size of the drawing area and for drawing lines whose geometry conforms to the spacing of the dots in the grid. Many floor plans have a separate grid, created specifically for the project, and made up of lines running vertically and horizontally through key structural parts of the building. At one end of each grid line, a circle or hexagon is placed and a letter or number is centered in the shape to identify it. This kind of grid is usually reserved for large, complex drawings, but we will put a small grid on the cabin floor plan to learn the basic method for laying one out.

1. Create a new layer called Grid. Assign it a color and make it current.

2. Type **z** ↵ **.6x** ↵ to make more room around the floor plan.

3. Offset the upper roof line up 10'. Offset the left roof line 10' to the left. Offset the lower roof line down 2'. Offset the right roof line to the right 4'. Pan and zoom as necessary.

4. Set Endpoint and Perpendicular Osnaps to running. Then start the Line command.

5. Draw lines from the upper-left and upper-right corners of the building up to the horizontal offset line. Then draw lines from the left upper and lower corners of the building to the vertical offset line on the left (Figure 10.11).

FIGURE 10.11:   The first grid lines

6. Now you need to draw grid lines through the middle of the interior walls. Zoom into the bathroom area and draw a short guideline across the interior wall between the bathroom and bedroom, where this wall meets the exterior wall (Figure 10.12).

7. Use Realtime Zoom and Pan to set up the view so that it contains the bathroom and the offset roof lines above and to the left of the floor plan.

8. Draw two vertical lines, and one horizontal line, from the middle of the interior walls out to the offset roof lines. Use Midpoint Osnap and pick one of the jamb lines, or the guideline, to start each line from the middle of a wall (Figure 10.13).

SKILL
10

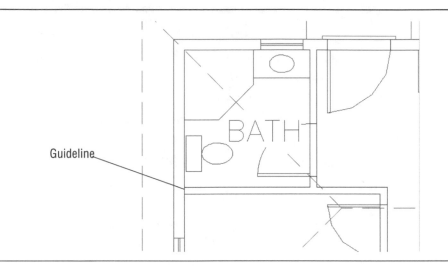

Guideline

FIGURE 10.12: A guideline for drawing a grid line through one of the interior walls

FIGURE 10.13: Drawing the grid lines

9. Erase the guideline you drew in step 6, then zoom out to a view that includes the floor plan, the grid lines, and all the offset roof lines (Figure 10.14a).

TIP TIP TIP TIP TIP TIP TIP TIP TIP TIP TIP TIP TIP TIP TIP TIP TIP TIP TIP TIP TIP TIP TIP TIP

When erasing the guideline, use a regular selection window to select it.

10. Use the Extend command to extend the seven grid lines to the right or down, and use the offset roof lines on those sides of the floor plan as boundary edges (Figure 10.14b).

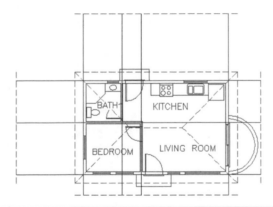

FIGURE 10.14:   Zoomed view for completing the grid lines (a), and the completed grid lines (b)

This completes the grid lines. To finish the grid, you need to add a circle with a letter or number in it to the left, or upper, end of the lines. We'll use letters across the top and numbers running down the side.

1. Erase the four offset roof lines. Zoom out a little.

2. Type **c ↵ 2p ↵**, then pick the upper end of the left-most vertical grid line.

3. Type **@2'<90** ↵. A 2-foot diameter circle is placed at the top of the grid line (Figure 10.15a).

4. Start the Copy command. Select the KITCHEN text and press ↵.

5. For the base point, pick the Insert Osnap on the Object Snap toolbar. Then click anywhere on the KITCHEN text.

6. For the second displacement point, pick the Center Osnap and click the circle on the grid. The KITCHEN text is placed on the circle with the lower-left corner of the text at the center of the circle (Figure 10.15b).

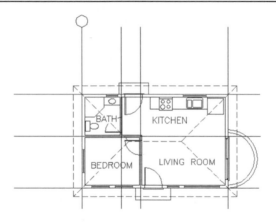

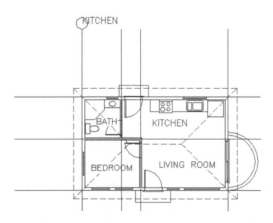

FIGURE 10.15: The circle on the grid line (a), and the KITCHEN text copied to the circle (b)

7. Click the copy of the KITCHEN text that's now on the grid. Then click the Properties button on the Standard Properties toolbar. The Properties dialog box comes up, and Text is displayed on the drop-down list at the top, telling you that you have selected a text object. Be sure the Categorized tab is active.

8. Use the Categorized tab of this dialog box to change the KITCHEN text as follows:

   A. Change the Layer from Text1 to Grid.

   B. Change the Contents from KITCHEN to the letter *A*.

   C. Change the Justify setting from Left to Middle.

For each change, follow these steps in the Properties dialog box:

1. First click the category in the left column that needs to be changed. If the setting is on a drop-down list, an arrow will be highlighted in the right column.

2. Click the down arrow to open the list. In the case of the KITCHEN text, just highlight it, as there is no drop down list.

3. Click the new setting, or type it in.

4. When finished, close the dialog box and press Esc twice to remove the grip.

SKILL
10

The KITCHEN text changes to the letter *A*, is centered in the grid circle, and moves to the Grid layer (Figure 10.16).

NOTE NOTE NOTE NOTE NOTE NOTE NOTE NOTE NOTE NOTE NOTE NOTE NOTE NOTE

This may at first seem like a roundabout method for generating letters for the grid symbols, but the exercise is meant to show you how easy it is to use text from one part of the drawing for a completely different text purpose. It's a handy technique, as long as you want to use a font that has been chosen for a previously defined text style. Several of the exercises in the book are designed to illustrate an important feature, though there may be faster ways to accomplish the same goal in AutoCAD. I'll make note of this when it is occurring.

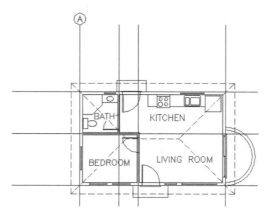

FIGURE 10.16:   The grid circle with the letter *A*

You used the Insertion Osnap on the KITCHEN text to position its justification point at the center of the circle. Then you modified the justification point from the Left position (which is actually short for Lower Left) to the Middle position (short for Center Middle). The Middle position is the middle of the line of text, horizontally and vertically; therefore, this had the effect of centering the text in the circle. Let's look at Text Justification briefly.

Text Justification

Each line of single line text is an object. It has a justification point that is similar to insertion points on blocks. When drawing, you can use the Insert Osnap to precisely locate the justification point of text (or the insertion point of blocks), and thereby control their position on the drawing. When you use the Dtext command, the default justification point is the lower-left corner of the line of text. At the Dtext prompt (`Specify start point of text or [Justify/Style]:`), if you type **j** ↵, you get the prompt `Enter an option [Align/Fit/Center/Middle/Right/TL/TC/TR/ML/MC/MR/BL/BC/BR]:`. These are your justification options.

Most of these options are represented in Figure 10.17. The dots are in three columns—left, center, and right—and four rows—top, middle, lower, and base. The names of the justification locations are based on these columns and rows. So you have, for example, TL for Top Left, MR for Middle Right, etc. The third row down doesn't use the name lower. It simply goes by left, center, and right. Left is the default justification position. (So it's not in the list of options.) The Middle position will sometimes coincide with the Middle Center position, but not always. For example, if a line of text has *descenders*—lower case letters that drop below the base line—the Middle position will drop below the Middle Center position. Finally, the lowest row—the *Base row*—sits just below the letters at the lowest point of any descenders.

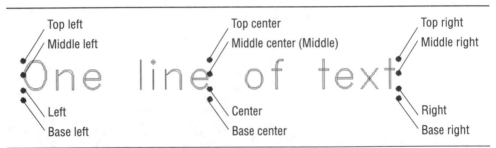

FIGURE 10.17: The justification points on a line of text

Finishing the Grid

To finish the grid, you need to copy the grid circle with its text to each grid line, then change the text.

1. Be sure Endpoint Osnap is still running. Then, at the `Command:` prompt, click the letter *A*, then click the circle. Grips appear.

2. Click the grip at the bottom of the circle to activate it.

3. Press the space bar once to get to the Move command, then type **c** ↵ to activate the copy option.

4. Pick the top end of each vertical grid line. Then type **x** ↵ (Figure 10.18).

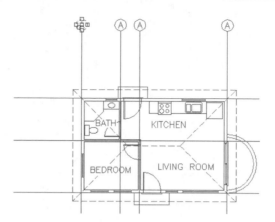

FIGURE 10.18: Grid circle and letter are copied to the top of all three vertical lines.

5. Move back to the original grid circle and select the grip on the right side of the circle to activate it.

6. Press the space bar once to get to the move command. Then type **c** ↵.

7. Pick the left end of each horizontal grid line. Type **x** ↵ and press Esc twice to remove the grips. Now you'll use the *Text Edit command* to change the text in each circle.

8. Be sure Caps Lock is on. Pick Modify ➤ Text. Select the letter *A* in the second grid circle from the left on the top row. The Edit Text dialog box comes up.

TIP TIP TIP TIP TIP TIP TIP TIP TIP TIP TIP TIP TIP TIP TIP TIP TIP TIP TIP TIP TIP TIP

This command can also be started by typing ddedit ↵ at the command line.

9. With Caps Lock on, type **b** ↵. The *A* changes to B.

10. Click the *A* in the next circle to the right, then type **c** ↵. The *A* changes to C.

11. Repeat this process for the remaining four grid circle letters, changing them to D, 1, 2, and 3. Press ↵ to end the Edit Text command. The letters and numbers are all in place, and the grid is complete (Figure 10.19).

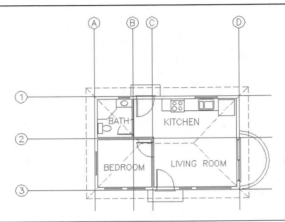

FIGURE 10.19: The completed grid

12. Zoom to Extents, then zoom out a little to get a view of the entire drawing with the grid completed (Figure 10.20).

13. Save this drawing as Cabin10a.

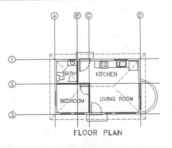

FIGURE 10.20: The Cabin10a drawing

Often it is easier to copy existing text and modify it than to create new text; and grips are a handy way to copy text. The Edit Text command (technically called Ddedit) is a quick way to modify the wording of short lines of text, consisting of a word or a few letters. The Properties dialog box is very useful for changing all aspects of a line of text.

For the final exercise with text, you get a chance to set up some more new text styles, place text precisely, and use the Ddedit command again to modify text content. Also, you'll get to work with the other kind of text: multiline text. This will all be done as you develop a title block for your drawing.

Creating a Title Block and Border

The first step in creating a title block and border for the cabin drawing is deciding on a sheet size for printing the final drawing. Because many people have access to an 8½×11-inch format printer, we will use that sheet size. If we print the drawing at a scale of ⅛" = 1'-0", will it fit on the sheet?

To answer that question, we have to ask ourselves: How big of an area will fit on an 8½×11-inch sheet at 1" = 8'-0" scale? The answer is really quite simple: If every inch on the sheet represents 8', you multiply each dimension of the sheet in inches by 8' per inch. For this sheet, you multiply 8½"×8' per inch to get 68'. And you multiply 11"×8' per inch to get 88'. So the 8½×11-inch sheet represents a rectangle with dimensions of 68'×88'. That should be plenty of room for your cabin drawing. This is the information we need to start the title block.

Drawing the Border

The border of the drawing will be set in from the edge of the sheet.

1. Create a new layer called Tblk1. Leave the default color assigned and make this layer current.

2. Start the Rectangle command (it was used in Skill 4 to make the doors).

3. At the prompt, type **0,0** ↵. Then type **68',88'** ↵. A rectangle is drawn that extends off the top of the screen (Figure 10.21a).

4. Use Realtime Zoom to zoom out until the entire rectangle is visible in the drawing area (Figure 10.21b). You need to fit the drawing into the rectangle, as if you were fitting it on a sheet of paper—the easiest and safest way to do this is to move the rectangle over to the drawing.

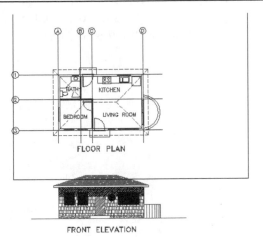

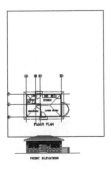

FIGURE 10.21: Creating the rectangle (a), and zooming out to include the entire rectangle (b)

5. At the Command: prompt, click the rectangle to turn on the grips. Grips appear at the corners of the rectangle.

6. Click the lower-left grip. Press the space bar once. Then move the rectangle over the drawing (Figure 10.22a).

SKILL
10

7. When the rectangle is approximately in the position shown in Figure 10.22b, click. Then press Esc twice to turn off the grips. The rectangle is positioned around the drawing and represents the edge of the sheet.

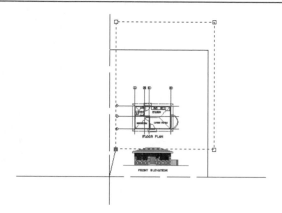

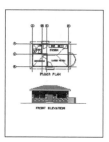

FIGURE 10.22: Moving the rectangle with grips (a), and the results (b)

8. You need a border set in from the edge. Offset the rectangle 3' to the inside. (With a scale of 8'-0" = 1", which is another way of expressing the scale of ⅛" = 1'-0", each 1'-0" on the drawing will represented by ⅛" on the sheet. So a 3-foot offset distance will create an offset of ⅜" on the printed sheet.)

9. Select the inside rectangle. Then click the Properties button on the Standard toolbar.

10. In the list of Geometry settings in the Properties dialog box, change the Global Width from 0" to 3". Close the Properties dialog box and press Esc twice to remove the grips.

11. Zoom to Extents, then zoom out a little to create a view in which the drawing with its border nearly fills the screen. You now have a border for the drawing (Figure 10.23). The outer rectangle represents the edge of the sheet of paper, while the thicker, inner rectangle is the sheet's border.

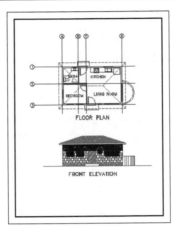

FIGURE 10.23: The drawing with its border

Constructing a Title Block

The title block is a box that contains general information about the drawing, such as the name of the project, the design company, the date of the drawing, and so on. It will be set up in the lower-right corner of the border and will use the same special line—the polyline—that was used in the Rectangle command.

Polylines

We first used the Rectangle command in Skill 4 for drawing the doors. At that time, it was mentioned that rectangles created with the Rectangle command were made up of a polyline whose four segments were grouped as one object. In step 10 of the previous section, you saw that these segments can have varying widths.

There is also a *Polyline command*, nicknamed the *Pline command*, which allows you to draw continuous straight and curved line segments of varying widths, with all segments behaving as if they were one object.

SKILL
10

When you explode a polyline using the Explode command, the segments lose any width they had and become independent lines. The ability of a polyline to have a width makes it useful in constructing title blocks. We'll use the Pline command to draw the various lines that make up the title block. Then we'll fill in the text.

1. Zoom into a view of the lower part of your drawing, including the bottom of the border. Be sure Endpoint and Perpendicular Osnaps are running.

2. Start the Polyline command. To do this, type **pl** ↵ or pick the Polyline button on the Draw toolbar or select Draw ➤ Polyline. The `Specify start point:` prompt appears in the Command window.

3. Be sure Ortho is on. Then select Temporary Tracking Point Osnap. Click the lower-left corner of the border and hold the cursor directly above that point. When the vertical tracking path appears along the left boundary line, type **12'** ↵. This starts a polyline on the left side of the border 12' above the lower-left corner.

4. Notice the bottom two lines in the Command window. The upper one tells you the current width set for polylines. The lower one displays the options for the Polyline command, with the default option being to pick a second point. You need to set the line width.

5. Type **w** ↵, then type **3** ↵ ↵. This sets the starting and ending width of polyline segments to 3". The original Polyline command prompt returns, and you can pick a point to define the line segment (Figure 10.24a).

6. Hold the crosshair cursor on the right side of the border. When the perpendicular icon appears on the borderline, click. Then press ↵. The first polyline segment is drawn (Figure 10.24b). The 3-inch width setting will stay until you change it, and will be saved with the drawing file.

7. Restart the Polyline command. Choose the Midpoint Osnap and start a new segment at the midpoint of the line you just drew.

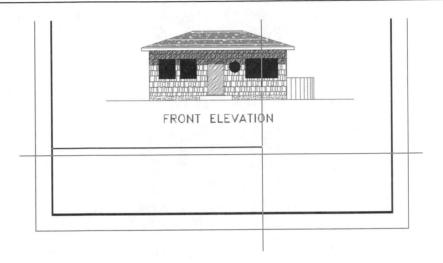

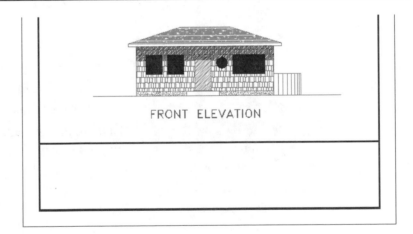

FIGURE 10.24: Drawing a polyline: setting the width (a), and completing the segment (b)

SKILL
10

8.   Click the bottom of the border near its midpoint. The running Perpendicular Osnap is activated, and the left edge of the title block is drawn (Figure 10.25a). Press ↵ to end the Polyline—or Pline—command.

9.   Trim the left half of the first Pline drawn back to the Pline just drawn.

10. Offset the horizontal Pline down 4'. Then offset this new line down 3'. Then offset this new line down 2'-6" (Figure 10.25b).

11. Start the Pline command. Using Midpoint Osnap, start a Pline at the midpoint of the third horizontal line down. Then end the segment at the bottom of the border, taking advantage of the Running Perpendicular Osnap. Press ↵ to end the Pline command.

12. Trim the right side of the line just above the bottom of the border, back to the line you just drew (Figure 10.25c).

The lines for the title block are almost done. Some of the Plines may look wider than others. This almost certainly is caused by the monitor distorting the picture at the current view. By zooming in, you can assure yourself that everything is correct.

1.   Zoom into a close view of the title block. Notice that the intersection of the outer lines in the upper-left corner doesn't seem clean.

2.   Zoom into that corner using a zoom window (Figure 10.26a). The lines don't intersect in a clean corner. They need to be joined.

3.   Type **pe** ↵ to start the Polyline Edit command and select one of the two lines. You must place the pickbox on the edge of the polyline to select it—not in the middle of it.

4.   Type **j** ↵. Then pick the other Pline and press ↵. The corner is corrected (Figure 10.26b). Type **x** ↵ to end the Pedit command.

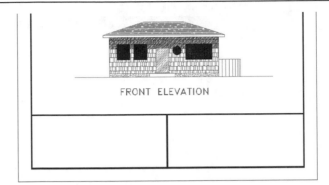

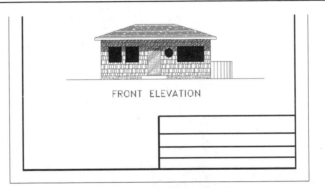

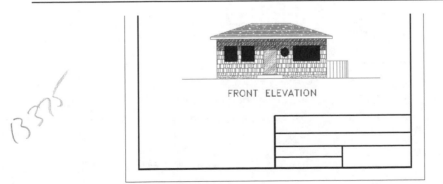

FIGURE 10.25: Building the title block: the left edge (a), the horizontal lines (b), and the last line trimmed (c)

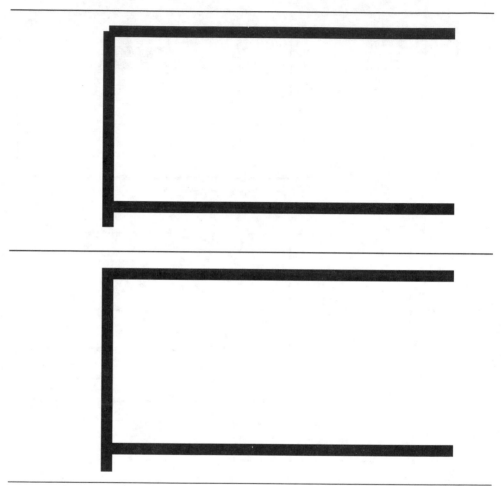

FIGURE 10.26: Zoomed into the upper-left corner (a), and the corner corrected (b)

5. Zoom previous once. Then use Realtime Zoom to zoom out just enough to see the Front Elevation text at the top of the screen (Figure 10.27).

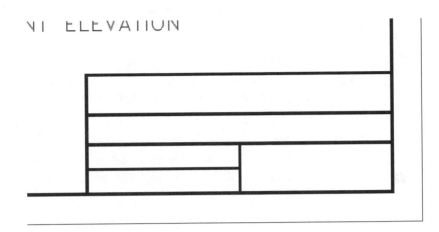

Putting Text in the Title Block

The title block has five boxes that will contain distinct pieces of information. The large one at the top will contain the name of the project. Below that will be the name of the company producing the drawing—your company. Below that on the left will be the name of the person who drew this drawing—you—and below that, the date. In the lower-right corner will be the sheet number, in case more than one sheet is required for this project. This follows a standard format, but many title block layouts will contain this and more information as well, depending on the complexity of the job.

You need to put labels in some of the boxes to identify what information will be shown there. For this, you need to set up a new text style.

1. Type **st** ↵. The Text Style dialog box appears. The Label text style should still be current.

2. Click New and type **tblk-label** and click OK. Leave the font set to romans.shx, but change the height to 8". Then click Apply and Close. Tblk-Label is the current text style.

If you press Enter after changing the height, the Apply button ghosts out. Pressing Enter at this point has the same effect as clicking the Apply button.

3. Be sure Caps Lock is on, then type **dt** ↵ to start the Dtext command. Click the None Osnap button. Then pick a point in the upper-left corner of the upper box of the title block. It doesn't have to be the perfect location now; you can fix it after you see the text.

4. Press ↵ at the rotation prompt. Type **project:** ↵ ↵. PROJECT: will be placed in the upper box (Figure 10.28a).

5. If necessary, move this text to the upper-left corner, as far as possible, while still allowing it to be readable. It will help if Ortho and Osnap are temporarily turned off.

If you have running Osnaps and need to have them off for one pick, you can pick the None Osnap button. This cancels all running Osnaps for the next pick. If you need running Osnaps turned off for several picks, click the Osnap button on the Status bar. Click it again when you want the running Osnaps to become active.

6. Use the Copy command to copy this text to the bottom two boxes on the left, using the Multiple option and the endpoint of the horizontal lines above each of the boxes as the base and displacement points. This will keep each piece of text in the same position relative to the upper-left corner of each box.

7. Pick Modify ➤ Text to start the Ddedit command. Then click the upper of the two copies of text. The Edit Text dialog box appears with PROJECT: highlighted.

8. Type **drawn by:** and click OK. Pick the lower copy of text. The Edit Text dialog box returns.

9. Type **date:** and click OK. Press ↵ to end the Ddedit command. The text is changed and three of the boxes have their proper label (Figure 10.28b).

The Ddedit command is a quick way to change the wording of text and make spelling corrections. You have to change one line at a time, but the command keeps running until you stop it.

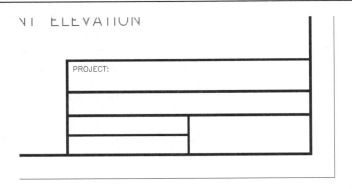

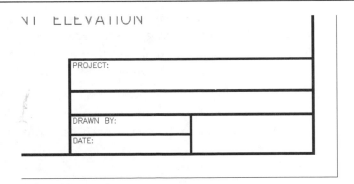

FIGURE 10.28: One line of text placed (a), and the text changed to the correct wording (b)

The next area to work on is the lower-right box. This is where the sheet number is located, and it is usually displayed in such a way that the person reading the drawing can tell not only the page number of the current sheet, but also the number of sheets being used for the project. We will create a new text style for this box.

1. Start the Style command. In the Text Style dialog box, click New.

2. Type **Sheet_No** and click OK. For the font, select romand.shx. Change the height to 1'-3". Click Apply, then click Close. Sheet_No is now the current text style.

3. You will need to center the text horizontally in the box. This will require breaking the horizontal line running across the top of this box at the upper-left corner of the box. To do this, click the Break button on the Modify toolbar. Then select the line to break at a point where no other lines are touching it.

4. Type **f** ↵ to select the first point of the break. Then use the running Osnap to pick the upper-left corner of the box.

5. At the Enter second break point: prompt, type @ ↵. This forces the second point to coincide with the first point, and the line is broken without leaving a gap.

6. Start the Dtext command and type **j** ↵. Then type **tc** ↵. Pick Midpoint Osnap and pick a point on the line across the top of the box.

7. Press ↵ at the rotation prompt. With Caps Lock on, type **sheet no.:** ↵ **1 of 1** ↵ ↵. (When you get to the *of*, turn Caps Lock off.) For clarity, leave a double space after the first *1* and before the second *1*. The text is inserted into the box and is centered horizontally (Figure 10.29a).

8. With Ortho on, use the Move command to move the text down and center it vertically in the box (Figure 10.29b). Remember, when you select the text to move it, you have to pick each line because they are two separate objects.

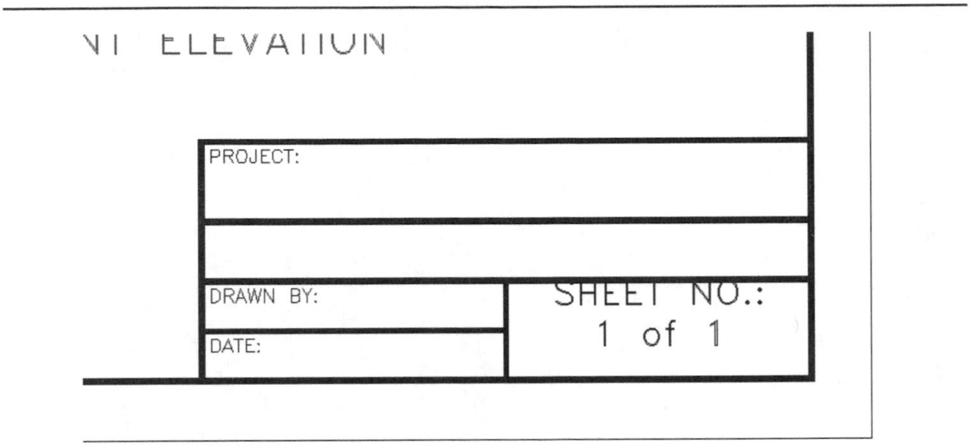

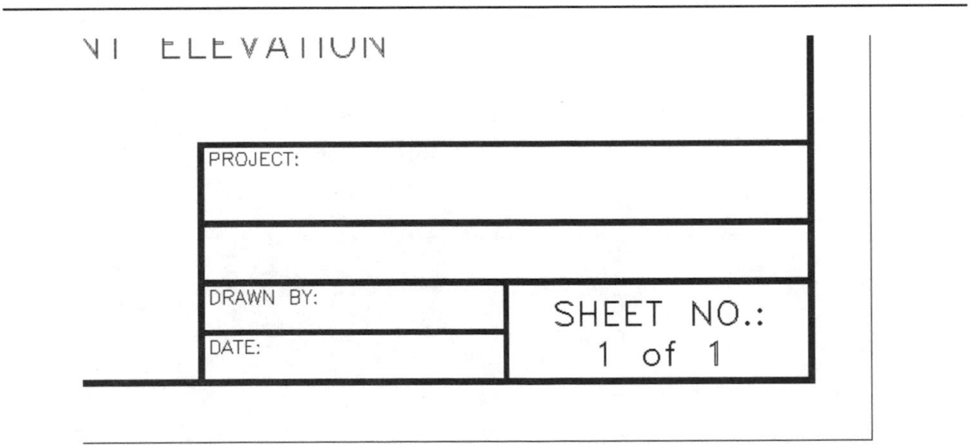

NI ELEVATION

PROJECT:

DRAWN BY: SHEET NO.:
                                1 of 1
DATE:

NI ELEVATION

PROJECT:

DRAWN BY: SHEET NO.:
                                1 of 1
DATE:

FIGURE 10.29: The text after being inserted (a), and after centering vertically (b)

Now it's time for you to experiment. Use the same techniques you just went through to fill in the text for the other four boxes. Feel free to try other fonts, but you will have to adjust the height for each text style so that the text fits in its box. Here are some guidelines for height:

Box	Recommended Height of Text
Project:	2'-6"
Company:	1'-3"
Drawn By:	1'-0"
Date:	1'-0"

If you don't have a company name, make one up.

You will have to set up a new style for each new font or height you choose, unless you set up a style with a height of 0'-0". In that case, you will be prompted for the height each time you start to place text in the drawing. This is the recommended way to operate for the top two boxes because it will give consistency to the text even when heights vary. You might try several fonts, then come back to this technique at the end. I also recommend that you use a relatively simple font for the text in the Drawn By and Date boxes—something a little larger and possibly bolder than the labels in those boxes.

Try these fonts:

- **romant.shx** or **romanc.shx**

- any of the **swis721** series

- **Times New Roman**

- **Technic**

- **SansSerif**

- **CityBlueprint** or **CountryBlueprint**

- **Arial**

In the top two boxes, the text can be centered vertically and horizontally if you draw a line diagonally across the box, choose Middle as a justification for the text, and use Midpoint Osnap to snap to the diagonal line when you start the text. For the Drawn By and Date boxes, centering the text horizontally is not advisable because the label text already in the boxes takes up too much space. You can use the same technique with the diagonal line to center it, however, then put Ortho on and move the text to the right until it makes a good fit. This will keep it verti-cally centered.

Be careful in your use of running Osnaps as you position text. If you are "eye-balling" the final location, it is best to have no running Osnaps. On the other hand, if you are precisely locating justification points by snapping to lines and other objects, you might try having the following Osnaps running: Endpoint, Intersection, Perpendicular, and Insertion, with Midpoint optional.

When you finish, your title block should look something like Figure 10.30. In this sample, romant.shx font was used for a style that was set to zero height, then applied to the top two boxes at the recommended heights. The romand.shx font was used for the Drawn By and Date boxes, also at the recommended height.

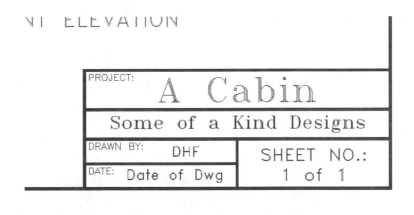

FIGURE 10.30: The completed title block

If you are going to design your own company title block, be ready to spend a little time setting it up and deciding which fonts will give the look that best reflects the image you want to project. You can then use this title block on all your subsequent projects.

Zoom to Extents, then zoom out a little to view the entire drawing. Save this drawing as Cabin10b (Figure 10.31).

The final part of the skill will introduce you to multiline text, which you will also work with as you learn about dimensions in the next skill.

SKILL
10

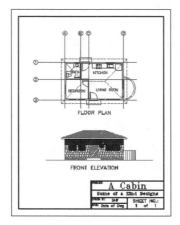

FIGURE 10.31: The latest version of the cabin drawing

Using Multiline Text

Multiline text (often referred to as MText) is a more complex form of text than single line text. It can be used the same way single line text has been used in this chapter, and it can do more. If you have several lines of text, or if you need certain words within a line of text to appear differently than the adjacent words, multiline text is the best thing to use.

A paragraph of multiline text is a single entity. The text will wrap around and the length of a line can be easily modified after the text has been placed in the drawing. Within the multiline text entity, all text is fully editable and behaves as if it were in a word processor. A special word or letter of the text can be given its own text style or color. Everything you have learned about defining a new text style also applies to multiline text, as both kinds of text use the same text styles. Just as polylines become lines when exploded, multiline text is reduced to single line text when exploded.

Dimensions use multiline text, and any text that is imported into an AutoCAD drawing from a word processing document or text editor will become multiline text in the drawing. In this section, you will learn how to place a paragraph of multiline text in the cabin drawing and then modify it. In Skill 11, *Dimensioning a Drawing*, you will work with dimension text and text with leader lines, both of which use multiline text. We will start by adding a note in the lower-left corner of the drawing, using Multiline text.

1. Click the Make Object's Layer Current button on the left end of the Object Properties toolbar. Then click the FRONT ELEVATION text to make the Text1 layer current. Zoom into the blank area to the left of the title block in the lower-left corner of the cabin drawing.

2. Click the Osnap button on the Status bar to temporarily disable any running Osnaps. Then type **t** ↵, or click the Text button on the Draw toolbar, or pick Draw ➤ Text ➤ Multiline Text. Any of these will start the Multiline Text Command. At the Command window, you are shown the name of the current text style and height, and are prompted to specify a first corner.

3. Pick a point near the left borderline in line with the top of the title block. The prompt now reads "Specify opposite corner or [Height/Justify/ Line spacing/Rotation/Style/Width]:." These are all the options for the Multiline Text command.

4. If the current style is Label, go on to step 5. Otherwise type **s** ↵ for the style option and type **label** ↵.

5. Drag open a window that fills the space between the left border and the left side of the title block. This defines the length of line for the multiline text (Figure 10.32). Click to finish the window.

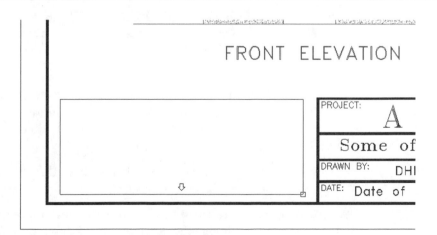

FIGURE 10.32: Making a Multiline text window

6. The Multiline Text Editor dialog box opens, and you can see a long blank area with a flashing cursor in it. This is where you will type in the text. In the drop-down lists at the top, you can see the font and height of the current text style.

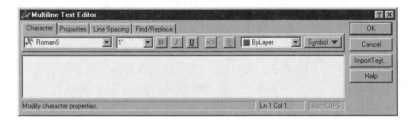

7. Type in the following text, using single spacing and pressing Enter only at the end of the first line and at the end of each note:

   GENERAL NOTES:

   1. **All work shall be in accordance with the 1990 Ed. Uniform Building Code and all local ordinances.**

   2. **Roof can be built to be steeper for climates with heavy snowfall.**

   3. **Solar panels available for installation on roof.**

   4. **All windows to be double-paned.**

NOTE NOTE NOTE NOTE NOTE NOTE NOTE NOTE NOTE NOTE NOTE NOTE NOTE NOTE NOTE
The Multiline Text Editor dialog box can be resized to accommodate more lines of text and a greater line length.

When finished, press OK. The text is placed in the drawing (Figure 10.33a). The window you specified was only used to define the line length. Its height does not control how far down the text will come, as that is determined by how much text you enter.

8. Pick anywhere on the new text. Then Pick Modify ➤ Text. The Multiline Text Editor dialog box comes back up.

9. Move the cursor to the upper-left corner of the window containing the text and in front of the G in the first word. Hold down the left mouse button and drag it to the right and down until all the text is highlighted. Release the

mouse button. Be sure the Character tab is active, then change the Text Height from 1" to 9" and click OK. The text is redrawn smaller and now fits better in the space available (Figure 10.33b).

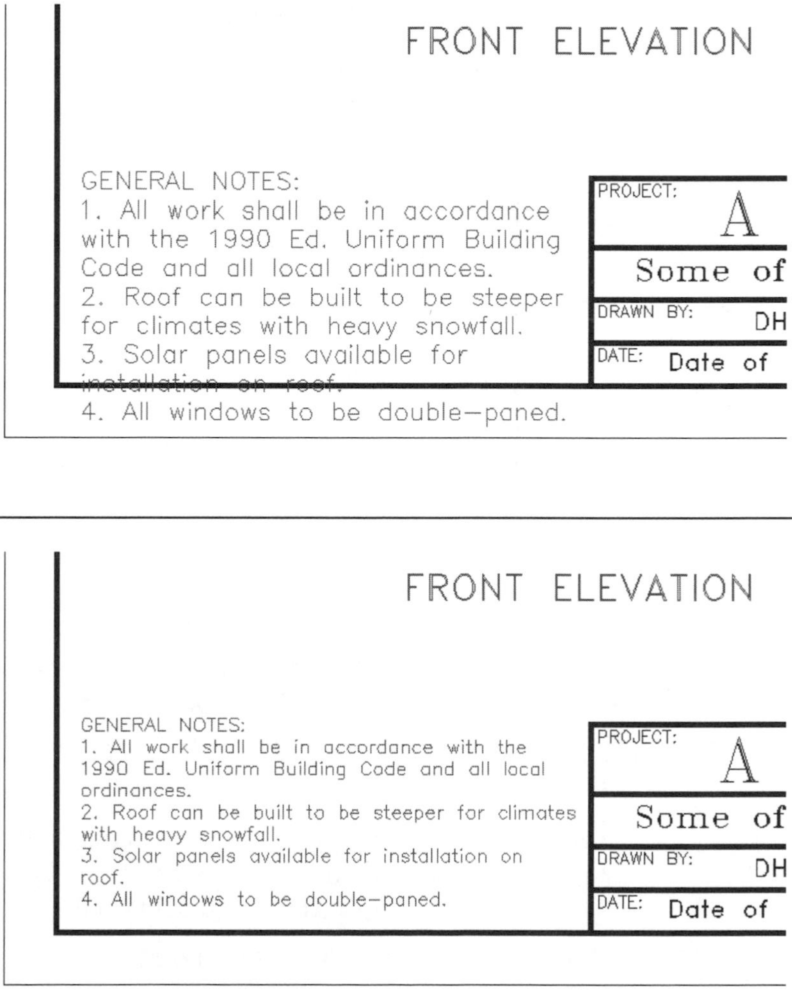

FRONT ELEVATION

GENERAL NOTES:
1. All work shall be in accordance with the 1990 Ed. Uniform Building Code and all local ordinances.
2. Roof can be built to be steeper for climates with heavy snowfall.
3. Solar panels available for installation on roof.
4. All windows to be double—paned.

PROJECT: A

Some of

DRAWN BY: DH

DATE: Date of

FRONT ELEVATION

GENERAL NOTES:
1. All work shall be in accordance with the 1990 Ed. Uniform Building Code and all local ordinances.
2. Roof can be built to be steeper for climates with heavy snowfall.
3. Solar panels available for installation on roof.
4. All windows to be double—paned.

PROJECT: A

Some of

DRAWN BY: DH

DATE: Date of

FIGURE 10.33: MText in the drawing (a), and modified to be smaller (b)

SKILL
10

10.   Click on the Mtext again. The Multiline Text Editor dialog box comes up.

11. Highlight all the text again. In the fonts drop-down list at the left side of the Character tab, select SansSerif to be the current font. The selected text changes to the new font.

12. Click OK. The MText in the drawing has become more compact and there is room for more notes (Figure 10.34).

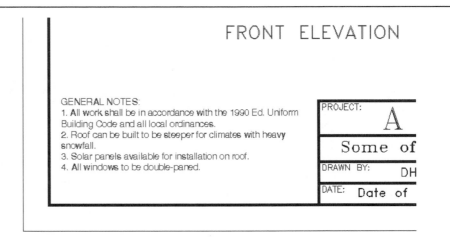

FIGURE 10.34: The results of a font modification

The SansSerif is a TrueType font supported by Windows. When used in AutoCAD drawings, it can be italic or boldface. To see how to change individual words within the text, we will underline and boldface the Uniform Building Code text.

1. Click the Mtext again. The Multiline Text Editor dialog box appears again.

2. Use the same technique used earlier to highlight the Uniform Building Code text. Then click the Bold (**B**) and Underline (**U**) buttons on the Character tab. The selected text is underlined and boldfaced.

3. Click OK. Then press ↵ to end the Edit Text command. The text is redrawn with the changes (Figure 10.35).

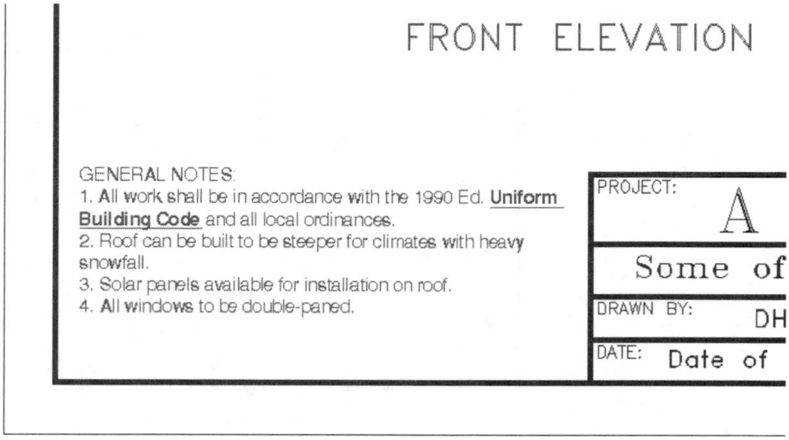

FRONT ELEVATION

GENERAL NOTES:
1. All work shall be in accordance with the 1990 Ed. **Uniform Building Code** and all local ordinances.
2. Roof can be built to be steeper for climates with heavy snowfall.
3. Solar panels available for installation on roof.
4. All windows to be double-paned.

PROJECT:	A
	Some of
DRAWN BY:	DH
DATE:	Date of

FIGURE 10.35: The MText with individual words modified

Individual words can also be italicized and given a different color or height than the rest of the MText, by using the other tools at the top of the Multiline Text Editor dialog box. You are encouraged to experiment with all these tools to become familiar with them.

The length of a line can be easily altered to make the MText fit more conveniently on the drawing. Let's say you've decided to put your company logo to the left of the title block. You need to squeeze the text into a narrower space. You have some extra room at the bottom, so you should be able to do it.

1. At the Command: prompt, select the text. Four grips appear at the corners of the body of MText.

2. On the Status bar, be sure Polar, Osnap, and Otrack are off; and Ortho is on. Then click the upper-right grip to activate it.

3. Slowly move the cursor to the left, stopping periodically until the defining rectangle appears. When the bottom of the rectangle gets close to the bottom line of the border, you will have moved about ⅓ of the way to the left borderline (Figure 10.36a).

4. Click the mouse button, then press Esc twice. The text is squeezed into a narrower space but still fits on the page (Figure 10.36b).

**SKILL
10**

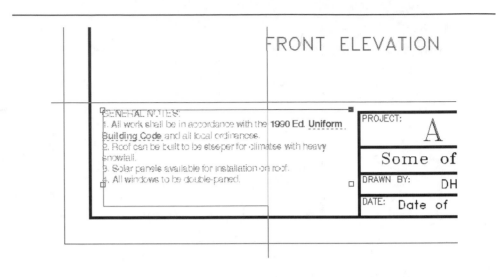

FRONT ELEVATION

GENERAL NOTES:
1. All work shall be in accordance
with the 1990 Ed. **Uniform Building
Code** and all local ordinances.
2. Roof can be built to be steeper
for climates with heavy snowfall.
3. Solar panels available for
installation on roof.
4. All windows to be double-paned.

PROJECT:
A
Some of

DRAWN BY: DH

DATE: Date of

FIGURE 10.36: Modifying the MText line length with grips (a), and the results (b)

5. Zoom to Extents, then zoom out a little to a view of the whole drawing (Figure 10.37). You won't be able to read the MText at this magnification, but it will look fine when you print your drawing.

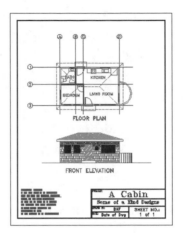

FIGURE 10.37: The full drawing

6. Save this drawing as Cabin10c.

MText has justification points similar to those of single line text, and they behave the same way. The default justification point for MText, however, is the upper-left corner of the body of text, and the available options are for nine points distributed around the perimeter of the body of text and at the center (Figure 10.38).

This completes the exercises for this skill. If you want to play around with the MText, it can be edited with the Multiline Text Edit dialog box by picking Modify ➢ Text and selecting the text you need to edit.

With both MText and single line text, you can add special characters—degree symbol, diameter symbol, etc.—which are not included in most font character packages. You will have a chance to do this in the next skill.

SKILL
10

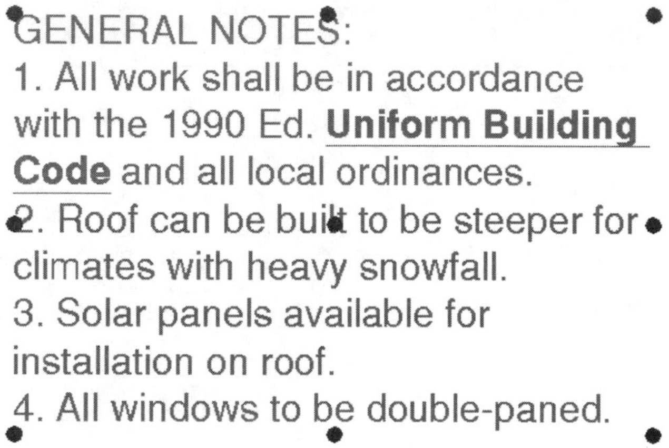

GENERAL NOTES:
1. All work shall be in accordance with the 1990 Ed. **Uniform Building Code** and all local ordinances.
2. Roof can be built to be steeper for climates with heavy snowfall.
3. Solar panels available for installation on roof.
4. All windows to be double-paned.

FIGURE 10.38: Justification points for MText

Are You Experienced?

Now you can . . .

- ☑ set up text styles
- ☑ place single line text in a drawing for titles and room labels
- ☑ create a grid for a drawing
- ☑ modify single line text
- ☑ construct a title block and place text in it
- ☑ place MText in a drawing
- ☑ modify MText in several ways

Dimensioning a Drawing

- Setting up a dimension style
- Dimensioning the floor plan of the cabin
- Modifying existing dimensions
- Modifying existing dimension styles

Dimensions are the final ingredient to be added to your drawing. To introduce you to dimensioning, we are going to follow a pattern similar to the one we used in the previous skill on text.

Dimension Styles

Dimension styles are similar to text styles, but are more complex. They are set up the same way, but there are many parameters controlling the various parts of dimensions, including the dimension text.

Before you start setting up a dimension style, you need to make a few changes to your drawing to prepare it for dimensioning.

1. Open up Cabin10c and zoom into the upper half of the drawing.

2. Create a new layer called Dim1. Assign it a color and make it current.

3. Freeze the Grid layer.

4. Set Endpoint Osnap to be running.

5. Right click any button on any toolbar on the screen to bring up the on-screen toolbar menu. Click Dimension. The Dimension toolbar comes up on the drawing area in the form of a floating toolbar.

6. Move the Dimension toolbar to the top center of the drawing area, being careful to avoid docking it. (In Skill 1, *Getting to Know AutoCAD*, you learned about moving toolbars around on the screen.) Your drawing will look like Figure 11.1.

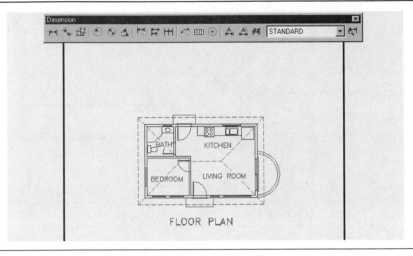

FIGURE 11.1: The floor plan of Cabin10c with the Dimension toolbar centered at the top of the drawing area

Making a New Dimension Style

Each dimension has several components: the dimension line, arrows or tick marks, extension lines, and the dimension text (Figure 11.2). The appearance and location of each of these components is controlled by an extensive set of variables that is stored with each drawing file. You will work with these variables through a series of dialog boxes that have been designed to make setting up a dimension style as easy and trouble-free as possible. Remember that AutoCAD has been designed to be useable by drafters from many trades and professions, each of which has its own standards for drafting. To satisfy the widely varied dimensioning needs of these folks, Auto-CAD dimensioning features have many options and settings for controlling the appearance and placement of the dimensions in your drawings.

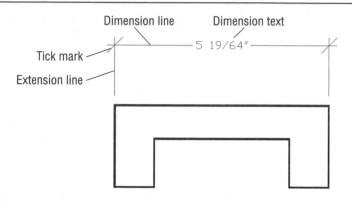

FIGURE 11.2: The parts of a dimension

Naming a Dimension Style

Every dimension variable has a default setting, and these as a group comprise the default Standard dimension style. As in defining text styles, the procedure is to make a copy of the Standard dimension style and rename the copy—in effect, making a new style that is a copy of the default style. Then you make changes to this new style so it has the settings you need to dimension your drawing.

1. Click the Dimension Style button on the Dimension toolbar. The Dimension Style Manager dialog box comes up (Figure 11.3). On the top left in the Styles list box, Standard is listed.

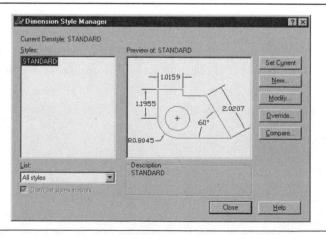

FIGURE 11.3: The Dimension Style Manager dialog box

2. Click the New button on the right side of the dialog box. The New Dimension Style dialog box appears.

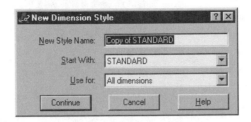

3. In the New Style Name text box, Copy of Standard is highlighted. Type **DimPlan** but don't press ↵ yet. Notice that Standard is in the Start With drop-down list just below. Because it is the current and only dimension style in this drawing, the new dimension style you are about to define will begin as a copy of the Standard style. This is similar to the way in which new text styles are defined (Skill 10, *Controlling Text in a Drawing*). The Use For drop-down list allows you to choose the kinds of dimensions to which the new style will be applied. In this case, it's all dimensions, so we don't need to change this.

4. Click the Continue button. The New Dimension Style dialog changes into a large dialog box with the same name, but with DimPlan added to the title bar (Figure 11.4). It has 6 tabs. You have created a new dimension style that is a copy of the Standard style, and now you will make the changes necessary to set up DimPlan to work as the main dimension style for the floor plan of the cabin.

5. Be sure the Lines and Arrows tab is active (on top). If it's not, click it.

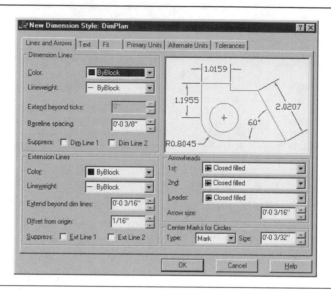

FIGURE 11.4: The New Dimension Style dialog box with DimPlan as the current style and Lines and Arrows as the active tab

Using the Lines and Arrows Tab

You will use the Lines and Arrows tab to control the appearance of the dimension and extension lines, the arrowheads, and the center marks.

1. In the Arrowheads area, click the down arrow in the first list to open the drop-down list of arrowheads.

2. Click Architectural Tick. The drop-down list closes with Architectural Tick displayed in the first and second drop-down lists. In the preview window above, a graphic displays the new arrowhead type.

3. In the Arrow Size text box, use the down scroll arrow to change 0'-0 ³⁄₁₆" to 0'-⅛".

4. Move to the Dimension Lines area. Change the Extend Beyond Ticks setting from 0" to ³⁄₃₂" by highlighting the 0 and typing in the new setting. This will extend the dimension line past the tick mark a short distance.

5. In the Extension Line area, use the down scroll arrow to change the Extend Beyond Dim Lines setting from 0'-0 ³⁄₁₆" to ⅛". This controls how far the extension line will extend beyond the dimension line.

Before saving these changes, make some more modifications to the DimPlan style.

Making Changes in the Text Tab

The settings in the Text tab control the appearance of dimension text and how it is located relative to the dimension and extension lines.

1. Click the Text tab on the New Dimension Style dialog box. There are three areas with settings that affect the appearance and location of dimension text. Look ahead to Figure 11.5 for a graphic of the Text tab. The preview window appears in all tabs and is updated automatically as settings are modified. Move to the Text Appearance area in the upper-left corner of the dialog box where there are five settings that control how the text looks. We are concerned about only two of them.

2. Click the Browse button that sits at the right end of the Text Style drop-down list. The Text Style dialog box opens. Set up a new text style called Dim that has the following parameters:

    -   Romand.shx font
    -   0'-0" height
    -   0.8000 width factor
    -   All other settings at their default

    If you need a reminder on creating text styles, refer to Skill 10, *Controlling Text in a Drawing*. Apply this text style to make it current, then close the Text Style dialog box.

3. Back in the Text tab, open the Text Style drop-down list and select the new Dim style from the list.

4. Change the Text Height setting from ³⁄₁₆" to ³⁄₃₂".

5. Move down to the Text Placement area. These settings determine where the text is located, vertically and horizontally, relative to the dimension line. There are two settings to change.

6. Open the Vertical drop-down list and select Above. At this setting, the text will sit above the dimension line and not break the line into two segments. Set the Offset From Dim Line setting to ¹⁄₁₆".

7. Now move to the Text Alignment are. There are three radio buttons that control whether dimension text is aligned horizontally or with the direction of the dimension line. The ISO Standard option varies text alignment depending on whether the text can fit between the extension lines. Only one of the buttons can be active at a time. Horizontal should already be active. Click the Aligned with Dimension Line button. Notice how the appearance and location of the text has changed in the preview window. This finishes our work in this tab. The settings should look like Figure 11.5.

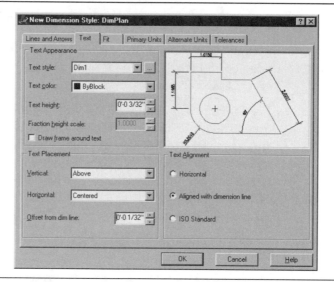

FIGURE 11.5: The Text tab with settings for the DimPlan style

There are four more tabs with settings, but we'll be making changes in only two of them: Fit and Primary Units.

Working with Settings in the Fit Tab

The settings in the Fit tab control the overall scale factor of the dimension style and how the text and arrowheads are placed when the extension lines are too close together for both text and arrows to fit.

1. Click the Fit tab on the New Dimension Style dialog box. Look forward to Figure 11.6 for a graphic of the Fit tab.

2. In the upper-left corner—in the Fit Options area—click the Text radio button.

3. In the Text Placement area, click the Over the Dimension Line, Without a Leader radio button.

4. Make no changes in the Fine Tuning area for now. Move to the Scale for Dimension Features area. Be sure Use Overall Scale Of radio button is active. Set the scale to 96. (Use the highlight–and–type-in method described in step 4 of "Using the Lines and Arrows Tab.") The settings in the Fit tab should look like Figure 11.6.

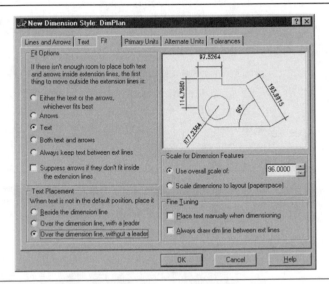

FIGURE 11.6: The new settings in the Fit tab

Setting Up the Primary Units Tab

In the preview window, you may have noticed that the numbers in the dimension text were maintaining a decimal format with 4 decimal places, rather than the feet and inches format of the current Architectural units. Dimensions have their own units setting, independent of the basic units for the drawing as a whole. In the next tab, you will set the dimension units.

1. Click the Primary Units tab and take a peek ahead at Figure 11.7 to see how it's organized. There are two areas: Linear and Angular Dimensions. Within each of these areas are a few settings and one or two nested areas.

2. In the Linear Dimensions area, starting at the top, make the following changes:

   A. Change the Unit Format setting from Decimal to Architectural.

B. Change the Fraction Format setting to Diagonal.

C. In the Zero Supression sub-area, uncheck 0 Inches.

NOTE NOTE NOTE NOTE NOTE NOTE NOTE NOTE NOTE NOTE NOTE NOTE NOTE NOTE NOTE NOTE

Zero Supression controls (a) whether or not the zero is shown for feet when the dimensioned distance is less than one foot, and (b) whether or not the zero is shown for inches when the distance is an even number of feet. For the Cabin drawing, we will supress the zero for feet, but we will show the zero for inches. So 9" will be shown as 9", and 3' will be shown as 3'-0".

3. In the Angular Dimensions area, leave Decimal Degrees as the Units Format and change Precision to two decimal places, as you did for the basic draw-ing units in Skill 3. For now, leave the Zero Supression sub-area as it is. After these changes, the Primary Units tab will look like Figure 11.7.

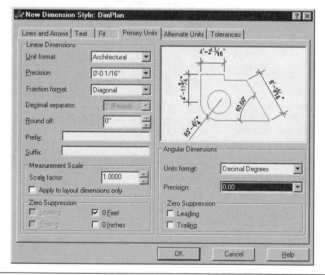

FIGURE 11.7: The Primary Units tab after changes have been made

The last two tabs—Alternate Units and Tolerances—are advanced settings that we won't need to change to dimension the cabin. It's time to save these setting changes to the new DimPlan dimension style and begin dimensioning the cabin.

1. Click the OK button at the bottom of the New Dimension Style dialog box. You will be returned to the Dimension Style Manager dialog box (Figure 11.8). DimPlan is displayed in the Styles list box, along with Standard. In the lower-right corner of the dialog box, in the Description area, the following information is presented about the new style: the name of the original style that the new style is based upon and changes that were made to the original style to create the new style.

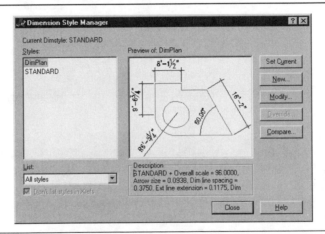

FIGURE 11.8: The Dimension Style Manager dialog box with DimPlan listed

2. Click DimPlan to highlight it. Then click the Set Current button. Finally, click the Close button. You are returned to your drawing, and the Dimension toolbar now displays DimPlan in the Dim Style Control drop-down list. This indicates that DimPlan is now the current dimension style.

You have made changes to 15 settings that control dimensions. This is not too many, considering that there are over 50 dimension settings. Here is a summary of the changes you've made to make the dimensions work with the cabin drawing:

Tab	Setting	Default Setting	DimPlan
Lines and Arrows	Arrowheads	Closed Filled	Architectural Tick
	Arrowhead size	³⁄₁₆"	⅛"
	Dim Line Extension	0"	³⁄₃₂"
	Ext. Line Extension	³⁄₁₆"	⅛"
Text	Text Style	Standard	DimPlan
	Text Height	³⁄₁₆"	³⁄₃₂"
	Text Vert. Justification	Centered	Above
	Offset from Dim Line	³⁄₃₂"	¹⁄₁₆"
	Text Alignment	Horizontal	Aligned with Dimension Line
Fit	Fit Options	Either—whichever best	Text
	Text Placement	Beside dim line	Over dim line, no leader
	Overall scale	1.0000	96.0000
Primary Units	Unit Format	Decimal	Architectural
	Fraction Format	Horizontal	Diagonal
	Zero Suppression	Feet, Inches	Feet only
	Angular Precision	No decimal places	Two decimal places

You will change a few more settings throughout the rest of this skill as you begin to dimension the cabin in the next set of exercises.

Placing Dimensions on the Drawing

Upon returning to your drawing, it should still look almost exactly like Figure 11.1, and it should have the following:

- A new layer called Dim1, which is current

- A new dimension style called Dimplan, which is current and is now displayed in the drop-down list on the Dimension toolbar

- The Grid layer frozen

- Endpoint Osnap running

- A new text style called Dim, which is current

Horizontal Dimensions

First, you will dimension across the top of the plan, from the corner of the building to the center of the interior wall, then to the other corner. Then you'll dimension the roof.

1. Click the Linear button at the left end of the Dimension toolbar to activate the *Dimlinear command*. The prompt reads `Specify first extension line origin or <select object>:`.

2. Pick the upper-left corner of the cabin walls. The prompt changes to `Specify second extension line origin:`. At this point, zoom into the bathroom area until you can see the wall between the bathroom and kitchen, as well as the back wall, close up.

3. Type **.x** ↵ to start point filters.

4. Activate Midpoint Osnap and click the upper jamb line of the bathroom door opening when the triangle appears at the jamb's midpoint (Figure 11.9).

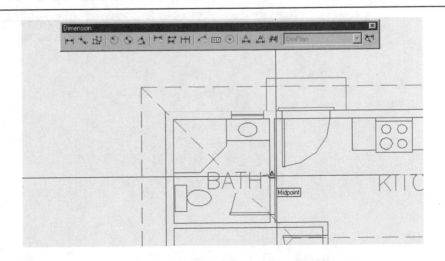

FIGURE 11.9: Selecting the jamb with Midpoint Osnap

5. Click the upper-left corner of the cabin walls again. The dimension appears in ghosted form attached to, and moving with, the cursor (Figure 11.10a). Notice that the right extension line starts just outside the outer wall line. This is the result of using the point filters.

6. Pan the drawing down until there's room to place the dimension. Move the cursor until the dimension line is about 3' above the back step. Click to place it (Figure 11.10b).

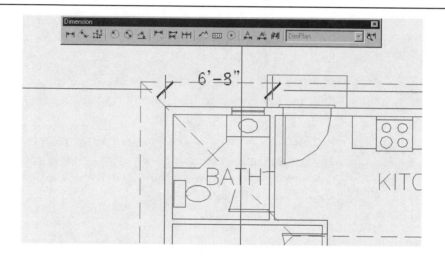

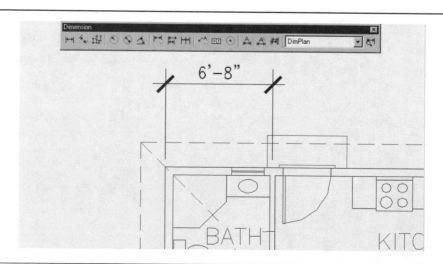

FIGURE 11.10: The dimension attached to the cursor (a), and placed (b)

Your first dimension is completed.

When dimensioning walls, you usually dimension to the outside of the exterior ones and to the center of the interior ones. The next dimension will run from the right side of the first dimension to the right corner.

NOTE NOTE NOTE NOTE NOTE NOTE NOTE NOTE NOTE NOTE NOTE NOTE NOTE NOTE NOTE

When dimensioning buildings that have 2x4 or 2x6 stud walls, architects usu-ally make the dimensions show the distance to the face of the stud for the out-side walls, but we are not able to go into that level of detail in this book. (Studs are the small, upright members in the framing of a wall.)

The Continue Command

AutoCAD has an automatic way of placing adjacent dimensions in line—the *Continue command.*

1. Zoom out and pan until you have a view of the upper wall and roof line, with space above them for dimensions (Figure 11.11).

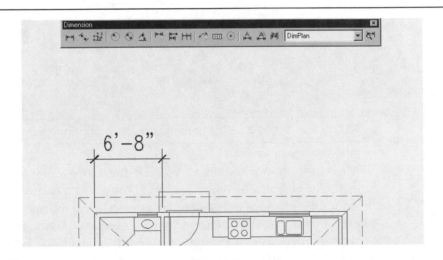

FIGURE 11.11: The result of zooming and panning for a view of the top of the floor plan

2. Select the Continue button of the Dimension toolbar. The prompt reads `Spec-ify a second extension line origin or [Undo/Select] <Select>:`. All you need to do here is pick a point for the right end of the dimension—in this case, the upper-right corner of the walls.

3. Click the upper-right corner of the house. The second dimension is drawn in line with the first (Figure 11.12). Note that the same prompt has returned to the Command window. You could keep picking points to place the next adjacent dimension in line, if there was need of one. Press Esc to cancel the Continue command.

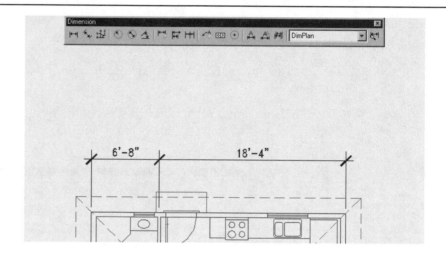

FIGURE 11.12: The completion of the Continue command

With the Continue command, you can dimension along a wall of a building very quickly, just by picking points. AutoCAD assumes that the last extension line specified for the previous dimension will coincide with the first extension line of the next dimension. If the extension line you need to continue from is not the last one specified, press ↵ at the prompt, then pick the extension line you want to continue from, and continue the command.

Another automatic routine that can be used with linear dimensions is called Baseline.

The Baseline Command

The *Baseline command* gets its name from a style of dimensioning called baseline, in which all dimensions begin at the same point (Figure 11.13). Each dimension is stacked above the previous one. Because of the automatic stacking, you can use the Baseline command for overall dimensions. AutoCAD will stack the overall dimension a set height above the incremental ones.

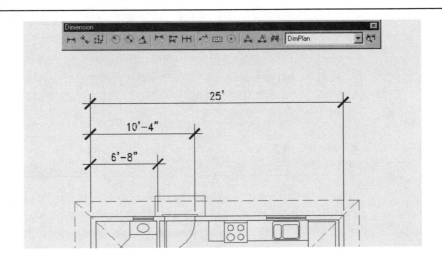

FIGURE 11.13: Example of baseline dimensions

1. Pick the Baseline button on the Dimension toolbar. The prompt reads "Specify a second extension line origin or [Undo/Select] <Select>:", just like the first prompt for the Continue command.

2. Press ↵ to choose the Select option.

3. Pick the extension line that extends from the upper-left corner—the first extension line of the first dimension.

4. Pick the upper-right corner of the walls, then press Esc to cancel the Baseline command. The overall dimension is drawn above the first two dimensions (Figure 11.14). (The Baseline command will keep running until you cancel it, just like the Continue command.)

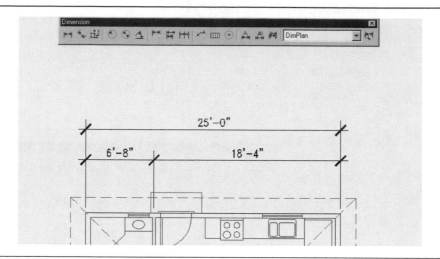

FIGURE 11.14: The completion of the overall dimension with the Baseline command

The Baseline command assumes the baseline is the first extension line of the last dimension. For the cabin, that would be the extension line that extends to the center of the interior wall. You want the baseline to be the extension line above the upper-left corner of the walls, so you pressed ↵ to select that extension line to be the baseline.

It would be nice to have a dimension for the roof spaced the same distance above the overall dimension as the overall dimension is spaced above the incremental dimensions. The Baseline command can help you do this.

1. Start the Baseline command again and press ↵ for the Select option.

2. Pick the extension line for the upper-left corner of the walls as the baseline.

3. Pick the upper-right corner of the roof. A dimension is placed above the overall dimension (Figure 11.15a). Press Esc to cancel the Baseline command. To finish it, you need to move the left extension line of this last dimension to the upper-left corner of the roof.

4. Click the text of the roof dimension. Grips appear in five places on the dimension, and the dimension ghosts (Figure 11.15b).

5. Click the grip at the bottom of the left extension line to activate it.

6. Click the upper-left corner of the roof, then press ↵ twice. The extension line moves, and the dimension text is updated to display the full length of the roof (Figure 11.15c).

This completes the horizontal dimensions for the floor plan.

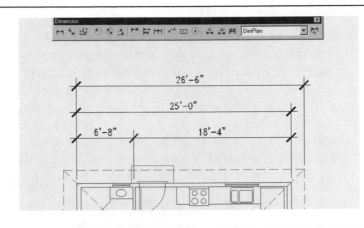

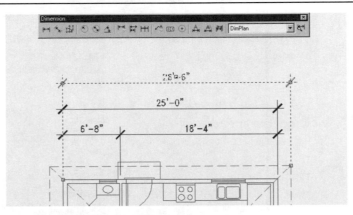

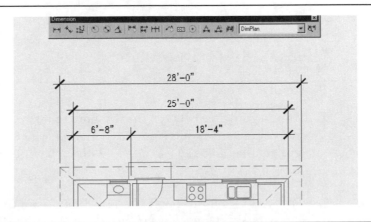

FIGURE 11.15: The result of the second use of the Baseline command (a), starting grips to modify the dimension (b), and the results (c)

Vertical Dimensions

Because the Linear command can be used for vertical and horizontal dimensions, you can follow the same steps as above to do the vertical dimensions on the left side of the floor plan. The only difference here from the horizontal dimensioning is that there is no jamb line that can be used with point filters to establish the center of the interior wall between the bedroom and bathroom. You will draw a guideline—the same one you drew in the last skill to help make the grid. The following steps will take you through the process of placing the first vertical dimension. Then you'll be able to finish the rest of them by yourself.

1. Pan and zoom to get a good view of the left side of the floor plan, including the space between the roof and the border (Figure 11.16).

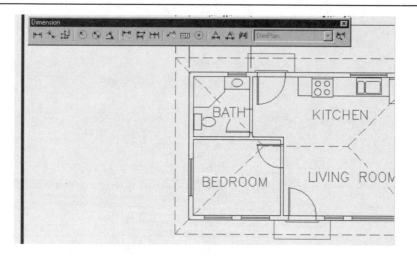

FIGURE 11.16: The result of zooming and panning for a view of the left side of the floor plan

2. Draw a guideline between the two horizontal interior wall lines where they meet the exterior wall (Figure 11.17a). Endpoint Osnap should be running, and you should be able to do this without having to zoom in.

3. Click the Linear button. Then pick the upper-left corner of the walls.

4. Type **.y** ↵ to start the point filters. Pick Midpoint Osnap and move the cursor to the short guideline you just drew. When the triangle appears on the line, click the mouse.

5. Click again on the upper-left corner of the walls to complete the point filter process. The vertical dimension appears in ghosted form, attached to the cursor.

6. Move the dimension line to a point about 3' to the left of the roof line and click. The first vertical dimension is drawn (Figure 11.17b).

7. Erase the short guideline from between the interior walls.

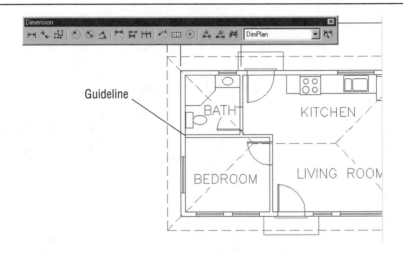

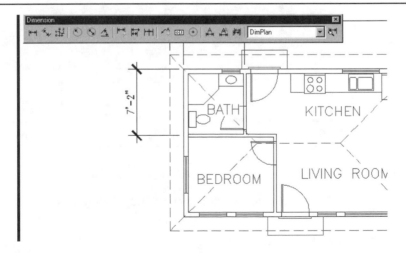

FIGURE 11.17: A guideline is drawn to help find the center of an interior wall (a), and the first vertical dimension is placed (b).

Finishing the Vertical Dimensions

The rest of the vertical dimensions are placed using the same procedure as was used to complete the horizontal dimensions. Here is a summary of the steps:

1. Use the Continue command to dimension the bedroom.

2. Use the Baseline command to place an overall dimension.

3. Use the Baseline command to place a roof dimension to the left of the overall dimension.

4. Use grips to move the first extension line of the roof dimension to its corner.

Refer back through the previous section if you need more detailed instructions. The completed vertical dimensions will look like Figure 11.18.

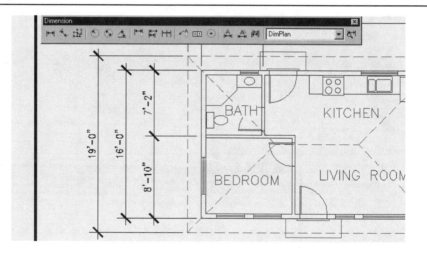

FIGURE 11.18: The completed vertical dimensions

The next area to dimension will be the balcony.

1. Pan to a view of the balcony. Include some space below and to the right of it.

TIP TIP TIP TIP TIP TIP TIP TIP TIP TIP TIP TIP TIP TIP TIP TIP TIP TIP TIP TIP TIP TIP TIP TIP

When you have a floating toolbar on the screen, using the Zoom Window command doesn't take into account the area that the floating toolbar takes up. It's better to use Realtime Pan and Zoom to adjust your view in this situation when you can.

2. Start the Linear command and pick the lower-right corner of the building walls.

3. Use Quadrant Osnap and pick near the right-most edge of the outside balcony wall.

4. When the dimension appears, move it down below the roof line and place it there (Figure 11.19).

This will be enough on vertical and horizontal linear dimensions for now. Take a look at some other kinds of dimensions.

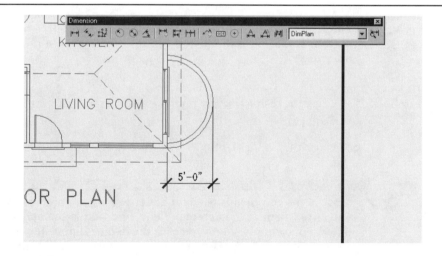

FIGURE 11.19: The horizontal balcony dimension

Other Types of Dimensions

AutoCAD provides tools for placing linear dimensions that are neither vertical nor horizontal, as well as radial and angular dimensions. You'll use the *Radial command* to dimension the inside radius of the balcony.

Radial Dimensions

On the Dimension toolbar, there are icons for Radius and Diameter dimensions. They both operate the same way and are controlled by the same settings.

Radius   Diameter

TIP TIP TIP TIP TIP TIP TIP TIP TIP TIP TIP TIP TIP TIP TIP TIP TIP TIP TIP TIP TIP TIP TIP TIP

The icons on the toolbars don't really look like buttons until you move the pointer cursor onto them. In this book, we'll refer to them as both icons and buttons.

1. Click the Osnap button on the status bar to temporarily disable any running Osnaps.

2. Click the Radius Dimension button to start the Dimradius command.

NOTE NOTE NOTE NOTE NOTE NOTE NOTE NOTE NOTE NOTE NOTE NOTE NOTE NOTE NOTE

Most of the commands used for dimensioning are prefaced with a "dim" when you enter them at the command line, and that is the actual name of the command. For example, when you click the Radius Dimension button on the Dimension toolbar, or pick Dimension ➢ Radius on the menu bar, you will see _dimradius in the Command window to let you know that you have started the Dimradius command. The same command can be started by typing dimradius ↵ or dra ↵ (the shortcut alias).

3. Click the inside arc of the balcony. The radius dimension appears in ghosted form. Its angle of orientation is by where you pick the arc, but the text follows the cursor (Figure 11.20).

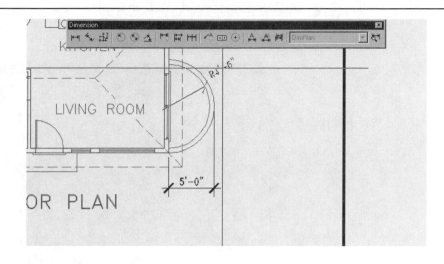

FIGURE 11.20: The radius dimension initially positioned in the arc

4. Notice that the tick mark used for linear dimensions is used here also. We must have an arrowhead for the radial dimension. Press Esc to cancel the command.

We will have to alter the dimension style to specify an arrowhead for radial dimensions.

Parent and Child Dimensioning Styles

The DimPlan dimension style you set up at the beginning of this chapter applies to all dimensions and is called the *parent* dimension style. But you can change settings in this dimension style for particular types of dimensions, like, say, the radial type. This makes a *child* dimension style. The *child* version is based on the *parent* version, but has a few settings that are different. In this way, all your dimensions will be made using the DimPlan dimension style, but radial dimensions will be using a child version of the style, while most other dimensions will be using the parent version of the style. Once you create a child dimension style from the parent style, you then refer to both styles by the same name, but you call them a dimension style family.

1. Click the Dimension Style button on the Dimension toolbar to bring up the Dimension Style Manager dialog box. It will look like Figure 11.21.

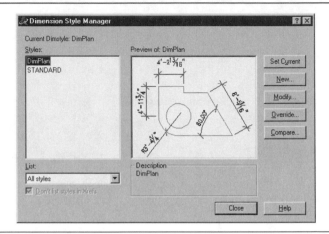

FIGURE 11.21: The Dimension Style Manager dialog box with DimPlan current

2. Be sure DimPlan is highlighted in the Styles list. Then click the New button. The New Dimension Style dialog box will come up.

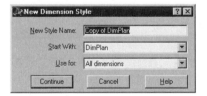

3. Open the Use For drop-down list and select Radius Dimensions. Then click the Continue button. The New Dimension Style dialog box gets larger and now has the six tabs you worked with earlier. Its title bar now includes Radial, and the preview window shows a radial dimension.

4. Activate the Lines and Arrows tab. Then move to the Arrowheads area and open the first Arrowhead drop-down list.

5. Select Right-Angle. Notice how the preview window now illustrates a radial dimension with a right-angle arrowhead. Click OK to close the New Dimension Style: DimPlan: Radial dialog box.

6. In the Dimension Style Manager dialog box, notice the Style list. Radial is now a sub-style of DimPlan. Radial is referred to as a "child" style of the "parent" style DimPlan. Click Close to close the Dimension Style Manager dialog box.

7. Click the Radius button on the Dimension toolbar.

8. Click the inside arc of the balcony at a point about 15° above the right quadrant point. The radius dimension appears in ghosted form, and it now has an arrow instead of a tick mark.

9. Move the cursor to the outside of the balcony, and place the dimension text so that it looks similar to Figure 11.22.

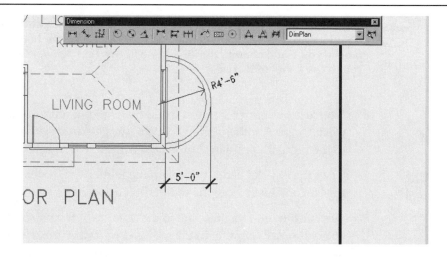

FIGURE 11.22: The radius dimension for the balcony

When placing the dimension, you have control over the angle of the dimension line by where you pick the arc, and the location of the dimension text by where you pick the second point.

The balcony also needs to be identified in the drawing as the rooms are.

Leader Lines

You can use the *Leader command* to draw an arrow to the balcony and place the text outside the arcs. The Leader Line dimension also requires an adjustment of a few dimension style settings.

1. Click the Dimension Style button on the Dimension toolbar.

2. With DimPlan highlighted, click New.

3. In the New Dimension Style dialog box, open the Use For drop-down list and click Leaders and Tolerances. Then click Continue.

4. Activate the Lines and Arrows tab, then move to the Arrowheads area and open the Leader drop-down list. Click Right-Angle.

5. Click the Text tab. In the Text Placement area, change Above to Centered. Then click OK.

TIP TIP TIP TIP TIP TIP TIP TIP TIP TIP TIP TIP TIP TIP TIP TIP TIP TIP TIP TIP TIP TIP TIP

If you wanted the Balcony label text to be of the same text style as the room labels, you could change the Text Style in the Text Appearance area of the Text tab to the Label text style.

6. Notice how Leader is now a Child Style, along with Radial, in the Styles list. Click Close. Another child DimPlan dimension style is created. It's identical to the regular DimPlan style except for the two settings you just changed.

7. Click the Quick Leader button on the Dimension toolbar. Pick a point inside the balcony just below the radial dimension line.

8. Turn Ortho off. Drag the line to the outside of the balcony, making the line approximately parallel to the radius dimension line, and pick a point (Figure 11.23a).

9. Press ↵. Then, at the `Specify text width <0">:` prompt, press ↵ again. At the next prompt, with Caps Lock on, type **balcony** ↵. The prompt changes to read "`Enter next line of annotationtext:`." Now you can enter multiple lines of text for the leader. Press ↵. The leader line is completed, and BALCONY is placed at the end of the line (Figure 11.23b).

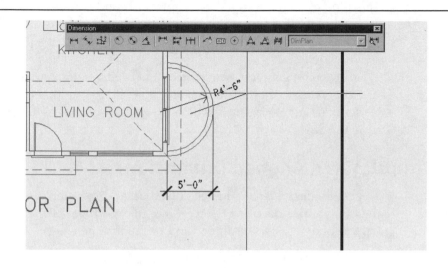

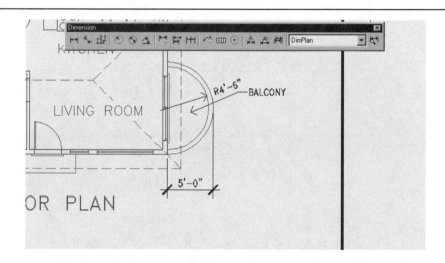

FIGURE 11.23: The leader line being drawn (a), and the completed leader (b)

NOTE NOTE NOTE NOTE NOTE NOTE NOTE NOTE NOTE NOTE NOTE NOTE NOTE NOTE NOTE

If the angle of the leader line is steeper than 15°, a short horizontal line called a *dogleg* or *hook line* is added between the leader line and the text.

10. Zoom to extents, then zoom out a little and pan to view the whole drawing with dimensions.

11. Save this drawing as Cabin11a.

This exercise gets you started using the Leader command. Later in this skill, in the section on modifying dimensions, you will get another chance to work with leader lines and their text. Next, I have two more types of dimensions to introduce to you.

Angular and Aligned Dimensions

To get familiar with the Aligned and Angular dimension types, play around with the two commands, using the roof lines to experiment. Here's how to set up Cabin11a to work with Aligned and Angular dimensions:

1. Make the Roof layer current.

2. Freeze all other layers by following these steps:

    A. Click the Layers button.

    B. In the Layer Properties Manager dialog box, place the cursor on the 0 layer and right-click. A small menu comes up.

    C. Click Select All on the menu. Then click one of the suns in the Freeze column.

    D. Click OK in the warning box. The sun icon changes to a snowflake for all the layers except the Roof layer (because it is the current layer).

    E. Click OK to close the dialog box and return to the drawing. Everything has disappeared except the roof lines.

3. Zoom in to a closer view of the roof.

4. Create a new layer called Dim2. Keep the black/white color and make it current.

5. Set Endpoint Osnap to be running. Now you are ready to dimension.

Aligned Dimensions

Aligned dimensions are linear dimensions that are not horizontal or vertical. They are placed in the same way that horizontal or vertical dimensions are placed with the Linear command. You can also use the Baseline and Continue commands with aligned dimensions.

Use the *Aligned command* to dimension a hip line of the roof. Try it on you own. Follow the prompts. It works just like the Dimlinear command.

Start the Aligned command by picking the Align button on the Dimension toolbar.

Angular Dimensions

The angular dimension is the only basic dimension type that uses angles in the dimension text instead of linear measurements. Generally, tick marks are not used with angular dimensions, so you'll need to create another child dimension style for this type of dimension. Follow the steps listed previously in this skill for setting up the Radial and Leader child styles. The only changes you need to make is in the Lines and Arrows tab: replace the Architectural Tick with the Right-Angle arrowhead.

Try making an angular dimension on your own. You can start the Angular command by clicking the Angular button on the Dimension toolbar. Follow the prompts and see if you can figure out how this command works.

Figure 11.24 illustrates angular and aligned dimensions on the roof. Give it a try on your own and see how you do.

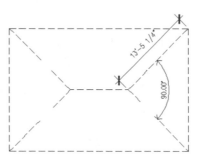

FIGURE 11.24: The roof with angular and aligned dimensions

When settings for a dimension style are changed, dimensions created when that style was current will be automatically updated to reflect the changes. You'll do more modifications of dimensions in the next part of this skill.

You have been introduced to the basic types of dimensions—linear, radial, leader, and angular—and some auxiliary dimensions—baseline, continue, and aligned—that were special cases of the linear type. The Baseline and Continue dimensions can also be used with angular dimensions.

The final part of this skill will be devoted to teaching you a few methods for modifying various parts of dimensions.

Modifying Dimensions

Several commands, as well as grips, can be used to modify dimensions, depending on what the desired change is. You can:

- Change the dimension text content.

- Move the dimension text relative to the dimension line.

- Move the dimension or extension lines.

- Change the dimension style settings for a dimension, or group of dimensions.

- Revise a dimension style.

The best way to understand how modifications of dimensions are achieved is by making a few yourself.

1. Thaw all layers and make the Dim1 layer current again.

2. Freeze the following layers:

    - Dim2

    - Grid

    - Hatch-plan-floor

    - Hatch-plan-wall

3. Zoom and pan until your view of the floor plan is similar to Figure 11.25.

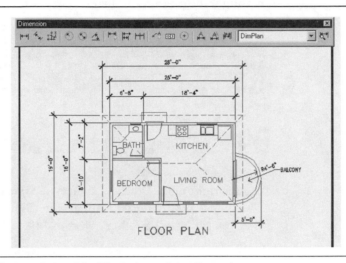

FIGURE 11.25: Modified view of the floor plan

Modifying Dimension Text

Any aspect of the dimension text can be modified. We'll look at how the content is changed first.

Editing Dimension Text Content

To change the content of text for one dimension, or to add text before or after the actual dimension, use the Ddedit command. (You used this command in Skill 10 to modify text.) We'll change the text in the horizontal dimensions for the roof and walls.

1. Type **ddedit** ↵. Then select the horizontal roof dimension at the top of the drawing. The Multiline Text Editor dialog box appears. The angle brackets in the editing box represent the existing text in the dimension, or 28'-0". You

can highlight the brackets and enter a new dimension, or enter new text before or after the brackets.

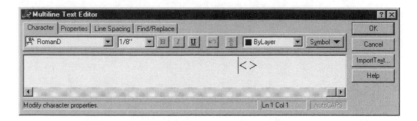

2. Click to the right of the brackets, then type *(space)***verify in field** and click OK. The phrase is added to the dimension (Figure 11.26a). The prompt tells you that you can select another object to edit.

3. Click the dimension just below the roof dimension.

4. In the Multiline Text Editor dialog box, click to the right of the angle brackets again. Then click the Symbol button in the upper-right corner. A drop-down list gives three special characters and some other choices.

5. Select Plus/Minus. The ± symbol is now in the edit box.

6. Click OK. The dimension now has a ± after it (Figure 11.26b). Press ↵ to end the Ddedit command.

If you need to change the text of several dimensions at once, use the *Dimedit command*.

1. Click the Dimension Edit button on the Dimension toolbar.

2. At the Enter type of dimension editing [Home/New/Rotate/ Oblique] <Home>: prompt, type **n** ↵ to replace the existing text or add to it.

3. In the Multiline Text Editor dialog box, highlight the angle brackets.

4. Type **Unknown** and click OK.

5. In the drawing, click the 6'-8" and 18'-4" dimensions. Then press ↵.

6. The two dimensions now read Unknown (Figure 11.26c).

Next, you'll learn about moving the dimension text.

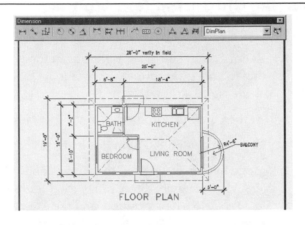

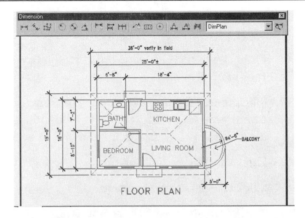

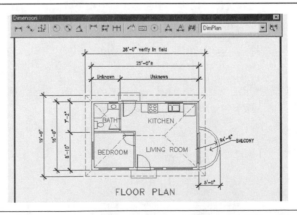

FIGURE 11.26: Adding a phrase to dimension text (a), adding a special character (b), and editing more than one dimension text at a time (c)

Moving Dimension Text Around

You can use grips to move dimension text and the dimension line.

1. Zoom into a view of the right side of the floor plan until you have a view that includes the entire balcony and its three dimensions, as well as the entire right cabin wall.

2. At the Command: prompt, click the 5'-0" dimension. Grips appear.

3. Click the grip on the right tick mark to activate it.

4. Move the cursor up until the dimension text is above the balcony. Then click again to fix it there. Press Esc twice (Figure 11.27a). The dimension, line, and text move to a new position, and the extension lines are redrawn to the new position.

5. Click the leader line. Then click the word *Balcony*. Two grips appear on the leader line, and one appears on the text.

6. Hold down the Shift key and click the two grips near the text. Then release the shift button.

7. Click one of the two activated grips. Then move the cursor down to reposition the leader and text slightly below the Quadrant point of the balcony arcs. Then click to fasten them there. Press Esc twice (Figure 11.27b).

8. Click the 4'-6" radial dimension. Three grips appear.

9. Click the grip at the arrowhead.

10. Pick Nearest Osnap. Then move the cursor to the inside arc and below the just relocated leader line until the radial dimension line displays in a clear space. Then pick that point.

11. With grips still on the radial dimension, click the grip in the middle of the dimension text.

12. Drag it down and to the right until it clears the leader line and its text. Then click again to fix it there. Press Esc twice (Figure 11.27c).

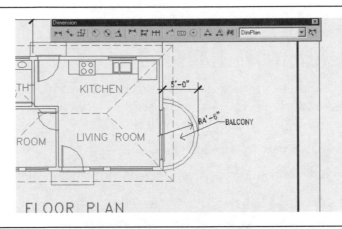

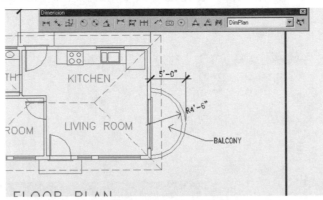

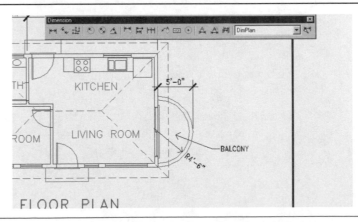

FIGURE 11.27: Moving the balcony dimensions with grips: the linear dimension (a), the leader (b), and the radial dimension

To finish the changes to the balcony, you need to suppress the left extension line of the 5–foot–0–inch dimension because it overlaps the wall and header lines.

Dimension Overrides

Suppression of the left extension line will be done with the Properties command, which allows you to change a setting in the dimension style for one dimension without altering the style settings.

1. Freeze the Headers layer.

2. Click the Properties button on the Standard toolbar.

3. Click the 5–foot–0–inch dimension.

4. In the Properties dialog box, move to the Lines and Arrows heading and click the + sign to the left of it. The settings of the Lines and Arrows tab appear.

5. Click **Ext line 1**. Then click the down arrow in the right column to open up the drop-down list. Click Off. The left extension line on the linear balcony dimension is suppressed.

6. Close the Properties dialog box. Press Esc twice to remove the grips (Figure 11.28).

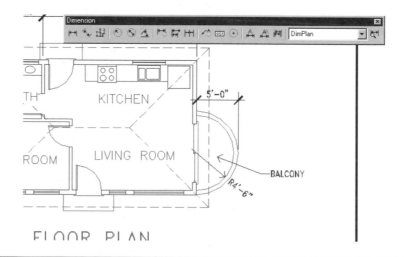

FIGURE 11.28: The 5–foot–0–inch dimension with the left extension line suppressed

The bedroom needs a horizontal dimension. Because of a shortage of space outside the floor plan, you'll place the dimension inside the bedroom and suppress both extension lines with an override to the current dimension style.

1. Pan the drawing over until the bedroom is fully in view.

2. Open the Dimension Style Manager dialog box and click the Override button.

3. Activate the Lines and Arrows tab. In the Extension Lines area, put a checkmark in the Ext Line 1 and Ext Line 2 checkboxes. Then click OK.

4. In the Dimension Style Manager dialog box, click Close.

5. Click the Linear button on the Dimension toolbar.

6. Pick the lower-left inside corner of the bedroom, then pick the lower-right inside corner. The dimension appears in ghosted form, attached to the cursor.

7. Suppress the running Osnaps for one pick. Then move the dimension up to a position below the BEDROOM text and above the lower wall, and click to fix it there. Move the dimension up to a position below the window and click to fix it there. The dimension is placed, and both extension lines are suppressed (Figure 11.29).

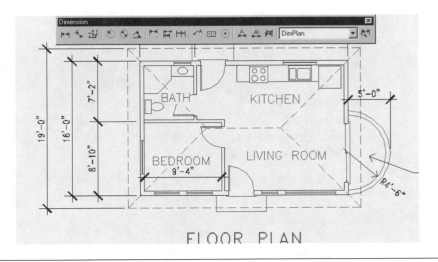

FIGURE 11.29: The completed bedroom dimension

8. Open the Dimension Style Manager dialog box. In the Styles list, the current style is the sub-style under DimPlan called <style overrides>. We can delete this style now, as it is no longer needed.

9. Click DimPlan in the list. Then click the Set Current button. A warning window appears. You are warned that the override settings will be deleted if you make DimPlan the current dimension style. Click Yes. The style overrides are deleted.

10. Click Close to close the dialog box.

TIP TIP TIP TIP TIP TIP TIP TIP TIP TIP TIP TIP TIP TIP TIP TIP TIP TIP TIP TIP TIP TIP TIP

If you set a style override that you later decide should be incorporated into the parent dimension style, highlight <style overrides> in the Styles list, right-click, and then click Save to Current Style on the small menu that appears.

Extension lines are usually about the thinnest lines in a drawing, so it is usually not critical that they be suppressed in most cases. However, if a print were made with the Headers layer frozen, the left extension line of the 5'-0" dimension for the balcony would have to be suppressed or moved so it would not be visible spanning the sliding door opening.

Dimensioning Short Distances

When you have to dimension distances so short that the text and arrows (or tick marks) can't both fit between the extension line, a dimension style setting determines where they are placed. To see how this works, you'll redo the horizontal dimensions above the floor plan, this time dimensioning the distance between the roof line and wall line, as well as the thickness of the interior wall. When we set up the DimPlan dimension style before, the setting changes that we made in the Fit tab then will help us now.

1. Zoom out to a view of the upper portion of the floor plan so that the horizontal dimensions above the floor plan are visible (Figure 11.30).

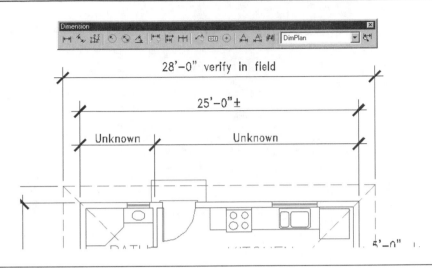

FIGURE 11.30: The new view of the upper floor plan and its dimensions

2. Use the Erase command to erase the four dimensions that are above the floor plan. Each dimension is a single object, so you can select them with four picks, or one crossing window.

3. Select the Linear button and pick the upper-left corner of the roof. Then pick the upper-left corner of the wall lines. Place the dimension line about 3' above the upper roof line (Figure 11.31a).

4. Select the Continue button. Click the upper end of each interior wall line, then click the upper-right corner of the wall lines, and, finally, click the upper-right corner of the roof (Figure 11.31b). Press Esc to cancel the Continue command.

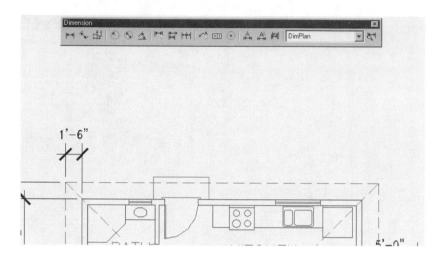

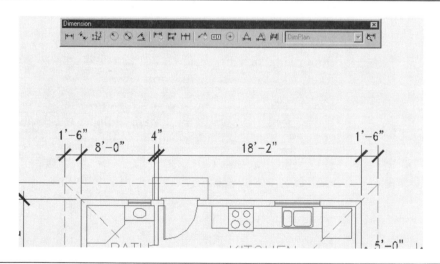

FIGURE 11.31: The first dimension is placed (a), and the other dimensions (b)

5. Click the Baseline button. Press ↵ and then pick the left extension line of the 1-foot–inch dimension on the left end.

6. Click the upper-right corner of the roof. The overall dimension is placed a set distance above the lower dimensions (Figure 11.32a). Press Esc to cancel the Baseline command.

Because some of the text in the smaller of the lower dimensions was placed higher than normal, the overall dimension needs to be raised to clear that text.

1. Click the overall dimension. Grips appear. Click the grip at the intersection of the right extension line and the dimension line to activate it.

2. Move the cursor up until the dimension line clears the higher text on the lower dimensions. Press Esc twice (Figure 11.32b). The text of the two 1-foot–6-inch dimensions crosses over the outer extension lines.

3. You can move dimension text with grips. Click the right 1-foot–6-inch dimension. Grips appear. Click the grip right in the middle of the text. Be sure Ortho is on. Then move the text to the left until it clears the extension line and click to place it.

4. Click the left 1-foot–6-inch dimension and repeat step 3, this time moving the text to the right.

5. When the text is where you want it, press Esc twice to clear the grips (Figure 11.32c).

SKILL
11

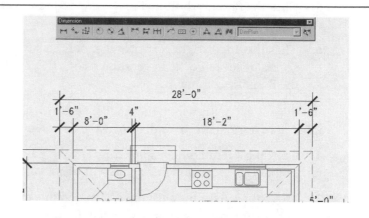

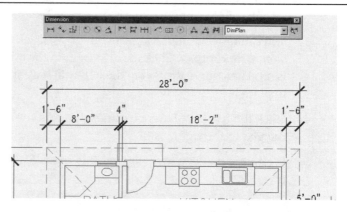

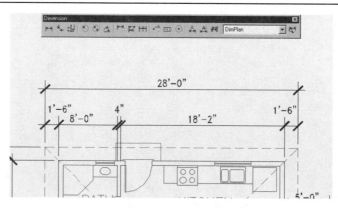

FIGURE 11.32: The overall dimension is placed using Baseline (a), raised using grips (b), and the 1-foot–6-inch dimensions are moved to clear the extension lines (c)

This concludes the exercises for dimensions in this skill. The current drawing won't be used in future skills, so feel free to experiment with the dimensioning commands you have just learned. When you finish a drawing session, before you save, it is a good habit to zoom to extents and then zoom out a little so all visible objects are on the screen. This way, the next time you bring up this drawing, you will have a full view of it at the beginning of your session.

1. Click the X in the upper-right corner of the Dimension toolbar to close it.

2. Zoom to extents, then zoom out a little to a full view of the cabin (Figure 11.33).

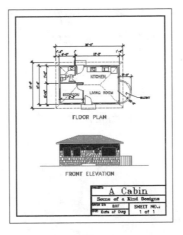

FIGURE 11.33: The full view of the cabin drawing with dimensions complete

3. Save this drawing to your training folder as Cabin11b.

4. Take a break. You deserve one!

Working successfully with dimensions in your drawing requires an investment of time to become familiar with the commands and settings that control how dimensions appear, how they are placed in the drawing, and how they are modified. The exercises in this skill have led you through the basics of the dimension processes. For a thorough treatment of AutoCAD's dimensioning features, see *Mastering AutoCAD 2000*, by George Omura (Sybex, 1999).

The next skill will introduce you to external references, a tool for viewing a drawing from within another drawing.

Are You Experienced?

Now you can . . .

- ☑ create a new dimension style
- ☑ place vertical and horizontal dimensions in a drawing
- ☑ use radial, aligned, and angular dimensions
- ☑ create leader lines for notes
- ☑ modify dimension text
- ☑ override a dimension style
- ☑ modify a dimension style

Managing External References

- → **Understanding external references**
- → **Creating external references**
- → **Modifying external references**
- → **Converting external references into blocks**

*E*xternal references are .dwg files that have been temporarily connected to the current drawing and are used as reference information. The externally referenced drawing is visible in the current drawing. Its layers, colors, linetypes, and visibility can be manipulated, and its objects can be changed. But it is not a permanent part of the current drawing.

External references are similar to blocks in that they both behave as single objects and are inserted into a drawing in the same way. But blocks are part of the current drawing file and external references are not.

Blocks can be exploded back to their component parts, but external references cannot. In Skill 7, you were able to modify the window block and, in so doing, updated all instances of the window block in the drawing. This was done without having to explode the block. With an external reference—usually referred to as an *Xref*—the same mechanism can be applied. In order to be able to manage external references, you need to learn how to set up an Xref, manipulate its appearance in the host drawing, and update it. Before you set up the Xref, you will create a site plan for the cabin. Then you will Xref the cabin drawing into the site drawing (Figure 12.1). In this figure, the lines of the cabin floor plan comprise the Xref, and the rest of the objects are part of the host drawing.

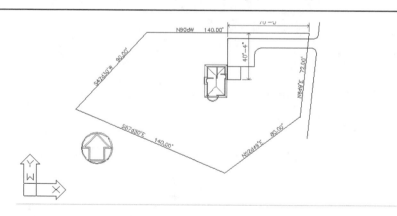

FIGURE 12.1: The site plan with the cabin as an external reference

Drawing a Site Plan

The site plan you will use has been simplified so that you can draw it with a minimum of steps and get on with the external referencing. Essential elements are:

• Property lines

- Access road to the site

- North arrow

- Indication of where the building is located on the site

The first step is to draw in the property lines.

Using Surveyor Units

Property lines are drawn using surveyor units for angles and decimal feet for linear units. In laying out the property lines, you will use relative polar coordinates, so the form of the coordinates you enter will be @*distance*<angle where the distance is in feet and hundredths of a foot, and the angle is in surveyor units to the nearest minute.

Surveyor Units

Surveyor units, called bearings in the civil engineering field, describe the direction of a line from its point of beginning. The direction, which is described as a deviation from the north or south to the east or west, is given as an angular measurement in degrees, minutes, and seconds. The angles used in a bearing can never be greater than 90°, so bearing lines must be headed in one of the 4 directional quadrants: north-easterly, north-westerly, south-easterly, or south-westerly. If north is set to be at the top of a plot plan, then south is down, east is to the right, and west is to the left. Thus, when a line from its beginning goes up and to the right, it will be headed in a north-easterly direction. And when a line from its beginning goes down and to the left, it is headed in a south-westerly direction, etc. A line that is headed in a north-easterly direction with a deviation from true north of 30° and 30 minutes is shown as N30d30'E in AutoCAD notation.

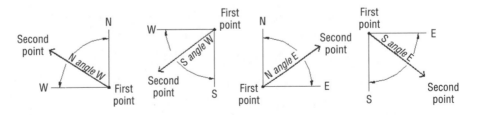

With the surveyor unit system, a sloping line that has an up-and-to-the-left direction would have a down-and-to-the-right direction if you started from the opposite end. So, for property lines, it is important to move in the same direction (clockwise or counterclockwise) as you progress from one segment to the next.

Laying Out the Property Lines

You will set up a new drawing, and then start at the upper-right corner of the property and work your way around in a counterclockwise direction.

1. Open Cabin11a from your training folder. Use File ➤ Save As to save the drawing as Cabin12a.

2. Click the New button on the Standard toolbar. In the Create New Drawing dialog box, click Start from Scratch, and then click OK.

3. From the menu bar, select Format ➤ Units. In the Drawing Units dialog box, change the Precision in the Length area to two decimal places (0.00).

4. In the Angle area, open the Type drop-down list and select Surveyor's Units. Then change the precision to the nearest minute (N 0d00' E). Click OK. You will need an area of about 250' × 150' for the site plan.

5. Open the Format menu again and pick Drawing Limits. Press ↵ to accept the default 0.00,0.00 for the lower-left corner. Type **250,150** ↵. Don't use the foot sign.

6. From the menu bar, click Tools ➤ Drafting Settings. Activate the Snap and Grid tab if it isn't already. Change the Snap Spacing to 10.00 and the Grid to 0.00. Then click in the Grid checkbox to turn the grid on. Click OK.

7. In the drawing, type **z** ↵ **a** ↵. Then zoom to .85× to see a blank space around the grid (Figure 12.2).

8. Create a new layer called Prop_line. Assign it a color and make it current.

9. Start the Line command. For the first point, type **220,130** ↵. This will start a line near the upper-right corner of the grid.

10. Be sure Snap is turned off. Then type:

    @140<n90dw ↵

    @90<s42d30'w ↵

    @140<s67d30'e ↵

@80<n52d49′e ↵

c ↵

The property lines are completed (Figure 12.3).

FIGURE 12.2: The site drawing with the grid on

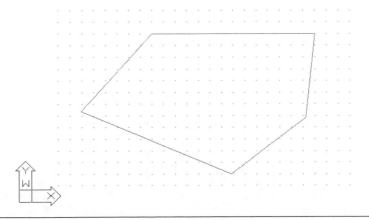

FIGURE 12.3: The property lines on the site drawing

Drawing the Driveway

The driveway is 8-feet wide and set 5' from the horizontal property line. The access road is 8' from the parallel property line. The intersection of the access road line and the driveway lines forms corners, each with a 3-foot radius. The driveway extends 70' in from the upper-right corner of the property. Let's lay this out now. First, switch to Architectural units and Decimal angular units.

1. Select Format ➤ Units from the menu bar. Change the units to Architectural and the angular units to Decimal degrees. Then set the Length precision to ¹⁄₁₆" and the angular precision to 0.00. Because of the way AutoCAD translates decimal units to inches, your drawing is now only ¹⁄₁₂th the size it needs to be. (Use the Distance command to check it.) You will have to scale it up.

2. Click the Scale button on the Modify toolbar.

> NOTE NOTE NOTE NOTE NOTE NOTE NOTE NOTE NOTE NOTE NOTE NOTE NOTE NOTE NOTE
> **The Scale command can also be started by selecting Modify ➤ Scale from the menu bar, or by typing sc ↵.**

3. Type **all** ↵↵. For the base point, type **0,0** ↵.

4. At the `Specify scale factor or [Reference]:` prompt, type **12** ↵. Then click Grid on the Status bar to turn the grid off.

5. Zoom to Extents, then zoom out a little. The drawing looks the same, but now it's the right size. Check it with the Distance command. (You were introduced to the Distance command in Skill 7, *Using Blocks and Wblocking*.)

6. Offset the upper, horizontal property line 5' down. Offset this new line 8' down.

7. Offset the right-most property line 8' to the right (Figure 12.4a).

8. Create a new layer called Road. Leave it assigned the default color and make it current.

9. Use the Property button to move the driveway and road lines to the Road layer.

10. Extend the driveway lines to the access road line. Trim the access road line between the driveway lines.

11. Fillet the two corners where the driveway meets the road, using a 3-foot radius (Figure 12.4b).

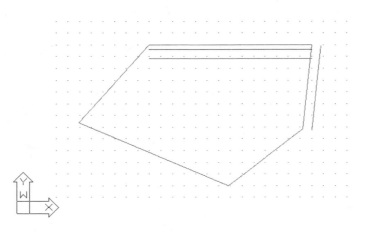

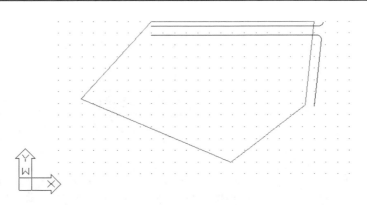

FIGURE 12.4: Offset property lines (a), and the completed intersection of the driveway and access road (b)

Finishing the Driveway

A key element of any site plan is information that shows how the building is positioned on the site relative to the property lines. Property lines are staked out by surveyors. Then the building contractor will take measurements off the stakes to locate one or two corners of the building. In this site, you only need one corner because we are assuming the cabin is facing due west. A close look at Figure 12.1 will reveal that the end of the driveway lines up with the outer edge of the back step of the cabin. Below the driveway is a square patio, and its bottom edge lines up with the bottom edge of the back step. So the bottom corner of the back step coincides with the lower-left corner of the patio. This locates the cabin on the site (Figure 12.5).

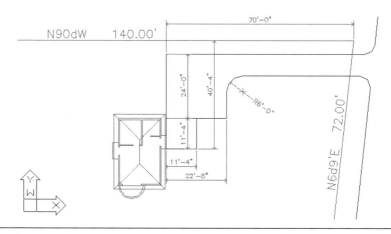

FIGURE 12.5: The driveway and patio lined up with the cabin

NOTE NOTE NOTE NOTE NOTE NOTE NOTE NOTE NOTE NOTE NOTE NOTE NOTE NOTE NOTE
Imagine the site being on a bluff of a hill overlooking land that falls away to the south and west, offering a spectacular view in that direction. To accommodate this view, we will want to change the orientation of the cabin when we Xref it into the site drawing.

1. Be sure Ortho is on. Then draw a line from the upper-right corner of the property lines straight up to a point near the top of the screen.

2. Offset this line 70' to the left. This will mark the end of the driveway.

3. Draw a line from the lower endpoint of this offset line down a distance of 40'-4". Then, with Ortho on, continue this line 11'4" to the right.

---

4. Offset the 40-foot-4-inch line 11'4 to the right. Offset the newly created line 11'-4" to the right as well.

5. Offset the upper driveway line 24'-0" down. These are all the lines you need to finish the site plan (Figure 12.6a).

6. By using the Trim and Fillet commands as you have in several previous skills, you can finish the driveway and patio (Figure 12.6b). The radius of the corner to fillet is 6'.

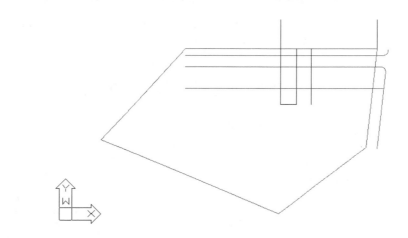

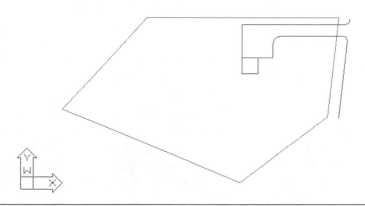

FIGURE 12.6: The offset lines (a), and the finished driveway and patio (b)

7. Make the 0 layer current, then draw a north arrow and place it in the lower-left corner.

8. Open the Layer Control dialog box and change the linetype for the Prop_line layer to Phantom. (You will have to load it—see Skill 6, *Using Layers to Organize Your Drawing*.)

9. Type **ltscale** ↵, then type **100** ↵. You will see the phantom linetype for the property lines.

10. Save this drawing in your training folder as Site12a.

This completes the site plan. The next step is to insert the Cabin drawing as an external reference into the site plan.

Setting Up an External Reference

When you set up an external reference, you go through a process similar to that of inserting a drawing into another drawing, like you did in Skill 7. You will select the drawing to be referenced and specify the location of its insertion point. There are options for the X scale factor, Y scale factor, and rotation angle—just as for inserting blocks. And here, as with blocks, you can set the command up so that it uses the defaults for these options without prompting you for your approval.

The External Reference Dialog Box

All external reference operations can be run through the Xref Manager dialog box, which is brought up by selecting Insert ➤ Xref Manager from the menu bar, or by typing **xr** ↵. To set up a new external reference, use the Insert ➤ External Reference command. There is also a Reference toolbar that has five command buttons related to Xrefs. You can bring it up the same way you brought up the Dimension toolbar in the last skill: Right-click any button on the screen, then pick Reference from the menu that comes up. However, I don't recommend using the Reference toolbar while working through this skill unless you're an advanced user, for two reasons. First, there are seven other buttons on the toolbar used for Image commands that allow you to import raster drawings into AutoCAD—an operation not covered in this book. Second, the toolbar does not include all of the Xref commands we will be covering. If you have already brought this toolbar up, click the X in the upper-right corner to turn it off.

1. With Site12a as the current drawing, create a new layer called Cabin. Use the default color of White/Black and make it current.

2. Pick Insert ➤ External Reference from the menu bar. The Select Reference File dialog box appears.

3. Locate the Training Data folder (or the folder your training files are stored in) and select Cabin12a.dwg. Then click Open. The External Reference dialog box comes up.

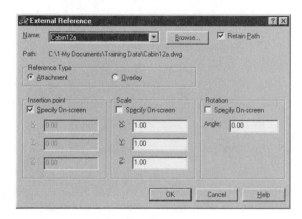

The file being referenced—Cabin12a—is displayed in the drop-down list at the top of the dialog box, with the full path of the file's location just below. The bottom half contains three options for the insertion process—similar to those in the Insert dialog box that you used for inserting blocks in Skill 7. Note that only the insertion point is specified on screen. The Scale and Rotation options are preset to use the default settings. If they are not set up this way click in the appropriate checkboxes so they are.

1. Click OK. An AutoCAD Message dialog appears. It has a technical message that doesn't concern us right now.

2. Click OK to close it. You return to your drawing and the cabin drawing appears and moves with the crosshair cursor.

3. Pick any point within the property line and to the left of the patio, to be the insertion point. The Xref drawing is attached and appears in the site plan (Figure 12.7).

The attached Xref appears exactly as it did when it was the current drawing. When we use this file as part of a site plan, we don't want all of the information in Cabin12a to be visible. In fact, we want most of the information invisible. We will accomplish this by freezing many of the layers in the Xref drawing.

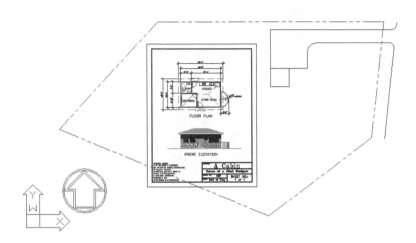

FIGURE 12.7: The Cabin12a drawing attached to the Site12a drawing

Controlling the Appearance of an Xref

Xref layers will be part of the list of layers for the current, or host, drawing. But the name of the Xref file is added to the front of the layer's previous name, separated from the layer's previous name by a vertical bar (|).

1. Click the Layer button on the Object Properties toolbar. The Layer Control dialog box comes up. Layers from the Xref drawing all have *Cabin12a* and a vertical bar before the name of the layer, as in Cabin12a | Balcony.

2. Freeze all layers beginning with Cabin12a *except:*

    Cabin12a | Balcony

    Cabin12a | Roof

    Cabin12a | Steps

    Cabin12a | Walls

TIP TIP TIP TIP TIP TIP TIP TIP TIP TIP TIP TIP TIP TIP TIP TIP TIP TIP TIP TIP TIP

You can resize the Layer Properties Manager dialog box to display more layers at a time. Depending on the size of your screen and your screen resolution, you might be able to view all Xref layers at once.

The drawing will now look like Figure 12.8.

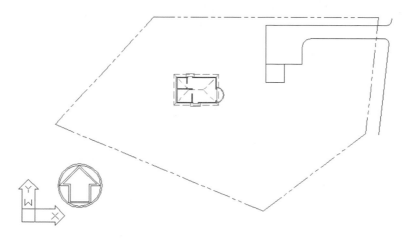

FIGURE 12.8: The site plan with most of the cabin layers frozen

Because we want the visible parts of the cabin to read as a unit, we will assign the same color to all the thawed cabin layers.

3. Click the Layer button again, and highlight the Cabin12a | Balcony layer. Then hold down the Ctrl key and click the other cabin layers listed in step 2. Change the color of one of the selected layers to a dark green. The rest of the selected layers will also change to a dark green. Click OK.

4. Finally, in the site plan, the roof should have a continuous line instead of the dashed line it currently has. Click the Layer button again. Highlight the Cabin12a | Roof layer and change its linetype to Continuous.

5. Click OK. The cabin is now all one color and the roof has continuous lines. Now the cabin needs to be moved and rotated to its position next to the patio.

6. Zoom into a view where the cabin and the left side of the patio are visible.

7. Start the Rotate command and click the cabin. The entire cabin is selected. Press ↵.

8. Click anywhere near the middle of the cabin, then type **-90** ↵. The cabin is rotated to the correct orientation (Figure 12.9a).

9. Be sure Endpoint Osnap is running. Then use the Move command to move the lower-right corner of the back step to the lower-left corner of the patio (Figure 12.9b).

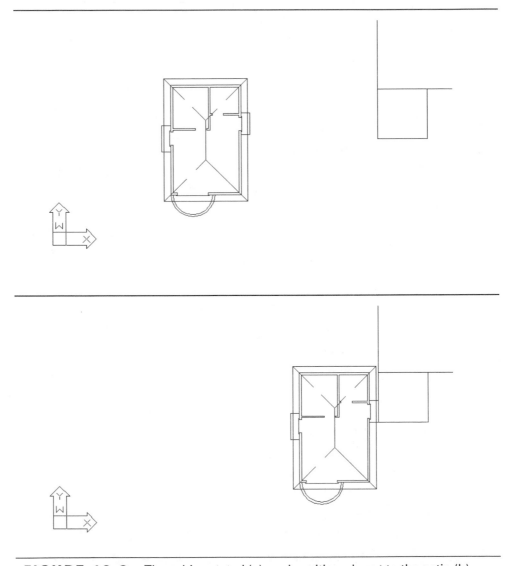

FIGURE 12.9: The cabin rotated (a), and positioned next to the patio (b)

10. Zoom previous to a view of the whole site. The cabin is oriented correctly on the site (Figure 12.10).

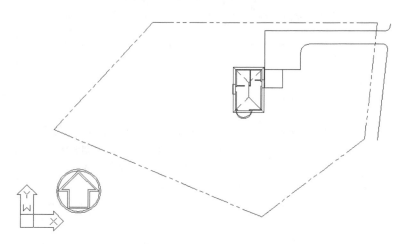

FIGURE 12.10: The cabin Xref is located on the site drawing.

You have established Cabin12a as an external reference in this drawing and modified the appearance of some of the Xref's layers. The next step is to make some revisions to Cabin12a and see how this affects the Xref.

Modifying an Xref Drawing

You can modify Cabin12a either by making it the current drawing or by using a special command while the host drawing is current. We'll start by bringing up Cabin12a and making an addition to it. Then we'll make Site12a current again and modify Cabin12a as an Xref. Before we do anything, however, we need to change a setting so that the changes we make to the layers of the Xref are saved with the host file.

1. Type **visretain** ↲. If the value in the angle brackets is set to 1, press ↲. Otherwise, type **1** ↲ to set the value to 1. This will allow you to save the layer settings of the Xref layers with the current file.

2. Use File ➤ Save As to save the current file as Site12b.

3. Click the Window menu. At the bottom of the menu, Cabin12a should be displayed next to 1. Click it to make it the current drawing.

Modifying an Xref by Making It the Current Drawing

Because we found such a spectacular site for the cabin, we want to add a deck around what is now the west-facing entrance (previously the front entrance).

1. Zoom into the area that includes the floor plan and the area between it and the front elevation.

2. Create a new layer called Deck. Assign it a color and make it current. Next, give yourself some room to make this revision.

3. Freeze the following layers:

   Dim1

   F-elev

   Tblk1

   Text1

   Any Hatch layers that aren't already frozen

4. The drawing will look like Figure 12.11. Use the Pline command to draw a deck across the front of the cabin that extends down 10'. (The Polyline command was introduced in Skill 10, *Controlling Text in a Drawing*.)

FIGURE 12.11: The view with selected layers frozen

5. Make sure the Endpoint Osnap is running. Then select the Polyline button from the Draw toolbar and pick the lower-left corner of the cabin walls to start the Pline.

6. Type **w** ↵. Then type **0** ↵↵ to reset the Pline width to zero.

7. Be sure Ortho is on. Then hold the crosshair cursor straight down below the first point picked and type **10'** ↵.

8. Click the Otrack button on the Status bar to turn Otrack mode on. Then hold the crosshair cursor on the lower-right corner of the cabin walls for a moment, until a cross appears there. When it does, begin moving the crosshair cursor directly down and stay on the tracking path. A small × will appear at the intersection of the vertical tracking path and the horizontal line segment now being drawn (Figure 12.12a). When you see the small ×, click once to establish the second line segment. A horizontal line is drawn that parallels, and is 10' below, the front wall of the cabin.

8. Finally, pick the lower-right corner of the cabin to complete the outline of the deck. Press ↵ to end the Pline command.

9. Offset this polyline 6" to the inside (Figure 12.12b). When a polyline is offset, all segments are automatically offset together and filleted to clean up the corners. (The fillet radius is 0" for this operation, even if it's currently set to a non-zero value.) This concludes the modifications we will make to the Cabin12a drawing. Now we can return to the Site12b drawing.

10. It is important to save this file at this point. Keep the name as Cabin12a—otherwise the Xref in the Site12b drawing will not be updated to include the deck. This is a revision to the Cabin12a drawing that has been externally referenced into the Site12b drawing. Save Cabin12a, then click Window ➤ Site12b to switch back to the site drawing.

NOTE NOTE NOTE NOTE NOTE NOTE NOTE NOTE NOTE NOTE NOTE NOTE NOTE NOTE NOTE NOTE

A host drawing reads the latest saved version of a drawing that is externally referenced to it.

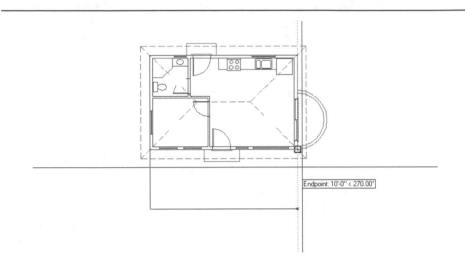

Endpoint: 10'-0" < 270.00"

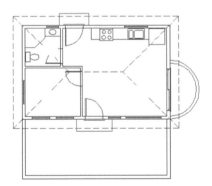

FIGURE 12.12: The vertical tracking path (a), and the offset deck line (b)

11. On the pull-down menus, click Insert ➤ Xref Manager. The Xref Manager dialog comes up.

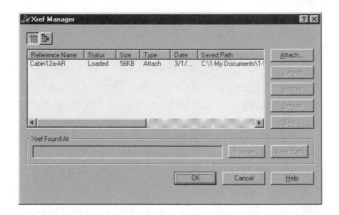

Once an External Reference has been set up, you will use this dialog box to control the linkage between the Xref and the host drawing. We need to update the Cabin12a Xref to reflect the changes we made to the Cabin12a drawing.

1. In the list of Xref files, click on Cabin12a to highlight it. All the buttons on the right side of the dialog box are now available.

2. Click the Reload button, then click OK. You are returned to the Site12a drawing; the new deck has been added (Figure 12.13).

3. Save this drawing. It's still called Site12b.

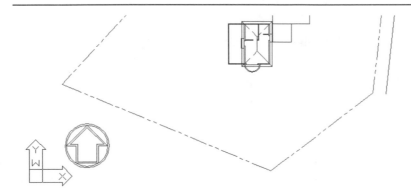

FIGURE 12.13: The Site12b drawing with the revised Xref of the cabin

In this exercise, you have seen how a host drawing is updated when the drawing that is externally referenced is made current, modified, and updated as an Xref. You've also seen how the appearance of objects in the Xref drawing can be controlled from the host drawing by working with the Xref layers. This is a good example of the power of layers. They can be set up one way in the actual drawing and another way in the Xref of that drawing in a host file. In fact, you can Xref the same drawing into any number of host files and have the layer characteristics of visibility, color, and linetype be different in each host file, and saved as such with each host file. Xref is a powerful feature of AutoCAD, and you will learn more about the possible applications of this tool towards the end of this Skill.

Modifying an Xref from within the Host Drawing

There is a powerful tool for editing an Xref while the host drawing is the current drawing. You can't create a new layer and draw new objects with this tool, but many of the regular editing commands are available to you when this tool is used. We'll make a few modifications related to the new deck to illustrate this feature.

1. Use the Window Menu to switch to Cabin12a. Then close this file. Site12b will return to the drawing area. (Click File ➢ Close.)

2. Zoom into the cabin floor plan on the site plan (Figure 12.14a). We need to erase the old front step and fill in the roof lines that were broken out to make room for the room label text.

3. On the pull-down menus, click Modify ➢ In-place Xref and Block Edit ➢ Edit Reference. You are prompted to select the Xref to edit.

4. Click anywhere on the cabin—it's all one object for now. The Reference Edit dialog box comes up. It lists Cabin12a as the selected Xref, and there is a preview window to illustrate the Xref drawing.

5. Click OK. At the Select nested objects: prompt, click on the six roof hip lines that need repair, the roof ridge line, and the three lines that make up what was formally the front step (10 picks in all). Then press ↵. The Command: prompt returns to the command window. The Refedit toolbar appears.

You are now free to use most of the modification commands that are normally available to edit the objects of the Xref that we just selected.

6. Use the Erase command to erase the three lines of the front step and the three broken roof line segments that connect to the ridgeline.

7. Use the Fillet command to extend the three remaining broken roof line segments to the ridgeline (Figure12.14b).

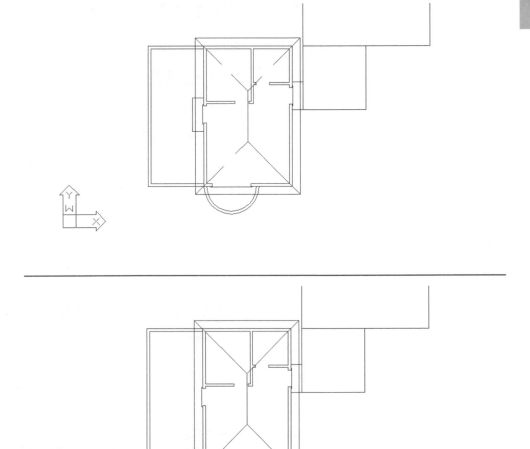

FIGURE 12.14: Zooming in for a close-up view of the Xref cabin (a), and the Xref cabin with the step erased and the roof lines filled in

TIP TIP TIP TIP TIP TIP TIP TIP TIP TIP TIP TIP TIP TIP TIP TIP TIP TIP TIP TIP TIP TIP TIP TIP

The bottom fillet will require you to use the ridgeline as one of the lines to fillet, rather than the unbroken hip line, because this latter line was not selected to be part of the Xref edit in Step 4 of the previous section.

8. Move to the Refedit toolbar. On the far-right end of the toolbar, click the Save Back Changes to Reference button. When the warning dialog box comes up, click OK.

9. Zoom to Extents, then zoom out a little to a view of the whole (Figure 12.15). Save this drawing. It is still named Site12b.

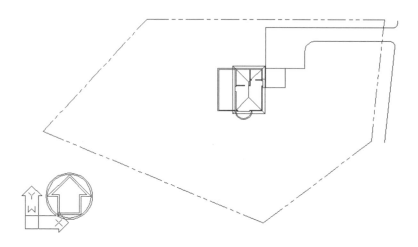

FIGURE 12.15: The Site12b drawing with the revised Xref of the cabin

In this exercise, you have seen how a host drawing is updated when its external reference is changed, and how the appearance of objects in the Xref drawing can be controlled from the host drawing by working with the Xref layers. You also saw how modifications can be made to objects in the Xref from the host drawing by using the In-place Xref Edit tool. A drawing can serve as an External Reference in several host drawings at the same time and have a different appearance in each one. The results of in-place Xref editing, however, must be saved back to the original drawing in order to be viewed in the Xref. So, in this case, when you open the Cabin12a, the front step will be missing. Also, the roof hip lines will be drawn over the room label text, as they were before they were broken in Skill 10. In-place

Xref editing, then, is usually done only when the results are meant to be permanent changes in the original source drawing. We used it in this case just to show you how the feature works.

Applications for Xrefs

The applications for external references are diverse. A description of two common applications for Xrefs will illustrate their range of use.

   If you are working on a project as an interior designer and are a sub-contractor to the architect of the project, the architect can give you a drawing of a floor plan that is still undergoing changes. You would load this file onto your hard drive, in a specially designated folder, then Xref it into your drawing as a background—a drawing to be used as a reference to draw over. Now you can proceed to lay out furniture, partitions, etc., while the architect is still refining the floor plan. At an agreed upon time, the architect will give you a revised version of the floor plan. You will overwrite the one you have on your computer with the latest version. Then you can reload the Xref into your furniture layout drawing and the newer version of the floor plan will now be the background. In this example, the architect may also be sending these same versions of the floor plan to the structural and mechanical engineers and the landscape architect, all of whom are working on the project and using the architect's floor plan as an Xref in their respective host drawings (Figure 12.16).

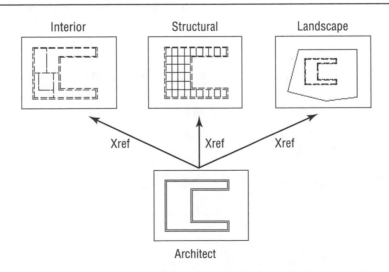

FIGURE 12.16: A single floor plan as an Xref to three sub-contractors

Another example of how Xrefs are often used takes place all in the same office where a network is in place. A project could involve work on several buildings all on the same site. Each building can be externally referenced to the site plan. This will keep the site plan drawing file from getting too large, and will allow the project work to be divided up to different work stations, while the project manager could open the site plan, or host, drawing on their computer and keep track of progress (Figure 12.17).

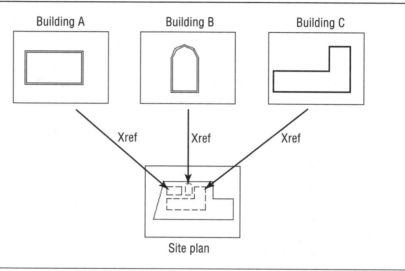

FIGURE 12.17: Three buildings as Xrefs to a single site plan

Additional Features of External References

You have seen how properties of layers in an Xref can be changed and how modifications to an Xref can be made. There are a few other features of external references that deserve mention.

The Xref Path

When you attach an Xref to the host drawing, AutoCAD stores the name of the Xref and its path.

NOTE NOTE NOTE NOTE NOTE NOTE NOTE NOTE NOTE NOTE NOTE NOTE NOTE NOTE NOTE
The path of a drawing file is the name of the drive, folders, and sub-folders where a file is stored, followed by the name of the drawing. C:\TRAINING\SITE12B.DWG is the path of the current drawing file.

Each time you bring up the host drawing, AutoCAD is directed to search and find any Xrefs saved with the host file and to bring them up in the host drawing. If the Xref drawing is moved to a new folder after the Xref has been attached, AutoCAD won't be able to find the Xref and can't bring it up in the host drawing.

To correct this situation, you must update the host drawing with the new path to the Xref file. We'll go through a quick exercise to illustrate how this works.

1. Close the Site12b drawing momentarily.

2. Use My Computer or Windows Explorer to create a new sub-folder called Xref within the Training folder you have previously set up. Move Cabin12a to this folder.

3. Bring up Site12b again. The Xref does not show up, but there's a little line of information in the host drawing where the insertion point of the Xref was located. If you zoom in a couple of times, you will be able to read the information. It says "Xref C:\1-My Documents\Training Data\Cabin12a.dwg." This is the original path of the Xref.

4. Press F2 to switch to the AutoCAD text screen for a moment and note the line that says "Can't find C:\1-My Documents\Training Data\Cabin12a.dwg." AutoCAD is unable to find the Xref because the path has changed. Press F2 again.

5. Type **xr** ↵ to bring up the Xref Manager dialog box. In the large box where Xrefs are listed, the path is listed for each Xref under the heading Saved Path. You can slide the scroll bar to the right to see the full path.

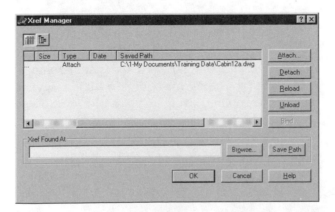

6. Click the `Cabin12a` Xref to highlight it.

7. Next to the Xref Found At text box, click Browse. Find `Cabin12a` in the new Xref folder. Highlight it and click Open.

8. Back in the Xref Manager dialog box, the path has been updated for `Cabin12a`. Click OK. Zoom previous. The Xref is restored in your drawing.

TIP TIP TIP TIP TIP TIP TIP TIP TIP TIP TIP TIP TIP TIP TIP TIP TIP TIP TIP TIP TIP TIP TIP

When you're working with a lot of Xrefs, it is important to be very careful where you store files that are acting as Xrefs to other files.

Binding Xrefs

There are occasions when you will want to permanently attach an Xref to the host drawing. If you send your drawing files to a printing service to be plotted, having to send a whole set of files that are Xrefs can make things complicated. Also, for archiving finished work, it's better to reduce the number of files. As well, there will be occasions when the Xref has been revised for the last time and no longer needs to be a separate file. In all these situations, you will use the Bind command to convert an external reference into a block that can be inserted into the host drawing.

1. Type **xr** ↵ to open the External Reference dialog box and highlight the Cabin12a Xref.

2. Click the Bind button. The Bind Xrefs dialog box comes up.

The two options in the Bind Type area have to do with how layers are treated when an Xref is bound to the host drawing. The default is Bind. It sets the Xref layers to be maintained as unique layers in the host drawing. With the Insert option, layers that have the same name in the two drawings will be combined into one layer. None of the layers in `Cabin12a` have the same name as any layers in `Site12b`. Let's use the Insert option.

3. Change the Bind Type to Insert and click OK. The Xref disappears from the list of Xrefs.

4. Click OK. Your drawing looks unchanged.

5. Select the List button from the Inquiry flyout and select the cabin. Press ↵. The text screen shows that the cabin is now a block reference.

6. Press F2 and click the Layer button on the Object Properties toolbar. The cabin's layers have all become layers in the Site12b drawing, and no longer have the Cabin12a | prefix.

7. Click OK, then pick Insert ➤ Block. In the Insert dialog box, open the Name drop-down list. Cabin12a is listed here as a block, along with the window and two door blocks that you created in Skill 7. There are a couple of other blocks on the list. These blocks are used by the dimensions in the drawing.

8. Close the drop-down list by clicking on a blank portion of the dialog box. Then click Cancel again to return to your drawing. The cabin is now a permanent part of the Site12b drawing. If you need to make changes to the drawing, you can explode it and use the modify commands to make those changes. Or you can use the In-place Xref and Block Edit tool that you used previously in Skill 7 to modify the window block, and again in this skill to modify the roof lines and erase the front step.

9. Save this drawing as Site12c.

This has been a quick tour of the basic operations that are used to set up and control external references. There are more features and commands for working with Xrefs than have been covered here, but you now have enough to get you started working with them.

Other Features of Xrefs

What follows are a few additional operations and features that you may find useful when you delve more deeply into external references. Play around a little and see what you can do.

- Externally referenced drawings can have drawings externally referenced to them. These are called *nested* Xrefs. There is no limit to the number of levels of nested Xrefs that a drawing can have.

- You can't explode an Xref, but you can detach it from the host. The Detach command is a button on the Xref Manager toolbar.

- You can bind Blocks, Layers, and Text and Dimension styles of an Xreffed drawing to the host drawing without binding the objects themselves. Use the *Xbind command* for this. Type **xbind** ↵, or pick the External Reference Bind button from the Reference toolbar, to start this command.

- Large, complex drawings that are Xreferenced often have their insertion points coordinated in such a way that all Xreferences are attached at the 0,0 point of the host drawing. This helps keep drawings aligned properly. By default, any drawing that is Xreferenced into a host drawing uses 0,0 as its insertion point. But you can change the coordinates of the insertion point with the *Base command*. With the drawing you want to change current, type **base** ↵ and enter the coordinates for the new insertion point.

- You can limit which layers and, to some degree, which objects in a drawing are Xreferenced in the host drawing by using *Indexing* and *Demand Loading*.

- A host drawing can be Xreferenced into the drawing that has been Xreferenced into the host. This is called an *overlay* and is an option in the Attach Xref dialog box. Overlays ignore nested Xreferences.

- If you freeze the layer that was current when an Xref was attached, the entire Xref is frozen.

- The Unload button in the External Reference dialog box allows you to deactivate Xrefs without detaching them from the host file. They stay on the list of Xrefs and can be reloaded at any time with the Reload button. This can be a time-saver in complex drawings.

Are You Experienced?

Now you can . . .

- ☑ **draw a basic site plan**
- ☑ **use Surveyor units to lay out property lines**
- ☑ **attach an external reference**
- ☑ **control the appearance of an external reference by modifying layers**
- ☑ **use Visretain to save Xref layer changes**
- ☑ **revise a drawing that is externally referenced**
- ☑ **modify and Xref from the host drawing**
- ☑ **update an Xref path**
- ☑ **bind an Xref to a host file**

Using Layouts to Set Up a Print

- ➔ **Putting a title block in a Layout**
- ➔ **Setting up viewports in a Layout**
- ➔ **Aligning viewports**
- ➔ **Controlling visibility in viewports**
- ➔ **Setting up a text style for a Layout**
- ➔ **Adding text in a Layout**

In the previous skill, we introduced external references—useful and powerful tools. Although the commands for Xrefs are a little tricky, the overall concept is fairly straightforward—in effect, you are viewing another drawing from within the current drawing. The concept of the *Layout* display mode is a little difficult to understand, but the commands are fairly simple. While external references help you combine several drawings into a composite, Layouts allow you to set up and print several views of the same file. The Layout is a view of your drawing as it will sit on a sheet of paper when printed.

Each Layout has a designated printer and paper size for the print. You adjust the positioning of the drawing and the scale of the print. The part that is hard to understand is the way two scales are juxtaposed in the same file: the scale of the drawing on the printed paper (This is usually a standard scale used by architects, like ¼" = 1'-0".) and the scale of the Layout, which is almost always 1:1, or the actual size. One way to visualize how a Layout works is to think of it as a second drawing, or a specialized layer that has been laid over the top of your current drawing. Each Layout that you create will have a scale of 1:1, or actual size, and will contain the border and title block, and possibly some other information like notes, the scale, etc.

Think for a moment about drawing the floor plan of a building on a traditional drafting table. You will draw the building to a scale, like ⅛" = 1'-0". Then, on the same sheet of paper, you will print out a note using letters that are, say ⅛-inch high. If you look at those letters as being in the same scale as the building, they would measure as 1-foot high, and that's what we've been doing on the cabin drawing so far. But in traditional drafting, you don't think that way; instead, you work with two scales in the drawing without thinking about it. So a letter is ⅛-inch high (actual size) and a part of the building that measures ⅛" on the paper is thought of as being 1-foot long (at a scale of ⅛" = 1'-0"). Layouts are designed to let you juggle two (or more) scales in a drawing in the same way, in order to set the drawing up to be printed.

Setting Up Layouts

We will begin working with Cabin11a, which is the drawing we used for basic dimensioning in Skill 11. This drawing is essentially complete and ready to print. You will print it in the next skill, just as it is right now (Figure 13.1), without using Layouts. To begin this skill, you will modify this drawing and create a Layout for it to get a basic understanding of what Layouts are and how they are activated and set up. Then, in the next skill, you'll print this same drawing using a Layout.

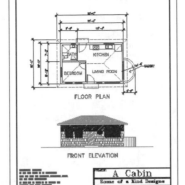

FIGURE 13.1: Cabin11a ready to print

In setting up a new Layout, we will use an 8 $\frac{1}{2}$×11-inch sheet.

1. Open Cabin11a. Notice the border of the drawing and the rectangle just outside the border that represents the edge of the sheet of paper on which the print will be made. If you remember (from Skill 10, *Controlling Text in a Drawing*) when you constructed the border and title block for this drawing, you had to make a calculation to determine that the size of the border for a scale of ⅛" = 1'-0" (⅛-inch scale) was based on a rectangle 68-feet wide×88-feet high that was then offset 3' to make the border. With Layouts, you don't have to make this kind of calculation—you draw the border actual size.

2. Create a new layer called Tblk-L1. Assign it a color and make it current. Look at the lower-left corner of the drawing area.

3. There is a Model tab, and there are one or two Layout tabs. Click the Layout1 tab. The Page Setup–Layout1 dialog box comes up. It has two tabs. The Plot Device tab should be active. If it's not, click to make it active (Figure 13.2a).

This is where you associate the new Layout with a printing device. The example shows a laser jet printer in the Plotter Configuration area, but yours may be different. If your computer is linked to more than one printer, make sure you choose a printer that can take 8 ½×11-inch paper.

NOTE NOTE NOTE NOTE NOTE NOTE NOTE NOTE NOTE NOTE NOTE NOTE NOTE NOTE NOTE

Print and *Plot* are used interchangeably in this book, as are *printer* and *plotter*. In the past, *plot* and *plotter* referred to large-format devices and media, but that's no longer necessarily so. *Print* and *printing* are more widely used now because of changes in the technology of the large-format devices.

4. Click the Layout Settings tab. This tab has six areas containing settings that control how the drawing will fit on the printed paper.

5. In the Paper Size and Paper Units area, be sure the Paper Size drop-down list is set to Letter 8 ½×11 in. Below that, the Printable Area for the chosen printing device is displayed. This shows the maximum area your printer can print on an 8 ½×11-inch sheet of paper and, thereby, gives you an idea about how close to the edge of the paper the printer will print. Jot down the Printable Area. In this example, it's 8.00×10.54 inches.

6. Move to the Drawing Orientation area and select Portrait for the orientation.

7. The Plot area contains five radio buttons for selecting what is to be plotted. Some are disabled. Be sure that Layout is checked.

8. In the Plot Scale area, the scale to be used is 1:1. If it's not already selected, open the Scale drop-down list and select it from the 26 preset scale choices. The Layout Settings tab should look like Figure 13.2b.

9. In the upper-right corner of the Page Setup–Layout1 dialog box, in the Page Setup Name area, click Add. The User Defined Page Setups dialog box comes up. In the New Page Setup Name text box at the top, type **Cabin11a-L1**. Then click OK. Your setting changes are named and saved.

10. Click OK to close the Page Setup–Layout1 dialog box. You are returned to your drawing and Layout1 is displayed (Figure 13.3).

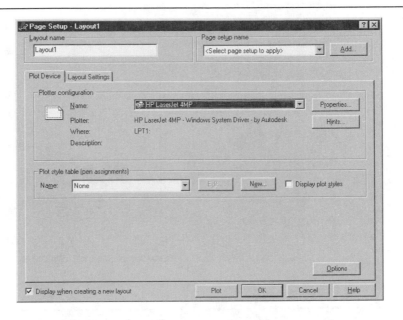

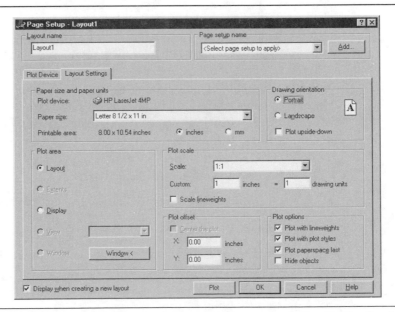

FIGURE 13.2:   The Page Setup–Layout1 dialog box with the Plot Device tab
(a), and with the Layout Settings tab (b)

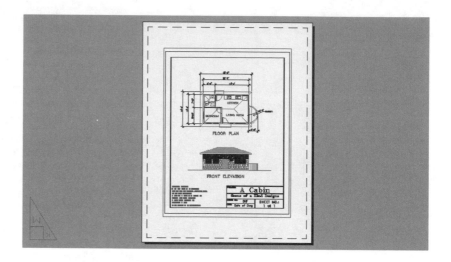

FIGURE 13.3: Layout1 for `Cabin11a`

The drawing area now displays a white sheet of paper resting on a grey background. The drawing of the cabin is centered on the paper with its border and outer rectangle defining the edge of the paper. We'll be changing this momentarily. Outside this rectangle, there is another rectangle. This is a *viewport* that was automatically created when you set up Layout1. The viewport is a new AutoCAD object that creates a hole (or window) in the Layout so that you can see through the Layout to the drawing of the building. You can think of the building as residing "underneath" the Layout.

Look to the lower-left corner of the drawing area at the Model and Layout tabs. Note that the Layout1 tab is now the active tab.

1. Click the Model tab. A view of `Cabin11a`, without Layout1, is shown.

2. Click the Layout1 tab. The Layout returns.

Throughout the book so far, you have been drawing in the Model tab (sometimes called *Model space*). You have put some information—some of the text, the title block, and the border—on the Model tab that is usually put on the Layout if you're using the Layout feature.

Notice the triangle in the lower-left corner of the drawing area. This icon indicates that your cursor is currently residing on the active Layout. In this setup, you cannot select any part of the cabin to work on, and any new objects you create will be on the Layout. To work on the cabin itself, you need to move the cursor to the Model tab, and there are two ways of doing that. One is to click the Model tab. This temporarily removes the Layout, and you are left with just the drawing or *model*. The other way is to switch to the Model space while a Layout tab is active. We'll try this latter method now.

1. Move the crosshair cursor around and notice that it can be placed at any point on the Layout.

2. On the far right end of the Status bar, click PAPER. The Paper Button changes to become the Model button. Continue moving the cursor around the drawing area. The cursor becomes a crosshair only when it is placed inside the viewport surrounding the cabin drawing (Figure 13.4). Otherwise the cursor changes to a pointer arrow, as it does when it is placed on the toolbars and menus. When the cursor is within the viewport, the lines of the crosshair extend only to the edge of the viewport. This is the boundary of where you may pick points to draw when working on the cabin.

NOTE NOTE NOTE NOTE NOTE NOTE NOTE NOTE NOTE NOTE NOTE NOTE NOTE NOTE

If the lines of your crosshair cursor don't normally extend to the edges of the drawing area, click Tools ➢ Options and select the Display tab. In the lower-left corner, where it says Crosshair Size, push the slidebar all the way to the right. The new setting will be 100.

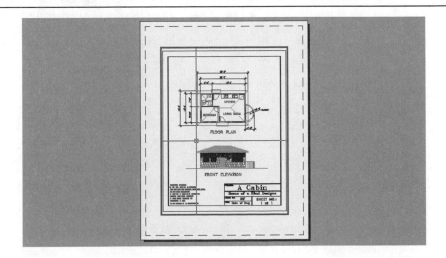

FIGURE 13.4: The crosshair cursor in Model space with Layout active

TIP TIP TIP TIP TIP TIP TIP TIP TIP TIP TIP TIP TIP TIP TIP TIP TIP TIP TIP TIP TIP TIP TIP TIP TIP

When you activate Model space while a Layout is active, it is like opening a window and reaching through the opening to touch the drawing of the building behind the window.

Once Layouts are set up, you will find it practical to make the Model tab active when making major changes to the drawing. This will temporarily disable the Layout and make it invisible. To make minor changes to the cabin (or other buildings), leave the Layout tab active and click the Paper button on the Status bar to make Model space active while the Layout is still visible.

You need to transfer the title block and border from Model space to Layout. We'll start by drawing a new border on the Layout.

Drawing a Border on a Layout

The border for a Layout is drawn at the actual size that it will be when it is printed, as the Layout is the actual size of the paper on which the drawing will be printed—or, 8 ½×11".

1. Click the Model button on the Status bar. This moves the crosshair cursor back to the Layout.

2. Start the Rectangle command and type **0,0** ↵. Then type in the Printable Area number that you jotted down in Step 5 above. For the example here, type **8,10.54** ↵. A rectangle is drawn that coincides with the dashed lines representing the Printable Area of the sheet (Figure 13.5).

3. We want the border to be set in from the rectangle you just drew about ⅛". Offset the new rectangle ⅛" to the inside.

4. Erase the outer rectangle. The dashed lines become visible again. The border should be a line ½-inch wide.

5. Type **pe** ↵ to start the Pedit command. Select the inner rectangle. Type **w** ↵, then type **1/32** ↵. The lines of the offset rectangle are now ½-inch wide and will serve as the new border (Figure 13.6).

6. Type **x** ↵ to end the Pedit command.

7. Click the Model tab. Layout1 is temporarily deactivated and you are back in the Model space. Take note of the title block.

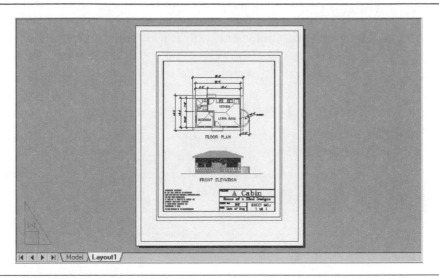

FIGURE 13.5: Layout1 with a rectangle drawn on the boundary of the printable area

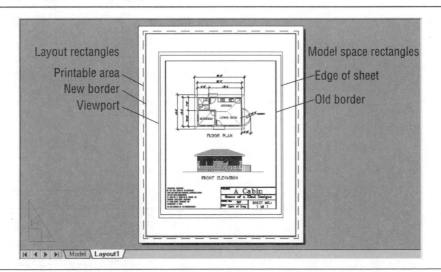

FIGURE 13.6: The new border in the Layout, among a lot of rectangles

There are a lot of rectangles around the drawing of the cabin, but you will be removing some of them soon. You have a border and a rectangle in the Model space, the latter of which indicates the edge of the sheet of paper. These will be removed. But first you need to put a title block in the Layout, connected to the border that you just created. Let's look at the title block you've already drawn.

Designing a Title Block for a Layout

The original title block was drawn to a size that could be plotted at ⅛-inch scale, so its dimensions are quite large (Figure 13.7a). You will need to make the size of the new title block much smaller to make it fit on the border that you just drew. How much smaller? The dimensions of the new title block drawn at actual size are shown in Figure 13.7b.

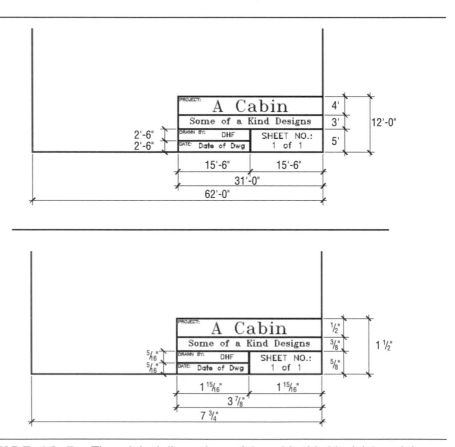

FIGURE 13.7: The original dimensions of the cabin title block (a), and the new, actual size dimensions in the Layout (b)

The text, too, has to be made smaller to fit into the new title block. The following is a chart showing the heights of the various text used in the two title blocks:

Text	Original Title Block	Layout1 Title Block
A Cabin	2'-6"	5/16"
Some of a Kind Designs	1'-3"	5/32"
DHF	1'-0"	1/8"
Date of Dwg	1'-0"	1/8"
SHEET NO.: 1 of 1	1'-3"	5/32"
PROJ.:, DRAWN BY:, DATE:	8"	1/12"

SKILL 13

This may seem complicated at first, but think about the discussion we had near the beginning of this skill in which we talked about using two scales in the same drawing. Traditional drafting uses a scale for the lines that represent the building. The text, title block, and border are drawn at actual size. In CAD drafting without Layouts, you have the convenience of being able to draw the building at full size; but you have to draw the text, title block, and border larger than they will eventually be in the finished plot because there is only one scale for the drawing. With Layouts, you can return to the method used by traditional drafters. The Layout is the part of the drawing where you put everything that relates to the actual size of the sheet, and Model Space is where the building lines and objects representing building components reside. You'll see shortly how the two spaces work together to make a complete drawing.

Let's get back to this title block and finish making one on the Layout. You need to look at the change of size of the title block and text from the original title block to the new one. Because Cabin11a is set up to be printed at a scale of ⅛"=1'-0", the text, border, and title block have all been drawn larger than their actual size by the scale factor of ⅛-inch scale. And what is the scale factor of ⅛-inch scale? It's the true ratio of the scale and is found by dividing the smaller number on one side of the equation into the larger number on the other side of the equation. If you divide ⅛" into 1'-0" (or 12"), you will get the scale factor—96. We did this in Skill 10: *Controlling Text in a Drawing*. The text border and title block are all 96 times larger in the original than they need to be in Paper Space, where they will be actual size.

After scaling the original title block down by a factor of 96, you will have a new title block that will be actual size. Then you will need to put it in the Layout, and attach it to the border. You can easily do both the scaling and the moving in one operation by using the Cut and Paste tools in AutoCAD.

Cutting and Pasting in AutoCAD

When you use the Windows Cut and Paste tools that have been customized to work with AutoCAD, the objects that are cut (or copied) can have an insertion point and can be inserted as a block back into the drawing or into another drawing. With Layout1 deactivated, the Cabin11a drawing is visible on the screen.

1. Select Edit ➤ Copy with Base Point from the menu bar. Use Endpoint Osnap and pick the lower left corner of the title block as the base point. Use a regular selection window to select the title block and all of its text, but not the border. (Selection windows were described in Skill 6, *Using Layers to Organize Your Drawing*, when you were selecting the kitchen and bathroom fixtures to move them onto the Fixtures layer.) Press ↵.

2. Click the Layout1 tab again, click the Paper button on the status bar, then erase the original before activating Layout1 again, erase the original border and title block, and the outer rectangle representing the edge of the sheet— all of which were created in the original Cabin11a drawing. The two rectangles and the original title block disappear (Figure 13.8a).

3. Click the Model button (on the Status bar) to reactivate Layout1 and move the cursor back to it.

4. Select Edit ➤ Paste as Block from the menu bar. Part of the image of the title block appears in the drawing, attached to the cursor. It's huge—you can see only the end of one line. Remember that we drew the original title block and border in a scaled-up fashion so that they would fit with the drawing's scale. The original scale factor we used to scale it up was 96 for ⅛-inch scale, so we'll use the reciprocal of that to scale it down.

5. Use Nearest Osnap and pick a point anywhere on the left half of the bottom borderline as the insertion point. Now we'll use the scale command to scale the title block down.

6. Start the Scale command. Select the large polyline by picking it on its edge, then press ↵. At the Specify base point: prompt, move the cursor to the center of the bottom edge of the polyline. When the Endpoint Osnap symbol appears there, click. Then type **1/96** ↵ (Figure 13.8b).

7. Start the Move command. Be sure Ortho is on. Using Endpoint and Perpendicular Osnaps, move the title block to the right until the right end of the top line in the title block (Endpoint) meets the right side of the border (Perpendicular). This will position the title block correctly on the border (Figure 13.8c).

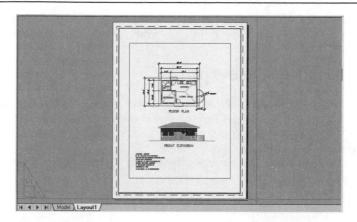

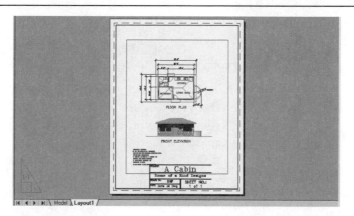

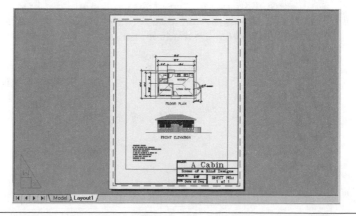

FIGURE 13.8: Removing the title block and border rectangles (a), pasting the title block into Layout1 (b), and positioning it correctly (c)

8. Use the Explode command to explode the title block. Then use the Properties button to move the title block lines and its text to the Tblk-L1 layer. This completes the transfer of the title block from Model Space to Layout1.

Adjusting a Viewport

The last step in using the Layout feature to set up Cabin11a to print is to adjust the size of the default viewport to more closely fit into the border, and to set the scale of the cabin drawing to ⅛" = 1'-0".

1. Click the viewport rectangle. Grips appear. Then click the Osnap button on the Status bar to temporarily deactivate any running Osnaps.

2. Click the upper-right grip to activate it.

3. Move the cursor to a point near the upper-right corner of the border, but still inside of it, then click.

4. Click the lower-left grip. Then move, as in Step 3, to a point close to the lower-left corner of the border and click to set it.

5. Press Esc twice to remove the grips. The viewport is now about as large as it can be on the page (Figure 13.9). To complete the last step, you need to adjust the scale of the cabin drawing to be ⅛" = 1'-0", and make the viewport border invisible.

6. Create a new layer called Vports-L1. Assign it a color that really stands out, like purple. Don't make this new layer current.

 TIP TIP TIP TIP TIP TIP TIP TIP TIP TIP TIP TIP TIP TIP TIP TIP TIP TIP TIP TIP TIP TIP TIP TIP

It's useful to assign a color that will stand out in your drawing to the Vport-ps layer, so you are reminded that the viewports are not an essential part of the drawing and can be made invisible.

7. Click the viewport to select it. Then click the Properties button on the Standard toolbar.

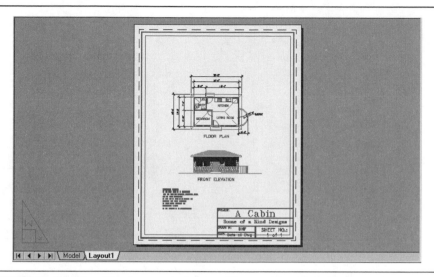

FIGURE 13.9: The Layout1 of the Cabin11a drawing with the viewport enlarged to nearly the size of the border

8. In the Properties dialog box, Viewport should be in the drop-down list at the top. In the list of properties, click Layer. Then open the drop-down list next to Layer and select Vports-L1.

9. Close the Properties dialog box and press Esc twice to remove the grips. The viewport is now on the Vports-L1 layer.

10. Click Paper on the Status bar to move to Model space, then type **z** ↵. Type **1/96xp** ↵. The cabin drawing is reset to a scale of 1:96, or ⅛" = 1'-0".

11. Use Realtime Pan to pan the drawing so it fits properly within the new border.

12. Click Model on the Status bar to return to Layout1. Tblk-L1 should be current. Freeze the Vports-L1 layer (Figure 13.10). The drawing looks very much like the original Cabin11a before Layouts were introduced, but we now have the title block and border on a Layout at 1:1 scale.

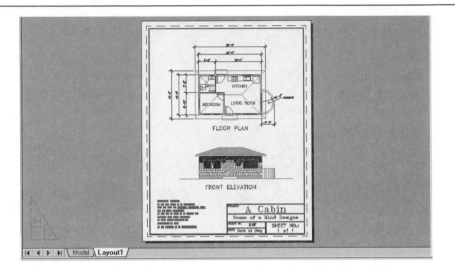

FIGURE 13.10: Cabin11b with the title block and border on Layout1

Switching between Model Space and a Layout

Let's look at our drawing for a moment to see what happens when you switch from Model space to a Layout. Currently, Layout1 is active.

1. Start the Erase command and pick the top dimension to erase. Try to pick something on the front elevation. You will find that you cannot pick anything in the cabin drawing. The only objects you can pick are the title block and the borderlines, which are on Layout1. When Layout1 is current, only objects on the Layout can be selected. The triangle icon in the lower-left corner of the drawing area is visible when a Layout is current. Press Esc to cancel the Erase command.

2. Click Paper on the Status bar. Paper changes to Model, and the triangular Paper Space icon disappears.

NOTE NOTE NOTE NOTE NOTE NOTE NOTE NOTE NOTE NOTE NOTE NOTE NOTE NOTE NOTE

When a Layout is active, the Paper/Model button on the Status bar controls whether the current Layout or Model space portion of the drawing is active. If Model space is active, the Status bar always displays the Model button. If you click the Model button when Model space is active, the last current Layout becomes active, and the button on the Status bar changes to the Paper button.

3. Restart the Erase command and try to select objects in the cabin drawing again. This time you are able to select anything inside the viewport.

NOTE NOTE NOTE NOTE NOTE NOTE NOTE NOTE NOTE NOTE NOTE NOTE NOTE NOTE NOTE
The cursor always resides in the active portion of the drawing. Work can be done only in one of the two portions (Model Space or a Layout) at any given time.

4. Try to select the viewport boundary line, the border, or the title block. You can't select anything on the Layout when Model Space is current. Cancel the Erase command.

SKILL
13

NOTE NOTE NOTE NOTE NOTE NOTE NOTE NOTE NOTE NOTE NOTE NOTE NOTE NOTE NOTE
The viewports in Layouts are called *floating* viewports because they can be moved around. There is another kind of viewport in AutoCAD called *tiled* viewports, which are fixed and exist only in Model Space. For brevity, in this skill, we will refer to floating viewports as viewports. Floating viewports always reside in the Layout portion of the drawing.

5. Click the Model tab. The Layout disappears, and you now view your drawing without a title block or border. We transferred them to Layout1, so they are no longer visible when the Model tab is active.

6. Zoom into the front door of the elevation, then click the Model button on the Status bar. Layout1 returns with the previous view of the cabin that you had when Layout1 was active.

7. Click the Model tab again. Zoom to Extents. Click the Layout1 tab. Save this drawing as Cabin13a.

NOTE NOTE NOTE NOTE NOTE NOTE NOTE NOTE NOTE NOTE NOTE NOTE NOTE NOTE NOTE
When a Layout tab is active, this is sometimes referred to as being "in Paper space." Conversely, when the Model tab is active, this is often called being "in Model space." In previous versions of AutoCAD, Layouts were not used, and the user was either in Model or Paper space. When a Layout is active (i.e. when you are in Paper space) you can switch to Model space while keeping the Layout visible, by clicking the Paper button. The button will change to the Model button, and you can work on the portion of your drawing that is visible in the viewport. Then you can click the Model button and switch back to the Layout (or Paper space).

Picturing your drawing as two drawings in one is still a useful way to understand Layouts, and will help you to understand how Layouts and Model space work together.

Once you have set up a title block, border, and viewport in a Layout, you can deactivate the Layout and work on your drawing from within Model space. Then, when you are ready to plot it out, reactivate the Layout. The orientation and magnification of your drawing relative to the Layout border will be preserved. You can also work on your drawing while the Layout is active by clicking the Paper button (as mentioned in the Note). However, you should not zoom while in Model Space because that changes the relationship between Model Space and the Layout that you set up by zooming to *1/scale factorxp*. The 1/scale factorxp zoom must be preserved so that the drawing plots at the correct scale. So, if you want to zoom into your drawing at this point, zoom while a Layout is active, then switch to Model space to work on the drawing. When finished, switch back to the Layout and zoom previous. This way, 1/scale factorxp zoom won't be affected.

NOTE NOTE NOTE NOTE NOTE NOTE NOTE NOTE NOTE NOTE NOTE NOTE NOTE NOTE NOTE

When a Layout is active, you can also switch back and forth between the Layout and Model space by typing ps ↵ or ms ↵.

This may seem like too much work to be worth the effort for a small drawing like this one, but be patient. As you start working on larger drawings, you will see what Layouts are capable of doing for you.

Working with Multiple Viewports in a Layout

The previous exercises introduced you to Layouts and taught you how they work. I used the example of a single viewport within a border and title block, all of which were on Layout1. This is the way Layouts are used much of the time, even in large projects. A title block is developed for a project. Each sheet in a set of drawings is a .dwg file with a title block on a Layout and one viewport, which encompasses most of the area inside the border, where you view the building components in Model space. But this is certainly not the only way Layouts are used. At times, more than one viewport will be used in a border. The rest of the exercises in this skill will lead you through an exploration of the advantages and techniques of using single and multiple viewports in Layouts.

Setting Up Multiple Viewports

You'll start by creating a new Layout with two viewports using the Layout Wizard. Then you'll adjust the views of the cabin on the Layout sheet.

1. Create a new layer called Tblk-L2. If you have a Layout2 tab in the lower-left corner of the drawing area, type **layout** ↵, then type **d** ↵, then type **layout2** ↵. Assign Tblk-L2 a color and make it current. Then, with Layout1 enabled and active, go to the pull-down menus and click Insert ➤ Layout ➤ Layout Wizard. The Create Layout dialog box appears, and Begin is in the title bar (Figure 13.11a). On the left side, a list of the steps for creating a new Layout is displayed, and an arrow points at Begin. In a text box on the bottom right of the dialog box, Layout2 is highlighted as the name of the new Layout.

2. Leave Layout2 in the box and click Next>. The dialog box now displays a list of possible printers on the right. The pointer on the left is now pointing at Printer (Figure 13.11b). If you have DWF Classic.pc3 in the list of printers—or any printer that takes an 11×17-inch sheet of paper—highlight it and click Next again.

3. As the pointer indicates, the next step is to specify paper size. Open the drop-down list near the upper-right corner and select ANSI B (11.00×17.00 Inches). Then click Next again.

4. In the Orientation step, select Landscape, if it isn't already selected. Click Next again.

5. The next step is to choose a predrawn title block, or pick None and make your own. Click a few choices to see how they look in the preview port. We will make our own, so, when finished browsing, highlight None. Then click Next.

6. Next, set up viewports in the new Layout (Figure 13.11c). Open the Viewport Scale drop-down list and select ⅛" = 1'-0" (don't select 1:8). In the Viewport Setup area, there are four choices. Since we want two viewports side-by-side, we'll use the Array option. Click Array. The Array specification boxes become enabled below the Viewport Setup area. Change the number of rows to 1, and leave the other three boxes as they are. Then click Next.

7. Now the pointer is indicating Pick Location. Click the Select Location button on the right. You are returned to the drawing and Layout2 is displayed at the correct orientation. You are prompted to `Specify first corner`. This means that you need to create a window in the Layout that will encompass the area to be taken up with the new viewports. Make a window similar to the one in Figure 13.12a.

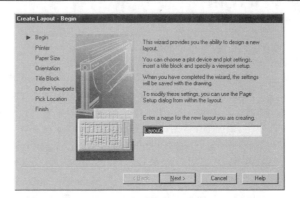

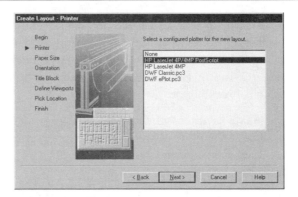

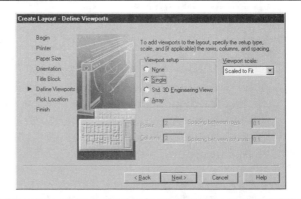

FIGURE 13.11: Three pages in the Layout Wizard: Begin (a), Printer (b), and Define Viewports (c)

8. Back in the Create Layout dialog box, you move to the last step. Click Finish. In the drawing, two identical viewports are drawn with the cabin drawing in each one, both displayed at a scale of ⅛" = 1'-0" (Figure 13.12b).

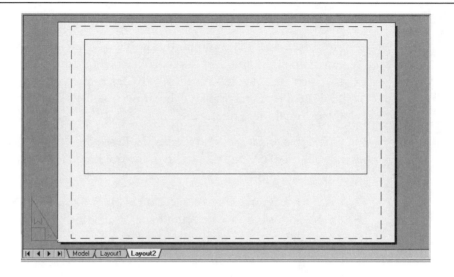

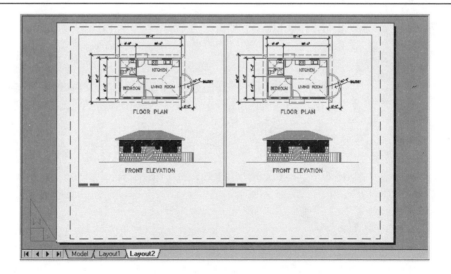

FIGURE 13.12: Windowing the viewport area in Layout2 (a), and the new viewports (b)

We'll work on the viewports momentarily, but first we need to create a border and title block for Layout2.

1. Click File ➤ Page Setup. In the Page Setup–Layout2 dialog box, be sure the Layout Settings tab is active. In the Paper Size and Paper Units area, note the Printable Area for the current printer and jot it down. Click OK.

2. Start the Rectangle command. Type **0,0** ↵. Then enter the two numbers that define the Printable Area as coordinates. For example, if the printable area is 15.66×10.60" (as it is for the DWF Classic.pc3 printer), you would type **15.66,10.6** ↵. A rectangle will be drawn over the dashed line that represents the printable area on the Layout.

3. Offset this rectangle ⅛" to the inside. Erase the outer rectangle. Use the Pedit command to change the width of the polyline of the new rectangle to ¹⁄₃₂" (Figure 13.13a).

4. Click the Layout1 tab to switch to Layout1. Be sure the Model/Paper button on the Status bar is displaying Paper. If it's not, click the button to change it. Then click Edit ➤ Copy with Base Point.

5. Click the Osnap button on the Status bar to activate the running Osnaps. Use Endpoint Osnap to pick the lower-right corner of the border as the base point.

6. Use a regular selection window to select the title block without the border. Press ↵.

7. Click the Layout2 tab to switch back to Layout2. Click Edit ➤ Paste as Block and pick the lower-right corner of Layout2's border as the insertion point. The title block has been copied from Layout1 to Layout2 (Figure 13.13b).

8. Explode the title block. Then use the Properties button to move the title block objects onto the Tblk-L2 layer.

Now we're ready to work on the viewports.

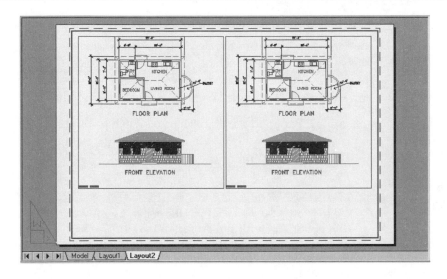

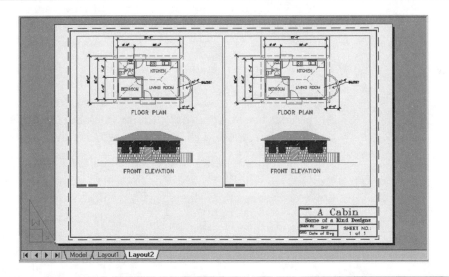

FIGURE 13.13: The new border for Layout2 (a), and the copied title block from Layout1 (b)

Aligning Viewports

We want the floor plan to be displayed in the left viewport and the front elevation to be displayed in the right viewport. We also want the titles of these two views to line up with each other horizontally. To accomplish this, we will need to perform some steps in Model space and some on the Layout, so we'll be switching back and forth while keeping Layout2 visible.

1. Click Paper on the Status bar to switch to Model space. Then move the crosshair cursor onto the viewports. The one that is active is the one where the crosshair cursor is visible.

TIP TIP TIP TIP TIP TIP TIP TIP TIP TIP TIP TIP TIP TIP TIP TIP TIP TIP TIP TIP TIP TIP TIP

When Model Space is active, there can be only one active viewport at a time. This is the one with the crosshair cursor. The active viewport's border is also highlighted. You can manipulate objects in the active viewport. To make a viewport active, place the arrow cursor in the viewport and click.

2. Be sure Ortho is on, then click in the right viewport to make it active. Use Realtime Pan to pan the drawing so that the front elevation is positioned halfway between the top and bottom boundary lines.

3. Type **mvsetup** ⏎. Then type **a** ⏎ to select the Align option.

4. Type **h** ⏎ to select the Horizontal option.

5. At the `Specify basepoint:` prompt, click the Insert Osnap. Then activate the right viewport and click the FRONT ELEVATION text.

6. At the next prompt, click Insert Osnap again. Click the left viewport and then click the FLOOR PLAN text. The floor plan in the left viewport is panned down so that its title is aligned with the title of the front elevation in the right viewport (Figure 13.14).

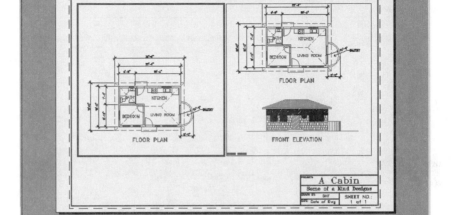

FIGURE 13.14: The text in the two viewports is aligned.

There are one or two more things to do to finish the Layout.

Finishing the 11×17-Inch Drawing

We want to make the floor plan in the right viewport invisible, and we want to add the Mtext that was in the lower-left corner of the original drawing (Cabin11a) to the lower-left corner of Layout1. We'll use grips to adjust the right viewport.

1. Click the Model button on the Status bar to move the cursor back to Layout.

2. Click the right viewport. Grips will appear at its corners.

3. Turn off running Osnaps. Click the upper-right grip to activate it.

4. Move the crosshair cursor down along the right edge of the right viewport until the horizontal line of the crosshair sits between the floor plan and the elevation, then click. The viewport now only extends to just above the elevation.

5. Click the lower-right grip. Move it up slightly so that the top of the note text in the lower-left corner of the viewport is no longer visible, then click. Press Esc twice. Now the right viewport displays only the front elevation (Figure 13.15).

6. If necessary, select the left viewport and adjust it so only the floor plan is visible.

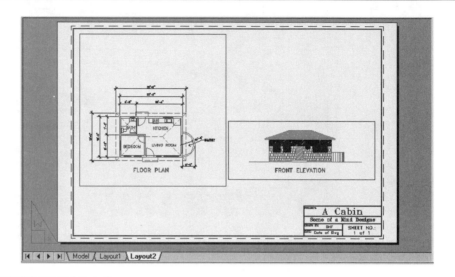

FIGURE 13.15: The right viewport showing only the front elevation after adjustments

To finish this drawing, you need to place the note text in the lower-left corner. You will accomplish this by creating a third viewport.

1. Click View ➤ Viewports ➤ 1 Viewport.

2. Pick two points in the lower-left corner to create a square viewport. The entire Model Space drawing appears in the viewport (Figure 13.16a).

3. Click the Paper button to switch to Model space.

4. Be sure the new viewport is active. If not, click in it, then pan the drawing in the new viewport until the note text is in the middle of the viewport. Press Esc to cancel Realtime Pan.

5. Type **z** ↵. Then type **1/96xp** ↵. The text is now the right size.

6. Do any additional panning necessary to get the text positioned in the corner near the border. If necessary, click the Model button to switch back to the viewport, then use grips to resize the Layout, and use Move to move it.

7. Click the Model button to switch to the Layout if you haven't already (Figure 13.16b).

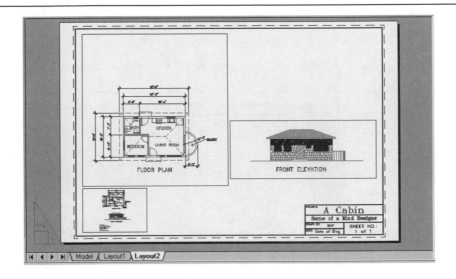

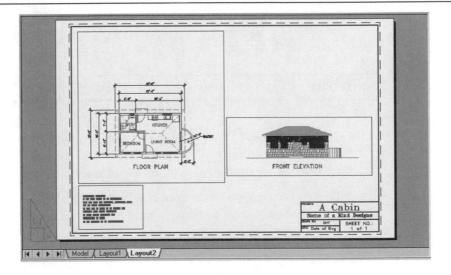

FIGURE 13.16: A third viewport is created (a), and the results of panning and zooming the view (b)

8. Create a new layer called Vports-L2 and assign it a color. Don't make this new layer current. Click OK.

9. Select the three viewports. Then pick the Properties button and move the viewports onto the Vports-L2 layer. Close the Properties dialog box and press Esc twice to remove the grips.

10. With the Tblk-L2 layer current, freeze the Vports-L2 layer (Figure 13.17).

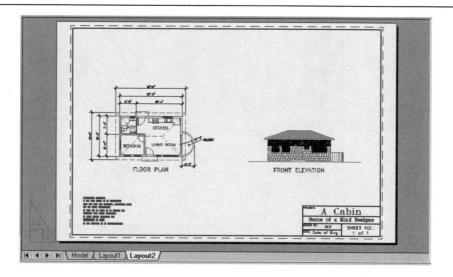

FIGURE 13.17: The completed 11×17-inch drawing with Layout2

11. Click the Layout1 tab to view the smaller Layout sheet. Click the Model tab to view the original drawing without its border and title block. Click the Layout2 tab again. All three views are of the same drawing.

12. Save this drawing to your training folder as Cabin13b.

Now you have two prints set up in Layouts, both based on the same drawing in Model space. There is room for more views in the larger of the two, possibly another elevation or a detail, but we're going to move on to a larger drawing.

Setting Up Viewports in Different Scales

In the next set of exercises, you will create a new Layout for a 30×42-inch sheet for the site plan you created in Skill 12. Then you will create several viewports that have drawings of different scales. Because the site plan has the cabin drawing Xreferenced into it, you will also have a chance to see how external references are handled in a drawing that is using Layouts.

**SKILL
13**

Setting Up a Layout for a 30×42-Inch Drawing

To set up a 30×42-inch Layout, you will use almost the same procedure you used earlier. The title block will be different, but you won't take the time to fill in a complete title block—just indicate its location in the drawing.

1. Close Cabin13b, then open Site12b.

2. Create new layers called Tblk-L1 and Vports-L1. Assign colors to them. Then make the Tblk-L1 layer current.

3. Click the Layout1 tab in the lower-left corner of the drawing area. A blank Layout will appear on the screen for an instant. Then the Page Setup-Layout1 dialog box comes up.

4. Activate the Plot Device tab. In the Plotter configuration area, open the Name drop-down list and select DWF ePlot.pc3, or any large-format plotter you may have set up to use.

5. Click the Layout Settings tab. In the Paper Size and Paper Width area, open the Paper Size drop-down list and scroll down to ARCH E1 (30.00×42.00 Inches). Select that size. Jot down the Printable Area setting (in the example, it's 40.66×29.60 Inches).

6. Drawing Orientation should be Landscape; Plot Area should be Layout; Plot Scale should be 1:1. When these are set, click Add in the upper-right corner of the dialog box. Enter **Site12b-L1**. Then click OK. Click OK again to close the Page Setup dialog box. You will be returned to your drawing. Layout1 is displayed. There is a viewport whose boundary is set in from the edge of the sheet. Site12b is zoomed to Extents within the viewport (Figure 13.18).

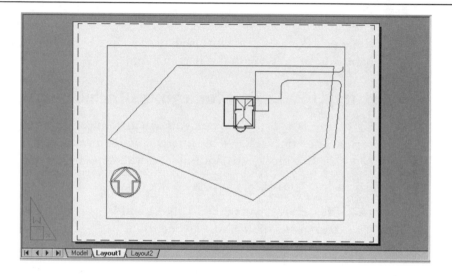

FIGURE 13.18: Site12b within Layout1

7. Use the Rectangle command to draw a rectangle from 0,0 to the point you jotted down in Step 5 (in the example, 40.66,29.60).

8. Offset the rectangle ⅛" to the inside. Zoom into a corner, then erase the outer rectangle and zoom previous to a full view of the Layout (Figure 13.19a).

9. Click the border rectangle to turn on the grips. Hold down the Shift key and select the two grips on the left side to activate them. Be sure Ortho is on and running Osnaps are off. Click one of the two active grips. Hold the cursor directly to the right of the selected grips and type **1** ↵. The left side of the border is moved to the right 1", leaving room for a binding on the left edge of the sheet. Press Esc twice. The large sheet sizes usually have their title block on the right side, turned at 90°. We will draw a guideline to indicate the title block.

10. Offset the border rectangle 4" to the inside. Then explode the new rectangle. Erase the top, bottom, and left lines of this new rectangle. Then use the Extend command to extend the remaining line up and down to the rectangle that will serve as the border (Figure 13.19b).

TIP TIP TIP TIP TIP TIP TIP TIP TIP TIP TIP TIP TIP TIP TIP TIP TIP TIP TIP TIP TIP TIP TIP TIP

Don't worry about the fact that the left side of the title block almost coincides with the right edge of the viewport. This is a coincidence. It makes it a little more difficult to pick the lines, but you know techniques now that can help you with this problem.

11. Start the Pedit command (type **pe** ↵) and select the rectangle that is the new border. Use the Width option to change the width of the borderline to ¹⁄₁₆". Type ↵ ↵ to stop and restart the Pedit command. Then pick the new line that represents the left side of the title block. When asked if you want to make this line into a polyline, press ↵ to accept the default of Yes. Use the Width option again and set this line to the same width as you used for the border. You now have a border and title block area set up in Layout1 and are ready to work with the viewports (Figure 13.19c).

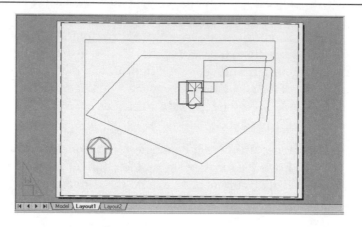

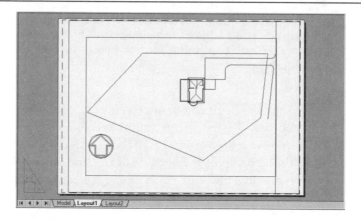

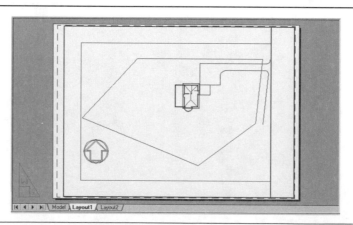

FIGURE 13.19: Creating the new title block and border: the border rectangle (a), the offset rectangle with title block (b), and the finished title block and border (c)

Adjusting a Viewport for the Site Plan

On this 30×42-inch sheet, we already have a large viewport. We'll move it and resize it to fit into the upper two-thirds of the Layout in order to view the site plan at ⅛-inch scale. Then you'll make smaller viewports across the bottom for viewing the floor plan and front elevation at ¼-inch scale, and to view a closeup view of the bathroom. We'll resize and reposition the larger viewport first.

1. Click the viewport in Layout1. Grips appear. Click the grip on the upper-left corner to activate it.

2. Turn Ortho and Running Osnaps off. Press the spacebar once. The Move command begins. Move the crosshair cursor to a point near the upper-left corner, just inside the border, then click. The viewport is moved to the upper left.

3. Click the lower-right grip. Then move the cursor to a point about one third of the way up from the bottom boundary line to the top boundary line, next to the title block (Figure 13.20a).

4. Click to position the second corner of the viewport. Then click the Properties button and use the Properties dialog box to move the viewport to the Vports-L1 layer. Close the Properties dialog box. Finally, press ↵ twice to remove the grips. The viewport is resized, repositioned, and on its proper layer (Figure 13.20b).

5. Click Paper on the Status bar, then type **z** ↵ **1/96xp** ↵. The site plan gets slightly smaller and looks like it will fit in the resized viewport.

6. Use Realtime Pan to reposition the Site12a drawing more centrally within the viewport. If you need to enlarge the size of the viewport, click Model on the Status bar and use grips to stretch the viewport to a size that will allow you to fit the site plan in the viewport at ⅛-inch scale. (Figure13.20c).

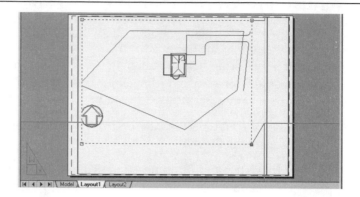

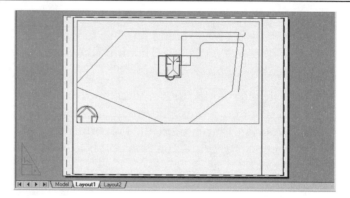

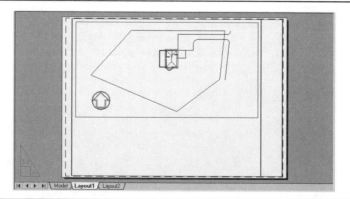

FIGURE 13.20: Adjusting a Viewport with grips on (a), after the adjustment (b), and after the zoom (c)

The view of the site plan is just like the drawing before Paper Space was activated. Remember that the cabin in this drawing is an external reference. Many of the cabin layers are frozen and the visible ones are all the same color, except the new deck. This will have to change when we set up other viewports for the floor plan and front elevation.

Adding Multiple Viewports to a Layout

Now we'll add three new viewports to the empty space below the first viewport, then modify each of them in terms of:

- Viewport size

- Content of each viewport

- Scale of objects within each viewport

- Visibility and color of layers within each viewport

We'll create the three viewports together, then modify them individually, starting with the left-most viewport where we'll place the floor plan of the cabin.

1. Be sure that the Model/Paper button on the Status bar is set to Paper. Then set the Vports-L1 layer to be current. Click View ➤ Viewports ➤ 3 Viewports. At the [Horizontal/Vertical/Above/Below/Left/Right] <Right>: prompt, type **V** ↵. You will be prompted to Specify first corner or [Fit]:. This means you need to make a window that the three new viewports will fit inside of, side-by-side.

2. Make a window that fills the open area below the existing viewport (Figure 13.21a). When you click the second point to define the window, the three new viewports are created and each has a view of the Site12a drawing zoomed to extents (Figure 13.21b).

3. Click the Model/Paper button on the Status bar to move to Model space and click in the left-most viewport. Type **ucs** ↵ **z** ↵ **−90** ↵. Then type **plan** ↵ ↵. The site plan is rotated 90° counterclockwise. The cabin is now oriented the way it was before being inserted as an external reference into the site plan (Figure 13.22a).

4. Pan the cabin to the middle of the viewport, then zoom its view to ¼-inch scale by typing **z** ↵ **1/48xp** ↵. The floor plan fills the viewport (Figure 13.22b).

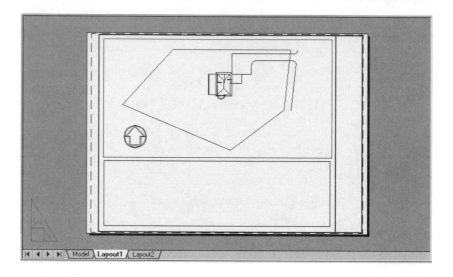

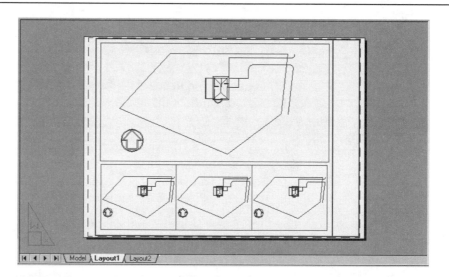

FIGURE 13.21: Windowing the area in which to insert the viewports (a) and the inserted viewports (b)

SKILL
13

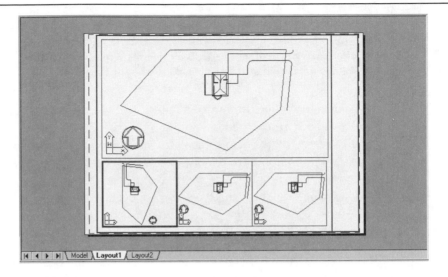

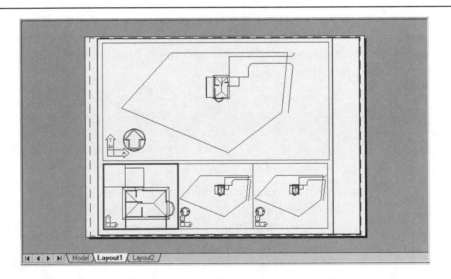

FIGURE 13.22: The left viewport with a rotated site plan (a), and the site plan zoomed to 1/4-inch scale in the viewport (b)

NOTE NOTE NOTE NOTE NOTE NOTE NOTE NOTE NOTE NOTE NOTE NOTE NOTE NOTE NOTE

The visibility of the UCS icon can be controlled in each viewport and in Paper Space by picking View ➤ Display ➤ UCS Icon, and then clicking On. When the checkmark is visible, the UCS icon is displayed. When the Layout is active, the icon is a triangle and sits outside the Layout.

There are a couple of things that need to be done to this view to complete it. You'll need to resize the viewport and pan the view to get everything that you want to see visible. You also need to determine which layers you want visible in this viewport and freeze the ones whose objects you don't want to see. We'll work with the layers first because we need to make all the objects to be displayed visible in order to tell how big the viewport needs to be.

Controlling Layers in Viewports

You can control which layers are visible in each viewport, so two viewports can have a different combination of layers visible. The way this is done is to first thaw all frozen layers. Then, with Model Space current, you make a viewport active and freeze the layers you don't want visible in that viewport. When finished, you move to the next viewport and freeze layers you don't want visible in that viewport. In this situation, you'll eventually have to reset the visibility of the layers in all viewports.

1. On the Layout1 tab, be sure that Model Space is active and the lower-left viewport is current. Then click the Layers button on the Object Properties toolbar. When the Layer Properties Manager dialog box opens, click and drag the right edge of the dialog box to the right to widen it enough to see the Active column on the far right.

2. Thaw all currently frozen layers. (Right-click any layer, then pick Select All off the menu that appears in the drawing area. All layers are highlighted. Then click a snowflake in the Freeze column. All layers are thawed. Scroll back to the top and click the Cabin layer. The rest of the layers are de-selected.) Now that all layers are visible, you need to go down the list of layers. When you see a layer that needs to be frozen in the current viewport, click the sun in the Active column for that layer. The smaller viewport is current, so let's start with the layers for that one.

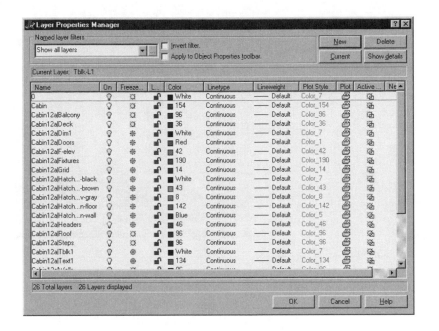

3. Move down the list and click the sun in the Active column for the following layers:

   - The following Cabin12a | layers: Dim1, F-elev, Roof, Tblk1, Text1, and all the hatch layers *except* Hatch-plan-wall

   - Prop-line and Road layers

   Click OK when finished. You are returned to your drawing (Figure 13.23a). The smaller viewport looks OK, but it needs resizing. All the layers are visible in the other two small viewports and in the larger one. Let's set the layers for the larger viewport now.

4. Click in the larger viewport to make it active. Then click the Layers button again. In the Layer Properties Manager dialog box, go down the list again, clicking the suns in the Active column, as you did before, to make the following layers invisible in this viewport: all Cabin12a | layers except Balcony, Deck, Roof, Steps, and Walls. Click OK when finished. The drawing in this viewport is what we want (Figure 13.23b). Now you need to adjust the size and view of the smaller-left viewport. You're going to stretch it up to a point where it will overlap the larger viewport, so, while the larger viewport is active, move the north arrow to the other side of the site plan.

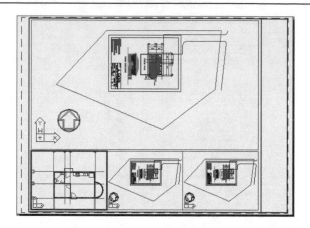

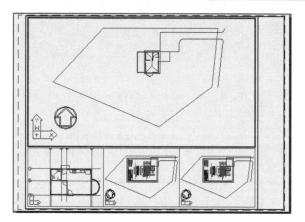

FIGURE 13.23: Layer changes made in the smaller left viewport (a), and in the larger viewport (b)

5. Start the Move command and select the north arrow. Press ↵. Click in the middle of the arrow and click again to place it in a clear space in the lower-right corner of the larger viewport.

6. Type **ps** ↵ to switch to Layout1 (or Paper Space). Click the small viewport on the left to make grips appear.

7. Click the upper-right grip. With Ortho off, move the cursor up and to the right at about a 45-degree angle and pick a point just below the property line (Figure 13.24a). Press Esc twice to remove the grips.

8. Type **ms** ↵ to switch to Model Space. Click in the lower-left viewport to make it active. Use the Pan command to move the floor plan around in the viewport until the deck and the grid are completely visible. Leave some room below the deck for text. Press Esc to end the Pan command. Switch back to Paper Space and do a final adjustment of the size with grips, making the viewport as small as possible while still showing everything (Figure 13.24b). Press Esc twice to remove the grips.

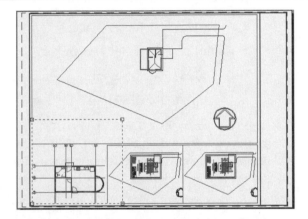

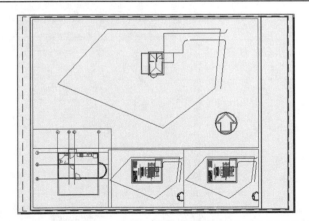

FIGURE 13.24: Stretching the viewport with grips in the Layout (a), and panning the view in Model space (b)

The layers are now set up so they are visible in all viewports (the Freeze column), except where frozen in particular viewports (the Active column). The other two small viewports have all layers visible, because we haven't yet made them current, and frozen layers in the Active column that we don't want visible in these particular viewports. Let's move to those viewports now and set them up using the procedures we've just used for the first two.

1. Type **ms** ↵ to switch to Model Space. Click in the smaller viewport that's in the middle to make it active. Then click the Layers button. Freeze all layers in the Active column, except the following layers:

    - Cabin
    - Cabin12a I F-elev
    - Cabin12a I Hatch-elev-black
    - Cabin12a I Hatch-elev-brown
    - Cabin12a I Hatch-elev-gray

    Click OK to return to the drawing.

2. Type **ucs** ↵ **z** ↵ **–90** ↵. Then type **plan** ↵ ↵. Pan the front elevation to the middle of the viewport. Then type **z** ↵ **1/48xp** ↵. Pan the drawing again until the ground line approximately lines up with the bottom line of the deck in the floor plan on the left.

3. Move to the Layout and resize the viewport so that it includes the entire front elevation and nothing more (Figure 13.25).

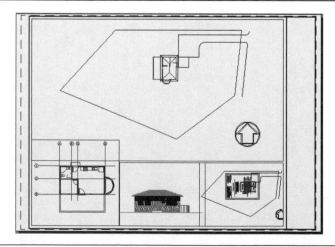

FIGURE 13.25: The front elevation in the middle small viewport

4. Now move to the viewport in the lower-right corner and make adjustments to display the bathroom at a scale of 1"=1'-0". Follow these steps:

   A. Switch to Model space and activate the right, small viewport.

   B. Use the UCS and Plan commands to rotate the drawing 90° counter-clockwise.

   C. In the Active column of the Layer Properties Manager dialog box, freeze the following layers: All the Cabin12a | layers, except for Doors; Fixtures; Hatch-plan-floor; Hatch-plan-wall; Headers; Walls; and Windows; all layers not prefaced by Cabin12a except the Cabin and 0 layers.

   D. Zoom to 1/12xp.

   E. Pan the drawing until the bathroom is centered in the viewport. Try to line up the bottom bathroom wall with the ground line in the front elevation.

   F. Switch to the Layout (click the Model button) and adjust the size and position of the viewport. Try to make the right and bottom boundary lines of the viewport coincide with the right and bottom edges of the wall lines. Zoom in close if you need to. Then zoom out to a view of the entire Layout when finished.

 NOTE NOTE NOTE NOTE NOTE NOTE NOTE NOTE NOTE NOTE NOTE NOTE NOTE NOTE NOTE
Once a viewport is zoomed to a scale with 1/xp, the final adjustment has two steps: panning the drawing in Model space, and adjusting the size and location of the viewport with grips in Layout.

   G. While in Layout, zoom into the bathroom door in the right small viewport. Switch to Model space and make the 0 layer current. Draw an arc to fill in the blank space in the door swing that you broke out for text in Skill 10. Switch back to Layout, then zoom previous to a full view of the Layout. Be sure Ortho is on. If necessary, move any of the small viewports horizontally to space them evenly on the layout.

The results should look something like Figure 13.26.

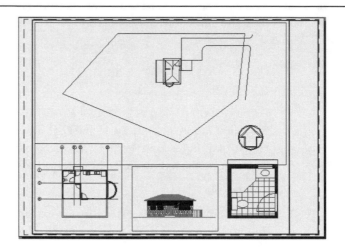

FIGURE 13.26: All viewports completed

TIP TIP TIP TIP TIP TIP TIP TIP TIP TIP TIP TIP TIP TIP TIP TIP TIP TIP TIP TIP TIP TIP TIP
Since viewports are usually made invisible, it isn't important to line them up evenly. Viewports can overlap each other as long as the objects *in* the viewports do not overlap.

Adding Text to Paper Space

Now you'll add titles to the views in a style that matches the style of the front elevation title. Underneath each title we will put the scale of the view.

1. Type **ms** ↵. Make the viewport containing the front elevation active. Then thaw the Cabin12a | Text1 layer in the active column. The FRONT ELEVATION text appears.

TIP TIP TIP TIP TIP TIP TIP TIP TIP TIP TIP TIP TIP TIP TIP TIP TIP TIP TIP TIP TIP TIP TIP
If the FLOOR PLAN text also appears, you can stretch this viewport up to hide it the next time Layout is active.

2. Create a new layer called Text-L1. Assign it the same color as the Cabin12a | Text1 layer and make it current.

3. Create a new text style called Title-L1. (Recall that the Style command is started by picking Format ➤ Text Style on the menu bar.) We want the new style to be identical to the Title text style we used in Model Space, but the height has to be adjusted for Layout. It was 1-foot-6-inches high in Model Space. The front elevation is now at ¼-inch scale. If you divide 1'-6" by 48, you have the Paper Space text height—⅜". Assign this text style the romand.shx font and a ⅜-inch height. Click Apply, then click Close.

4. Type **ps** ↵. Then select Draw ➤ Text ➤ Single Line Text from the menu bar. Type **j** ↵, then type **c** ↵. Then, to activate point filters, type **.y** ↵.

**SKILL
13**

5. Pick the Insert Osnap and click the FRONT ELEVATION text. Pick Midpoint Osnap and click one of the horizontal deck lines in the floor plan.

6. Press ↵ for the Rotation prompt. With Caps Lock on, type **floor plan** ↵ ↵. The floor plan title is placed on the drawing. Zoom in to see it better (Figure 13.27a).

7. With Ortho on, copy this text down ¾". Use the Properties button to change this text to be ¼-inch high and to SCALE: 1/4" = 1'-0" (Figure 13.27b). Leave an extra space before and after the = sign.

8. Zoom previous. Use the Insertion Osnap to copy the scale to the front elevation.

9. With Ortho on, use the Copy command with the Multiple option to copy both the view title and the scale from the floor plan to the bathroom viewport. Then turn Ortho off and continue using the same command to copy the view title and the scale to the site plan.

10. Select Modify ➤ Text to start the Ddedit command. Use this command to change the titles to BATHROOM and SITE PLAN, and to change the scales to 1" = 1'-0" and ⅛" = 1'-0", respectively.

11. Freeze the Vports-L1 layer. The results should look like Figure 13.28a. The drawing looks complete. The only problem is that the property line in the site plan looks continuous. With Paper Space, you need to set the global linetype scale setting to 1. Then AutoCAD will adjust the linetype scale for each viewport, depending on the scale it's zoomed to.

12. Type **ltscale** ↵ **1** ↵. The phantom linetype is now visible (Figure 13.28b).

You added one line of text on Layout, then copied and changed it to make six more lines of the text.

NOTE NOTE NOTE NOTE NOTE NOTE NOTE NOTE NOTE NOTE NOTE NOTE NOTE NOTE NOTE

If you have been using a black Model space background, some of your colors may appear faded out on the Layout. Feel free to modify them by assigning darker colors to the layers.

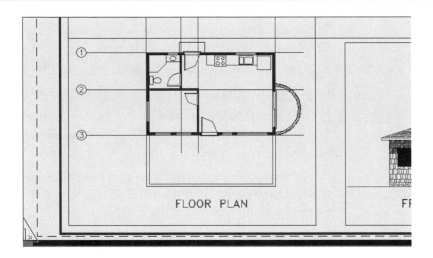

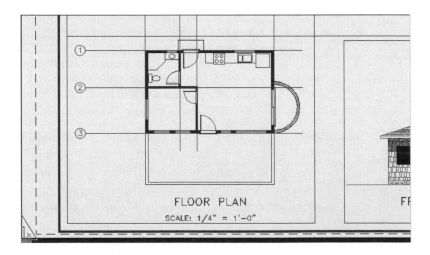

FIGURE 13.27: A title is placed on the floor plan (a), and a scale is added (b).

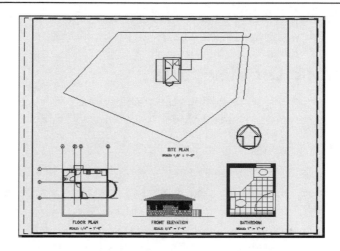

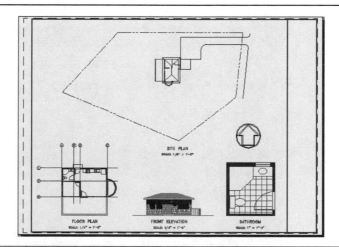

FIGURE 13.28: The 30×42-inch drawing complete with titles and scales of views (a), and with the ltscale setting adjusted for Paper Space (b)

As you have just seen, text and lines on a Layout can be put on top of viewports. The viewport is like a window through which you can view the Model space drawing, but the window has a transparent surface, like glass or cellophane, on which you can place text or other AutoCAD objects.

A layer can have some objects on Layout and some in Model space. But arranging the drawing like this is not a good practice to get into because it can make the drawing harder to manage.

Turning Off Viewports

Beyond just controlling the visibility of layers in each viewport, you can turn off a viewport so that all Model space objects within the viewport are invisible.

1. Thaw the Vports-L1 layer for a moment.

2. Select the three small viewports, then click the Properties button.

3. In the Properties dialog box, under Misc, click On. Then open the drop-down list next to On and click No. Close the Properties dialog box. Then press Esc twice to remove the grips. All selected viewports go blank, and all that's visible is their borders and the text that's on the Layout (Figure 13.29).

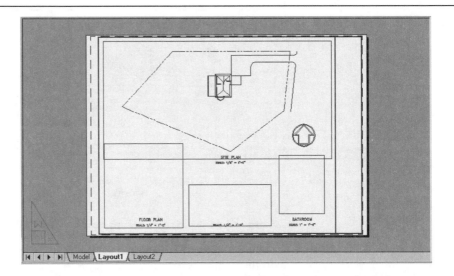

FIGURE 13.29: Layout1 with the smaller viewports turned off

4. Reselect the three small viewports and use Properties to turn them back on. Freeze the Vports layer again. Your drawing should look like Figure 13.28b.

5. Save this drawing as Site13.

Being able to turn viewports off can be an advantage for a complex drawing with many viewports, or one with a lot of information in each viewport. Remember that, even though all four views in this drawing are based on one drawing, AutoCAD is drawing at least part of that drawing in each viewport. In a complex drawing, this can slow down the computer, so it's handy to be able to temporarily turn off any viewports you are not working on.

We will work with the viewports and Layouts again in the next skill where you will round out your knowledge of AutoCAD by learning the principles of plotting and printing AutoCAD drawings.

SKILL
13

Are You Experienced?

Now you can . . .

- ☑ create a Layout
- ☑ draw a border and title block on a Layout
- ☑ set up viewports on Layouts
- ☑ cut and paste in AutoCAD
- ☑ zoom to a scale in a viewport
- ☑ align viewports
- ☑ control layer visibility in individual viewports
- ☑ control the visibility of viewport boundaries
- ☑ copy viewports
- ☑ set up a text style for Layouts
- ☑ add text to a Layout
- ☑ turn viewports off and on

Printing an AutoCAD Drawing

- ⊖ **Setting up a drawing to be printed**
- ⊖ **Using the Plot dialog box**
- ⊖ **Assigning lineweights to layers in your drawing**
- ⊖ **Selecting the part of your drawing to print**
- ⊖ **Previewing a print**
- ⊖ **Printing a Layout**

First of all, with today's equipment, there is no difference between printing and plotting. Printing used to refer to the smaller format printers, and plotting used to refer to the pen plotters, most of which were for plotting large sheets. But the terms are now used almost interchangeably. Pen plotters have a few extra settings that other printing devices do not have. Otherwise, as far as AutoCAD is concerned, the differences between plotters and laser jet, ink jet, dot matrix, and electrostatic printers, are minimal. So I'll refer to all printing and plotting processes as printing.

Getting your drawing onto paper can be very easy or very hard, depending on whether your computer is connected to a printer that has been set up to print AutoCAD drawings, and whether AutoCAD has been configured to work with the printer to which you have access. If these initial conditions are met, printing can be handily managed with the tools you will learn in this skill. If you do not have the initial setup, you will need to get some help to either set up your system to make AutoCAD work properly with your printer, or to find out how your system is already set up to print AutoCAD drawings. Then dive into this skill.

We will be using a couple of standard setup configurations between AutoCAD and printers to move through the exercises. You may or may not be able to follow through each step to completion, depending on whether you have access to an 8½×11-inch laser jet or desk jet printer, or a larger format printer, or both.

We have four drawings to print:

- Cabin11a—a drawing with Model space only, to be printed on an 8 ½×11-inch sheet at ⅛-inch scale

- Cabin13a—the same drawing as Cabin11a, except with the title block and border on Layout1, to be printed from Layout1 on an 8½×11-inch sheet at a scale of 1:1.

- The 11×17-inch drawing—in Cabin13b, to be printed on an 11×17-inch sheet from a Layout

- Site13, to be printed on a 30×42-inch sheet from a Layout

If your printer won't allow you to print in all these formats, I would advise you to follow along with the text anyway. You'll at least get to preview how your drawing would look if printed in these formats, and you will be taking large strides towards learning how to set up and run a print for your drawing. The skill is written to give you the basic principals for printing whether or not you have access to a printer.

The Plot Dialog Box

The job of getting your AutoCAD file onto hard copy can be broken down into five tasks. You will need to specify to AutoCAD:

- The printing device you will use

- The lineweight assigned to each object in your drawing

- The portion of your drawing you are printing

- The sheet size you are printing onto

- The scale, orientation, and placement of the print on the sheet

Most of these tasks will be handled through the Plot dialog box.

SKILL
14

1. Open Cabin11a. Zoom to Extents, then zoom out a little (Figure 14.1). This drawing is not quite ready to print.

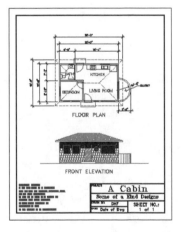

FIGURE 14.1: Cabin11a zoomed to Extents, then zoomed out a little

2. Click the Print button on the Standard toolbar. The Plot dialog box appears. This dialog box is a near duplicate of the Page Setup dialog box that you worked with in Skill 13: *Using Layouts to Set Up a Print*. It has the same two tabs: Plot Device and Plot Settings (called Layout Settings in the Page Setup dialog box). Be sure the Plot Settings tab is active here (Figure 14.2).

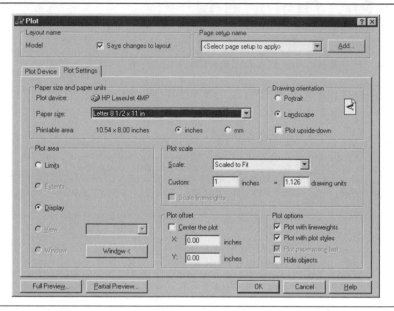

FIGURE 14.2: The Plot dialog box with the Plot Settings tab active

NOTE NOTE NOTE NOTE NOTE NOTE NOTE NOTE NOTE NOTE NOTE NOTE NOTE NOTE NOTE

The Plot dialog box can also be brought up by selecting File ➤ Print, by typing Ctrl+P, or by typing plot ↵ or print ↵.

You worked in the same dialog box when you set up Layouts, and, when we get to the point in this skill where we are printing Layouts, you'll find that much of the setup work has already been done. But before we start printing, let's take a quick tour of this dialog box. Then we'll start setting up to print.

Most of the work you have to do in this dialog box is on the Plot Settings tab. There are six areas of settings on this tab. Some of the buttons and boxes won't be activated. Others will be mentioned only in passing, as their functions are for more advanced techniques than those covered in this book.

Paper Size and Paper Units

In the Paper Size and Paper Units area, the current Plot Device is displayed at the top (in this case it's the HP LaserJet 4MP). Just below the Plot Device is the Paper Size drop-down list. It will contain paper sizes that the current plot device can handle. Below that is the Printable Area of the selected paper size on the selected plot device. We used this data to set up Layouts in the previous skill.

1. Click the Plot Device tab to make it active (Figure 14.3).

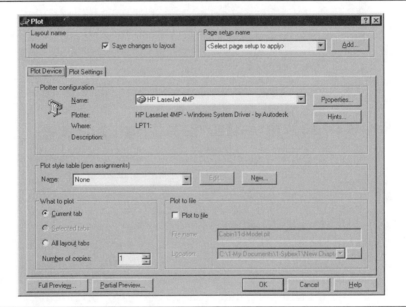

FIGURE 14.3 The Plot dialog box with Plot Device tab active

2. In the Plotter Configuration area at the top of the dialog box, the Name drop-down list contains the various printing devices to which AutoCAD has been configured, with the current one—in this case, the HP LaserJet 4MP—displayed. Just below the list, the name of the driver and port are displayed for the selected printer. The Properties button to the right opens up the Plotter Configuration Editor, which has three tabs of data specific for the current printer. Most of these will already be set up by your Windows

operating system. The other areas in the lower part of the tab contain more advanced tools for:

- Selecting a previously named and saved group of plot settings, or creating a new one

- Controlling which tabs, and how many copies, are printed

- Directing AutoCAD to make and save the print as a file, rather than to send it to a printer

If you find yourself repeatedly using the same setup for the same printer, you will need to get at least a little familiar with these areas, but we won't be using these features in this book. We will, however, come back to the Plot Device tab when we set up prints for large format drawings in the last half of this skill.

2.   Click the Plot Settings tab to make it active, so we can finish our tour.

Drawing Orientation and Plot Scale

To the right of the Paper Size and Paper Units area of the Plot Settings tab on the Plot dialog box is the Drawing Orientation area. The settings here are self-explanatory. The radio buttons serve as a toggle between the Portrait and Landscape orientation, and the Plot Upside-down checkbox serves as an on/off toggle.

Moving down, we come to the Plot Scale area, where you control the scale of the plot. The Scale drop-down list contains 33 preset scales to choose from, including Custom and Scaled to Fit. With this latter choice selected, AutoCAD will take whatever area you have chosen to print and automatically scale it so that it will fit on the selected page size. Some of the scales in the list are displayed as pure ratios, such as 1:50. Others are shown in their standard format, such as ¼" = 1'0". Below the drop-down list is a pair of text boxes for setting up a custom scale. When a preset scale is chosen, these text boxes display the true ratio of the current scale.

To set up a custom scale, you enter a plotted distance in the Inches text box. Enter the distance on the computer drawing file that will be represented by the first distance in the Drawing Units text box. The Inches distance will be an actual distance on the plotted drawing, while the Drawing Units distance is the distance the plotted units represent. For ¼-inch scale (¼" = 1'-0") you could enter several combinations:

Inches	Drawing Units
¼	1'
1	4'
1	48

Layouts are plotted at a scale of 1:1. We'll come back to this and other scale issues as we prepare a drawing for printing.

Plot Offset and Plot Options

Below the Plot scale area are two small areas: Plot Offset and Plot Options. The Plot Options area has four miscellaneous on/off settings that don't concern us now. In the Plot Offset area, you have the on/off Center the Plot checkbox. When selected, the plot is centered on the printed sheet. If it is not selected, by default, AutoCAD will place the lower-left corner (or the Origin) of the area you have specified to plot at the lower-left corner (or Origin) of the printable area of the current paper size. By changing the settings in the X and Y text boxes, you can move the drawing horizontally or vertically to fit on the page as you wish. When the Center the Plot checkbox is selected, the X and Y text boxes display any movement from the lower-left corner of the sheet that was necessary to center the drawing.

Just as each drawing has an origin (0,0 point), each plotter creates an origin for the plot. Usually it's in the lower-left or upper-left corner, but not always. When the plot is being made, the printer first locates the origin and starts the print there, moving outward from the origin. If the origin is in the lower-left corner, the print may come out looking like Figure 14.4a. If the origin is the upper-left corner, the print will look like Figure 14.4b.

By using the X Origin and Y Origin setting in the Plot Offset area, you can make one margin wider for a binding. To center your drawing on the page check the Center the Plot check box (Figure 14.4c).

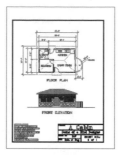

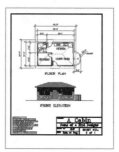

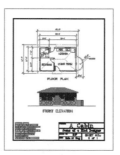

FIGURE 14.4: A print with its origin in the lower-left corner (a), in the upper-left corner (b), and with the drawing centered (c)

Usually printers of the 8½×11-inch format are configured to the portrait orientation. If your drawing is also that orientation, the origin of the plot will be in the lower-left corner. If your drawing is in the landscape orientation, the plot origin will move to the upper-left corner of the page because the plot has been rotated to fit on the page.

Setting the origin accurately will be a result of trial and error, and getting to know your printer well. We will return to this area shortly, when we get ready to print.

Plot Area

On the left side of the Plot Area, there are five radio buttons for the five methods of specifying what to print in your drawing. We have already made some decisions about what to print by deciding which layers will be visible when the print is made, and by freezing the layers whose objects we don't want to print. Now we must decide how to designate the area of the drawing to be printed. As we go through the options, it will be useful to think about the choices with regard to two printing possibilities: printing the whole drawing and printing just the floor plan.

To illustrate how these options work, we will make a couple of assumptions: First, the Scaled to Fit option is selected in the Scale drop-down list in the Plot Scale area, so AutoCAD will try to fill the sheet with the drawing. Second, the drawing will be in portrait orientation.

Limits

Do you remember the drawing limits for the cabin drawing that you set in Skill 3, *Setting Up a Drawing*? For a reminder, perform the instructions that follow.

1. Select Cancel to cancel the plot.

2. Click the Grid button on the status bar to make the grid visible. It's still there, around the floor plan, just as you first set it in Skill 3 (Figure 14.5a). When you print to Limits, AutoCAD will print only what lies within the limits, and it will push what's within the limits to the corner that is the origin of the print (Figure 14.5b). This doesn't work here because the limits don't cover the entire drawing. Printing to Limits can be a good tool for setting up a print, but you will usually reset the limits from their original defining coordinates for the actual print.

3. Press F7 to turn off the grid.

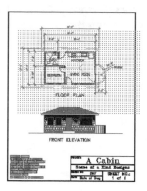

FIGURE 14.5: The grid showing the limits of Cabin11a (a), and the drawing printed to Limits (b)

Extents

When you select the Extents option, AutoCAD tries to fill the sheet with all visible objects in the drawing. If you print Cabin11a using the Extents method of selecting what to print, the results would look like Figure 14.6. This is a good method to use if the border has been drawn with the same proportions as the sheet. It was in this case because you offset a rectangle that represented the sheet to make the border, but the rectangle that represented the sheet was also printed, and we didn't want that. You would have to erase that rectangle before printing to Extents.

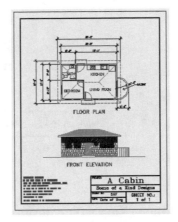

FIGURE 14.6: The Cabin11a drawing printed to Extents

Display

The Display option will print what's currently on the screen, including the blank area around the drawing. With both drawing and sheet in portrait orientation, and with the origin in the lower-left corner of the sheet, the plot would look like Figure 14.7, with the dashed lines representing the edge of what was the drawing area on the screen. If the drawing were rotated, it would fit better on the sheet, because the screen is wider than it is tall. Printing to Display is a good method if the drawing is in landscape orientation and is proportional in size to the drawing area.

FIGURE 14.7: The Cabin11a drawing printed to Display

View

When printing to View, you tell AutoCAD to print a previously defined view that was saved with the drawing. Right now the View radio button is greyed out because we haven't defined and saved any views yet. We'll save a view, and then we'll see what the print will look like.

1. Pick View ➤ Named Views. The View control dialog box comes up.

2. Click the New button. In the New View dialog box, type **plot1**. Click the Define Window radio button. Then move to the right and click the Define View Window button.

3. Back in the drawing, make a window around the left half of the floor plan, not including the dimensions, as in Figure 14.8a.

4. Click the OK button. The saved view, called Plot1, is listed in the Views list box of the View dialog box.

5. Click OK to return to the drawing. Then click the Print button and continue reading along.

Now, to plot the Plot1 view of this drawing, click the View button in the Plot area of the Plot dialog box. Then move to the right and select Plot1 from the drop-down list of saved views. At the settings for scale and orientation we have been using, the print will look like Figure 14.8b. This is a valuable tool for prints of parts of a drawing that you might want to redo at a later point in the progress of the project.

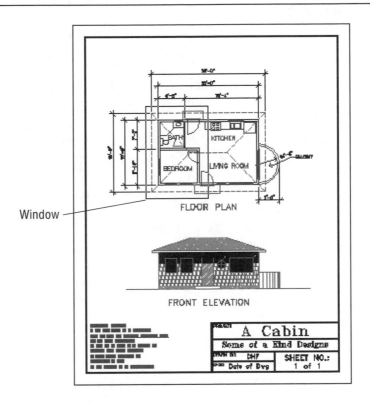

Window

FIGURE 14.8: Using a window to define a view (a), and the print to this
view (b)

Window

Using a window to define the area of a plot is the most flexible method of the five being described. It's like using zoom window in the drawing. AutoCAD will take the area you window and put it into the print. To select this option, click the rectangular Window radio button. In your drawing, make a window around the area you want to print. AutoCAD will print only what is in the window you made, regardless of how it fits on the sheet. This method is similar to the View method, discussed previously. The difference lies in the fact that the View method prints a previously defined view (one that was possibly defined by a window, but could also be defined in other ways), and the Window method prints what is included in a window that you define as you are setting up the plot. The window used by the Window method can't be saved and recalled at a later time.

These are the five ways to specify what to print. We'll use the Window option in the first exercise that follows.

We have taken a quick tour of the Plot dialog box, and we still have a drawing—Cabin11a—to print. Let's print this drawing. As we set up the print, refer back to this section for explanation of the steps, if necessary.

Printing a Drawing

Our task is to print Cabin11a.dwg at a scale of ⅛" = 1'-0" on an 8½×11-inch sheet. In this exercise, we will use the default system printer, which is set up for an 8½×11-inch format laser jet printer. If you have an 8½×11-inch format printer, you should be able to follow the steps. If you don't have a printer, you can still get familiar with printing by following along with the steps in the book.

The first step is to assign lineweights to the visible layers.

Determining Lineweights for a Drawing

Look at the Cabin11a drawing as a whole. We need to decide on weights for the various lines. The floor plan is drawn as if a cut were made horizontally through the building just below the tops of the window and door openings. Everything that was cut will be given a heavy line. Objects above and below the cut will be given progressively lighter lines, depending on how far above or below the cut the objects are located. In this system, the walls, windows, and doors will be heaviest. The roof, headers, fixtures, and steps will be lighter. For emphasis, we'll make the walls a little heavier than the windows and doors. In the front elevation, the hatch pattern will be very light and the outline of the various components will be heavier, for emphasis. Text and the title block information will use the default lineweight.

These are general guidelines—weights will vary with each drawing.

We will use four lineweights for this drawing:

Weight	Thickness In Inches
very light	0.005
light	0.008
medium	0.010
heavy	0.013

SKILL
14

There are fifteen layers in Cabin11a that are visible in the drawing as it is presently set up. Their lineweights will be assigned as follows:

Layer	Lineweight
Balcony	light
Dim1	very light
Doors	medium
F-elev	medium
Fixtures	light
Hatch-elev-42	very light
Hatch-elev-black	very light
Hatch-elev-gray	very light
Headers	light
Roof	very light
Steps	light
Tblk1	medium
Text1	medium
Walls	heavy
Windows	medium

When we look at the lineweights presently assigned to these layers, and at the thickness we need these lineweights to be, we can generate a third chart that will show us what layers need to be assigned to each particular thickness:

Thickness	Layers
0.005	Dim1, all visible hatch layers, Roof
0.008	Balcony, Fixtures, Headers, Steps
0.010 (default)	Doors, F-elev, Tblk1, Text, Windows
0.014	Walls

Now it's time to assign the lineweights to the layers in the drawings.

1. Click the Layers button on the Object Property toolbar. The Layer Properties Manager dialog box comes up.

2. Click the Dim1 layer to highlight it. Hold down the Ctrl key and click the three Hatch-elev layers and the Roof layers to select them. Then release the Ctrl key.

3. In the Lineweight column, click one of the highlighted Default words. The Lineweight dialog box comes up.

NOTE NOTE NOTE NOTE NOTE NOTE NOTE NOTE NOTE NOTE NOTE NOTE NOTE NOTE NOTE

If the lineweights listed in the Lineweight dialog box are in millimeters, type lw ↵. Then in the Lineweight Settings dialog box, click the Inches radio button in the Units for Listing area and click OK.

4. Click **0.005"**. Then click OK. The Lineweight dialog box disappears. In the Layer Property Manager dialog box, the five highlighted layers now have a lineweight of 0.005" assigned to them.

5. Click on the Balcony layer near the BALCONY.

6. Hold down the Ctrl key and click on Fixtures, Headers, and Steps.

7. Click one of the highlighted Default words. The Lineweight dialog box reappears.

8. Click **0.008"**. Then click OK. The newly highlighted layers now have a lineweight of 0.008" assigned to them.

9. You can leave Default as the linetype for the Doors, Windows, and Text1 layers because the thickness they need is the default thickness of 0.010". Click the Walls layer and use the same procedure to assign it the thickness of 0.014".

10. Click OK to close the Layer Properties Manager dialog box.

11. Type **lw** ↵ to open the Lineweight Settings dialog box.

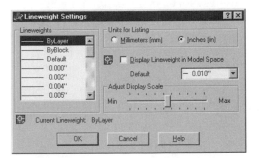

Notice the Default drop-down list on the right side. 0.010" is displayed. This tells you that the default lineweight thickness is 0.010", which is what we are assuming.

12. Click Cancel to close the dialog box.

The lineweights have been assigned. When the print is complete you can judge whether these lineweight assignments are acceptable or if they need to be adjusted. In an office, much time is invested in developing a lineweight standard that can be used in most drawings.

Setting Up the Other Parameters for the Print

Now that we have set the lineweights, it's time to move to the Plot dialog box and complete the setting changes we need to make in order to print this drawing. We will use the Window option for selecting what we will print.

1. Click the Print button on the Standard toolbar.

SKILL
14

2. In the Plot dialog box, be sure the Plot Settings tab is active. Check the Paper Size and Paper Units area to be sure you have the correct printer listed as the Plot Device as, and 8½×11 as the selected paper size. Then move down to Plot Area and click the Window button.

3. In the drawing, disable any running Osnaps. To start the window, pick a point outside the border, as close to the lower-left corner of the border as you can without touching it.

4. To complete the window, click a point above and to the right of the border, also as close to the border as you can without touching it. Back in the Plot dialog box, the Window radio button in Plot Area will be selected.

5. Move to the right side of the dialog box. Be sure Portrait is selected in the Drawing Orientation area at the top.

6. In the Plot Scale area, open the Scale drop-down list and select **1/8" = 1'0"**. Notice that the text boxes next to Custom now read **1** and **96**: the scale factor for ⅛-inch scale.

7. In the Plot Offset area, click the Center the Plot checkbox.

   This completes the setup for the first plot. Before we waste paper, let's preview how it will look as a result of our setup changes.

Previewing a Print

There are two ways of previewing a plot: Partial and Full. The Partial Preview method is a diagram and takes very little time to be generated by AutoCAD. The Full Preview method shows you exactly what you are going to get. We'll do both for this plot.

1. In the lower-left corner of the Plot dialog box, click the Partial Preview button. The Partial Plot Preview dialog box comes up (Figure 14.9). At the top is a diagram of the sheet being plotted. The white area is the actual sheet of paper. The dashed line near the perimeter is the printable area boundary. The blue rectangle is your drawing. The red triangle indicates the origin of the plot.

    In the middle of the dialog box, information on the size of the paper, the printable area, and the actual area taken up by the drawing (effective area) is listed. At the bottom of the dialog box, there is a warning box that will give you information if your drawing doesn't fit on the page properly.

Everything looks fine in this preview.

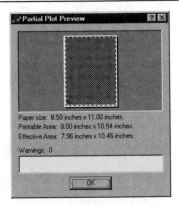

FIGURE 14.9: The Partial Plot Preview dialog box

2. Click OK to close the dialog box.

3. Click the Full Preview button. The computer takes a moment to calculate the plot. Then a full view of your drawing as it will fit on the page is displayed (Figure 14.10).

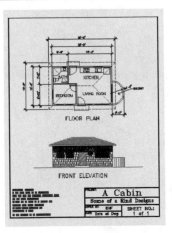

FIGURE 14.10: The Full Preview of Cabin11a, ready to print

4. Press ↵ to return to the Plot dialog box. If your print was oriented correctly on the sheet, you are ready to print. If not, recheck the setup steps for errors.

5. At the bottom of the Plot dialog box, click OK. The computer will begin calculating the print and eventually send it to the printer.

6. After the print is done, save this drawing as Cabin14a.

NOTE NOTE NOTE NOTE NOTE NOTE NOTE NOTE NOTE NOTE NOTE NOTE NOTE NOTE NOTE NOTE

You can change a setting in the Lineweight Settings dialog box to be able to see lineweights in your drawing before it's printed, but they are not very accurate. For the most part, you have to print out the drawing to see how the lineweights display.

When your print comes out, it should look similar to Figure 14.10. Take a close look at the border. Is the space outside the border equal on the left and right, or up and down? It should be, if you put a check in the Center the Plot checkbox. If not, or if you need to widen one of the margins to make room for a binding, go to the Plot offset area of the Plot dialog box and change the settings for X and Y. Just be sure you don't move the drawing to a point where one of the border lines gets lopped off. It takes a little trial and error. The Preview Features will help you. Figure 14.11 illustrates what you will see in the Partial and Full Previews when you try to print Cabin11a with the landscape orientation.

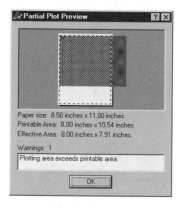
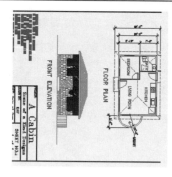

FIGURE 14.11: The Partial Preview (a), and Full Preview (b) of Cabin11a set up to be printed in the wrong orientation

Check the lineweights of the various components on the print. You may have to make adjustments for your particular printer.

Next you'll plot a similar drawing that uses Layouts for its border and title block.

Printing a Drawing Using Layouts

As a comparison to the previous exercise, we'll print a drawing that has a Layout set up. When a Layout tab has been set up properly and is active, you print at a scale of 1:1. The elements of the drawing on the Layout are then printed actual size, and the Model space portion of the drawing is printed at the scale to which the viewport has been zoomed.

1. Save the current drawing as Cabin14a.

2. Open Cabin13b. Be sure the Layout1 tab is active. This drawing is similar to Cabin11a. The only difference in appearance is that this one displays the dashed lines just outside the border, and the sheet is resting on the grey background with a shadowing effect, similar to how a Full Preview appears (Figure 14.12). This drawing, however, has a Layout containing the title block and border, with a viewport through which the model of the cabin is seen. The viewport is on a layer that's been frozen, so you can't see its border. (See Skill 13: *Using Layouts to Set Up a Print* for a review of Layouts and viewports.)

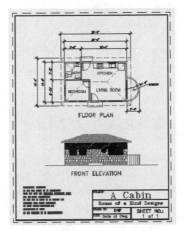

FIGURE 14.12: The Cabin13a drawing ready for printing

3. Open the Layer Property Manager dialog box and set the lineweights for the layers as you did for Cabin11a. Then Click OK.

4. Type **print** ⏎ to start the Print command. The Plot dialog box appears. All the parameters you set for the last print will still be in effect, so you have to determine what settings need to be changed to accommodate Paper Space.

5. We are using the same printer, paper size, and orientation, so those stay the same.

6. Notice that in Plot Area the top radio button is labeled Layout instead of Limits. Layout is also the active button. AutoCAD has sensed that this drawing has Layouts set up, and makes this change automatically.

7. In the Plot Scale area, the scale has been set to 1:1. This is what we want.

8. In the Plot Offset area, the Center the Plot checkbox is greyed out. It is not necessary when using a Layout to plot.

9. There are no changes to make. Because Layout1 has been set up for printing when it was created, all the settings in the Plot dialog box are automatically taken care of.

10. In the Print Preview Area, select Full. Click the Preview button. Your preview should look like Figure 14.10.

11. Press ⏎ or Esc to return to the dialog box. Click OK to start the print. If you don't have a printer, or if you are just following along, click Cancel to cancel the print at this point.

This exercise was intended to show you that once a Layout has been created, most of the setup work for printing is already done for you. This greatly simplifies the printing process because the scale of the print is determined before the Print command begins.

Printing a Drawing with Multiple Viewports

Multiple viewports in a Layout don't require any special handling. The print will be made with the Layout active at a scale of 1:1. For the next print, you will use a different printer—one that can handle larger sheet sizes. If you don't have access to a large format printer, you can still configure AutoCAD for one and preview how the print would look. In fact, that's what we did in Skill 13, *Using Layouts to Set Up a Print*, in order to set up Layout2, so this task is already completed.

Printing with a Large Format Printer

The procedure here varies little from the one you just followed to print Layout1.

1. Save the current drawing to your training directory as Cabin14b, but don't close it yet.

2. This drawing has two Layout tabs. We just printed Layout1. Layout2 consists of a 11×17-inch drawing in landscape orientation. You'll print this one, so be sure Layout2 is active (Figure 14.13).

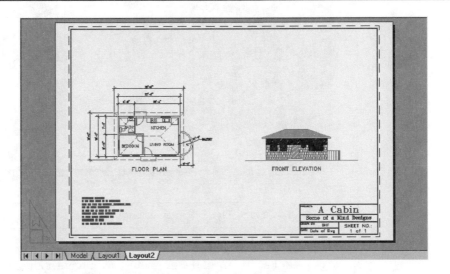

FIGURE 14.13: Cabin13b with the Layout2 tab active

3. Check in the Layer Properties Manager dialog box to see that the lineweight assignments you made for Layout1 are still there.

4. Click the Print button on the Standard toolbar to start the Print command.

5. In the Plot dialog box, make sure the Plot Settings tab is active. Look in the Paper Size and Paper Units area. The Plot Device is now listed as DWF Classic.pc3, or that of your own large-format plotter. Also the paper size has been set for 11×17. This was all done when you set up Layout2 in the previous skill.

6. Note the orientation of the drawing. It's now Landscape.

7. In the rest of the dialog box, the settings are the same as they were for Layout1. There are no changes to be made. Again, by setting up a Layout, all parameters for printing are done in advance.

8. Select the Full Preview button. The preview looks fine (Figure 14.14).

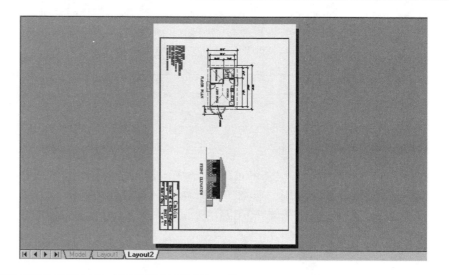

FIGURE 14.14: The Full Preview of Layout2

9. Press ↵ or Esc to cancel the preview. If you have a large format printer configured and can plot this drawing on an 11×17-inch sheet, click OK to start the print. Otherwise click Cancel.

10. Resave this drawing as Cabin14b.

For the last exercise in the book, you will set up a print for Site13, using the large format printer.

Printing the Site Plan

The site plan was also set up with a Layout and based upon a 30×42-inch sheet in landscape orientation. As in the last two prints, we shouldn't have to do much to print this drawing. Follow along even if you can't make the print.

1. Open Site13. The Layout1 tab should be active. If it's not, click it to activate it.

2. Open the Layer Property Manager dialog box and make the following lineweight assignments to these layers:

    - Prop_line—0.014"
    - Tblk-L1—0.031"
    - Cabin12 ⏐ roof—0.014"

    Click OK to close the dialog box.

3. Type **print** ↵. The Plot dialog box comes up. There are no changes that need to be made.

4. Click Full Preview. You see how the print sits on the sheet (Figure 14.15a). We want the margins to be the same on the top and bottom, and the right side to be as small as possible so that there is extra room on the left side for the binding strip.

5. Press ↵ or Esc to return to the Plot dialog box. In the Plot Offset area, change the *X* setting from 0.00 to 0.15.

6. Click Full Preview again. The drawing is positioned fairly well (Figure 14.15b). Feel free to make minor adjustments to the origin settings. You could also use the Stretch command to move the left side of the border a little to the right in order to gain a little more space for the binding. Because the border so closely fits the Printable area, we could move the drawing on the sheet only a little more than ⅛" without lopping off the right side, so the results are barely noticeable. Normally, you make these adjustments when you set up the Layout.

7. When finished making adjustments, return to the Plot dialog box. Click OK to start the print, or click Cancel to cancel it.

8. Save this drawing as Site14a.

Getting consistently good output from your AutoCAD drawings involves an investment of time by you, or the office CAD expert, to set up the best configuration of your printers and AutoCAD. Layouts provide a very good tool for setting up plots, once the configuration is right.

This concludes the exercises for this skill, and for the book. The Appendices that follow contain tutorials and discussion about drawing in 3D and using Attributes. You will find a glossary of terms, related to AutoCAD, building construction, and design, that have been mentioned in the book. I do hope you have found the book useful in learning AutoCAD 2000.

SKILL
14

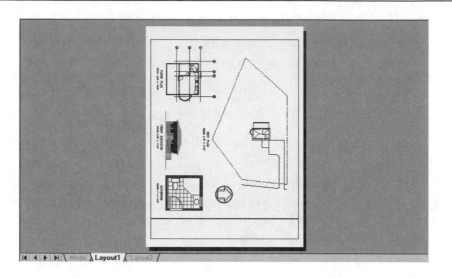

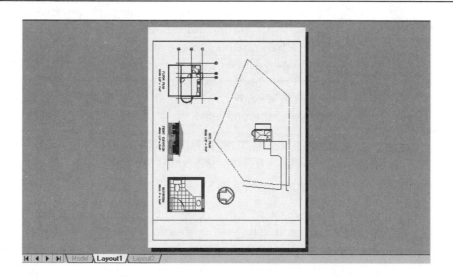

FIGURE 14.15: The first print preview (a), and the preview with the origin adjusted (b)

Are You Experienced?

Now you can . . .

- ☑ set up a drawing to be printed
- ☑ assign lineweights to layers in your drawing
- ☑ select the area of your drawing to print
- ☑ choose a sheet size to print your drawing on
- ☑ control the orientation and origin of the print
- ☑ set the scale of the print
- ☑ preview a print
- ☑ print a Layout

SKILL
14

Appendix A:
A Look at Drawing in 3D

Nothing in CAD is quite so fascinating as drawing in 3D. When you compare the traditional 3-D rendering of a building on a drafting board, using vanishing points and projection planes, with a true 3D model of a building on the computer that can be rotated and viewed from any angle, as well as from the inside, there is a world of difference. Many architectural firms still use the drafting board to create 3D presentation drawings, even though they may use AutoCAD for their construction drawings. More and more firms, however, are using AutoCAD's 3D features to either create perspective drawings, or to create simple 3D models that are then traced over by hand in the process of creating the final presentation drawing. So it's useful to acquire some skills in working in 3D. It's also a lot of fun.

Constructing a 3D model of a building requires the use of many of the tools you have been using throughout this book, and some new ones that you will be introduced to in this appendix. Your competence in using the basic drawing, editing, and display commands is critical to your successful study of 3D for two reasons: First, drawing in 3D is more complex and difficult than drawing in 2D, and can, for this reason, be very frustrating. If you aren't familiar with the basic commands, you will become that much more frustrated. Second, accuracy is critical in 3D drawing. The effect of errors is compounded, so you must be in the habit of using tools, like the Osnap modes, to maximize your precision.

Don't feel discouraged, just warned. Drawing in 3D is a truly fascinating and enjoyable process, and the results you get can be astounding. I sincerely encourage you to make the effort to learn some of the basic 3D skills presented here.

There are many 3D software packages on the market today; some are better for drawing buildings than others. Many times, because of the precision that AutoCAD provides, a 3D .dwg file will be exported to one of these specialized 3D packages for further work, after being laid out in AutoCAD. Other drawings will be created in 2D, converted into a 3D drawing, and then refined into a shaded, colored, and textured rendering with specific lights and shadows. We will look at two basic methods of creating 3D models—surface modeling and solid modeling—but we won't be covering the rendering portion of the process. For a more in-depth discussion of the entire process, including rendering, see *Mastering AutoCAD 2000* (Sybex, 1999) and *Mastering AutoCAD 3D* (Sybex, 1996) by George Omura.

Surface Modeling

Our approach will be to begin building a 3D model of the cabin, using several techniques for creating 3D surfaces. Along the way, you will get more familiar with the User Coordinate System (UCS), learn how the UCS is used with 3D, and begin using a basic method of viewing a 3D model. Then you see a second method of viewing 3D models, and a demo of how a 3D model of the cabin can be constructed with the solid modeling commands. By then, you will have enough of a taste of this world to take charge of your further education in 3D techniques, if you so desire.

Viewing a Drawing in 3D

We will start with Cabin06b. This version of the cabin has all the basic components of the floor plan on their respective layers, with no blocks or hatch patterns, and no front elevation or title block. If you haven't been following through the whole book and saving your work progressively, you can download this file from Sybex's Web page, at www.sybex.com. You can still follow along if you have another floor plan not too much more complex than that of the cabin to use for the exercise.

1. Open Cabin06b. When the floor plan comes up, make the Walls layer current and freeze all other layers. Your drawing will look like Figure A.1. You need to start thinking of your drawing in three dimensions: The entire drawing is on a flat plane parallel to the monitor screen. When you add elements in the third dimension, they will project straight out of the screen towards you if they have a positive dimension, and straight back through the screen if they have a negative dimension. The line of direction is perpendicular to the plane of the screen and is called the z axis. You are familiar with the x and y axes running left-to-right, and up-to-down, respectively. Think of the z axis for a moment as running in and out of the screen.

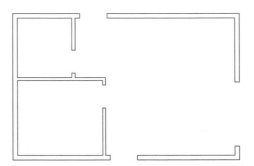

FIGURE A.1:   Cabin06b with all layers frozen except Walls

2. Pick View ≻ Display ≻ UCS Icon ≻ On. The UCS Icon appears again. It's been disabled since Skill 5, when it was not used and was in the way. We'll be using it in time. For now, just keep an eye on it as the drawing changes. Remember that the icon's arrows indicate the positive direction for the x and y axes.

3. Now you'll change the view from a plan view of the drawing—looking straight down at it—to one in which you are looking down at it from an angle. Pick View ≻ 3D Views ≻ SW Isometric. The view changes to look like Figure A.2. Notice how the UCS icon has changed with the change of view. The X and Y arrows still run parallel to the left side and bottom of the cabin; but the icon as a whole, as well as the floor plan, are at an angle to the screen.

4. Zoom out and pan down to give yourself some room to put the walls in 3D.

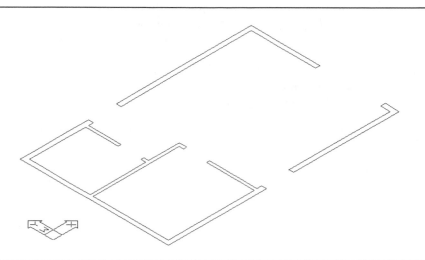

FIGURE A.2:   The walls as seen from the SW Isometric view

Creating a Wireframe 3D Model

Your next task is to create what is called a *wireframe* of the cabin in 3D. Wireframes are drawings in 3D in which the lines represent the intersection of walls or other planes. The 2D drawing is already a kind of wireframe because the wall lines represent the intersections of the walls and jambs with the floors. We are simply going to expand on this wireframe by creating lines that extend perpendicularly up from the floor to represent the intersections of the walls with each other, and with the jambs.

1. Set Endpoint Osnap to be running, and be sure Ortho is turned off. Then start the Line command and pick the lowest outside corner of the building to start a line.

2. Type @0,0,8' ↵↵. A line is drawn to represent the intersection of the two outside walls that meet at the corner you just picked (Figure A.3a). In this view, the positive x direction is diagonally up and to the right, the positive y direction up and to the left, and the positive z direction straight up. You just drew a line whose second point was 8' in the positive z direction.

3. Copy this line to the other three outside corners of the building, then draw a line connecting the upper endpoints of these four lines to each other. These lines now represent the outside walls of the building (Figure A.3b).

Now you have two tasks left to complete the wireframe of the walls: (a) Use this same technique to draw the inside walls. Then (b) draw in the doorway openings. But first, let's look at another technique for making objects in 3D, called *extrusion*.

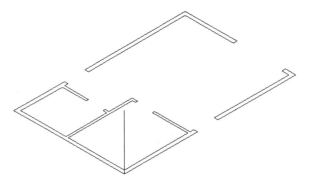

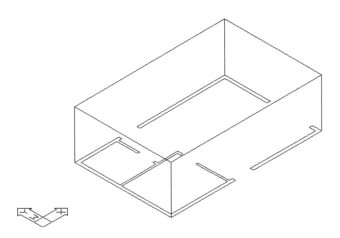

FIGURE A.3: The first line drawn in the positive *z* direction (a), and the outside walls completed (b)

Extruding Lines

Any lines drawn in the *xy* plane (in this case, any of the original wall and jamb lines) can be extended up, in a direction parallel to the *z* axis, to make a 3D wall surface. This way of making walls in 3D is useful only when you don't have door or window openings in the walls. In this exercise, we'll ignore the window openings and extrude all wall lines where there are no doorway openings. In the cabin, there are a total of 18 wall surfaces (4 exterior and 14 interior). Ten of them have doorway openings. Of the remaining eight wall surfaces, we will now extrude seven of them.

1. Select the seven wall lines that are shown as dashed in Figure A.4a. Zoom in if you need to. Then pick the Properties button.

NOTE NOTE NOTE NOTE NOTE NOTE NOTE NOTE NOTE NOTE NOTE NOTE NOTE NOTE NOTE

The eighth wall line without a doorway opening is the exterior wall line that spans across the bedroom and bathroom, on the left side of the building. We'll do something special with it later.

2. In the Properties dialog box, change the Thickness setting from 0" to 8'. Close the Properties dialog box. Press Esc twice to remove the grips. The seven lines are extruded in the direction of the positive *z* axis. Seven wall surfaces are created (Figure A.4b).

NOTE NOTE NOTE NOTE NOTE NOTE NOTE NOTE NOTE NOTE NOTE NOTE NOTE NOTE NOTE

To understand how thickness is used here, think of a metal plate with holes in it. The thickness of the plate extends in the *z* direction. In a building, the same extension would be called wall height, but in AutoCAD, both are called thickness.

3. Type **hi** ↵ to start the *Hide command*. The Hide command can also be started by selecting View ➤ Hide. The extruded walls become opaque and block your view of the objects behind them (Figure A.4c).

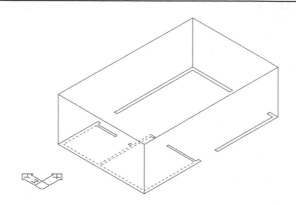

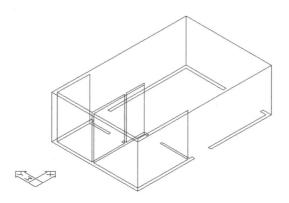

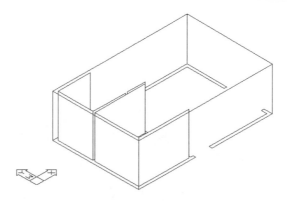

FIGURE A.4: The seven selected wall lines without showing the grips (a), the wall lines extruded (b), and the Hide command applied to the 3D model (c)

You have created seven interior wall surfaces in 3D, and you have created a wireframe to represent the four exterior wall surfaces. When you used the Hide command, the extruded walls became opaque, hiding objects behind them, while the wireframe didn't change. The wireframe contains no surfaces, just lines, so you can see directly through the surface they're representing. The extruded wall lines look just like the wireframe lines when you first perform the extrusion, but they are actually surfaces that become opaque when the Hide command is used. Extrusions and wireframes are two of the three primary elements used to construct a 3D model with surface modeling, which is the technique of displaying 3D objects by depicting the surfaces of the objects. You'll be introduced to the third element shortly.

Let's do some more work on the wireframe model.

1. Type **regen** ↵. This regenerates the drawing from scratch and the extruded walls are no longer opaque.

2. We want to copy one of the vertical 8-foot lines on the four exterior corners to the other corners in the interior of the cabin, but note how the inside and outside corners coincide for some of the corners. This will make it difficult to snap to those corners. We can alleviate this problem by giving our model a slight rotation.

3. Pick View ➤ 3D Views ➤ Viewpoint Presets. The Viewpoint Presets dialog box appears.

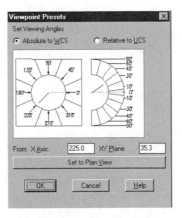

This dialog box allows you to control and change the view you have of your 3D model. You can rotate the view around the model, like a camera rotating around a person while always facing them, or you can move the camera higher or lower, again always facing the subject (in this case the cabin).

4. We just want to rotate the view slightly. In the dialog box, in the From X Axis text box, change the 225.0 to 240.0, then click OK. The model rotates slightly and the corners that were lined up no longer coincide (Figure A.5).

TIP TIP TIP TIP TIP TIP TIP TIP TIP TIP TIP TIP TIP TIP TIP TIP TIP TIP TIP TIP TIP TIP TIP

The Viewpoint Presets dialog box is an essential tool for working in 3D. Once you learn how to use it, you will be able to view your 3D model from any viewpoint.

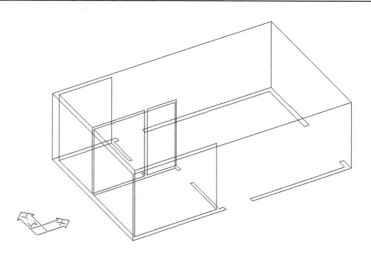

FIGURE A.5: The wireframe model slightly rotated

5. Use Copy Multiple to copy one of the 8-foot vertical lines in the wireframe to each of the remaining inside wall corners. There are four of them, all in the living room and kitchen. Zoom and pan as you need to. Don't worry about the doorway openings yet—we'll get to them shortly. Your drawing should look like Figure A.6a.

6. Draw lines to connect the upper endpoints of these lines to the corners of the extruded surfaces to complete the wireframe of the walls. You'll have to draw eight lines (Figure A.6b).

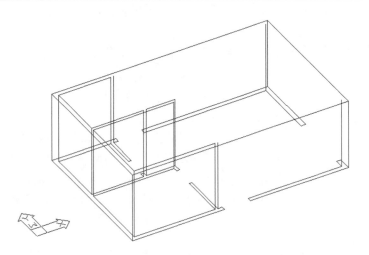

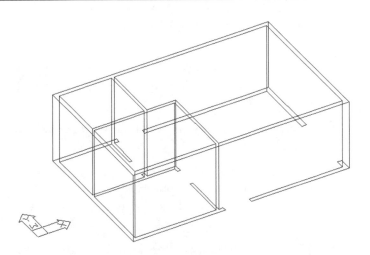

FIGURE A.6: The 8-foot corner copied to the remaining corners (a), and the completed wireframe of the walls (b)

TIP TIP TIP TIP TIP TIP TIP TIP TIP TIP TIP TIP TIP TIP TIP TIP TIP TIP TIP TIP TIP TIP TIP TIP TIP

Feel free to zoom and pan to facilitate picking any of the endpoints you need to pick.

The lines you have just drawn will serve an aid to help you visualize the actual form of the cabin rooms. The next task is to draw in the doorway openings.

Making the Doorway Openings

We have to draw in the jambs and the headers in 3D. There are no openings in the jambs, so we can extrude them. Selecting them for extrusion, however, is a problem.

1. Pick View ➤ 3D Views ➤ Top. Then zoom out a little to have a little blank space around the floor plan. Use five regular selection windows to select the five pairs of jamb lines. Then click the Properties button.

2. In the Properties dialog box, change the thickness from 0" to 6'-6". Then close the Properties dialog box and press Esc twice to clear the grips. Zoom previous twice to get the 3D view back. The jambs are all extruded (Figure A.7a).

NOTE NOTE NOTE NOTE NOTE NOTE NOTE NOTE NOTE NOTE NOTE NOTE NOTE NOTE NOTE

You can see from this task how important precision is. When selecting the jamb lines in the plan view, be careful not to select the 6-inch wall lines that extend from the jamb to the corner.

3. Thaw the Headers layer. Change its color to cyan, just like the Walls layer, and make it current. Then freeze the Walls layer. The drawing will look like Figure A.7b.

4. Select the five pairs of header lines with one window. Click the Properties button again.

5. In the Geometry section of the Properties dialog box, highlight the 0" for the Start Z setting and type **6'-6"**. Do the same for the End Z setting. Close the Properties dialog box. Press Esc twice to remove the grips. The headers are raised vertically to the tops of the openings.

6. Thaw the Walls layer and make it the current layer. The wireframe of the cabin is now complete (Figure A.7c).

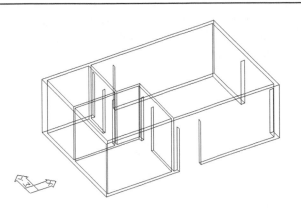

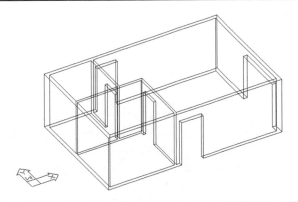

FIGURE A.7: The extruded jambs (a), the headers with the Walls layer frozen (b), and the completed wireframe of the walls (c)

7. Type **hi** ↵ to start the Hide command. The results of the hide are shown in Figure A.8. A close inspection of this view will reveal that the extruded walls and the vertical jambs are opaque, while the rest of the model is just a wireframe. You need to put surfaces on the bare parts of the wireframe.

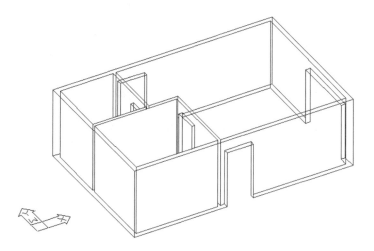

FIGURE A.8: The completed wireframe of the walls after a hide

> **NOTE** NOTE NOTE NOTE NOTE NOTE NOTE NOTE NOTE NOTE NOTE NOTE NOTE NOTE NOTE
>
> **Extruded lines are considered part of the wireframe model before the Hide command is invoked. After the Hide command, extruded lines become part of the surface model. The wireframe becomes partially covered with surfaces.**

3D Faces

We can add a new element, called a 3D face, to the wall surfaces that were not extruded. 3D faces are three- or four-sided areas that can be drawn over a wireframe model to make a surface model, like stretching a tent over its frame. They cannot have any openings in them. When applying them to a wall surface that does have an opening, the 3D faces must go around the opening. This may create joints between 3D faces that you don't want to be visible. Fortunately, you can make individual edges of a 3D face invisible. Let's put a 3D face on the front wall of the cabin to see how they work.

The front wall is no longer a rectangle after the front door opening has been cut into it. It is an upside-down U-shape that will require three 3D faces to cover it (Figure A.9a). When you draw a 3D face, you pick points in sequence around the perimeter. The command is set up to allow you to keep drawing additional faces whose first edge coincides with the last edge of the one previously drawn. If you can anticipate which edges will coincide with other faces, you can plan the sequence of points picked in such a way that you pick the fewest points necessary to define the 3D faces. For the front wall, a good sequence is shown in Figure A.9b.

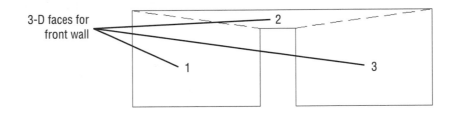

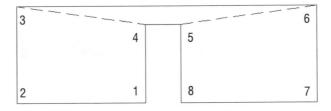

FIGURE A.9: The three 3D faces for the front wall (a), and the sequence for picking points to draw the faces (b)

1. Select Draw ➤ Surfaces ➤ 3D Face to start the 3D Face command. You can also start the command by opening the Surfaces toolbar and picking the 3D Face button, or by typing **3f** ↵.

2. Following the sequence in Figure A.9b, pick the eight pick points with End-point Osnap running, then press ↵.

TIP TIP TIP TIP TIP TIP TIP TIP TIP TIP TIP TIP TIP TIP TIP TIP TIP TIP TIP TIP TIP TIP TIP TIP

Having the Endpoint Osnap running is highly recommended when working in 3D.

3. Type **hi** ↵. The front wall is opaque, but the joints between the 3D faces are visible also.

4. Pick Draw ➤ Surfaces ➤ Edge. Then pick each of the two diagonal joints and press ↵. The joints disappear (Figure A.10).

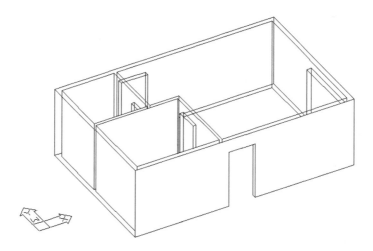

FIGURE A.10: The front wall with 3D faces and the Hide command running

NOTE NOTE NOTE NOTE NOTE NOTE NOTE NOTE NOTE NOTE NOTE NOTE NOTE NOTE NOTE

When using the Edge command, the running Endpoint Osnap is temporarily replaced by a running Midpoint Osnap, and a colored triangle appears when you touch the face edge. This facilitates your being able to select the edge you want.

This is the basic procedure for covering the wireframe with 3D faces. Each wall surface with a doorway opening needs three 3D faces. Each opening has two wall surfaces—one on each side—so there are nine more wall surfaces that need this procedure. We can do one of them from this view. After that we'll need to change the view to pick the correct points more easily.

1. Type **re** ↵ to regenerate the drawing. The opaqueness of the walls is gone and the whole drawing is now a wireframe model. Zoom in to a closer view of the wall that contains the opening for the sliding glass door.

2. Pick Draw ➤ Surfaces ➤ 3D Face to start the 3D Face command.

3. Pick the eight points on the inside wall containing the sliding glass door in the same sequence that you used for the outside front wall, then press ↵.

4. Pick Draw ➤ Surfaces ➤ Edge. Then pick each of the two diagonal joints and press ↵. You may have to use the Edge command twice and zoom in closer to be able to pick the shorter face joint. The joints disappear.

5. Hide the view (type **hi** ↵) to make the new faces opaque. Check your work (Figure A.11). Now you need to rotate the view to be able to place 3D faces on other parts of the wireframe.

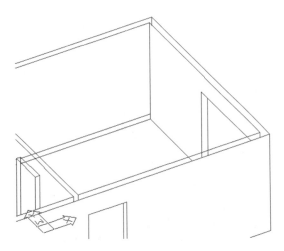

FIGURE A.11: The finished side wall after the Hide command is used

By now, you should realize how important it is to know the best place to place the cursor, with Endpoint Osnap running, to be able to accurately pick the correct corner.

6. Pick View ➤ 3D Views ➤ Viewpoint Presets. The Viewpoint Presets dialog box comes up. In the middle of the dialog box, there are two diagrams. The one on the left displays how the current view is rotated in the *xy* plane, while the one on the right shows the angle the current view is above or below the horizon. You can click in any of the pie segments in either diagram to reset the angles.

7. In the left diagram, click the 315-degree segment. In the right, click the 10-degree segment that's above the 0-degree segment, then click OK. Your view will look like Figure A.12. Notice that you are viewing the UCS icon almost on its edge. Also, note that the vertical lines, representing the inside and outside corners closest to you, are coinciding. We need to rotate the view a little more.

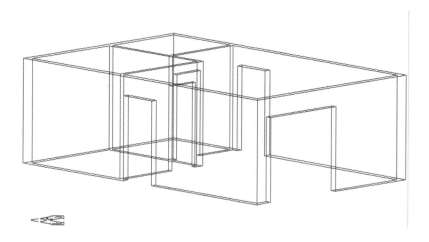

FIGURE A.12: The new view at 315-degree rotation and 10-degree angle above the horizon

8. Right click. A shortcut menu appears. Click Repeat Viewpoint Presets to bring up the Viewpoint Presets dialog box again. Under the diagram on the left, enter **305** in the From X Axis text box. Click OK. We can take care of a couple more walls in this view.

NOTE NOTE NOTE NOTE NOTE NOTE NOTE NOTE NOTE NOTE NOTE NOTE NOTE NOTE NOTE

Each time you reset the viewpoint, the model is zoomed to extents.

9. Zoom into the kitchen wall and type **3f** ↵. Pick eight points in the same locations and in the same sequence as you followed earlier, but this time for the inside back wall surface where the kitchen is. Press ↵ to end the 3D Face command.

10. Zoom previous. Restart the 3D Face command and pick eight more points in the same way, this time on the outside surface of the wall with the sliding glass door. Press ↵.

11. Type **edge** ↵. Pick the four diagonal joints between the 3D faces in the two walls. Press ↵.

12. Type **hi** ↵. The drawing will look like Figure A.13.

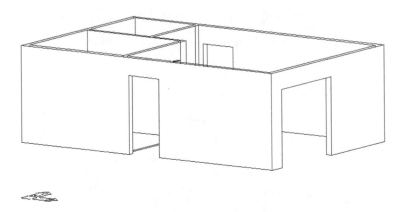

FIGURE A.13: The two new wall surfaces

NOTE NOTE NOTE NOTE NOTE NOTE NOTE NOTE NOTE NOTE NOTE NOTE NOTE NOTE

You cannot use Realtime Pan or Zoom when the Hide command is in effect. Type re ↵ first, then use those tools. Other zoom tools can be used, but any change of view cancels the effects of the Hide command, and your drawing reverts to the wireframe model.

Now it's your turn. Use the five commands—regen (type **re** ↵), Viewpoint Presets (Type **vp**), 3D Face (type **3f** ↵), Edge (type **edge** ↵), and Hide (type **hi** ↵)—to create 3D faces to cover the six remaining wall surfaces with door openings. I advise you to keep rotating the drawing approximately 90° and set the angle above the horizon at about 10° to 20°. Experiment with the Viewpoint Settings dialog box until you get familiar with how it works. You should be able to do four walls after the next rotation. Then you can finish up by rotating one more time and making the inside surfaces for the bathroom and bedroom walls that have door openings.

Here's a summary of the steps:

1. Type **re** ↵ to regenerate the drawing if you've just done a hide.

2. Use View ➤ 3D Views ➤ Viewpoint Presets to rotate the drawing in the *xy* plane.

3. Type **3f** ↵ to start the 3D Face command. Pick eight points on the wall. Then press ↵.

4. Zoom and pan as necessary.

5. Type **edge** ↵. Pick the two diagonal joints between faces. Then press ↵.

6. Type **hi** ↵ to check your work.

7. Type **re** ↵ to regenerate.

8. Do another wall or rotate the view, and continue.

If you make a mistake when putting on a 3D face, cancel the command, undo the command, or erase any incorrect faces, and try again. Faces can be a little bit of a problem to select because some of their edges coincide with lines and some coincide with edges of other faces. The regular selection window can be useful in these situations. Once selected, 3D faces will erase just like any other AutoCAD object. Take your time and be patient, as it is important to select the points of a 3D face accurately. The task of putting 3D faces on walls with openings is one of the most tedious procedures in 3D surface modeling.

1. When you're finished, use the Viewpoint Presets dialog box to set the rotation to 155° and the angle above the horizon to 30°.

2. Use the Hide command. Your drawing should look like Figure A.14. The outside wall surface next to the bathroom and bedroom has not been done. We'll use this wall to take a look at how window openings can be put into walls.

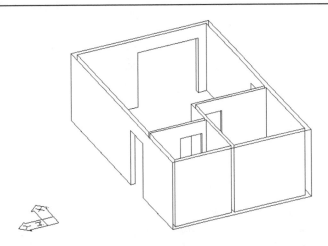

FIGURE A.14: The model at 140-degree rotation and 30-degree angle after a Hide

Creating 3D Faces around a Window Opening

We are using a drawing (Cabin06b) that was completed before Skill 7, *Using Blocks and Wblocking*, so there're no windows in the floor plan, no Windows layer, and no Win-1 block in the file. We'll create the Windows layer and insert the Win-1.dwg file, which we made in Skill 7, into the exterior bedroom wall on the side of the building currently facing us.

1. Create a new layer called Windows. Assign it an orange color (color number 30) and make it the current layer.

2. Select Insert ➤ Block. Then click Browse and open the Symbols folder in your training directory and select the Win-1.dwg file. Click Open. In the Insert dialog box, put select in the Specify On Screen for Scale and Rotation checkboxes. Click OK.

3. Zoom into a closer view of the side wall of the cabin that includes the bedroom and bathroom.

4. In the drawing, type **.xy** ↵. Then pick Midpoint Osnap to select the midpoint of the inside wall line of the exterior bedroom wall that is facing you in the current view. (This is the same location for the insertion point you used for this window in Skill 7.)

5. At the (need Z): prompt, type **3'** ↵.

6. For the *X* scale factor, enter **4**. For the *Y* scale factor, enter **1**. For the rotation angle, enter **90**. The Win-1 block is inserted inside the wall at the height of the sill (Figure A.15a).

7. Start the Copy command and select the window block, then press ↵. For the base point, pick any point on the screen. For the second point of displacement, type **@0,0,3'6** ↵. The window block is copied to a position in the wall, at a distance of 3'-6", directly above the original block insertion (Figure A.15b). You will snap to the endpoints of the jamb lines in these two blocks to create the 3D faces around this window opening. Start with the inside wall surface.

8. Select the extruded inside wall surface in the bedroom, where this window opening is going to go. Click the Properties button. In the Properties dialog box, change the thickness of this extrusion from 8' to 0". Close the dialog box and press Esc twice.

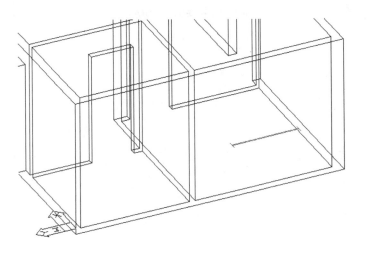

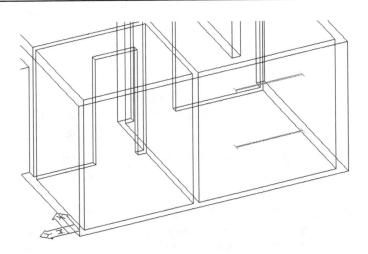

FIGURE A.15: The Win-1 block inserted in the wall (a), and the Win-1 block copied to the top of the window (b)

9. Now you can draw four 3D faces for the inside surface of the exterior bedroom wall. You will pick points in a sequence like this:

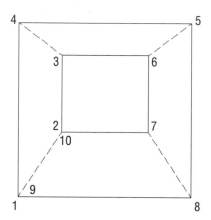

Start the 3D Face command (type **3f** ↵). Pick points in the sequential order shown here.

When you are finished, press ↵. The new faces will look like Figure A.16a.

10. Press ↵ to restart the 3D Face command, then repeat the same sequence of point selection for the outside wall surfaces, remembering that the left side of this wall surface extends to the left corner of the building in our current view. The results will look like Figure A.16b.

11. Type **edge** ↵. Pick the eight diagonal lines representing joints between 3D faces. Press ↵.

TIP TIP TIP TIP TIP TIP TIP TIP TIP TIP TIP TIP TIP TIP TIP TIP TIP TIP TIP TIP TIP TIP TIP

You can also make any edge of a 3D face invisible as you are drawing it. Before you pick the first point of the edge you want to be invisible, type i ↵, then pick the two points to define the edge.

12. Type **hi** ↵ to use the Hide command on the view. The results will look like Figure A.16c.

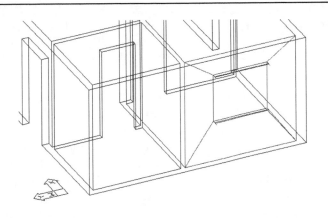

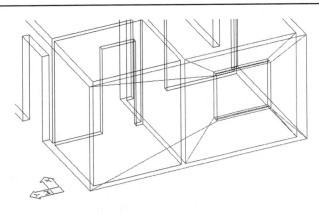

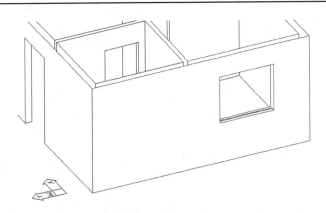

FIGURE A.16: The inside 3D faces (a), plus the outside 3D faces (b), and the view of the completed wall after using Hide (c)

NOTE NOTE NOTE NOTE NOTE NOTE NOTE NOTE NOTE NOTE NOTE NOTE NOTE NOTE NOTE
You could have drawn each face by itself rather than four in one cycle of the command. In some situations, the 3D geometry gets so complex that it's more reasonable to draw the faces individually.

To complete this window, you need to draw a 3D face for the window sill. Because the Win-1 block is still in the wall at the top and bottom of the window opening, you can explode the bottom Win-1 block and extrude the jamb lines, and one of the two glazing lines, up to make the window jamb surfaces and the glass. Then you could put the glass on a special layer that you freeze or thaw, depending on whether or not you want to be able to see through the glass. Go ahead and try that if you like. We're going to move on to the next task.

You may have noticed how adding the second color helps you to see your wire-frame model more clearly. Working in 3D can be made easier by setting up additional layers for building components, or parts of building components, and assigning the layers different colors. For example, you could have a layer for interior wall faces that's assigned green, and a second layer for exterior wall faces that's assigned dark green. Or you could have faces for one room be on one layer, and those for another be on a second layer. Using either method of organization, you can freeze layers containing the faces that you're not working on and are in your way. This technique is also valid for working on just the wireframe because wireframes can be full of lines that seem to coincide in a view, though they are on opposite sides of the building in the model. Making some of the lines invisible can help make snapping to points easier.

If you combine the technique for drawing faces around a door opening in a wall surface with the one you just learned for windows, you can put 3D faces on walls that have both doors and windows. In a wall with two doors and three windows, the faces could have a pattern like this:

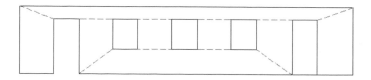

This may seem like a lot of trouble to go through to make walls with openings have the ability to be opaque after a hide, and you're right. It is a lot of trouble, and many times unnecessary. Whether it's worth the trouble will depend on whether you need the openings to really be openings. That is, would it be all right if the doors and windows were just drawings of doors and windows sitting on the surface of the wall, rather than actual holes in the wall?

Putting 2D Drawings on 3D Surfaces

Let's put the windows on the exterior front wall surface of the cabin as 2D drawings to see how this works. We'll get the windows from a previously saved drawing.

1. Pick View ➤ 3D Views ➤ SW Isometric to rotate the drawing around so you can see the front wall.

2. Type **vp** ↵ to bring up the Viewpoint Presets dialog box. In the From: X Axis: text box, change 225.0 to 240.0. Click OK.

3. Save this drawing as CabinA1.

4. Open Cabin08b if you have it saved. If not, open Cabin08a.

5. Zoom into a view of the front elevation. Make the F-elev layer current.

6. Draw a short diagonal line from the lower-left corner of the front wall at the height of the step (Figure A.17). This will be a guideline for inserting the windows.

FIGURE A.17: The front elevation with the diagonal guideline drawn

7.   Select Edit ➤ Copy with Base Point. Use Endpoint Osnap to select the lower-left endpoint of the diagonal line. Then select the four windows and the diagonal guideline. Press ↵.

8.   On the pull-down menus, click Window. Near the bottom of the list, select `CabinB1.dwg`.

We want to use the Windows paste tool to paste the windows on the front wall, but if we do it with the drawing set up the way it currently is, the windows will be parallel to the floor plane in the 3D model. Originally, all objects in the front elevation were drawn in the same plane as the floor plan, before any 3D objects were made. The User Coordinate System will solve this problem for us.

Setting Up a New User Coordinate System

Even though you have been drawing in 3D, the User Coordinate System (UCS) has remained the same as it was when you were drawing in 2D. This UCS is called the World Coordinate System, and it's the default UCS for all new drawings. A UCS defines the orientation of the x, y, and z axes. If we set up a new UCS lined up with the front wall surface, we can paste the windows right on the 3D faces of that surface. Then we'll save that UCS so we can easily restore it anytime we want to work on the front wall.

1.   Zoom out a little.

2.   Type **ucs** ↵. You'll see the prompt `Enter an option [New/Move /orthoGraphic/Prev/Restore/Save/Del/Apply/?/World] <World>:`. These options give you several tools for setting up a new UCS, as well as those for saving the current UCS or restoring a previously saved one. When you create a new UCS, you either pick a preset one, or pick points on the 3D model to define the new origin and the positive x and y directions for the new axes.

3. Type **g** ⏎ for the orthoGraphic option. Type **f** ⏎ for the front orientation. The UCS icon in your drawing has flipped up around the x axis, and the icon is now parallel to the front wall surface (Figure A.18a). The positive x direction hasn't changed because we rotated the UCS around the x axis. But the positive y direction is now upwards, and the positive z axis comes out of the screen at an angle that is down and to the right.

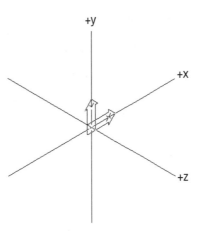

Now you can paste the window block in the correct dimension.

1. Select Edit ➤ Paste. The drawing appears in ghosted fashion with the lower-left endpoint of the guideline attached to the cursor.

2. Use Endpoint Osnap to pick the lower-left corner of the front wall. Then click. The windows are inserted as a block and pasted onto the front wall.

3. Erase the diagonal guideline.

4. Type **hi** ⏎. The drawing will look like Figure A.18b.

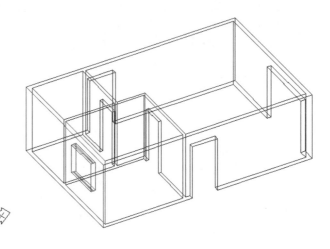

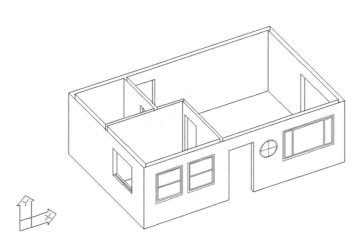

FIGURE A.18: The UCS icon rotated to its new position (a), and the windows after insertion (b)

The UCS icon, by its orientation, shows you the plane defined by the x and y axes. The two arrows in the icon show you the positive direction of these two axes. When you draw in 3D, you either snap to objects or, if you use relative coordinates, you draw in the *x* and *y* plane of the current UCS. You have seen that you can construct a good portion of the drawing without changing the default UCS, but some operations do require such a change.

You will have to decide whether to construct 3D faces around openings in walls, or to place a 2D drawing of the elevation on the 3D wall. One factor that will help you make your decision is whether you need to see inside the building from the outside, or whether you need views of the interior of the building, looking through a window or door to the outside or to another interior space. There are many levels of detail in which you can work in 3D, from creating the basic shape of the building, to making openings in walls, to putting in the window details. You could take the 4-foot–wide window opening you made in the wall with 3D faces and add detail in 3D to make it look like the windows you just pasted on the front wall. Then you would have the detail and you would be able to see through the windows, but you would have to spend more time to achieve that level of detail. Determining the level of detail depends on how you plan on using the 3D model.

We'll put the roof and balcony in 3D to complete this 3D surface model. Then we'll move on to other areas.

Getting the Roof into 3D

To get the roof into 3D, you can move it up to its actual height above the walls. Then extrude the edge down and stretch the ridge up.

1. Thaw the Roof layer. Change its linetype from Dashed to Continuous, and make it current.

2. Freeze the Walls and Headers layers, then zoom out a little (Figure A.19a).

3. Turn off any running Osnaps. Start the Move command. Select the nine lines that make up the roof and press ↵. Pick any point on the screen for the base point. For the point of displacement, type @8'6<90 ↵. ø. The roof moves up in the positive *y* direction of the current UCS (Figure A.19b).

NOTE NOTE NOTE NOTE NOTE NOTE NOTE NOTE NOTE NOTE NOTE NOTE NOTE NOTE NOTE
Moving the roof in the positive Z direction while using the current UCS is the same as moving it in the positive Z direction while using the default World Coordinate System. By using the current UCS, you were able to use relative coordinates to determine the distance and direction—something you wouldn't be able to do without the new UCS.

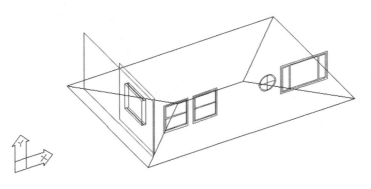

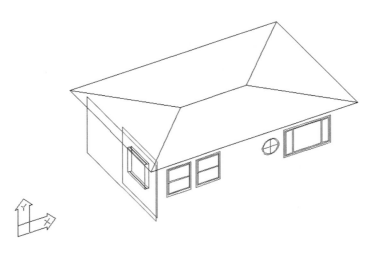

FIGURE A.19:   The model with the Roof layer current and the Walls and Headers layers frozen (a), and the model after the roof is moved up (b)

4.   Start the Stretch command. Use a crossing window to select the ridgeline and hip lines of the roof and press ↵. Pick any point on the screen for the

base point. For the point of displacement, type **@3'<90** ↵. The ridgeline is moved up, and the hip lines are stretched.

5. Type **ucs** ↵. Then type **s** ↵ to select the Save option. At the Enter name to save current UCS or [?]: prompt, type **front** ↵.

6. Press ↵ to restart the UCS command. Then press ↵ to select the default <World> option. The UCS icon returns to its former position, and the W returns to the icon.

NOTE NOTE NOTE NOTE NOTE NOTE NOTE NOTE NOTE NOTE NOTE NOTE NOTE NOTE NOTE

You don't have to save the World UCS. It's an integral part of your drawing by default. Making it the current UCS is like "going home."

7. Select the four eaves lines that form the edge of the roof, then click the Properties button. In the Properties dialog box, change the thickness from 0" to negative 6". Click OK. The roof's edge drops down. Close the Properties dialog box and remove the grips (Figure A.20).

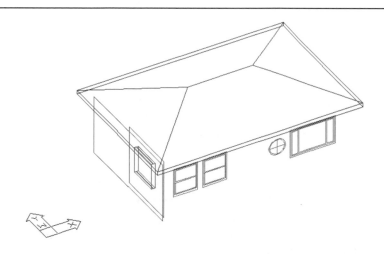

FIGURE A.20: The ridge is raised and the eaves line is dropped down.

8. Set the Endpoint Osnap to be running and make Roof the current layer. Start the 3D Face command (type **3f** ↵). Put a 3D face on each of the four planes on

the roof top. Do them individually, restarting the 3D Face command after each face. For the triangular areas, just click the third point twice. Press ↵ after each face is drawn to end the command, then press ↵ again to restart it.

9. Thaw the Walls and Headers layers.

10. Type **vp** ↵. Change the XY Plane text box from 35.3 to 20 and click OK.

11. Type **hi** ↵. The view is flatter (Figure A.21).

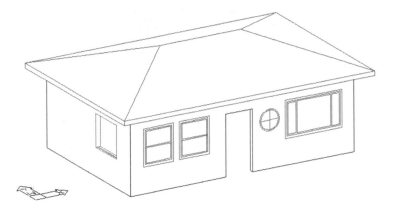

FIGURE A.21:   The finished roof after a Hide with the angle from the *xy* plane set to 20°

Some of the Modify commands are tricky to use in 3D, including the Stretch command. For the stretch to work, the direction of the stretch has to lie in the current *xy* plane. We had to have the Front UCS current because if the World UCS were current, the direction of the stretch would have been perpendicular to the current *xy* plane and wouldn't have worked. Other commands that behave this way are Mirror and Offset. Trim and Extend can also give unpredictable results, so it is very important that the UCS is set up properly.

Making a 3D Balcony

The balcony wall can be extruded just like the blank walls, but it will need a cap on the top.

1. Thaw the Balcony layer. Make it current. Freeze the Walls and F-elev layers.

2. Type **vp** ⏎. Change the X Axis angle from 240.0 to 340.0. The view rotates.

3. Zoom in to the balcony area (Figure A.22a).

4. Select the two semi-circles, then click the Properties button. Change the thickness from 0" to 3'. Close the dialog box and remove the grips.

5. Draw a guideline between the endpoints of the outside balcony wall at the top of the balcony wall (Figure A.22b).

6. Pick Draw ➤ Donut. Enter **9'** for the inside diameter and **10'** for the outside diameter. On the screen, pick Midpoint Osnap and select the straight guideline you just drew. The donut is placed. Press ⏎.

7. Start the Trim command. Select the guideline as a cutting edge and press ⏎. Pick the part of the donut that is not sitting on the balcony, then press ⏎. The donut is trimmed back to a semicircle.

8. Erase the guideline and thaw the Walls and F-elev layer, then type **hi** ⏎. The Drawing will look like Figure A.22c.

9. Save this drawing as CabinA2.

There are just a couple more steps necessary to finish the 3D surface model of the cabin building. It's time for you to do a little 3D work on your own.

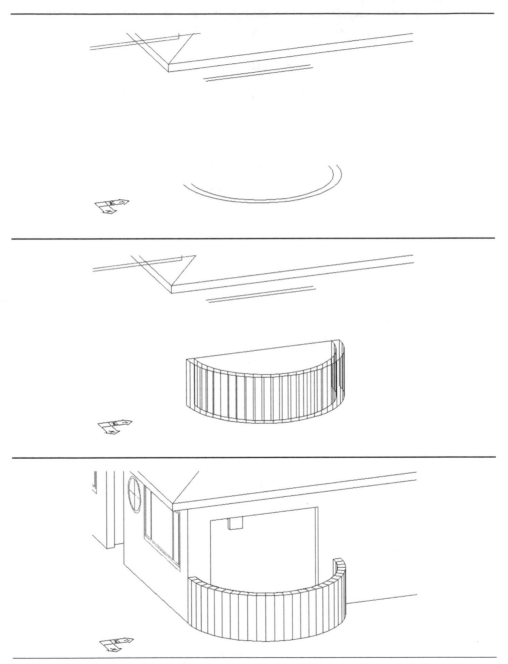

FIGURE A.22: The balcony area with the Walls layer frozen (a), the balcony walls extruded and a guideline drawn (b), and the completed balcony (c)

Finishing Up the 3D Surface Model

To finish the 3D model of the building, the following tasks need to be completed:

1. Create a 12-inch foundation wall around the building, below the walls.

2. Extrude and put a face on the front steps, the back steps, and the three thresholds.

3. Put in a set of 3D faces that will serve as the floor.

4. Apply 3D faces to the headers.

5. Drop the balcony down to the ground level.

You can use the commands, tools, and techniques discussed in this skill so far to finish these tasks. The foundation wall is a little tricky because of the way it has to mesh with the steps and thresholds. You will have to draw some extra faces and make some of the edges invisible at those places. The thresholds are 2-inches thick, and the steps start at the bottom of the threshold and drop 10". For the floor, you simply draw 3D faces in each room and doorway opening, then make the adjacent edges invisible. The headers require only one face each.

To drop the balcony, use the Move command then change the thickness from 3' to 4'.

If you have time, give it a try. It's great practice. The completed drawing will look something like Figure A.23. If you get that far, save this drawing as CabinA3.

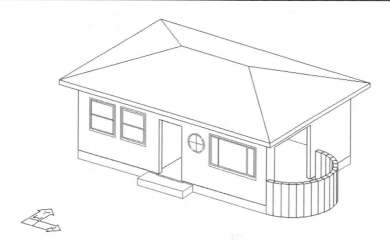

FIGURE A.23: The completed 3D model of the cabin after a Hide

Finally, you can try to draw the objects on the fixtures layer. Before you do that, read on to the end of this appendix, where I introduce another way of drawing in 3D.

With the completion of this final exercise, you have finished a whirlwind tour of the features and commands used for drawing 3D surface models. In generating a 3D model of the cabin, you have been introduced to the most basic commands for creating 3D surfaces. The following is a brief discussion about other tools used for working in 3D.

Using 3D Orbit

You have been using 3D Viewpoint to modify the view of the cabin while building the 3D model. There are several tools for manipulating views in this way, including the two you have used: a preset isometric view (SW Isometric) and the Viewpoint Presets dialog box. But there is another command called 3D Orbit that allows you to do much more.

We will use the 3D model of the cabin that you have been developing so far in this skill to take a quick tour of the 3D Orbit feature.

1. Type **re** ↵. Then zoom and pan until the entire cabin is centered in the drawing area. Click View ➤ 3D Views ➤ Viewpoint Presets. Be sure the X Axis setting is 340 and the XY Plane setting is 20. Click OK to close the Viewpoint Presets dialog box.

2. Click on View ➤ 3D Orbit. A circle appears in the middle of the drawing area with small circles at the four quadrant points of the larger circle. This is the 3D Orbit *Arcball* (Figure A.24). Notice how the UCS icon has changed.

3. Move the cursor to the inside of the large circle and notice the form that the cursor takes on. Move it to the outside of the circle and note its form here. Finally, move it onto one of the smaller circles. When the cursor is on the top and bottom small circles, it has lines going in one pattern. When it is on the two side circles, the lines are in a different pattern.

4. Move the cursor onto the right small circle and hold down the left mouse key. Move the cursor back and forth from left to right and note how the cabin seems to rotate horizontally.

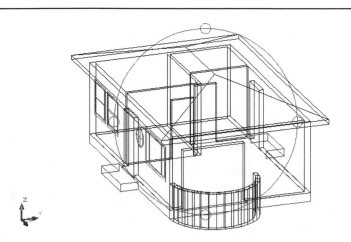

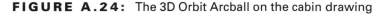

FIGURE A.24:   The 3D Orbit Arcball on the cabin drawing

5. Move the cursor back to the right small circle and release the left mouse button. Move the cursor up to the top small circle, hold down the left mouse button, and then move the cursor up and down a few times. Note how the cabin rotates vertically to different views of it from above and below.

6. Move the cursor back to the top small circle and release the left mouse button. Now move the cursor to the outside of the circle and hold down the left mouse button. Move the cursor around the outside of the circle and note how the cabin seems to rotate around a line perpendicular to the screen.

7. Release the left mouse button. Finally, move the cursor to a place inside the large circle and hold down the left mouse button. Move the cursor around inside the circle and note how the cabin seems to rotate around in no particular pattern.

Steps 4 through 7 illustrate the four ways of using the Arcball to change the view of the cabin. Now we'll look at some other features of 3D Orbit.

1. Right click. A short-cut menu appears, click Shading Modes ➢ Hidden. The Hide command is applied to the drawing. Surfaces become opaque.

2. Right click again. This time pick Visual Aids ➢ Grid. A lined grid appears.

3. Use the four rotating tools described in Steps 4–7 to change the view of the cabin. Play around with it for a while and try to get a view similar to Figure A.25.

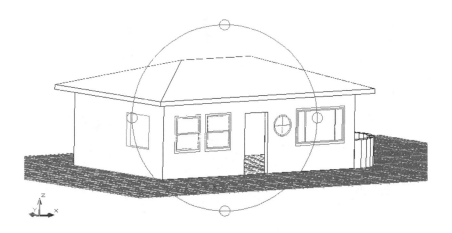

FIGURE A.25: A view of the cabin using 3D Orbit with Hidden and Grid on

4. Right-click again and this time click on Shading Modes ➢ Gourard Shading. The surfaces of the cabin are shaded with the color assigned to their layers in a rendered effect. Right-click and select Shading Modes ➢ Hidden again.

5. Finally, right-click and then click More ➢ Continuous Orbit. Click and drag a short distance to the left or right, then release the mouse button. The cabin begins to rotate horizontally and continues to do so (Figure A.26).

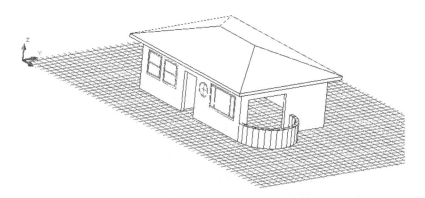

FIGURE A.26: The rendered cabin as it rotates on the screen

6. To stop the rotation, right click and select Exit on the short-cut menu to end 3D Orbit.

7. Use the Viewpoint Presets to change the view back to one of the views you had before. Save the drawing as `CabinA4`.

This has been a very short tour for the 3D Orbit feature. Feel free to experiment with other tools that work with 3D Orbit. These tools are accessed from the short-cut menu that comes up when you right-click after 3D Orbit has started.

We are now going to take a brief look at the concepts involved in Solid Modeling.

Solid Modeling

We can't leave the subject of 3D without at least mentioning *solid modeling*. For many years, this feature was an additional piece of software that you could opt to purchase with AutoCAD. It is now included as part of the AutoCAD program, and has been since Release 13. While the faces and meshes are tools for surface modeling and help describe the surface of objects, solid modeling describes shapes as solid objects made up of more simple shapes that have been added together or subtracted from each other. You can read the following discussion as a demo: It's not meant to be an exercise.

To construct the walls of the cabin with solid modeling, you would first make a box that was 25-feet long, 16-feet wide, and 8-feet high (Figure A.27a). Think of it as a solid block. Then you would make four boxes for the three rooms (two for the living room and kitchen) and put them inside the big box (Figure A.27b). Then you would subtract the four interior boxes from the big box (Figure A.27c). This creates all the 8-foot walls for the cabin. The next step would be to create boxes for the windows and door and place them in their proper location inside the walls. Then you would subtract the windows and doors from the solid object that is the walls.

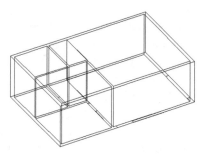

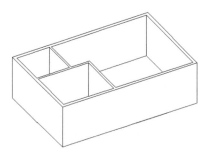

FIGURE A.27: Solid modeling the cabin walls: the outside box (a), the inside boxes added (b), and after the subtraction (c)

Now you have openings in walls, and the walls can be made opaque with the Hide command (Figure A.26). This is much easier than using the 3D faces. In addition to the boxes we just used to form the cabin walls, you have five other basic shapes you can use in combination with boxes to build up a 3D solid model: sphere, cylinder, cone, wedge, and torus. These six basic shapes are called *primitives*. The processes of adding, subtracting, and intersecting the primitives to create complex solid shapes are called *boolean* operations. Solid shapes can also be generated by extruding a 2D shape along a line or revolving it around an axis. In solid modeling, however, the line of extrusion can be curved, or it can have curves and straight segments in it.

You can apply some of the standard Modify commands, like Fillet, to solids to produce special effects. There is also a Slice command that allows you to cut through a solid at any angle. The tools and shapes you have to work with will allow you to build any shape you want. If you experiment with these tools for a little while, you will find yourself wondering as you look at any object, "How could I build that as a solid model?"

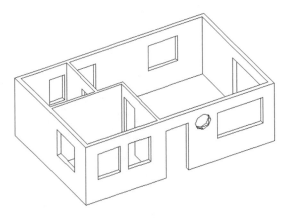

FIGURE A.28: The completed walls after subtracting window and door openings

The solid modeling commands are found on the Draw menu in a sub-menu called Solids. The three Boolean commands (Union, Subtract, and Intersect) are found on the Modify menu in a sub-menu called Solids Editing. This menu also contains several other commands for modifying solids. There are also two toolbars that contain commands for most solid modeling operations: the Solids toolbar that has the primitive shapes and most of the solids modeling commands, and the Solids Editing toolbar that contains the modification commands. You will find Solids Modeling tools handy in constructing a 3D model of almost anything. Try using them to create 3D models of some of the fixtures in the cabin.

Summary

This appendix is a brief introduction to 3D drawing and its concepts. The main features you've covered here are:

- Two methods of viewing a 3D model—Viewpoint Presets and 3D Orbit
- The basic surface modeling operations: wireframe construction, extrusion, and drawing 3D faces
- The User Coordinate System (UCS)
- Solids modeling concepts

APPENDIX B

Appendix B:
An Introduction to Attributes

A*ttributes* are a special type of AutoCAD object made up of text that resides inside a block. Attributes are different from text in several ways, two of which are:

- The text content of attribute text can be extracted from an AutoCAD drawing and manipulated as data in a database, spreadsheet, or word processor.

- Attributes must be part of a block definition in order to function.

Because attributes exist as part of a block, they have several applications in CAD drawings. They are frequently used to attach information to geometric objects that are blocked. Information that you would normally find in a door or window *schedule* can be stored with the individual doors or windows.

NOTE NOTE NOTE NOTE NOTE NOTE NOTE NOTE NOTE NOTE NOTE NOTE NOTE NOTE NOTE

A schedule is a chart in a drawing that contains logically organized information about a particular building component, such as doors, windows, or room finishes. Each of these would have their own schedule. Possible information in a door schedule, for example, would be size, material, finish, location, and type of jamb.

In fact, the information in schedules can be generated from the attributes in the drawing. Number or letter symbols in column grids are easier to set up and update with attributes than with the regular text you used in Skill 10, *Controlling Text in a Drawing*, when you created a grid for the cabin floor plan. Title blocks can be easily standardized for a project so that the text that is the same on each sheet uses regular text, and the text that might be different from sheet to sheet—like page number, date, scale, etc.—will use attributes.

In this appendix, you'll have a chance to set up attributes for the grid you created in Skill 10. Then you'll go through a set of exercises to learn a basic application for attributes, and you'll extract the information contained in the attributes that you create for the drawing.

Using Attributes for a Grid

The grid lines for a building usually are located at centerlines of structural components, like walls or columns. Columns in buildings can then be identified by the letter and number identifying the two grid lines intersecting at their location.

In the cabin drawing, we used the grid lines to indicate the outside edge of exterior walls and the center lines of interior walls. Grids generally have a circle or hexagon with a number or letter in it at the end of each grid line, with the numbers running in one direction (horizontal or vertical) and letters in the other.

A very simple but handy use of attributes is to make the letter or number in the circle an attribute, then make a block out of the attribute and circle. By redoing the grid symbols in the cabin drawing, you will learn how attributes are set up.

1. Open Cabin10a. The drawing consists of the floor plan with a grid and the front elevation. Be sure the Grid layer is current.

2. Zoom into the floor plan, keeping the grid visible. In this case, the letters run horizontally across the top, and the numbers run vertically along the side.

3. Erase all the circles, letters, and numbers in the grid except those for *A* and *1*. Leave the grid lines intact (Figure B.1).

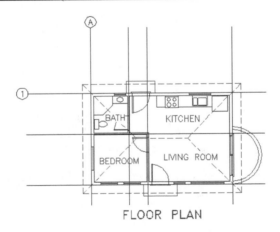

FLOOR PLAN

FIGURE B.1: The floor plan of Cabin10a with all but two grid symbols erased

4. Type **li** ↵ to start the List command. Select the letter *A*, then press ↵. The text window displays information about the text. You need to know the text style and height: Label and 12".

5. Erase the letters *A* and *1*, but not the circles.

6. Type **sc** ↵ to start the Scale command. Select the circle on the top and press ↵.

7. Use Endpoint Osnap and pick the endpoint of the grid line where it meets the circle. Type **1.25** ↵. The circle is enlarged.

8. Repeat steps 6 and 7 for the circle on the left side.

9. Select Draw ➤ Block ➤ Define Attributes. The Attribute Definition dialog box appears.

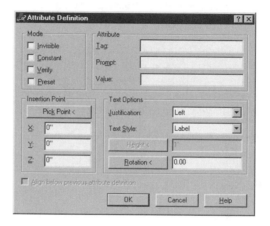

In the Attribute area, there are three text boxes: Tag, Prompt, and Value. The cursor is flashing in the Tag text box. Think of the letter in the grid circle: The Tag is the type of thing that the letter or number is.

10. Type **grid_letter**. Don't press ↵. Press Tab to move to the Prompt text box. Here you enter a prompt for the future user who's setting up a grid.

11. Type **Enter grid letter**. Press Tab to move to the Value prompt. Here you enter a default or sample value to help the future user. You want it capitalized, so enter **A**. This sets up the attribute so that the drafter setting up the grid will be prompted to enter the grid letter, and will be given a default of *A*. The *A* will let him know it should be an uppercase letter.

12. The lower portion of the dialog box is where you set up parameters for the attribute text: location in the drawing, justification, text style, height, and rotation. Click the Justification drop-down list and select Middle.

13   Be sure Label is in the Text Style list box. If not, open the drop-down list and select Label. Since the Label text style has a height set to 12", the height text box in the Attribute Definition dialog box is faded out.

14.   In the Insertion Point area, click the Pick Point button. This returns you to the drawing to pick an insertion point. Back in the drawing, use Center Osnap and click the circle at the top of the grid. You are returned to the dialog box.

15.   Back in the Attribute Definition dialog box, click OK. GRID_LETTER is centered in the circle (Figure B.2).

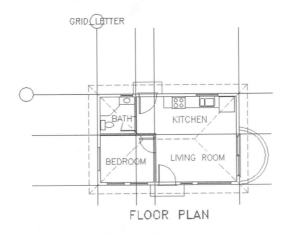

FIGURE B.2: The first attribute definition placed in the grid circle

   The text in the circle is called the attribute definition and has a similar function in AutoCAD as a block definition. When you made the Win-1 block for the windows, the definition was a 12-inch–long window with an insertion point. When the Win-1 block was inserted, you could make windows with various sizes from the original block definition. The same is true for the attribute definition: when it becomes part of a block that's inserted, the attribute can be any letter you like. You'll see that happen in just a minute. First, make a similar attribute definition for the numbered grid symbol.

1.   Type **att** ↵ to start the Attribute definition command. The Attribute definition dialog box appears again.

2. Repeat steps 10 through 15, using the following guidelines:

    A. Enter **grid_number** for the tag.

    B. Type **Enter grid number.** for the prompt.

    C. Enter **1** for the value.

    D. Select Middle justification.

    E. Click the Pick Point button, use Center Osnap, and click the grid circle on the left.

    F. Click OK in the Attribute Definition dialog box.

   The second attribute definition will be centered in the circle on the left side (Figure B.3).

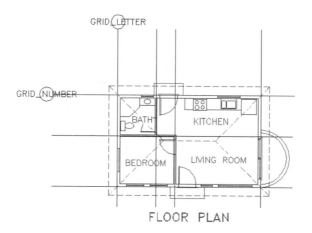

FIGURE B.3: The second attribute definition is placed.

   You now have two attribute definitions and are ready to make each of them part of a block that will include the circle they are presently centered in.

Defining Blocks with Attributes

We have to define two blocks for the grid symbols and their attributes. The block used for the top of the grid will need its insertion point to be at the lowest point of the circle. The one for the left side will need its insertion point to be at the point on the circle furthest to the right.

1. Click the Make Block button on the Draw toolbar to start the block command. The Block Definition dialog box comes up.

2. In the Name drop-down list, enter **grid-v** (for vertical), then click the Pick Point button in the Base Point area.

3. In the drawing, use Endpoint Osnap and select the grid line that ends at the circle on top.

4. In the Block Definition dialog box, click the Select Objects button.

5. In the drawing, select the circle and attribute definition on the top. Press ↵.

6. In the Block Definition dialog box, be sure the Delete button is selected in the Objects area and click OK. The block is defined and includes the attribute definition. In the drawing, the top circle and attribute definition have been deleted.

7. Type **b** ↵ to start the Block command again. Repeat steps 2 through 6 to define a second block for the circle and attribute definition on the left side. Use the following guidelines:

   A. Enter **grid-h** in the Block name text box.

   B. Click Pick Point. Use Endpoint Osnap and pick the horizontal grid line that ends at the right-most point of the grid circle on the left of the floor plan.

   C. When selecting objects, select the circle on the left and its block definition.

When you complete the command, you will have a second block definition that includes an attribute definition. Your drawing will look like Figure B.4.

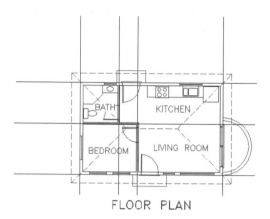

FLOOR PLAN

FIGURE B.4: The floor plan with grid circles and attribute definitions erased

Inserting Blocks with Attributes

Now you can insert these blocks (which are now grid symbols) at the endpoints of the grid lines and assign them the appropriate letter or number as you insert them.

1. Set Endpoint Osnap to running.

2. Select the Insert Block button on the Draw toolbar to start the Insert command.

3. In the Insert dialog box, open the Name drop-down list and select **grid-v**.

4. Be sure the Specify On-screen checkbox for Insertion point is marked, but not for Scale and Rotation. Click OK.

5. Click the left-most vertical grid line in the drawing. Note the command window. It says Enter grid letter <A>:. This is the prompt you entered in the Attribute Definition dialog box for the Prompt. <A> is the Value you entered as the default value. Press ⏎ to accept the default value for this grid line.

6. The grid symbol is inserted at the endpoint of the left-most vertical grid line (Figure B.5).

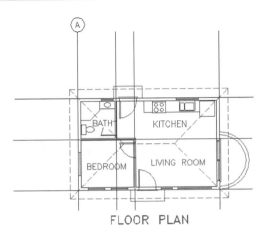

FLOOR PLAN

FIGURE B.5: The first grid symbol block is inserted.

7. Press ↵ to restart the Insert command. Click OK to accept grid-v as the current block to be inserted.

8. Click the grid line to the right of the one you just selected above.

9. At the `Enter grid letter <A>`: prompt, type **B** ↵, then click OK. The second grid symbol is inserted on a grid line and the letter *B* is located in the circle.

10. Repeat steps 7 through 9 to insert the other two grid symbols across the top of the floor plan.

11. Keep repeating steps 8 through 11, but select the **grid-h** block for the three grid symbols that run down the left side of the floor plan. The results should look like Figure B.6.

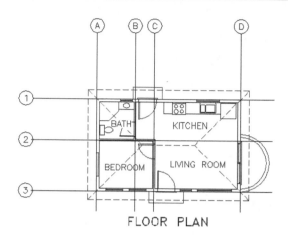

FLOOR PLAN

FIGURE B.6:   The grid with all symbols inserted

Editing Attribute Text

To illustrate how attribute text can be edited, we'll assume that a decision was made to change the C grid symbol to B1. The D symbol will then have to be changed to C.

1. Select Modify ➤ Attribute ➤ Single. This starts the Ddatte command.

2. Select the C grid symbol. The Edit Attributes dialog box appears. The attribute value is highlighted.

3. Type **B1**, then click OK. B1 replaces C in the grid.

NOTE NOTE NOTE NOTE NOTE NOTE NOTE NOTE NOTE NOTE NOTE NOTE NOTE NOTE NOTE
Because you set the justification point for the attribute text to middle and located it at the center of the grid circle, the B1 text is centered in the circle just like the single letters.

4. Press ↵ to restart the Ddatte command, then select the D grid symbol.

5. In the Edit Attributes dialog box, change the D to C and click OK. The attributes have been updated (Figure B.7)

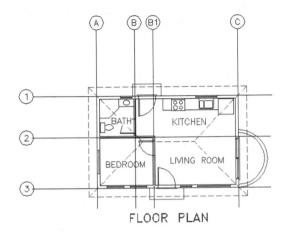

FIGURE B.7: The grid symbols after being updated

The above exercises have illustrated the basic procedure for defining, inserting, and changing attributes. You can apply these same procedures to the process of setting up a title block in which attributes are used for text that will change from one drawing to the next. We can now move to a more complex application of the attribute feature to see its full power.

Setting Up Multiple Attributes in a Block

In the cabin, we have three rooms and a balcony, with the kitchen and living room sharing a room. Each room has a different area and floor covering. This information, along with the room name, can be stored in the drawing as attributes. We will set up a block that will consist of three attributes. Then we'll insert the block back into the floor plan. If you remember, the text style for the room labels is LABEL. We'll use that for the attributes.

We have to erase the room labels for now, but it would be nice if we could mark where their justification points presently are. That way we can insert the attribute exactly where the text is now.

1. Start the Line command and pick Insertion Osnap, then click the Living Room label. A line is started at the justification point.

2. Draw the marker line to a blank point not too far away. The first endpoint of the line will be the location of the insertion point of the block that contains the attributes.

3. Repeat this for the Bedroom and Bath labels. We don't need one for the Kitchen because it will remain as is and have no attributes. The balcony doesn't have text in this drawing, so we can place the attribute anywhere we want.

4. Erase the Living Room, Bedroom, and Bath labels. The drawing should look like Figure B.8.

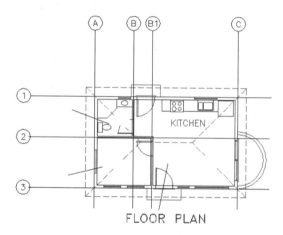

FIGURE B.8: The floor plan with markers for insertion points and three room labels erased

5. Make the 0 layer current. Select Draw ➤ Block ➤ Define Attributes. The Ddattdef command starts and the Attribute Definition dialog box appears.

6. For the tag, enter **rm_name**. For the prompt, type **Enter room name**. For the value, enter **LIVING ROOM**. (This default value will remind the user to use all uppercase letters.)

7. In the bottom half of the dialog box where the settings for the text are, everything is going to stay the same, so go to the Insertion Point area and click Pick Point.

8. In the drawing, use Endpoint Osnap and click the right end of the grid line that has the number *1* in the circle. In the dialog box, click OK. The first attribute definition is placed in the drawing (Figure B.9). Since we're going to make a block out of it and reinsert it into the rooms, we don't have to place the attribute definition where the room labels are; any place on the edge of the drawing is fine.

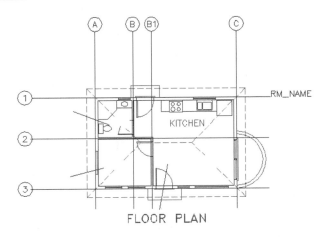

FLOOR PLAN

FIGURE B.9: The room name attribute definition placed in the drawing

9. Press ↵ to restart the Ddattdef command. For this attribute, in the Tag text box, enter **rm-area**. For the prompt, type **Enter area of room**, and for the value, enter **10.00 Sq. Ft**. This will show the user the format you want the area to be in.

10. In the Mode area, click to activate Invisible. The Invisible mode will make the attribute values invisible in the drawing, but they are still stored there.

11. In the lower-left corner of the dialog box, click in the checkbox next to Align Below Previous Attribute Definition. All the text options fade out. The style will be the same as the first attribute, and this attribute definition will be placed right below the first one.

12. Click OK. The second attribute definition is placed in the drawing below the first one.

13. Repeat steps 9 through 13 to define the third attribute. For the tag, enter **rm-floor**. For the prompt, type **Enter floor material of room**. For the value, enter **Wood Parquet**. Activate the Invisible mode and click in the checkbox next to Align Below Previous Attribute Definition. Click OK. All three attribute definitions are now in the drawing (Figure B.10).

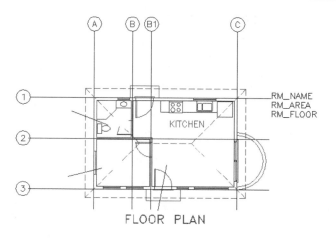

FIGURE B.10:   The floor plan with all three attribute definitions

Now we will make a block out of the three attributes.

Defining a Block with Multiple Attributes

A block with attributes usually includes lines, or other geometrical objects, along with the attribute definitions, but it doesn't have to. In this case, the three attribute definitions are the sole content of the block, and the block's insertion point will be the justification point for the first attribute—the room label text.

1. Start the Block command (type **b ↵**).

2. In the Block Definition dialog box, for the Name, enter **room_info**.

3. Click the Pick Point button. In the drawing, use Insertion Osnap and click the first attribute definition. This aligns the justification point of this attribute with the insertion point of the block.

4. Back in the Block Definition dialog box, pick the Select Objects button. In the drawing, pick each attribute definition in the order you created them. By picking them in this order, you will be prompted for their values in this

order when the block is inserted. Press ↵ after selecting them, then, in the dialog box, click OK. The Room_Info block is defined, and the attribute definitions are deleted from the drawing.

You are almost ready to insert the Room_Info block in each of the three rooms and near the balcony. But first, you need to calculate the area of each room.

Calculating Areas

You can calculate areas in a drawing by using the Area command. Because area calculations are made over and over again in design and construction, the Area command is an important tool. You can calculate an overall area and then subtract sub-areas from it, or you can add sub-areas together to make a total. For this exercise, you will use the command to simply calculate the areas of the four floor spaces in the floor plan. You will need to write down the areas after you make the calculations.

1. Type **undo** ↵, then type **m** ↵. This places a marker at the end of the sequence of steps you have been following up to now. After the next series of steps, you will undo the results until your drawing returns to the state it's in right now.

2. Make the Walls layer current. Freeze all the other layers, except Balcony. Your drawing should look like Figure B.11.

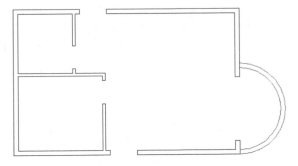

FIGURE B.11: The floor plan with all layers frozen except Walls and Balcony

3. Set Endpoint Osnap to be running, if it's not already.

4. Open the Inquiry flyout by clicking and holding down the Distance button on the Standard toolbar, and then moving to the Area button and releasing. At the `Specify first corner point or [Object /Add /Subtract]:` prompt, click the four inside corners of the bathroom, moving around the perimeter, then press ↵. The command line will display the results of your calculation: `Area = 5616.00 square in. (39.0000 square ft.), Perimeter = 25'-0"`.

5. Write down the area in square feet. Press ↵ to restart the Area command and click the four inside corners of the bedroom. It might be helpful to zoom in closer to pick the corners. Press ↵. The command line displays the area and perimeter. The area should be 76.2222 square feet. Write this number down (you can shorten it to two decimal places).

6. Repeat this for the living room, where you will have to pick six points. The area should be 236.6667 square feet. Write down 236.67.

7. Restart the Area command. Type **o** ↵ to select the Object option of the Area command, then click the inside arc of the balcony. You get this message in the Command window: `Selected object does not have an area`. The arc must be converted to a polyline to have its area calculated.

8. Press Esc to cancel the Area command. Pick Modify ➤ Polyline to start the Pedit command.

9. Click the inside arc of the balcony. The prompt now reads `Object selected is not a polyline Do you want to turn it into one? <Y>`. Press ↵ to accept the default of Yes. Then type **x** ↵ to exit the Pedit command.

10. Now you can click the Area button on the Standard toolbar to restart the Area command.

11. Type **o** ↵ to use the Object option, then click the inside arc again. You will get a calculation this time of 31.8086 square feet. Write down 31.81.

The area of polyline arcs will be calculated as if a straight line were drawn across the open side between endpoints of the arc.

B

12.   Type **undo** ↵, then type **b** ↵. The drawing is restored to the state it was in back at step 1.

The Add and Subtract options in the Area command prompt allow you to add areas together that you have calculated, and to subtract areas from each other. If you are going to add or subtract areas, type A ↵ after you start the command. Then, after each calculation you make, you will be given the Add and Subtract options. If you don't enter an A at the beginning, you can only make one calculation at a time.

Inserting the Room_Info Block

You have four areas calculated and recorded, and you are ready to insert the room _Info block.

1.   Make the Text1 layer current.

2.   Select Insert ➤ Block. In the Insert dialog box, select **room_info** from the Name drop-down list. Click OK. Endpoint Osnap should still be running. Select the end of the line that marks the justification point for the Living Room label text.

3.   The `Enter room name <LIVING ROOM>:` prompt appears in the command window. Press ↵ to accept the default.

4.   The prompt changes to `Enter area of room <10.00 Sq. Ft.>:`. Type **236.67 Sq. Ft.** ↵.

5.   For the last prompt concerning the floor material, click OK. The room_info block is inserted into the drawing in the living room. The room label is the only visible attribute (Figure B.12). We set the other two to be invisible.

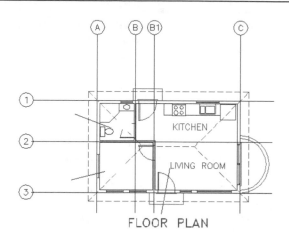

FLOOR PLAN

FIGURE B.12: The first room_info block is inserted.

6. Press ↵ to restart the Insert command. In the Insert dialog box, the room_info block should still be displayed in the Name drop-down list. Click OK.

7. In the drawing, click near the endpoint of the line marking the justification point of the Bedroom text label. The same three prompts as before appear in sequence at the command line with the same default values.

8. With Caps Lock on, type **bedroom** ↵ for the first prompt, then turn Caps Lock off. The command line changes to a prompt for the area of the room and displays the default for the second value.

9. Type **76.22 Sq. Ft.** ↵.

10. For the third prompt, type **Linoleum Tile** ↵. The second block is inserted in the bedroom. Again, only the room label text is visible.

11. Repeat steps 6 through 11 for the Bathroom, this time entering **BATH, 39.00 Sq. Ft.**, and **Ceramic Tile**.

12. Repeat steps 7 through 11 for the Balcony, this time entering **BALCONY, 31.81 Sq. Ft., and Wood Plank**. For the Specify insertion point prompt, place the Balcony label outside the balcony, a little above the middle of the arcs.

13. Erase the markers you used to locate the insertion points. Your drawing will look like Figure B.13.

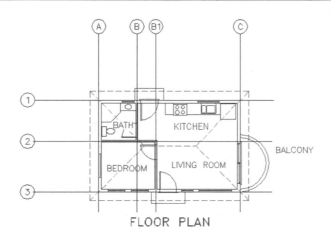

FIGURE B.13: All Room_Info blocks inserted

Controlling the Visibility of Attributes

The floor plan looks the same as it did at the beginning of this exercise, except for the addition of the balcony label. However, changes have taken place, and your drawing is "smarter" than it was before. What was regular text is now an attribute, and there's more than meets the eye.

1. Click View ➢ Display ➢ Attribute Display ➢ On. The invisible attributes are displayed with the room labels (Figure B.14).

2. Press ↵ to restart the Attdisp command, then type **off** ↵. All attributes disappear, including the room labels and the letters and numbers in the grid symbols.

3. Press ↵. Type **n** ↵ to change the setting back to Normal. The room labels, and grid numbers and letters, reappear. On and Off settings make all attributes visible or invisible, regardless of what was set for the visible/invisible mode in the attribute definition. The Normal setting allows attributes to be displayed only if the visible/invisible mode was set to visible in their definition.

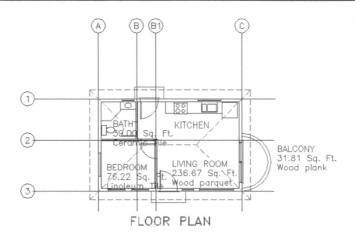

FLOOR PLAN

FIGURE B.14: The floor plan with all attributes displayed

Editing Attributes

Once attributes have been defined and inserted as blocks, you can easily edit any value using the same method you used at the beginning of this appendix to modify a grid number.

1. Select Modify ➤ Attribute ➤ Single to start the Attedit command. Select the Living Room label. The Edit Attributes dialog box appears, displaying both the visible and invisible attributes' values for the living room. You can now change any of the values.

NOTE NOTE NOTE NOTE NOTE NOTE NOTE NOTE NOTE NOTE NOTE NOTE NOTE NOTE NOTE

The Attedit command can also be started by typing ddatte ↵.

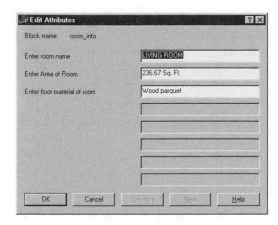

2. We won't make any changes right now. Press Cancel to cancel the Attedit command and return to the drawing.

3. Save this drawing in your training folder as CabinB1.

You can also edit more than one attribute at a time by using the –Attedit command. (The dash in front indicates that this is an older version of the Attedit command.) Start the command by picking Modify ➤ Attribute ➤ Global, or by typing **atte** ↵. The prompt will read Edit attributes one at a time? [Yes/No] <Y>. If you accept the default of Yes, you will be taken though of series of options for selecting attributes to edit. Select the attributes to edit. An x will appear on one of the selected attributes. At this point, you get the following prompt: Enter an option [Value/Position/Height/Angle/Style/Layer/Color/ Next] <N>:, allowing you to modify any of the characteristics listed in the prompt above for the attribute with the x. Press ↵ to move to the next selected attribute.

If you respond to the first prompt with No, you will be taken through a similar set of selection options. Then you are asked to enter a current value to be changed, and to enter the new value after the change. Values of attributes can be changed globally by using the Attedit command in this way.

The Properties dialog box can be used to edit (a) all properties of an attribute definition before it has become part of a block definition, and (b) attribute values after they have become part of a block definition. In the next section, you will extract the room information from this drawing to a text file.

Extracting Data from an AutoCAD Drawing

The extraction process allows you to take attribute data out of a drawing and put it into a text file, from which it can then be inserted into a database, word processor, spreadsheet, or even another AutoCAD drawing. You have to set up a template file to control the form the data is placed in when it comes out of the drawing. If you are familiar with databases, think of the attribute tag as the column or field of a database, and the values as records or rows. The template file sets up the columns by allowing them to be a certain width, and controlling whether the data in the rows is considered to be numerical data or not. We need to set up a template file for the four attributes that have information about the rooms, and we'll end up with a text file that will have three columns, one for each attribute, and four rows, one for each room that has attribute data. This text file will be based on the template file, which we will create first.

Creating a Template File for Data Extraction

1. Minimize AutoCAD and open the Notepad program that comes with Windows 95 and 98, or NT. (It can be found in the Accessories folder when you click Start ➤ Programs.) Notepad opens with a blank page and a flashing cursor.

2. Type **RM_NAME C015000** ↵ **RM_AREA C020000** ↵ **RM_FLOOR C020000** ↵. That's it. Be sure to press ↵ once, and only once, after typing the last line. You should have three lines of text.

3. Select File ➤ Save As and save this file as Room-1 in you training folder. It will be saved as Room-1.txt.

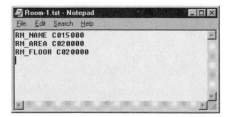

Take a moment to look at the new template file. Each line of text contains an attribute tag and a code. The code has three parts: the letter, the first three numbers, and the last three. The letter has to be a *C* or an *N*, designating whether the value of this attribute is numerical or a character. We will consider all our values for the three attributes to be non-numerical, even though the areas are numerical, because the words *Sq. Ft.* were added.

NOTE NOTE NOTE NOTE NOTE NOTE NOTE NOTE NOTE NOTE NOTE NOTE NOTE NOTE NOTE

The areas could be considered numerical if you set up the attributes to just have numbers and if you had not included the words *Sq. Ft.* Then you could add them together in a database or spreadsheet program.

The first three numbers following the *C* are where you enter how much space you need for this field in the table, from 0 to 999 characters. Our columns will be 15, 20, and 20 characters wide.

The last three numbers are where you enter the number of decimal places a numerical value can have, from 0 to 999. Since we have no numerical data, we leave this at 0.

Extracting Attribute Data

The next step is to perform the actual extraction.

1. Minimize Notepad and return to AutoCAD.

2. Type **ddattext** ↵. The Attribute Extraction dialog box appears.

There are five tasks you will accomplish with this dialog box:

- Choose one of the three extraction file formats.

- Select the template file you just made.

- Select an output file name and folder.
- Select objects in the drawing for the extraction to operate on.
- Execute the extraction.

3. Select the Space Delimited File (CDF) radio button. This mode will separate the columns of data with spaces.

4. Click the Template File button. Find the `Room-1.txt` file and click Open. The file will be displayed in the text box next to the Template File button.

5. By default, the Output file will be a `.txt` file with the same name as the current drawing file, in this case `CabinB1.txt`. You will have to direct Auto-CAD to save this file to your training folder, so click the Output File button and do that.

6. Click the Select Objects button. In your drawing, window the floor plan (Include the BALCONY text, but do not select the grid numbers and letters.) and press ↵. Back in the Attribute Selection dialog box, it will look like this:

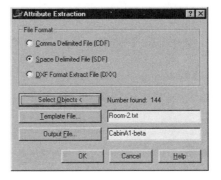

The Number Found: listing will vary, depending on how much of your drawing you selected.

7. Click OK. The Command window will say, "4 records in extract file." This tells you that the extraction was a success.

8. Minimize AutoCAD and bring up Notepad again. Pick File ➢ Open, then find and open `CabinB1.txt`. It will look like this:

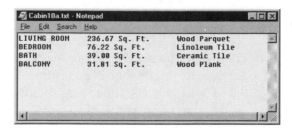

There are four rows of text. Each row contains the three pieces of information about a room. In this format, you can use Windows copy and paste tools to insert this as a schedule in the AutoCAD drawing or as a table in a word processor. Any text inserted into AutoCAD is placed as multiline text. Then it can be exploded into single line text and moved around. As easy as this is to do, it is difficult to line up the columns of data using this method. Use the process described next to link an Excel spreadsheet of extracted data back into an AutoCAD drawing.

To insert extracted data into a database or spreadsheet application, use the Comma Delimited File format in the Attribute Extraction dialog box. This will give you output like this:

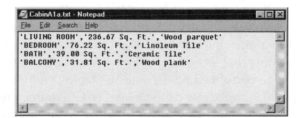

There are still four rows of data, but the columns are gone. The three pieces of data in each row are separated by commas and are in quotes. This format works well for databases and spreadsheets, though it is obviously difficult to read and would not make a good schedule or table in this form. Once imported into Excel, however, the data can be made visible in an AutoCAD drawing as a schedule, through a linking process known as OLE (Object Linking and Embedding). The data can then be updated in Excel, and the changes will show up in the AutoCAD drawing.

Summary

This has been quick tour of the various features of attributes and the commands used to set them up, modify them, and extract the data they contain. As well as being used for grid symbols, and room, window, and door schedules, attributes are widely used in standardized title blocks. One of the most frequent uses of attributes is in facilities management and interior design. Every piece of office furniture in a building can be specified with attributes. The data can then be extracted and sent to a furniture specifier who will input the data into their databases and complete the order. The big office furniture manufacturers sell their own proprietary software that works with AutoCAD and automatically sets up attributes when you insert their blocks of the furniture, which they have pre-drawn and included in the software package. Also, Architectural Desktop—an add-on software package that works with AutoCAD—can automatically create door and window schedules.

Attributes are also being used more and more in maps drawn in AutoCAD, which are then imported into Geographical Information System (GIS) software. When map features, such as buildings, are blocks containing an attribute, such as a building number, they are transformed in the GIS program in such a way that linkages can be set up between the map features (buildings) and database tables that contain information about the map features. In this way, analyses (such as locating buildings that have a total area greater than a specified square footage) can be performed on the database tables, and the results are automatically displayed graphically on the map. The GIS is an incredibly powerful tool of analysis and presentation, and many existing GIS projects use AutoCAD maps that have attributes set up in just this way.

Most architectural firms with which I've come in contact use the attribute feature for setting up title blocks, grids, and some symbols. Those involved in facilities management and interior design are more likely to use attributes in the process of generating specifications for office partitions and furniture.

In this appendix, you were introduced to the AutoCAD tools used for setting up and modifying attributes, and were shown several ways that they can be used in an AutoCAD drawing. You also looked at an advanced application for attributes—data extraction—and reviewed a couple of possible uses for that process. Finally, you learned how this feature is used in mapping and facility management. If you continue to work with attributes, you will find them to be a powerful tool and a way to link information in your AutoCAD drawing to other applications.

GLOSSARY

3D mesh

A set of adjacent flat surfaces that together form a geometrical depiction of a surface that occupies three dimensions.

3D model

An AutoCAD drawing file that contains Auto-CAD *objects* that occupy 3D space and represent building components or geometrical objects in the real world.

a

Absolute coordinates

Values for locating a point in space that describe its distance and direction from the *origin* (0,0,0) point of the drawing.

Alias

A shortcut for starting commands. It is a set of one or two letters that can be entered at the *command line* instead of the full command.

Aligned dimension

A linear dimension measuring the distance between two points. The dimension line for an aligned dimension is parallel to a line between the two points.

Angular dimension

A dimension that measures the angle between two lines or the angle inscribed by an arc segment.

Angular unit

The unit in which angle values are displayed. The choices are decimal degrees, degrees-minutes-seconds, grads, radians, or survey units.

Associative dimension

A dimension that updates automatically when the object being dimensioned changes size.

Associative hatch pattern

A hatch pattern that updates automatically when the shape of the hatched area is modified.

Attribute

An *object* inside a *block* that contains text data. The value of an attribute (*attribute value*) is specified when the block is inserted.

Attribute definition

A special AutoCAD *object* that is included in a *block definition* so that varying text information can be included in the *block reference* when a block is inserted in a drawing.

Attribute extraction file

A text file where extracted attribute data is stored.

Attribute extraction template file

A text file (`.txt`) that is used to organize the data in an *attribute extraction file.*

Attribute prompt

The part of the *attribute definition* that instructs the user what to enter at the *command line* or in a dialog box when they are entering *attribute values*.

Attribute tag

A part of the *attribute definition* that represents the field of the table into which attribute data is extracted.

Attribute value

The data that is the content of an attribute. It is always text and appears in the record or rows of the table into which attribute data is extracted.

AutoCAD object

See *Object*.

AutoSnap

A feature of AutoCAD that works with the Object Snap tools by displaying a symbol on the places in the drawing that can be snapped to. Each of these *Object Snap modes* has a different *Autosnap* symbol. The symbol appears when the cursor is near a location where the active Object Snap can be used.

b

Baseline dimension

A dimensioning option that allows you to do multiple measurements from a designated baseline.

Base point

1. The initial point of reference for a number of modify commands, including Copy, Move, Rotate, Stretch, and Scale. 2. The insertion point for a drawing, as designated by the Base command.

Blip marks

Small crosses that, when enabled, mark points in the *drawing area* that have been picked or specified, and where objects have been selected.

Block

See *Block reference*.

Block definition

The description of a grouping of AutoCAD objects that is stored with the drawing file and includes a name, an *insertion point*, and a listing of objects in the grouping.

Block reference

An instance of a grouping of objects that is inserted into a drawing and is based upon the block definition for that grouping. Casually called a block.

Bylayer

A property that can be assigned to colors and linetypes so that objects will receive their color and linetype properties according to the layer they are on.

c

Command line

A text window at the bottom of the screen that displays command prompts. This is where you see what you are entering through the keyboard. Also called the Command window.

Command prompt

A Command: *prompt* at the *command line*. When it is blank, no commands are currently running.

Command window

See *Command line*.

Continued dimension

A dimensioning option that allows you to place sequential dimensions that are adjacent to each other so that the dimension lines are aligned.

Crosshair cursor

A form of the *cursor* that consists of a horizontal line and a vertical line intersecting at their midpoints, resembling the crosshair in a sighting device.

Crossing window

A selection tool that selects an area defined by two points acting as opposite corners of a rectangle. All objects within or crossing the rectangle are selected.

Cursor

The pointing symbol on the computer monitor that is moved by moving the mouse. It can appear as, among other things, an arrow, a *pickbox*, and a *crosshair*.

Cutting edge

The role certain objects can be temporarily assigned to play in a trimming operation. If an object is designated as a cutting edge, lines or other objects being trimmed will be trimmed back to the point where they intersect the cutting edge.

d

Default

A value or option in a command that will be used unless you designate otherwise. In Auto-CAD, default values and options are enclosed in angle brackets (< >).

Dimension style

A collection of settings for *dimension variables* that is saved in a drawing under a specified name. Dimensions placed in the drawing will follow the settings of the current dimension style.

Dimension text

The text in a dimension. It expresses the measurement that the dimension is displaying.

Dimension variables

A group of settings and values that control the appearance of dimensions in AutoCAD.

Donut

A 2D wide polyline drawn in a circle and resembling a ring-shaped doughnut pastry.

Drawing area

The portion of the monitor screen where you draw objects and view your drawing.

Drawing extents

The minimum rectangular area with the same proportions as your *drawing area* that will enclose all visible objects in your drawing. When you *zoom* to extents, the rectangular area fills the drawing area.

Drawing limits

The area in a drawing that is covered by the *grid*. It can be defined by the user. It is stored as the coordinates of the lower-left and upper-right corner of the rectangular area covered by the *grid*.

Dwg

The file extension and format for the standard AutoCAD drawing.

e

Edge

1. The side of a *3D face* or a *3D mesh*. 2. A command for controlling the visibility of the edges of 3D faces.

Entity

See *Object*.

Explode

A command to undo a grouping of objects. It can be used on blocks, *multiline text*, *polylines*, and dimensions. Exploded multiline text becomes single line text. Exploded polylines become lines. Exploded blocks become the individual objects that make up the block.

External reference

A drawing file that has been temporarily attached to another drawing for read-only purposes. Also called an Xref.

External reference host file

The drawing file to which *external references* have been attached.

Extrusion

1. A 2D object that has been given *thickness*. 2. A 3D solid object created with the Extrude command, by sliding a closed 2D shape along a path that is usually perpendicular to the 2D shape. If you use the Path option of the Extrude command, the extrusion need not be perpendicular to the path.

f

Face

A triangular or four-sided flat surface that is the basic unit of a 3D surface.

Fill

A display mode that can be set to on or off. When it is set to on, it displays a solid color for shapes made with wide *polylines*, 2D solids, *donuts*, and *hatch patterns* using the Solid pattern. When it is set to off, the solid color area is invisible and only the boundary is displayed.

Floating viewports

Rectangular windows created in the *Paper Space* of a drawing that allows you to view a drawing in *Model Space*. See also *Paper Space* and *Model Space*.

Font

A group of letters, numbers, and other symbols all sharing common features of design and appearance.

Freeze

The Off portion of a setting called Freeze/Thaw that controls the visibility of objects on *layers* and determines whether AutoCAD calculates the geometry of these objects during a *regeneration.*

g

Graphical User Interface

See *Graphics window.*

Graphics Window

The appearance of your screen when Auto-CAD is running. It consists of the *drawing area* and surrounding *toolbars, menu bars, command window,* and *status bar.* Also called the Graphical User Interface.

Grid

1. A tool for drawing that consists of a regularly spaced set of dots in the *drawing area.* 2. A series of horizontal and vertical lines in a floor plan or section that locate the main structural elements of a building, such as columns and walls. Also called a column grid.

Grips

An editing tool that allows you to perform six modify commands on selected objects without having to start the commands. When grips are enabled, small squares appear on selected objects. By clicking a square, you activate the first of the available commands. You can cycle through the rest of the commands by pressing the space bar.

h

Hatch patterns

Patterns of lines, dots, and other shapes that fill in a closed area.

Host file

See *External reference host file.*

i

Insertion point

A reference point that is part of a *block* and is used to locate the block when it is inserted into a drawing. It is attached to the cursor while a block is being inserted. Once a block has been inserted, the insertion point can be snapped to with the Insertion *Osnap.*

Isometric view

A view of a 3D object in which all lines that are parallel on the object appear parallel in the view. See also *Perspective view.*

j

Jamb

A surface that forms the side or top of an opening for a door or window in a wall.

Justification Point

A reference point on a line of single line text, or a body of multiline text, that acts like the *insertion point* for blocks.

l

Layer

An organizing tool that operates like an electronic version of traditional transparent overlays on a drawing board. Layers can be assigned color and *linetype*, and their visibility can be controlled.

Layout

An optional interface that serves as an aid to the user in setting up a drawing for printing. It rests "on top of" the *Model space* in which the drawing of the building resides. It contains the title block, notes, scale and other adjunctory information. The user views their drawing through openings in the layout called *viewports*. A single drawing file may have multiple layouts, one for each print to be made from the file. The layout interface is sometimes referred to as *Paper space*.

Layout tab

A tab at the lower-left corner of the drawing area that is used to switch from a *Model space* view of the drawing to a Layout view.

Limits

See *Drawing limits*.

Linetype

The style of appearance of a line. These styles include continuous, dashed, dash dot, etc.

Linetype scale

A numerical value for non-continuous linetypes that controls the size of dashes and spaces between dashes and dots. In an AutoCAD drawing, there is a global linetype scale that controls all non-continuous linetypes in the drawing, and an individual linetype scale that can be applied to one or more selected lines.

m

Menu bar

The set of drop-down menus at the top of the AutoCAD graphics window.

Mirror

This command makes a copy of selected objects that are flipped around a specified line to make a mirror image of those objects.

Model space

The portion of an AutoCAD drawing that contains the lines representing the building or object being designed, as opposed to the notes and title block information, which are kept on a *Layout*.

Mtext

See *Multiline text*.

Multiline text

A type of text in which an entire body of text is grouped together as one object. Casually called Mtext, it can be edited with word-processing techniques. Individual characters or words in the Mtext can have different heights, fonts, and colors from the main body of Mtext. *Dimension text* is Mtext. When *exploded*, Mtext becomes *single line text*.

n

Named view

A view of your drawing that is saved and given a name so that it can be restored later.

o

Object

A basic AutoCAD graphical element that is created and manipulated as part of the drawing, such as a line, arc, dimension, block, or text. Also called an *entity*.

Object Snap mode

Any of a set of tools for precisely picking strategic points on an *object*, including Endpoint, Midpoint, Center, etc. It is casually called *Osnap*.

Object Snap Tracking

See *Tracking*.

Origin

The point with the coordinates 0,0,0, where the x, y, and z axes all meet.

Orthagonal drawing

A system of creating views in which each view shows a different side of a building or object, such as top, front, left side, right side, etc.

Ortho mode

An on/off setting that, when on, forces lines to be drawn and objects to be moved in a horizontal or vertical direction only.

Osnap

See *Object Snap mode*.

Otrack

See *Tracking*.

p

Pan

A command that slides the current drawing around on the drawing area without changing the magnification of the view.

Paper space

A term sometimes used to refer to the interface for a drawing that contains *Layouts*.

Path

The hierarchy of drive, folder, and subfolders where a file is stored, along with the file's name, such as C:\AUTOCAD-2000\TRAINING\CABIN8A.DWG.

Perspective view

A view of a 3D object in which parallel lines that are not parallel to the plane of the screen appear to converge as they move further away from the viewer, similar to the way objects appear in the real world, like railroad tracks in the distance. See also *Isometric view*.

Pickbox

A form of the cursor as a small square that occurs when AutoCAD is in *selection mode*.

Pick button

The button on the mouse (usually the left one) that is used to pick points, buttons, or menu items, as well as select objects on the screen.

Plan view

A view of a drawing in which the viewer is looking straight at the *xy plane* in a direction parallel to the *z* axis. In Plan view, the positive *x* and *y* directions are to the right and up, respectively.

Point filters

A set of tools that allow you to specify a point in the drawing by using some of the *x*, *y*, and *z* coordinates from another point or points to generate the coordinates for the point you are specifying.

Polar tracking

A tool for temporarily aligning the cursor movement to preset angles while drawing. See also *Tracking*.

Polyline

A special type of line that (a) treats multiple segments as one object, (b) can include arcs, (c) can be smoothed into a curved line, and (d) can have width in 2D applications.

Prompt

The text at the command line that asks questions or tells you what action is necessary to continue the execution of a command. The Command: prompt tells you that no command is presently running.

r

Redraw

A command to refresh the *drawing area* or a particular *viewport*, thereby ridding it of any *blip marks* or graphic distortions, called screen artifacts, that show up on the monitor while you're drawing.

Regeneration

A process in which the geometry for the objects in the current drawing file is recalculated.

Regular window

A selection tool that selects an area defined by two points acting as opposite corners of a rectangle. All objects completely within the rectangle are selected. See also *Crossing window*.

Relative coordinates

Values for locating a point in space that describe its distance and direction from the last point picked in the drawing rather than from the *origin*.

Rubberbanding

The effect of a line extending between the last point picked and the crosshair cursor, stretching like a rubber band as the cursor is moved.

Running Object Snap

An *Object Snap mode* that has been set to be continually activated until turned off.

S

Selection mode

The phase of a command that requires the user to select objects, and thereby build up a *selection set* of objects, to be modified by or otherwise used in the function of the command.

Selection set

Any object or group of objects that have been selected for modification, or have been selected to be used in a modification process.

Selection window

A tool for selecting objects whereby the user creates a rectangular window in the *drawing area* and objects are selected in two ways, depending on whether the selection window is a *crossing window* or a *regular window*. See also *crossing window*.

Single line text

A type of text *object* in AutoCAD in which each line of text is treated as a single object, with its own *justification point*, whether it be a sentence, word, or letter.

Snap mode

An on/off setting that locks the cursor onto a spatial grid, which is usually aligned with the *grid*, allowing you to draw to distances that are multiples of the grid spacing. When the grid spacing is set to 0, the grid aligns with the snap spacing.

Stud

A small, upright piece of lumber or metal used in framing walls. It is usually a 2×4 or 2×6 in cross dimension and extends the height of the wall.

t

Template drawing

A drawing that has been set up to serve as a format for a new drawing. This allows the user to begin a new drawing with certain parameters already set up because various settings have been predetermined.

Text style

A collection of settings that controls the appearance of text and is saved in a drawing under a specified name. Text placed in the drawing will follow the settings of the current text style.

Thaw

The On portion of a setting called Freeze/Thaw that controls the visibility of objects on *layers* and determines whether AutoCAD calculates the geometry of these objects during a *regeneration.*

Thickness

The distance a 2D object is *extruded* in a direction perpendicular to the plane in which it was originally drawn, resulting in a 3D object. For a floor plan of a building, wall lines can be extruded to a thickness that is the wall's actual height.

Tracking

The process by which the user sets up temporary points or angles as guides for the cursor, used to locate desired points in the process of drawing. *Object Snap Tracking* (or *Otrack*) creates the temporary points, and *Polar Tracking* sets the angles.

UCS

See *User Coordinate System.*

UCS icon

The double-arrowed icon in the lower-left corner of the *drawing area* that indicates the positive directions of the *x* and *y* axes for the current *User Coordinate System.*

User Coordinate System (UCS)

A definition for the orientation of the *x*, *y*, and *z* axes in space relative to 3D objects in the drawing or to the *World Coordinate System.* UCSs can be named, saved, and restored.

View

A picture of the current drawing from a particular user-defined perspective that is displayed on the screen or in a *viewport.* Views may be named, saved, and restored.

Viewport

A rectangular window through which the user can view their drawing or a portion of it. There are two kinds of viewports: *tiled viewports* and *floating viewports.* Tiled viewports are used in *Layouts.* Floating viewports are used in *Model space.*

W

Wireframe

The representation of a 3D object with lines that represent the intersections of planes or the corners of walls and other building components.

World Coordinate System

The *default User Coordinate System* for all new drawing files, in which the positive directions for the *x* and *y* axes are to the right and upwards, respectively, and in which the positive direction for the *z* axis is towards the user and perpendicular to the plane of the screen.

X

XY plane

The 2D flat surface, defined by the x and y axes, which is parallel to the monitor screen in a new, *default* AutoCAD drawing file.

Z

Zoom

The name of a command with several options, all of which allow the user to increase or decrease the magnification of the *view* of the current drawing in the *drawing area* or in a *viewport*.

Index

Note to the Reader: First level entries are in **bold**. Page numbers in **bold** indicate the principal discussion of a topic or the definition of a term. Page numbers in *italic* indicate illustrations.

Numbers and Symbols

3D drawings, 522–561
  adding 3D faces, **534–547**
    defined, **534**, **595**
    to front walls, 535–536, *535*, *536*
    hiding lines, 534, *534*, 537, *537*, 540
    making edges invisible while, 544, **595**
    overview of, 534–535, 540–541, *541*, 551
    rotating views, 538–539, *538*, *539*
    to side walls, 537–540, *537–539*
    starting 3D Face command, 535
    to window openings, 541–547, *543*, *545*
  creating wireframe models, **525–534**, **547–558**
    adding 3D faces to, 534–547
    adding details, 557–558, *557*
    balconies, 555, *556*, 557
    defined, **525**, **601**
    doorways, 532–534, *533*, *534*
    exterior walls, 525–526, *526*
    hiding lines, 527, *528*, 529
    interior walls, 527, *528*, 530, *531*
    overview of, 546–547
    pasting 2D windows onto, 547–551, *547*, *550*
    roofs, 551–555, *552–554*
    rotating views, 529–530, *530*
  Hide command and, 540
  overview of, 522, 564
  solid modeling method, 561–564, *562*, *563*
  surface modeling method, **523–558**
    adding 3D faces, 534–547
    color and, 546
    creating wireframe models, 525–534, 547–558
    defined, **529**
    elements in, 529
    extrusion in, 527, *528*, 532–534, *533–534*, **595**
    layers and, 546
    overview of, 523

User Coordinate System in, 524, *525*, 548–551, *550*
viewing in 3D
    3D Orbit View, 558–561, *559*, *560*
    overview of, 558
    SW Isometric View, 523–524, *524*, *525*, 558, **596**
    Viewpoint options, 529–530, *530*, 538–539, *538–539*
@ ("at" symbol) in entering coordinates, 30, 31
' (foot sign) in distance measures, 57
< ("less than" symbol) in entering coordinates, 31
+ (plus signs)
  in marking insertion points, 238–239, *239*, *240*
  in marking tracking points, 131, 138

A

absolute coordinates, 29, 592
alias keys, 19, 592
Aligned button on Dimension toolbar, 399
aligned dimensions, 398–399, *399*, **592**
aligning. *See also* centering; justification points
  multiple viewports, 466, *467*, 486
Alt key, 19
Angular button on Dimension toolbar, 399, *399*
angular dimensions, 398, 399–400, *399*, **592**
angular units. *See also* units
  defined, **592**
  setting for dimensions, 377–378, *378*
  setting for drawing areas, 50–53, *51–53*
ANSI hatch patterns, 292, **295**, 298–299, *299*
AR hatch patterns, 294, 295
Arc command. *See also* balconies; circles
  in drawing door swings, 98–101, *101*, 108
Arcball in 3D Orbit View, 558–559, *559*
Architectural units, 51–52, *52*, 54, 75
Area command, 579–581, *579*
Array command button on Modify toolbar, 303, *304*
arrows in dimensions, 374, *374*
associative hatch pattern, 315, 592

Attdisp command, 583, *584*
Attedit command, 584–585
Attribute button on Inquiry flyout, 580
Attribute Definition dialog box, 568–570, *569, 570*
Attribute Extraction dialog box, 587–588
attributes, **566–590**
  area calculations and, 579–581, *579*
  attribute definitions, **569**, **592**
  block definitions and, 569
  controlling visibility of, 583, *584*
  defined, **566**, **592**
  defining, 568–570, *569–570*, 575–578, *576–578*
  defining blocks for, 571, *572*, 578–581, *579*
  editing, 574–575, *575*, 584–586
  extracting into text files, 586–588, **592**
  inserting blocks of, 572–573, *573–574*, 581–583, *582–583*
  inserting extracted data into drawings, 589
  overview of, 566, 590
  setting up drawings for, 566–568, *567*
  versus text, 566
AutoCAD Text Window, 221, *221, 222*
Autosnap icons, 150, *150–151*, **593**

B

background color in drawing area, 7–9, *8*, 200
balconies, curved
  calculating area of, 580–581
  drawing in 3D, 555, *556*, 557
  in elevations
      drawing, 272, *273*
      hatching, 302–304, *302, 304–305*
  in floor plans
      dimensioning, 390–395, *391, 393–395*
      drawing, 133–137, *134–137*
      hatching, 313–314, *313, 314*
Base command, 442
Baseline button on Dimension toolbar, 385
baseline dimensions, 385–386, *385–387*, **593**
bathroom fixtures
  assigning to layers, 181, *182*
  overview of, 149, *149*
  shower units, 151–152, *152*
  sinks, 153–154, *154*
  toilets, 154–156, *157*
Bind command, 440–441
Bind Xrefs dialog box, 440
Blipmode feature
  blip marking block insertion points, 238–239, *239, 240*
  blip marks defined, **238**, **593**

  turning off, 239, 246
Block Definition dialog box, 208–209, *209*, 218
blocks, **206–252**, **344–359**. *See also* attributes
  block definitions, **207**, 210
  block insertion, **223**
  block references, **210**, 215, **593**
  copying to other drawings, **206**, 247–251, *248, 250*
  defined, **206**, *206*, **593**
  detecting
      with grips, 220
      with List command, 220–221, *221, 222*
      overview of, 219
      with Properties dialog box, 223, *224*
  door blocks, **207–219**
      creating, 208–210, *208–210*, 217, *218*
      inserting, overview of, 211–213, *211–213*, 217, 219
      inserting while flipping, 213–217, *215–216*
      insertion points for, 207, 211–212, *212*
      overview of, 207–208, *219*
  exploding, 244
  versus external references, 416
  insertion points, **596**
  layers and, 207
  options for, *209*, 218
  revising, 244–246, *245–247*
  rotating, 212–213, *213*
  saving, 247–248, *248*
  title blocks, **344–359**
      attributes and, 566
      cutting and pasting into Layouts, 454–456, *455*
      defined, **347**
      designing for layouts, 452–453, *452*, 464, *465*
      fonts, 358
      inserting text in, 353–357, *355, 357*
      justification points in, 358–359
      overview of, 359, *360*
      polylines in, 347–352, *349, 351–353*
      running Object Snaps and, 359
      scaling down, 452–453, *452*
      text height in, 358, 453
      view borders and, 344–347, *345–347*
  wblocking, **206**, 247–251, *248, 250*
  window blocks, **224–244**
      in 2D, pasting onto 3D surfaces, 547–551, *547, 550*
      converting from 2D into 3D, 541–547, *543, 545*
      creating, 224–228, *225–228*, 240–242, *241*, 243–244
      insertion points for, 227, 238–239, *239, 240*
      zooming to Extents, 243, *243*
  window blocks, inserting
      blip marking insertion points, 238–239, *239, 240*
      overview of, 228, 242, *242*

rotating while, 229–231, *229–231*
using guidelines, 227, *228*, 232–234, *233–235*
using point filters, 235–236, 237, **599**
X and Y scale factors and, 212–214, 217, 230, 244
bolding text, 364, *365*
Boolean operations, 563
borders
for elevation views, 344–347, *345–347*
for Layouts, 450–452, *451*, 464, *465*
boundaries for hatch patterns, 290, 293, *293*, 297
boundary edge lines, 42–43, *42*
Boundary Hatch dialog box, 291–295, *291–294*
Break command
breaking lines crossing text, 332–334, *333*
button on Modify toolbar, 333
in centering text in title blocks, 356
Browse button in dialog boxes, 248, 291
buttons. *See also* icons
defined, **211**
on Draw toolbar, *3, 24*
on Inquiry toolbar, *14*
on Modify toolbar, *3*
on Object Properties toolbar, *3, 4,* 164
on Object Snap toolbar, *94*
on Standard toolbar, *3, 4,* 11
in Startup dialog box, 2–3, *2*
on Status bar, *3,* 5–6
on toolbar flyouts, 11–13
Bylayer color and linetype setting, 175, 195, 201–202, **593**

C

Cartesian coordinates, relative, 29–30, *30*, 32, *33*
Categorized tab of Properties dialog box, 144–146, *145,*
339
centering. *See also* aligning; justification points
hatch patterns, 310–311, *311*
printing areas, 499, *500*
text in title blocks, 356
view titles, 325–328, *326–328*
child dimension styles, 393, 394–395, *394, 395*
Circle drop-down menu, 133
circles. *See also* Arc command; balconies
changing size of, 144, *145*, 146
in drawing balconies, 133–137, *134–137*
in drawing round windows, 271–272, *272*
in drawing stoves, 144–146, *145, 146*
moving, 134, *135*
color
in 3D models, 546
assigning to layers, 167–168, *167*

assigning to objects, 201–202
assigning to viewports, 456
of Autosnap symbols, 150–151
Bylayer color setting, **175**, 195, 201–202, **593**
of crosshair cursor, 7–9, *8*
of drawing area background, 7–9, *8*, 200
setting to be current, 201–202
Color Control drop-down list on Object Properties
toolbar, 201–202
Color Options dialog box, 8–9, *8*
Command window
defined, **593**
List command and, 221, *222*
overview of, *3,* 5, 9–10
prompt, 25–26, **594**
commands
activated by grips, 258–259, *260*
canceling, 36
restarting, 38
starting, 122
undoing effects of, 39, 139–140
using transparently, **104**
concrete hatch pattern, 296, *297*
Continue button on Dimension toolbar, 384
continued dimensions, 383–384, *383, 384,* **594**
coordinate, z, 28
coordinates, x and y. *See also* User Coordinate System
absolute coordinates, **29, 592**
coordinate readouts
drawing with Grid, Snap, and, 59–63, *61–63*
overview of, *3,* 5, 28–29
cursors and, 28–28
entering from keyboard, 27–34, *28, 30, 31, 33*
inserting window blocks using, 235–236, *237*
relative coordinates
defined, **29, 600**
formats for entering, 30, 31
relative Cartesian coordinates, **29–30**, *30,* 32, *33*
relative polar coordinates, 29, **31**, *31,* 33–34
Copy button on Modify toolbar, 102
Copy command
versus copying with grips, 258–259
copying swinging doors, 101–104, *103*
copying text, 338, *338*
Multiple option, 144, *145*
Copy option of Move command
copying lines with grips, 258–259, *260*
copying text with grips, 341–342, *342*
copying blocks to other drawings, 206, 247–251, *248, 250*
corners
cleaning up with Fillet command, 37–40, *38–39,* 72–73,
72–73, 76–78, *77–78*
cleaning up with Trim command, 77, 79–83, *79–83*

counters, kitchen, 138–140, *139*, *140*
Create Layout dialog box, 461–463, *462*, *463*
Create New Folder button in Save As dialog box, 64
crosshair cursor
    coloring, 7–9, *8*
    defined, **594**
    overview of, *3*, 4–5
    sizing, 449
crossing windows. *See also* window tools
    defined, **115**, *115*, **175**, **594**
    overview of, 175–176, *176*, 178, *179*
    selection sets and, 181, *182*
current colors and linetypes, 201–202
current dimension styles, 379, *379*
current layers, 172–173, 195
Current option of Plan command, 276
current text style, 322, **323**
Cursor menu, 20, 125, 325–326
cursors. *See also* icons
    crosshair cursor
        coloring, 7–9, *8*
        defined, **594**
        overview of, *3*, 4–5
        sizing, 449
    defined, **594**
    hand-shaped cursor, 154
    magnifying glass cursor, 154
    overview of, 5, 459
    pickbox cursor, **32**, **599**
    two-way arrow cursors, 9, 18
    x and *y* coordinates and, 28–28
curves. *See* Arc command; balconies; circles
cutting edges, **43**, *44*, 45, *46*, **594**
cutting and pasting. *See also* pasting
    title blocks into Layouts, 454–456, *455*

D

Ddattdef command, 576–578, *577*, *578*
Ddatte command, 574, *575*, 584
Ddattext command, 587–588
Ddedit command
    editing dimension text, 401–402, *403*
    editing text in floor plan grids, 342–344, *343*
    editing text in title blocks, 354–355, *355*
Decimal units, 50–52, *51*, 54, 75
decks, 430–431, *430*, *432*
deleting. *See* Erase command; Hide command; removing
Descartes, René, 30
descenders in text, **341**

Detach command, 441
detecting blocks. *See also* blocks
    with grips, 220
    with List command, 220–221, *221*, *222*
    overview of, 219
    with Properties dialog box, 223, *224*
diagonal reference lines, 279–280, *281*
Diameter button on Dimension toolbar, 392
dim (dimension) commands, **392**
Dimension drop-down menu, **11**
Dimension Edit button on Dimension toolbar, 402
Dimension Style button on Dimension toolbar, 372
Dimension Style Manager dialog box, 372–373, *372*,
    379–380, *379*, 394, *394*
Dimension toolbar, 370, *371*, 379
dimensions, 370–414
    angular dimensions, 398, 399–400, *399*, **592**
    dimension lines, 371, *372*
    dimension styles, **370–380**
        child styles, **393**, 394–395, *394*, *395*
        components of, 371, *372*
        defined, **594**
        lines and arrows options, 374, *374*
        naming, 372–374, *372*, *374*
        overriding, 406–408, *406*, *407*
        overview of, 371, 380, 400
        parent styles, **393**, 394–395, *394*, *395*
        preparing drawings for, 370, *371*
        scale options, 376–377, *377*
        setting as current, 379, *379*
        Standard style, 372–373, *372*
        text options, 375–376, *376*
        units options, 377–378, *378*
        Zero Suppression options, 378, *378*
    dimension text, 371, *372*, **594**
    dimension variables, **594**
    extension lines in, 371, *372*
    leader line dimensions, 396–398, *397*
    linear dimensions, **381–391**
        aligned dimensions, 398–399, *399*, **592**
        baseline dimensions, 385–386, *385*–*387*, **593**
        continued dimensions, 383–384, *383*, *384*, **594**
        horizontal dimensions, 381–386, *381*–*387*
        vertical dimensions, 388–391, *388*–*391*
    modifying, **400–412**
        dimension text, 401–402, *403*
        moving, 404–406, *405*
        overview of, 400, *401*
        for short distances, 408–411, *409*, *410*, *412*
        style settings, 406–408, *406*, *407*
    overview of, 380–381, 413, *413*

radial dimensions, 392–395, *393–395*
studs and, **383**, **600**
tick marks in, 371, *372*
Dimlinear command, 381–383, *382*
Dimradius command, 392–393, *393*
Direct Entry method, 125, 131, 138, *139*
Display option in printing, 503, *504*
Display tab of Options dialog box, 7, *7*
Distance command, 11–13, 220, 241
distance measures. *See also* Ortho mode
  changing offset distances, 75
  Direct Entry method for, 125, **131**
  formats for entering, 57, 74, 75
docked toolbars, 16
doglegs, 397
doors, 91–119. *See also* wall openings
  door blocks, **207–219.** *See also* blocks
    creating, 208–210, *208–210*, 217, *218*
    inserting, overview of, 211–213, *211–213*, 217, 219
    inserting while flipping, 213–217, *215–216*
    insertion points for, 207, 211–212, *212*
    overview of, 207–208, *219*
  door schedules, **566**
  in elevations, 267–269, *268–270*
  hatching, 297–298, *298*
  headers above, 186–188, *189*
  hinge point for, **99**
  overview of, 117–118, *118*
  sliding glass doors, **109–118**
    assigning to layers, 180, *180*
    Line command and, 111–112, *113*, 117
    Object Snaps and, 109–112, *110*, 117
    Offset command and, 111–112, *112, 113*
    overview of, 109, *118*
    Trim command and, 113–116, *114–116*
    Zoom Previous command and, 117, *118*
    Zoom Window command and, 109, *109*
  swinging doors, **91–108**
    Arc command and, 98–101, *101*
    assigning to layers, 178, *179*
    copying, 101–104, *103*
    creating, 91–92, *93*, 106–108, *107–108*
    mirroring, 104–106, *105, 106*
    Rectangle command and, 93–96, *94, 96*
    rotating, 96–97, *98*
    Zoom Window command and, 92, *93*
  thresholds, 130–133, *132*
  ways to illustrate, 91, *91*
Drafting Settings dialog box
  Object Snap tab, 92, 149–151
  Polar Tracking tab, 195–198, *196, 197*

Snap and Grid tab, 58–59, *58*
Drafting tab of Options dialog box, 150–151
drafting, traditional, 158, 162
Draw drop-down menu, 11, 99
Draw toolbar buttons, *3, 24*
drawing area grids, 54–63
  defined, **54, 56, 596**
  drawing lines using, 59–63, *61–63*
  overview of, 54–56, *55*
  setting drawing limits in, 54, 56–59, *57–59*, **595**
  sizing, 56–59, *57–59*
  spacing dots in, 58–59, *58, 59*
  zooming in and out of, 54, 55–56, *55*
drawing areas, 50–65. *See also* Graphics window
  adjusting view in, 154–155
  background color, 7–9, *8*, 200
  defined, **54, 594**
  overview of, *3*, 4–5
  panning, **154**, 598
  saving drawings, 63–65
  setting units in, 50–53, *51–53*
drawing extents, 594
drawing limits
  defined, **595**
  printing to, 501, *502*
  setting, 54, 56–59, *57–59*
drawing strategies, 68, *68*, 122, *123*
drawing units, 50–54
Drawing Units dialog box, 50–53, *51–53*
driveways, 420–424, *421–423*
drop-down lists, 51. *See also* Object Properties toolbar
drop-down menus. *See also* menus
  Arc menu, 99
  Circle menu, 133
  defined, **10**
  Draw menu, **11,** 99
  opening, 122
  overview of, 4, 10–11
Dtext command, 325, 354

E

eaves roof lines, **189**, 190–193, *191–193*
Edge command in 3D drawing, 536, *536*, 537, **595**
Edit Text dialog box, 342–344, *343*, 354–355, *355*
editing. *See also* modifying; revising
  attributes, 574–575, *575*, 584–586
  block references, 245–246, *246, 247*
  dimension text, 401–402
  objects with grips, 258–259, *260*

polylines, 350, *352*
text in floor plan grids, 342–344, *343*
text in title blocks, 354–355, *355*
elevations, 254–287. *See also* floor plans; site plans
  adding titles to, 325–328, *326–328. See also* title blocks
  defined, **254**
  front elevations, **254–273**
    adding details, 273, *273*
    balconies, 272, *273*
    copying lines with grips, 258–259, *260*
    doors, 267–269, *268–270*
    mirroring to rear elevations, 274, *275*
    overview of, 254–255, *255*
    roofs, 263–267, *264–267*
    setting up height lines, 256–257, *256, 257*
    steps and thresholds, 270, *271*
    transferring height lines, 279–283, *281–283*
    trimming lines, 261–263, *261, 262*
    windows, 267–269, *268–270,* 271–272, *272*
  hatching, **290–308**
    balconies, 302–304, *302, 304–305*
    doors, 297–298, *298*
    foundations, 296, *297*
    roofs, 291–294, *291–294*
    shaded surfaces, 300–302, *301*
    solid fills, 299, *299,* **595**
    walls, 298, *299*
    windows, 299, *299*
  interior elevations, 286, *287*
  left and right elevations, 279–284, *281–283,* 285
  moving views of, 284, *285*
  overview of, 254, 274, *285*
  rear elevations
    mirroring from front elevations, 274, *275*
    revising, 276–277, *278*
    rotating view 180-degrees, 274–276, *276*
    saving rotated views, 277, 279
  scale in, 285–286
Ellipse command on Draw toolbar, 153, *154,* 156, *157*
Endpoint Object Snap button, 95
Enter key, 26, 35
Erase command, 27, 32–33, *33. See also* Hide command; removing
Esc key, 34, 36, 53
Explode command
  button on Modify toolbar, 251
  defined, **595**
  exploding blocks, 244, 251
  exploding polylines, 348

exporting blocks to other drawings, 206, 247–251, *248, 250*
Extend command, 42–43, *42–43,* 85–86, *86–87*
extension lines in dimensions, 371, *372*
Extents
  drawing extents, **594**
  printing to, 502–503, *503*
  zooming to, **76,** 243, *243*
External Reference dialog box, 425
external references, 416–442
  applications for, 437–438, *437, 438*
  binding to host drawings, 440–441
  versus blocks, 416
  controlling appearance of, 426–427, *427,* 434
  defined, **416, 595**
  detaching from host drawings, 441
  host drawings and, **416, 595**
  inserting, 424–429, *426–429,* 442
  linking with host drawings, 433
  modifying
    by making current, 430–434, *430, 432, 433*
    overview of, 434, 436–437
    setting up for, 429
    from within host drawings, 434–436, *435, 436*
  moving and rotating, 427–428, *428, 429*
  nested Xrefs, **441**
  overview of, 441–442
  saving with host drawings, 429
  site plans and
    drawing driveways, 420–424, *421–423*
    drawing property lines, 417–418, *419*
    elements in, 416–417
    surveyor units in, **417**
  unloading and reloading, 441
  updating paths of, 438–440
extracting attributes into text files, 586–590

F

F keys, 19, 221
faces, 534, 595
Files tab of Options dialog box, *6*
Fillet command
  button on Modify toolbar, 37, 72
  cleaning up corners, 37–40, *38–39,* 72–73, *72–73,* 76–78, *77–78*
  kitchen counters and, 139–140, *140*
  versus Offset command, 73–74

roof lines and, 191–192, *192–193*, 198, *199*
undoing fillets, 39
fills. *See also* hatch patterns
defined, **290, 595**
solid fills, 299, *299*, 313–314, *314*
filters, point, 235–236, *237*, **599**
floating toolbars, 16, 391
floor plan grids. *See also* grids
attributes in
defining, 568–570, *569–570*
defining blocks for, 571, *572*
editing, 574–575, *575*
inserting blocks of, 572–573, *573–574*
setting up for, 566–568, *567*
defined, **334, 596**
drawing grid lines, 335–337, *335–337*
text in
copying, 341–342, *342*
editing, 342–344, *343*
inserting, 337–340, *338, 340*
moving, 341–342, *342*
floor plans. *See also* elevations; site plans
attributes in
controlling visibility of, 583, *584*
defining, 576–578, *577, 578*
defining blocks for, 578–579
editing, 584–586
inserting blocks of, 581–583, *582, 583*
setting up for, 575–576, *576*
calculating area in, 579–581, *579*
hatch patterns in
centering, 310–311, *311*
for floors, 308–313, *309, 311–313*
overview of, 308
parquet pattern, 312–313, *312, 313*
solid fills, 313–314, *314*, **595**
tile pattern, 308–311, *309, 311*
for walls, 313–314, *314*
labels in
adding, 328–332, *329–332*
breaking lines crossing, 332–334, *333*
defining as attributes, 568–570, *569–570*, 575–578, *576–578*
moving, 330–332, *331, 332*
setting up text style for, 322–323, *322*
overview of, 68, *68, 158*
flyouts on Standard toolbar, 11–13
fonts
defined, *323*, **596**

modifying, 364, *364*
options for, 323, 324, 358
foot sign (') for indicating distance, 57
Format drop-down menu, 10
formats, entry
for distance measures, 57, 74, 75
for relative coordinates, 30, 31
foundations, hatching, 296, *297*
freezing layers
defined, **596**
overview of, 183–185, *184–185*
in viewports, 480–481, *482*, 484
From Osnap tool. *See* Snap From Object Snap tool

G

garage addition, 119, *119*
Geographical Information System (GIS) software, 590
ghosting lines, 33
glazing (glass), 227
Graphics window. *See also* drawing areas
changing colors in, 7–9, *8*
defined, **596**
overview of, 2, *3–6*
removing elements from, 6–7, *6, 7*
grid tool in 3D Orbit View, 559, *560*
grids, drawing area. *See also* drawing areas
defined, **54, 56, 596**
drawing lines using, 59–63, *61–63*
overview of, 54–56, *55*
sizing, 56–59, *57–59*
spacing dots in, 58–59, *58, 59*
zooming in and out of, 55–56, *55*
grids, floor plan. *See also* floor plans
attributes in
defining, 568–570, *569–570*
defining blocks for, 571, *572*
editing, 574–575, *575*
inserting blocks of, 572–573, *573–574*
setting up for, 566–568, *567*
defined, **334, 596**
drawing grid lines, 335–337, *335–337*
text in
copying, 341–342, *342*
editing, 342–344, *343*
inserting, 337–340, *338, 340*
moving, 341–342, *342*

grips
    commands activated by, 258–259
    copying elevation lines using, 258–259, *260*
    copying text using, 341–342, *342*
    defined, **144**, *145*, **173**, *174*, **596**
    detecting blocks using, 220
    editing objects using, 258–259, *260*
    moving dimensions using, 404–406, *405*
    turning off, 146
GUI. *See* Graphics window
guide lines
    in drawing floor plan grids, 335–336, *336*
    in drawing sliding glass doors, 112, *113*
    for inserting blocks, 227–228, *228*, 232–234, *233–235*
    for locating stove burner centers, 143–144, *144*
    for placing dimensions, 388–389, *389*
    for placing text, 334–340
    for positioning toilets, 155, *157*

H

Hatch button on Draw toolbar, 291
Hatch Pattern Palette dialog box, 291, *292*, 294–295
hatch patterns, 290–316
    ANSI patterns, *292*, **295**, 298–299, *299*
    AR patterns, **294**, 295
    associative hatch pattern, **315**, **592**
    boundaries for, 290, 293, *293*, 297
    boundary problems, 310
    defined, **290**, **596**
    in elevations, **290–308**
        balconies, 302–304, *302*, *304–305*
        concrete foundations, 296, *297*
        curved surfaces, 302–304, *302*, *304–305*
        doors, 297–298, *298*
        roofs, 291–294, *291–294*
        shaded surfaces, 300–302, *301*
        walls, 298, *299*
        windows, 299, *299*
        wooden shingles, 298, *299*
    in floor plans, **308–314**
        centering, 310–311, *311*
        for floors, 308–313, *309*, *311–313*
        overview of, 308
        parquet pattern, 312–313, *312*, *313*
        tile pattern, 308–311, *309*, *311*
        for walls, 313–314, *314*
    ISO patterns, **295**
    layers for, 290–291
    modifying, 306, *307*, 315, *316*

    overview of, 306, *308*
    polar array (spoked) pattern, 302–303, *304*
    Predefined patterns, 291, *292*, 294–296
    scale of, 295–296
    solid fills, 299, *299*, 313–314, *314*, **595**
    User-defined patterns, 308–311, *309*, *311*
headers above doors and windows, 186–188, *189*
height
    of multiline text, 362–363, *363*
    of single line text, 358, 453
height lines in elevations, 256–257, *256–257*, 279–283, *281–283*
Hide command, 527, *528*, 529, 534, *534*, 540. *See also* Erase command; removing
highlighting (ghosting) lines, 33
highlighting multiline text, 362
hinge point for doors, 99
hip roof lines, 190, 195–200, *196*, *197*, *199*
hook lines, 397
horizontal dimensions, 381–386, *381–387*
host drawings. *See* external references
hotkeys, 19

I

icons. *See also* buttons; cursors
    Autosnap icons, 150–151, **593**
    defined, **211**
    snowflakes, 183, *184*, 185
    on toolbars, 392
    triangular arrows on Standard toolbar, 11–12
    User Coordinate System icon
        in 3D drawings, 524, *525*, 548–551, *550*
        defined, *3*, **5**, **601**
        displaying, 480, 524
        rotating view of, 274–276, *276*
        saving rotated views, 277, 279
        turning off, 54
        UCS defined, **548**, **601**
        World UCS default, **275**, 276, 277, 279, 548
    yellow suns, 183, *184*, 185
In-place Xref and Block Edit option, 245–246, *246–247*, 434–437, *435–436*
Inquiry flyout, 12–13
Inquiry toolbar
    buttons, *14*
    moving, 15–17, *15*, *17*
    opening, 13–14, *14*
    removing, 18
    reshaping, 17–18

Insert Block button on Draw toolbar, 211
Insert dialog box, 211–212, *211*
Insert drop-down menu, 10
inserting
  blocks
    of attributes, 572–573, *573–574*, 581–583, *582–583*
    door blocks, 211–217, *211–213*, *215–216*, 219
    in other drawings, **206**, 247–251, *248*, *250*
  external references, 424–429, *426–429*, 442
  text
    in floor plan grids, 337–340, *338*, *340*
    multiline text, 362
    in title blocks, 353–357, *355*, *357*
  window blocks
    marking insertion points, 227, 238–239, *239*, *240*
    overview of, 228, 242, *242*
    rotating while, 229–231, *229–231*
    using guide lines, 227, *228*, 232–234, *233–235*
    using point filters, 235–236, *237*, **599**
insertion points. *See also* justification points
  defined, **596**
  for door blocks, 207, 211–212, *212*
  for window blocks, 227, 238–239, *239*, *240*
interior elevations, 286, *287*
Intersection Object Snap tool, 144, *145*, 232–233, *234*
ISO hatch patterns, 295
Isometric View, 523–524, *524*, *525*, 558, **596**

J

jambs, 84, **597**
justification points. *See also* aligning; insertion points
  defined, **597**
  for multiline text, 367, *368*
  for single line text, 340–341, *341*
  in title blocks, 358–359

K

keyboard
  alias keys, **19**, **592**
  Alt key, 19
  Enter key, 26, 35
  entering coordinates with, 27–34, *28*, *30*, *31*, *33*
  Esc key, 34, 36, 53
  F2 key, 221
  F keys, 19

  hotkeys, **19**
  overview of, 19
kitchen fixtures, 137–149
  assigning to layers, 181, *182*
  counters, 138–140, *139*, *140*
  overview of, 137, *138*
  refrigerators, 141, *141*
  sinks, 147–148, *147*, *148*
  stoves, 141–146, *141–146*

L

labels in floor plans. *See also* attributes; text
  adding, 328–332, *329–332*
  breaking lines crossing, 332–334, *333*
  defining as attributes, 568–570, *569–570*, 575–578,
    576–578
  moving, 330–332, *331*, *332*
  setting up text style for, 322–323, *322*
Layer Properties Manager dialog box, 165–173. *See also*
    Object Properties toolbar; Properties dialog box
  Color column, 167–168, *167*
  Current button, 172–173
  Freeze column, 183–186, *184–186*, 480–481
  Layer list box, 164–169, *165–167*, *169*
  Linetype column, 170–172, *170–172*
  Lineweight column, 508–509
  New button, 166, *166*
  overview of, 164, *165*, 188, 426
layers, 162–189
  3D drawings and, 546
  assigning
    color to objects in, 201–202
    color to, 167–168, *167*
    linetypes to objects in, 201–202
    linetypes to, 170–172, *170–172*
    lineweights to, 506–509
  blocks and, 207
  controlling visibility of, 480–481, *482*, 484
  creating, 164–169, *165–167*, *169*
  current layer, 172–173
  defined, **597**
  freezing
    defined, **596**
    overview of, 183–185, *184–185*
    in viewports, 480–481, *482*, 484
  for hatch patterns, 290–291
  Headers layer, 186–188, *189*
  naming, 166, *166*, 168

overlays as, 162
overview of, 162–164, *163*
properties of, 165–166
selecting objects to assign to, **173–183**
   bathroom fixtures, 181, *182*
   doors, 178, *179*, 180, *180*
   kitchen fixtures, 181, *182*
   overview of, 173–175, *174*
   roof lines, 193
   selection sets in, 181, *182*, **600**
   using crossing windows, 175–176, *176*, 178, *179*, 181,
     182
   using regular windows, 176–177, *177*, 180, *180*, **599**
   wall lines, 182–183
status modes of, 166
for text styles, 320, *321*
thawing, 185, *186*, **601**
turning off, 183
Xref layer appearance, 426–427, *427*, 434
Layers buttons on Object Properties toolbar, 164, 173
Layers Control drop-down list on Object Properties
  toolbar, 173–175, *174*, 186–188, *189*
Layout tabs, *3*, 5, 445, **597**
Layout Wizard, 461–463, *462*, *463*
Layouts, 444–491
crosshair cursor and, 449
defined, **444, 597**
multiple viewports in, **460–491**
   adding to Layouts, 477–480, *478*, *479*
   adding titles to, 486–490, *488*, *489*
   adjusting linetype scale, 487, *489*
   aligning, 466, *467*, 486
   controlling layer visibility in, 480–481, *482*, 484
   creating, 460–463, *462–463*, 468–471, *469–470*, 477,
     478
   in different scales, 471–477, *472*, *474*, *476*
   moving, 475, *476*
   overview of, 460, 489–490
   printing, 514–517, *515–516*, *518*
   resizing, 467–468, *468*, 475, *476*, 481–485, *482–484*
   turning off, 490–491, *490*
printing
   on large format printers, 515–516, *515*, *516*
   with multiple viewports, 514–517, *515–516*, *518*
   overview of, 513–514, *513*
   site plan Layouts, 516–517, *518*
setting up, **444–458**
   with borders, 450–452, *451*, 464, *465*
   default viewport properties, 456–457, *457*, *458*
   overview of, 444–450, *445*, *447–449*

scale, 444, 446, *447*, 456–457
   with title blocks, 452–456, *452*, *455*, 464, *465*
switching between Model Space and, 449–451, *449*,
   458–460
UCS icon in, 480
viewports in
   assigning color to, 456
   defined, **448, 459, 601**
   floating viewports, **595**
   overview of, 460
   sizing, 456–457, *457*, *458*
   turning off, 490–491, *490*
   zooming to scale in, 460, 468, *469*, 477, *479*
leader lines, 396–398, *397*
limits, drawing
printing to, 501, *502*
setting in drawing areas, 54, 56–59, *57–59*
Line command, 22–34
button on Draw toolbar, 24
defined, **23**
entering coordinates with keyboard, 27–34, *28*, *30*, *31*, *33*
entering coordinates with mouse, 23–26, *24*, *26*
in Ortho mode, 125–126, *126*
overview of, 22–23, *22*, *23*
relative Cartesian coordinates, **29–30**, *30*, 32, *33*
relative polar coordinates, 29, **31**, *31*, 33–34
starting, 24–25
Linear command on Dimension toolbar, 381–383, *381*,
  382, 388
linear dimensions, 381–391. *See also* dimensions
aligned dimensions, 398–399, *399*, **592**
baseline dimensions, 385–386, *385–387*, **593**
continued dimensions, 383–384, *383*, *384*, **594**
horizontal dimensions, 381–386, *381–387*
vertical dimensions, 388–391, *388–391*
linear units. *See also* units
setting for dimensions, 377–378, *378*
setting for drawing areas, 50–53, *51–53*
lines
boundary edge lines, 42–43, *42*
breaking around text, 332–334, *333*
cleaning up in corners, 37–40, *38–39*, 77, 79–83, *79–83*
copying using grips, 258–259, *260*
diagonal reference lines, 279–280, *281*
drawing with Grid, Snap, and coordinate readouts,
  59–63, *61–63*
drawing with keyboard, 27–34, *28*, *30*, *31*, *33*
drawing with mouse, 23–26, *24*, *26*
erasing, 32–33, *33*
extending, 42–43, *42–43*

ghosting, 33
height lines in elevations, 256–257, *256–257*, 279–283, *281–283*
hiding, 527, *528*, 529
offsetting, 34–37, *35–37*
overlapping, 22, *23*
polylines
  defined, **599**
  editing, 350, *352*
  exploding, 348
  offsetting, 142
  overview of, 97, 141, 347
  setting width of, 348, *349*
  in title blocks, 347–352, *349*, *351–353*
property lines, 417–418, *419*
trimming, 43–47, *44–47*, 79–83, *79–83*
linetypes
assigning to layers, 170–172, *170–172*
assigning to objects, 201
Bylayer linetype setting, **175**, 195, 201–202, **593**
defined, **597**
linetype scale, **597**
non-continuous linetypes
  overview of, 170, *171*
  setting scale of, 193–194, *194*, 202, 487, *489*
setting to be current, 201–202
Lineweight dialog box, 508–509
Lineweight Settings dialog box, 508–509
lineweights, assigning to layers, 506–509
List command
button on Inquiry flyout, 13, 220
detecting blocks with, 220–221, *221*
overview of, 12–13
Load or Reload Linetypes dialog box, 170–171, *171*

M

Make Block button on Draw toolbar, 208
Make Object's Layer Current button on Object Properties toolbar, 195
Mastering AutoCAD 3D (Omura), 522
Mastering AutoCAD 2000 (Omura), 18, 65, 252, 315
measurement formats for distance, 57, 74, 75
Menu bar, 3, 4, **10**, 597
menus
Menu bar drop-down menus
  Arc menu, 99
  Circle menu, 133
  defined, **10**
  Draw menu, **11**, 99

opening, 122
overview of, *3*, 4, 10–11
right-click menus
  in 3D Orbit View, 559–561, *560*
  Osnap Cursor menu, 20, 125, 325–326
  overview of, 187–188
Midpoint Object Snap command, 111, 152, *152*
Mirror command
button on Modify toolbar, 104
defined, **597**
mirroring doors, 104–106, *105*, *106*
mirroring elevations, 274, *275*
mirroring roof lines, 198, *199*
using with grips, 259
mirror lines, 104, 105, *105*
Model Space
defined, **448**, **598**
switching between Layouts and, 449–451, *449*, 458–460
Model tab, 3, 5, 445, 448–450
Model/Paper button on Status bar, 3, 458, 459
Modify drop-down menu, 11
Modify Hatch command, 306, *307*
Modify Text command
editing single line text, 342–344, *343*, 354–355, *355*
modifying multiline text
  fonts, 364, *364*
  height, 362–363, *363*
  line length, 365, *366*
  overview of, 367
Modify toolbar buttons, *3*, 24
modifying. *See also* editing; revising
dimensions
  dimension text, 401–402, *403*
  moving, 404–406, *405*
  overview of, 400, *401*
  for short distances, 408–411, *409*, *410*, *412*
  style settings, 406–408, *406*, *407*
external references
  by making current, 430–434, *430*, *432*, *433*
  overview of, 434, 436–437
  setting up for, 429
  from within host drawings, 434–436, *435*, *436*
hatch pattern shape, 315, *316*
mouse
drawing lines with, 23–26, *24*, *26*
overview of, 19–20
right-click menus
  in 3D Orbit View, 559–561, *560*
  Osnap Cursor menu, 20, 125, 325–326
  overview of, 187–188

Move command
  button on Modify toolbar, 134
  Copy with grips option, 258–259, *260*, 341–342, *342*
  moving
      circles, 134, *135*
      external references, 428, *428*, *429*
      text in floor plans, 330–332, *331*, *332*
      viewports, 475, *476*
moving
  dimensions using grips, 404–406, *405*
  elevation views, 284, *285*
  toolbars, 15–17, *15*, *17*
multiline text, 360–368. *See also* text
  bolding, 364, *365*
  defined, **320**, **360**, **598**
  defining line length, 361, *361*, 362
  highlighting, 362
  inserting, 362
  justification points, 367, *368*
  modifying
      fonts, 364, *364*
      height, 362–363, *363*
      line length, 365, *366*
      overview of, 367
  overview of, 360, 367, *367*
  styling single words in, 364–365, *365*
  underlining, 364, *365*
Multiline Text command, 361–367, *361*, *363–368*
Multiline Text Editor dialog box, 362–367, *363–368*,
      401–402, *403*
Multiple Copy command option, 144, *145*

N

naming
  blocks, 209, *209*
  dimension styles, 372–374, *372*, *374*
  layers, 166, *166*, 168
  text styles, 322, *322*, 323
  views, 277, 279, **598**
Nearest Object Snap button, 225
nested Xrefs, 441
New button on Standard toolbar, 418
New Dimension Style dialog box
  Fit tab, 376–377, *377*
  Lines and Arrows tab, 374, *374*, 394–395
  overview of, 373, 394
  Primary Units tab, 377–378, *378*
  Text tab, 375–376, *376*

O

Object Properties toolbar. *See also* Layer Properties
      Manager dialog box; Properties dialog box; toolbars
  buttons, *3*, 4, 164
  Color Control drop-down list, 201–202
  Layers buttons on, 164, 173
  Layers Control drop-down list, 173–175, *174*, 186–188,
      189
  Linetype Control drop-down list, 201–202
  Make Object's Layer Current button on, 195
Object Snap tab of Drafting Settings dialog box, 92,
      149–151
Object Snap toolbar. *See also* toolbars
  buttons, *94*
  docking, 110, *110*
  overview of, 94–95, *94*
Object Snap tools
  Autosnap icons for, 150–151, **593**
  defined, **94**, **598**
  in drawing sliding glass doors, 109–112, *110*, 117
  in drawing steps, 124–125
  Endpoint tool, 95
  Intersection tool, 144, *145*, 232–233, *234*
  Midpoint tool, 111, 152, *152*
  Nearest tool, 225
  Perpendicular tool, 117, 129, *130*
  Quadrant tool, 134, *135*
  running Object Snaps
      defined, **149**
      setting up, 149–151
      title blocks and, 359
      turning off all, 156
      turning off for next pick, 153, 242, 263, 354
      turning off for several picks, 354
  Snap From tool, 128–129, *129*
  Snap to None tool, 263
  Temporary Tracking Point tool, 94, 131–133, *132*, 138,
      139, **601**
objects
  assigning linetype and color to, 201–202
  copying, 101–104, *103*
  defined, **598**
  displaying information on, 12, 220–221, *221*
  mirroring, 104–106, *105*, *106*
  rotating, 96–97, *98*
  selecting to assign to layers, 175–181, *176–177*, *179*, *180*,
      182
Offset command
  button on Modify toolbar, 70

changing offset distance, 75
versus Fillet command, 73–74
interior sides of exterior walls and, 34–37, *35–37*, 70–72, *71–72*
interior walls and, 74–76, *74–76*
kitchen fixtures and, 139–140, *140*, 147, *148*
marking wall openings, 40–41, *41*, 84–85, *85*
polylines and, 142
roof lines and, 190–191, *191*
sliding glass doors and, 111–112, *112*, *113*
starting, 70
steps and thresholds and, 126, *127*
Omura, George, 18, 65, 252, 315, 522
Options dialog box
Display tab, 7, *7*
Drafting tab, 150–151
Files tab, *6*
User preferences tab, 152
Orbit View, 3D, 558–561, *559*, *560*
origin
defined, **27**, *28*, **598**
in printing, 499–501, *500*
Ortho mode
button on Status bar, *3*
defined, **125–126**, *126*, **598**
overview of, 97, 127–128
using Tracking and Direct Entry with, 125, 138, *139*
orthoGraphic UCS option, 549, *550*
Osnap button on Status bar, *3*, 354
Osnap Cursor menu, 20, 125, 325–326
Osnaps. *See* Object Snap tools
overlays. *See also* layers
in external references, **442**
layers and, 162

P

Page Setup-Layout1 dialog box, 445–446, *447*
Pan Realtime command
button on Standard toolbar, 154
defined, **154**, **598**
Hide command and, 540
Paper Space, 459, **599**. *See also* Layouts
Paper/Model button on Status bar, *3*, 458, 459
parent dimension styles, 393, 394–395, *394*, *395*
parquet hatch pattern, 312–313, *312*, *313*
Partial Preview dialog box, 510, *511*
pasting. *See also* cutting and pasting
2D window blocks into 3D drawings, 547–551, *547*, *550*

paths, 438–440, **439**, **599**
Pedit command. *See* Polyline Edit command
Perpendicular Object Snap tool, 117, 129, *130*
Pick Point buttons
in Block Definition dialog box, 209, *209*
in Boundary Hatch dialog box, 293, *293*, 297
pickbox cursor, 32, **599**
Plan command, 276
Pline command. *See* Polyline command
Plot Device tab of Page Setup-Layout1 dialog box, 445–446, *447*
Plot dialog box, 495–506
Plot Device tab, 497–498, *497*
Plot Settings tab
Drawing Orientation area, 498
overview of, 495–496, *496*
Paper Size and Paper Units area, 497
Plot Area, 501–506, *502–505*
Plot Offset area, 499
Plot Options area, 499–501, *500*
Plot Scale area, 498–499
plotting. *See* printing
plus signs (+)
in marking insertion points, 238–239, *239*, *240*
in marking tracking points, 131, 138
point filters, 235–236, *237*, **599**
polar array hatch pattern, 302–303, *304*
Polar Tracking tab of Drafting Settings dialog box, 195–198, *196*, *197*
Polar Tracking tool. *See also* Temporary Tracking Point tool
defined, **599**, **601**
in drawing elevation lines, 279–280, *281*
in drawing roof lines, 195–198, *196*, *197*
Polyline button on Draw toolbar, 348
Polyline command, 347–350, *349*, *351*
Polyline Edit command, 350, *352*
polylines
defined, **599**
editing, 350, *352*
exploding, 348
offsetting, 142
overview of, 97, 141, 347
setting width of, 348, *349*
in title blocks, 347–352, *349*, *351–353*
positioning. *See* moving
Precision drop-down list, 51–52, *51*, *52*
Predefined hatch patterns, 291, *292*, 294–296
primitives, 563
Print button on Standard toolbar, 495

printing drawings, 494–518
  assigning lineweights to layers, 506–509
  overview of, 494, 506, 517
  previewing, 510–512, *511, 512*
  setting options, **495–506**
      Display, 503, *504*
      drawing orientation, 498, 512, *512*
      Extents, 502–503, *503*
      Limits, 501, *502*
      overview of, 495–496, *495–496*, 509–510
      paper size and paper units, 497
      plot area, 501–506, *502–505*
      plot offset, 499–501, *500*
      plotter configuration, 497–498, *497*
      scale, 498–499
      View, 504, *505*
      Window, 506
  starting prints, 512
  using Layouts
      on large format printers, 515–516, *515, 516*
      with multiple viewports, 514–517, *515, 516, 518*
      overview of, 513–514, *513*
      site plan Layouts, 516–517, *518*
prompt, Command, 25–26, **594, 599**
Properties button on Standard toolbar, 144
Properties dialog box. *See also* Layer Properties Manager
      dialog box; Object Properties toolbar
  Categorized tab, 144–146, *145*, 339
  changing text properties, 339
  detecting blocks with, 223, *224*
  overview of, 144–146, *145*, 223
  setting linetype scale, 202
property lines, 417–418, *419*

Q

Quadrant Object Snap button, 134, *135*
Quick Leader button on Dimension toolbar, 396
Quick tab of Boundary Hatch dialog box, 291–295,
      291–294

R

radial dimensions, 392–395, *393–395*
radio buttons, 2, *3*
Radius command button on Dimension toolbar,
      392–395, *393–395*
Realtime. *See* Pan Realtime command; Zoom commands
Rectangle command

      button on Draw toolbar, 93
      kitchen fixtures and, 141, *141*
      rectangle problems, 152
      sliding doors and, 93–96, *94, 96*
      toilet tanks and, 155, *157*
      walls and, 96
Redo command, 139
Redraw command, 239, 242, **599**
Refedit toolbar, 246, *246*, 434, 436
Reference Edit dialog box, 245–246, *246*, 434
Reference toolbar, 424
refrigerators, 141, *141*
regular selection windows, 175, 176–177, *177*, 180, *180*,
      599
relative coordinates. *See also* coordinates
  defined, **29, 600**
  formats for entering, 30, 31
  relative Cartesian coordinates, **29–30**, *30*, 32, *33*
  relative polar coordinates, 29, **31**, *31*, 33–34
Reload command, 441
removing. *See also* Erase command; Hide command
  Graphics window elements, 6–7, *6, 7*
  lines crossing text, 332–334, *333*
  toolbars, 18
revising. *See also* editing; modifying
  blocks, 244–246, *245–247*
  elevations, 276–277, *278*
right-click menus
  in 3D Orbit View, 559–561, *560*
  Osnap Cursor menu, 125, 325–326
  overview of, 187–188
roofs, 189–200
  assigning to layers, 193
  drawing in 3D, 551–555, *552–554*
  eaves lines, **189**, 190–193, *191–193*
  in elevations, 263–267, *264–267*
  hatching, 291–294, *291–294*
  hip lines, **190**, 195–200, *196, 197, 199*
  overview of, 189–190, *190, 200*
  ridgelines, **190**, 198, *200*
  setting linetype scale, 193–194, *194*, 202
Rotate command
  button on Modify toolbar, 97
  rotating swinging doors, 96–97, *98*
  using with grips, 259
rotating
  3D views
      in 3D Orbit View, 558–561, *559, 560*
      in Viewpoint dialog box, 529–530, *530*, 538–539,
          538–539
  blocks while inserting, 212–213, *213*, 229–231, *229–231*

elevation views, 274–276, *276*, 284, *285*
external references, 427–428, *428*, *429*
running Object Snaps. *See also* Object Snap tools
defined, **149**
setting up, 149–151
title blocks and, 359
turning off all, 156
turning off for next pick, 153, 242, 263, 354
turning off for several picks, 354

S

Save Back Changes to Reference button on Refedit toolbar, 246, 436
Save button on Standard toolbar, 64
Save Drawing As dialog box, 63–65
saving
blocks, 247–248, *248*
drawings, 63–65
elevation views, 277, 279
Xrefs with host drawings, 429, 436
scale
of dashed linetypes, 193–194, *194*, 202, 487, *489*
of dimensions, 376–377, *377*
in elevations, 285–286
of hatch patterns, 295–296, 306, *307*
in Layouts, 444, 446, *447*, 456–457
of multiple viewports, 471–477, *472*, *474*, *476*
in printing, 498–499
of text styles, 321
in title blocks, 452–453, *452*
true ratios of, 295–296
Scale command on Modify toolbar, 259, 420
Scale drop-down list in Boundary Hatch dialog box, 291, *291*, 293
schedules, 566
Select Color dialog box, 167, *167*
Select Linetype dialog box, 170–171, *170*, *171*
Select Objects button in Block Definition dialog box, 209, *209*
selection fences, **281**, *282*
selection mode, **600**
selection sets, 181, *182*, **600**
selection windows. *See also* window tools
crossing windows
defined, **115**, *115*, **175**, **594**
overview of, 175–176, *176*, 178, *179*
selection sets and, 181, *182*
defined, **600**

overview of, 173–175, *174*
regular windows, **175**, 176–177, *177*, 180, *180*, **599**
shaded surfaces, hatching, 300–302, *301*
shingles (shakes) hatch pattern, 298, *299*
shower units, 151–152, *152*
single line text, **324–360**. *See also* text
breaking lines crossing labels, 332–334, *333*
choosing styles, 328–329, *329*
defined, **320**, **600**
justification points, 340–341, *341*
labeling rooms, 328–332, *329–332*
moving labels, 330–332, *331*, *332*
titling views, 325–328, *326–328*
sinks
in bathrooms, 153–154, *154*
in kitchens, 147–148, *147*, *148*
site plans. *See also* elevations; floor plans
drawing driveways, 420–424, *421–423*
drawing property lines, 417–418, *419*
elements in, 416–417
in Layers, printing, 516–517, *518*
surveyor units in, **417**
Snap From Object Snap tool, 128–129, *129*
Snap and Grid tab of Drafting Settings dialog box, 58–59, *58*
Snap to Insert Object Snap tool, 271
Snap mode, **56**, 59–63, *61–63*, **600**
Snap to None Object Snap tool, 263
soffit, 257
solid fills, 299, *299*, 313–314, *314*, **595**. *See also* hatch patterns
solid modeling, 561–564, *562*, *563*
spoked hatch pattern, 302–303, *304*
Standard dimension style, 372–373, *372*
Standard text style, 322, *329*
Standard toolbar. *See also* toolbars
buttons, *3*, 4, 11
moving, 16–17, *17*
toolbar flyouts, 11–13
Start from Scratch button, 2, *3*
Startup dialog box, AutoCAD, 2–3, *2*
Status bar
buttons, *3*, 5–6
coordinate readout window, *3*, 5, 28–29
Paper/Model button, **3**, 458–459
status modes of layers, **166**
steps and thresholds, **123–133**
in elevations, 270, *271*
Object Snap tools and, 124–125
Offset command and, 126, *127*

Ortho mode and, 125–126, *126*, 127–129
overview of, 123–124, *124*, *125*
Perpendicular Osnap and, 129, *130*
Snap From Osnap and, 128–129, *129*
and thresholds, 123–124, *124*, 130–133, *132*
Tracking tool and, 131–133, *132*
stoves, 141–146, *141–146*
Stretch command
   button on Modify toolbar, 315
   defined, **258**
   modifying hatch pattern shape, 315, *316*
studs, 383, **600**
Style command, 320, 322–324, *322*
styles. *See* dimensions; text
surface modeling, 523–558. *See also* 3D drawings
   adding 3D faces, **534–547**
      defined, **534**, **595**
      to front walls, 535–536, *535*, *536*
      hiding lines, 534, *534*, 537, *537*, 540
      making edges invisible while, 544, **595**
      overview of, 534–535, 540–541, *541*, 551
      rotating views, 538–539, *538*, *539*
      to side walls, 537–540, *537–539*
      starting 3D Face command, 535
      to window openings, 541–547, *543*, *545*
   color and, 546
   creating wireframe models, **525–334**, **547–558**
      adding 3D faces to, 534–547
      adding details, 557–558, *557*
      balconies, 555, *556*, 557
      defined, **525**, **601**
      doorways, 532–534, *533*, *534*
      exterior walls, 525–526, *526*
      hiding lines, 527, *528*, 529
      interior walls, 527, *528*, 530, *531*
      overview of, 546–547
      pasting 2D windows onto, 547–551, *547*, *550*
      roofs, 551–555, *552–554*
      rotating views, 529–530, *530*
   defined, **529**
   elements in, 529
   extrusion in, 527, *528*, 532–534, *533–534*, **595**
   layers and, 546
   overview of, 523
surveyor units, 417
SW Isometric View, 523–524, *524*, *525*, 558, **596**
Sybex Web site, 523
symbols. *See* buttons; cursors; icons
Symbols folder, creating, 247–248

T

template drawings, 600
template files for attribute extraction, 586–590, **592**
Temporary Tracking Point tool. *See also* Polar Tracking
   tool
   button on Object Snap toolbar, 94, 131
   defined, **131**, **601**
   overview of, 131–133, *132*
   using with Ortho and Direct Entry, 138, *139*
text, 320–368. *See also* attributes
   versus attributes, 566
   in dimensions
      modifying, 401–402, *403*
      moving, 404–406, *405*
      options for, 375–376, *376*
      overview of, 371, *372*, **594**
   in floor plan grids, **334–344**
      copying text, 341–342, *342*
      defined, **334**
      drawing grid lines, 335–337, *335–337*
      editing text, 342–344, *343*
      inserting text, 337–340, *338*, *340*
      moving text, 341–342, *342*
   labels in floor plans
      adding, 328–332, *329–332*
      breaking lines crossing, 332–334, *333*
      defining as attributes, 568–570, *569–570*, 575–578,
         576–578
      moving, 330–332, *331*, *332*
      setting up text style for, 322–323, *322*
   multiline text, **344–368**
      bolding, 364, *365*
      defined, **320**, **360**, **598**
      defining line length, 361, *361*, 362
      highlighting, 362
      inserting, 362
      justification points, 367, *368*
      modifying fonts, 364, *364*
      modifying height, 362–363, *363*
      modifying line length, 365, *366*
      modifying, overview of, 367
      overview of, 360, 367, *367*
      styling single words, 364–365, *365*
      in title blocks, 344–360
      underlining, 364, *365*
   overview of, 320
   single line text, **324–344**
      breaking lines crossing labels, 332–334, *333*

choosing styles, 328–329, *329*
defined, **320**, **600**
in floor plan grids, 334–344
justification points, 340–341, *341*
labeling rooms, 328–332, *329–332*
moving labels, 330–332, *331, 332*
titling views, 325–328, *326–328*
text styles
current text style, 322, **323**
defined, **320**, **600**
fonts, 323, 324
Label text style, 322–323, *322*
layers for, 320, *321*
naming, 322–323, *322*
scale, 321
Standard text style, 322, *329*
Title text style, 323–324
title blocks, **344–360**
attributes and, 566
cutting and pasting into Layouts, 454–456, *455*
defined, **347**
designing for layouts, 452–453, *452*, 464, *465*
fonts, 358
inserting text in, 353–357, *355, 357*
justification points, 358–359
overview of, 359, *360*
polylines in, 347–352, *349, 351–353*
running Object Snaps and, 359
scaling down, 452–453, *452*
text height in, 358, 453
view borders and, 344–347, *345–347*
Text button on Draw toolbar, 361
Text Edit command, 342–344, *343*
Text Style dialog box, 322–323, *322*
Text Window, AutoCAD, 221, *221, 222*
thawing layers, 185, *186*, **601**
thickness, 527, **601**
thresholds. *See* steps and thresholds
tick marks in dimensions, 371, *372*
tile hatch pattern, 308–311, *309, 311*
tiled viewports, 459
title bar, *3, 4*
title blocks, 344–359. *See also* blocks; text
attributes and, 566
cutting and pasting into Layouts, 454–456, *455*
defined, **347**
designing for layouts, 452–453, *452*, 464, *465*
fonts, 358
inserting text in, 353–357, *355, 357*
justification points in, 358–359

overview of, 359, *360*
polylines in, 347–352, *349, 351–353*
running Object Snaps and, 359
scale of, 452–453, *452*
text height in, 358, 453
view borders and, 344–347, *345–347*
Title text style
setting up, 323–324
titling elevation views, 325–328, *326–328*
titling viewports, 486–490, *488, 489*
toilets, 154–156, *157*
tool tips, 12
toolbars. *See also* Object Snap tools
activating, 13–14, *14*
buttons/icons on, **211**
customizing, 18
Dimension toolbar, 370, *371*, 379
docking, 16, 18
Draw toolbar, *3, 24*
floating toolbars, 16, 391
Inquiry toolbar, 13–18, *14, 15, 17*
Modify toolbar, *3, 24*
moving, 15–17, *15, 17*
Object Properties toolbar
buttons, *3, 4*, 164
Color Control drop-down list, 201–202
Layers buttons on, 164, 173
Layers Control drop-down list, 173–175, *174*
Linetype Control drop-down list, 201–202
Make Object's Layer Current button on, 195
Object Snap toolbar
buttons, *94*
docking, 110, *110*
overview of, 94–95, *94*
Refedit toolbar, 246, *246*
Reference toolbar, 424
removing, 18
reshaping, 17–18
for solid modeling, 564
Standard toolbar
moving, 16–17, *17*
overview of, *3, 4*, 11
toolbar flyouts on, 11–13
Toolbars dialog box, 13–14, *14*
tools, 211
Tools drop-down menu, 10
tracking. *See* Polar Tracking tool; Temporary Tracking Point tool
transparent use of commands, 104

Trim command
  button on Modify toolbar, 44
  changing Edgemode variable, 116
  cleaning up corners, 77, 79–83, *79–83*
  cutting wall openings, 43–47, *44–47*, 86–88, *87–88*
  elevation lines and, 261–263, *261, 262*
  sliding glass doors and, 113–116, *114–116*
  starting, 44
  undoing trims, 263
true ratios of scales, 295–296
Type drop-down list, 51, *51*

U

U (Undo) command
  button on Standard toolbar, 139–140
  defined, **140**
  versus Undo command, 140
  using, 39, 45, 263
UCS. *See* User Coordinate System
underlining text, 364, *365*
Undo command, 140
units, linear and angular
  angular units defined, **592**
  Architectural units, 51–52, *52,* 54, 75
  Decimal units, 50–52, *51,* 54, 75
  setting for dimensions, 377–378, *378*
  setting for drawing areas, 50–53, *51–53*
units, surveyor, 417
Unload command, 441
updating Xref paths, 438–440
User Coordinate System (UCS) icon
  in 3D drawings, 524, *525,* 548–551, *550*
  defined, *3,* **5,** *601*
  displaying, 480, 524
  rotating view of, 274–276, *276*
  saving rotated views, 277, 279
  turning off, 54
  UCS defined, **548,** *601*
  World UCS default, **275,** 276–277, 279, 548
User preferences tab of Options dialog box, 152
User-defined hatch patterns, 308–311, *309, 311*

V

vertical dimensions, 388–391, *388–391*
View drop-down menu, 10

View option in printing, 504, *505*
Viewpoint Presets dialog box, 529–530, *530,* 538–539,
  538–539
viewports. *See also* Layouts
  assigning color to, 456
  defined, **448, 459, 601**
  floating viewports, *459,* 595
  multiple viewports, **460–491**
    adding to Layouts, 477–480, *478, 479*
    adding titles to, 486–490, *488, 489*
    adjusting linetype scale, 487, *489*
    aligning, 466, *467,* 486
    controlling layer visibility in, 480–481, *482,* 484
    creating, 460–463, *462–463,* 468–471, *469–470,* 477,
      478
    in different scales, 471–477, *472, 474, 476*
    moving, 475, *476*
    overview of, 460, 489–490
    printing, 514–517, *515, 516, 518*
    resizing, 467–468, *468,* 475, *476,* 481–485, *482–484*
    turning off, 490–491, *490*
  sizing, 456–457, *457, 458*
  tiled viewports, **459**
  turning off, 490–491, *490*
views
  3D views
    3D Orbit View, 558–561, *559, 560*
    overview of, 558
    SW Isometric View, 523–524, *524, 525,* 558, **596**
    of UCS icon, 524, *525,* 548–551, *550*
    Viewpoint options, 529–530, *530,* 538–539, *538–539*
  borders for, 344–347, *345–347*
  defined, **601**
  naming, 277, 279, **598**
  saving, 63–65, 277, 279
  titling, 325–328, *326–328*

W

wall openings, 40–47, 83–90. *See also* doors
  drawing in 3D, 532–534, *533, 534*
  Extend command and, 42–43, *42–43,* 85–86, *86*
  Offset command and, 40, *41,* 84–85, *85*
  overview of, 83–84, *84,* 88–90, *89–90*
  Trim command and, 43–47, *44–47,* 86–88, *87–88*
walls, 32–40, 69–83
  assigning to layers, 182–183
  exterior walls
    adding 3D faces to, 535–540, *535–539*

drawing in 3D, 525–526, *526*
drawing using Grid, Snap, and coordinate readouts, 59–63, *61–63*
drawing using Rectangle command, 96
drawing using relative coordinates, 32–34, *33*
Fillet command and, 37–40, *38–39*, 72–73, *72–73*
Offset command and, 34–37, *35–37*, 70–72, *71–72*
overview of, 69, *69*
hatching, 298, *299*, 313–314, *314*
interior walls
    drawing in 3D, 527, *528*, 530, *531*
    Fillet command and, 76–78, *77–78*
    Offset command and, 74–76, *74–76*
    overview of, 69, *69*, 83, *83*
    Trim command and, 77, 79–83, *79–83*
overview of, 69, *69*
wblocking, 206, 247–251, *248, 250*
width of polylines, 348, *349*
Window drop-down menu, 11
window tools
canceling, 53
crossing windows
    defined, **115,** *115,* **175, 594**
    overview of, 175–176, *176,* 178, *179*
    selection sets and, 181, *182*
for defining print areas, 504, *505,* 506
regular windows, **175,** 176–177, *177,* 180, *180,* **599**
for selecting objects, 175–182
Zoom Windows, 78–81, *79–81,* 92, *93,* 391
windows
in elevations, 267–269, *268–270,* 271–272, *272*
hatching, 299, *299*
headers above, 186–188, *189*
window blocks, **224–244, 540–551.** *See also* blocks
    converting into 3D windows, 541–547, *543, 545*
    creating, 224–228, *225–228,* 240–242, *241,* 243–244
    pasting onto 3D surfaces, 547–551, *547, 550*
    zooming to Extents, 243, *243*
window blocks, inserting
    marking insertion points, 227, 238–239, *239–240*
    overview of, 228, 242, *242*
    rotating while, 229–231, *229–231*
    using guide lines, 227, *228,* 232–234, *233–235*
    using point filters, 235–236, *237,* **599**
window schedules, **566**
wireframe models. *See* 3D drawings
wooden shingle hatch pattern, 298, *299*
World Coordinate System (World UCS), 275, 276, 277, 279, 548, **601**
Write Block dialog box, 248, *248*

X

X Origin and *Y* Origin print settings, 499–501, *500*
x and *y* coordinates. *See also* User Coordinate System
absolute coordinates, **29, 592**
coordinate readouts
    drawing with Grid, Snap, and, 59–63, *61–63*
    overview of, *3, 5,* 28–29
cursors and, 28–28
defined, **602**
entering from keyboard, 27–34, *28, 30, 31, 33*
inserting window blocks using, 235–236, *237*
relative coordinates
    defined, **29, 600**
    formats for entering, 30, 31
    relative Cartesian coordinates, **29–30,** *30,* 32, *33*
    relative polar coordinates, 29, **31,** *31,* 33–34
X and *Y* scale factors for blocks, 212–214, 217, 230, 244
Xbind command, 441
Xref Manager dialog box, 432–433, 439–440
Xrefs. *See* external references

Z

z coordinate, 28
Zero Suppression options for dimensions, 378, *378*
Zoom commands
defined, **602**
Hide command and, 540
Zoom All, 57–58, *57*
Zoom to Extents, **76,** 243, *243*
Zoom In, 56
Zoom Out, 55–56, *55*
Zoom Previous, 82, *82,* 102, 117, *118*
Zoom Realtime, 154, 155, 156, *158*
Zoom to Scale
    Zoom to 1/XP, 460, 468, *469,* 477, *479*
    Zoom to X, 76, 243, *243*
Zoom Window, 78–81, *79–81,* 92, *93,* 391

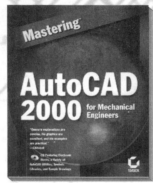

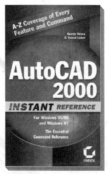